TOURISM AND
INFORMAL ENCOUNTERS
IN CUBA

New Directions in Anthropology

General Editor: **Jacqueline Waldren**, *Institute of Social Anthropology, University of Oxford*

Tourism and Informal Encounters in Cuba

Valerio Simoni

berghahn
NEW YORK · OXFORD
www.berghahnbooks.com

First published in 2016 by
Berghahn Books
www.berghahnbooks.com

Library of Congress Cataloging-in-Publication Data

Simoni, Valerio.
    Tourism and informal encounters in Cuba / Valerio Simoni.
        p. cm. — (New directions in anthropology ; volume 38)
    Includes bibliographical references and index.
    ISBN 978-1-78238-948-4 (hardback : alk. paper) -- ISBN 978-1-78238-949-1 (ebook)
    1. Tourism--Cuba. 2. Tourism--Social aspects--Cuba. I. Title.
    G155.C9S58 2015
    338.4'7917291--dc23

                                                                2015012545

British Library Cataloguing in Publication Data
A catalogue record for this book is available from the British Library

Printed on acid-free paper

ISBN: 978-1-78238-948-4 (hardback)
ISBN: 978-1-78238-949-1 (ebook)

To Lin

Contents

❧

ILLUSTRATIONS

✦

FOREWORD

This work is a methodological tour de force in the ethnography of tourism, carried out over a total of thirteen months between 2005 and 2014. As I pointed out some time ago (Graburn 2002), the ethnographic study of tourism faces challenges common to many other contemporary ethnographic fields: challenges of mobility and temporariness, altered states of consciousness, personal privacy in closed-door societies and political asymmetries, all of which are found in today's tourism in Cuba. In addition I noted the sensitive matters of racial, national and class identities that favoured anthropologists who shared these characteristics with their informant subjects. In Cuba, as Valerio Simoni makes clear, there are vast racial and ethnic gaps both within Cuba and between Cubans and the majority of tourists who, in this work, come predominantly from Europe. Yet here, Simoni has transcended most of these barriers by working with both men and women, and European visitors and multiracial Cuban hosts.

Within Cuban tourism, Simoni does not attempt to cover all types of international tourism. Indeed, as he shows us, his work complements, rather than duplicating, the considerable research already conducted on tourism in Cuba. He has chosen an important field he calls *informal encounters*, which is methodologically challenging, often marginal (or even illegal) to official structures and well-worn paths. These encounters, usually between younger unmarried (or unattached) tourists and young Cubans on the make 'with no visible means of support' involve intense intersubjective ambiguity. Simoni makes a good point: we are dealing with what could be 'friend-like' relationships, a field almost neglected by mainstream social anthropology, which has found it easier to deal with set structures and roles, even if informal. Thus the work is a methodological exemplar for contemporary anthropology, which needs to deal with the more fluid, short-term, interethnic or intercultural, and marginal relationships increasingly found in the modern world, such as those of lifestyle migrants, refugees, economic aspirants, backpackers and gap year travelers, self-seeking exiles (Graburn 2012) and so on.

The Cuban case is more problematic than most because of issues of ambivalence and (lack of) trust. The young Cuban 'entrepreneurs' hope to find friendship, economic support or even long-term relationships leading to emigration with a foreign partner to his or her homeland. Their situation emerged in the 'special period' of the 1990s after Cuba lost the massive support of the USSR (which consisted mainly of buying sugar at above-world prices) and was plunged into an economic crisis that consequently moved international tourism to the center of its international trade (as an 'export' industry, tourism brings in foreign currency that helps pay for imported goods and services). This emphasis broadened tourism from its traditional orientations to solidarity, culture and staid tropical luxury. Combined with more permissive privatization, tourism opened up a field of entrepreneurship for individual Cubans and households. For instance, in the (informal) economy tourists were for the first time allowed to stay in private homes, and prostitution was said to have flourished as never before, providing much-needed income for the underemployed. Meanwhile tourist numbers increased tenfold, and a new breed of younger, more exploratory tourists came to take advantage of the opportunity for 'authentic' relationships with ordinary Cubans, avoiding the formal role of following paid guides and eating and staying in government-run establishments.

During this period there emerged the phenomenon of *jineterismo*, a name given to the activities of outgoing Cubans who tried to make contact with tourists in order to gain something from the encounter, be it money, gifts, rewarded sex, privileged companionship and entry to 'tourist only' places, or in their wildest dreams, invitations to go abroad for employment or partnership such as marriage (Tanaka 2010). The word comes from *jinete*, jockey, with the implication that the *jinetero/a* is 'riding', i.e. directing, the tourist for his or her own advantage. The police often see such behavior as hassling or hustling and may go so far as to arrest the offender (unless bribed). This open-ended role is central to Simoni's ethnography, and he sensitively dissects the sequence of processes by which the tourist tries to avoid being 'taken' while finding friendship and intimacy and the *jinetero* tries to allay such suspicions by becoming a friend of the tourist in such a way as to also achieve his or her goals and desires. These private and secretive behaviors are revealed in a masterly 'quadripartite' ethnography that shows equally the viewpoints and strategies of men versus women and tourists versus Cubans; eventually, Simoni shows, male versus female gender roles take precedence over national differences.

The stories lay out the principles and guises of trust, friendship and market exchange in vignettes, also telling of both successes and failures by following individuals over time and consorting with many people on 'both sides'. This approach is both remarkable and eminently readable; the author shows how individuals keep a strong moral basis or at least a morally justifiable rationale while pursuing personal goals, all the while trying to maintain the appearance of moral behavior. For instance, a young Cuban woman is able to look down on taking money for sex by accepting twenty dollars in 'taxi money' after intimacy with a male tourist, rather than getting fifty dollars for patently 'transactional sex work' – even though she always walks or hitchhikes home. Unlike a few exceptional older and very experienced male tourists, visiting young men also refuse to 'pay for sex', even though they may pay for meals, drinks, taxis and so on to facilitate the consummation. Female tourists almost never pay a Cuban man, though they have the means to facilitate dance partnerships, friendship, intimacy or even permanent relationships to be continued back home in Europe. Cuban men, with the distant goal of marriage, may indulge the tourist's desires in order to be invited abroad; however, some men complained that they were just taken and used for sex, while others failed in their dream marriages and had to return home. This multi-sided ethnography only faltered, the author admits, in the examination of the behavior of *pingueros*, that is, Cuban male sex workers who have encounters with gay tourists. Some of these Cubans are straight men practising another variation of *jineterismo* in order to support their families.

Though the most flamboyant cases of *jineterismo* centre on sexual relationships, especially European males' desire for 'hot' black or *mulata* Cubans and European women's fantasies, the book's main concern is social processes and relationships. Indeed, the same kinds of games and negotiations, protestations and informal relationships involving mutual gain play out in rural Cuban tourism – sampling cigars, exchanging 'gifts', access to restaurants and so forth – where the same basic asymmetries of power and wealth hold. Not only do Cubans try to convince tourists of their honourable intentions and authentic friendship, but they are often rivals amongst themselves for tourists' attention and benefits, bad-mouthing other Cubans as untrustworthy or even handing them over to the police. The tourists, on the other hand, may eventually see that the Cubans have great economic needs that do not necessarily preclude genuineness in friendship; in fact, the two may well have to go together in touristic Cuba. Simoni stresses the relational idioms into which these encounters are seen to fit – idioms of friendship, romance and exceptionalism by which the partners eventually agree to a shared set of meanings that downplay the irregular details and facilitate their continuity. Immersed in situations where entertaining and cherishing relationships abide across differences and inequalities, readers can realize the debates, reflections and negotiations required in making their meanings as the actors construct their own worlds. This reopens the question of what kind of relationships can emerge from touristic encounters, which deserves to be put afresh at the forefront of anthropological research.

This work is an exemplar for contemporary ethnographers studying open-ended encounters in any series of relationship processes, taking into account self-interest, moral necessity, gender and power asymmetries, and political uncertainties. At the same time, the author is very aware of the unique historical and political context, showing how *jineterismo* emerged as a public concern during the critical period of Cuban economic weakness, and how it swelled the informal economy that so many Cubans had to depend on while also threatening the structures of a proud but struggling society that has had numerous anti-colonial conflicts. The official censure and the police surveillance and arrests of young Cuban 'entrepreneurs' perhaps cover an unofficial permissiveness born of necessity, but any appearance of dependence on, or selling out to, wealthy foreigners must be constantly subdued. In this complex work, the anthropology of tourism reaches full maturity and offers valuable lessons for today's social sciences.

Nelson Graburn

ACKNOWLEDGEMENTS

The research on which this book is based started about ten years ago, in the summer of 2004. Since then, my investigation and writing have benefited from the help of many people and institutions, to which I would like to express my gratitude here.

It all began at the Centre for Tourism and Cultural Change (CTCC), at Sheffield Hallam University and then at Leeds Metropolitan University (UK), where my researches benefited above all from the invaluable encouragement, expertise and guidance of Mike Robinson and Scott McCabe. At the CTCC, I was part of a close-knit group of colleagues with whom I continuously exchanged ideas and insights, and I would like to thank here in particular Josef Ploner, Fabian Frenzel, Sean Kim, Tamás Regi, Desmond Wee, Sonja Buchberger, Donata Marletta, Claudia Müller, Birgit Braasch, Ploysri Porananond, Martin Bastide, Jakob Calice, Suleiman Farajat, Sunyoung Hong, Yi Fu, Hannah C. Wadle, Mathilde Verschaeve, and Daniela Carl. At the CTCC, I profited from stimulating conversations with the more senior scholars David Picard and Simone Abram, with whom I have continued exchanging and collaborating, as well as with Phil Long and colleagues and advisors working in related fields in Sheffield and Leeds, including Rodanthi Tzanelli, Jenny Blain, John McCauley, Dorothea Meyer, Lucy McCombes, and Ko Koens. In Leeds I also had my first encounter with Nelson Graburn, who throughout the years would continue to provide insightful feedback on my work.

At the outset of my research in February 2005, I went to Cuba for a first, exploratory fieldwork stay of one month. There I met many of the friends and acquaintances with whom I am still in touch to this day, and who have helped me greatly in my work. To protect their anonymity as research participants, I will not mention their names, but I nevertheless wish to express my immense gratefulness for their help and collaboration in my study. None of this would have been possible without their willingness to spend time with me and tell me their stories. In Cuba I also established connections with anthropologists working on related themes, or at least interested in what I was doing, among whom were Pablo Rodríguez Ruiz, Avelino Couceiro Rodríguez, and Abel Sierra Madero. Year after year in my successive stays on the island, I visited and talked to them about the development of my research, and I am pleased to acknowledge the helpful insights of our conversations here.

While undertaking research in England, in 2006 and 2007 I also participated in a Swiss postgraduate programme in Ethnology/Anthropology that enabled me to come back regularly to Switzerland and continue my productive exchanges with Christian Ghasarian at the University of Neuchâtel. I am indebted to Ellen Hertz and Heinz Käufeler for directing and contributing to this postgraduate programme, which was a great platform for sharing the early findings of my investigation. Feedback from the participants in this programme improved the clarity and substance of my work, and here I wish to thank in particular Christian Giordano and Erhard Stölting (from the module on 'trust'), and Shalini Randeria and Jean and John Comaroff (who led the session on 'power'). Throughout these years within the Swiss academic community I benefited from stimulating exchanges with Géraldine Morel, Bastien Birchler, Séverine Rey, David Bozzini, Anne Lavanchy, Alain Mueller, Hervé Munz, Julie Perrin, Jérémie Forney, Anahy Gajardo, Aymon Kreil, and Alessandro Monsutti, among others.

In 2010 I left England to take on a research fellowship at the Centre for Research in Anthropology at Lisbon University Institute in Portugal (CRIA-IUL). In my four years there I had many fruitful exchanges and discussions with new colleagues, among whom I should acknowledge Francesco Vacchiano, Diana Espirito Santo, Anastasios Panagiotopoulos, Sofia Sampaio, Cyril Isnart, José Mapril, Anna Fedele, Peter Anton Zoettl, Ruy Blanes, Paulo Raposo, Micol Brazzabeni, Lorenzo Bordonaro, Chiara Pussetti, Vitor Barros, Ambra Formenti, Marianna Bacci Tamburlini, Lira Dolabella, Maria Cardeira da Silva, Miguel Vale de Almeida, Ramon Sarró, Paolo Favero, Filipe Reis, Antónia Pedroso de Lima, Manuela Ivone Cunha, Cristiana Bastos, Daniel Seabra Lopez, Paola Togni, Erin Taylor, Octávio Sacramento, Fernando Bessa, Ema Pires, and Eugenia Roussou.

Since the start of my research on tourism in Cuba, I have received invaluable feedback from participants in the various seminars, workshops and conferences I attended, some of whom were colleagues already acknowledged above. Though it would be impossible to thank all the other scholars that provided useful insights on my work here, I would like to mention at least some of them, grouped nonexclusively by research focus and themes. On the subject of tourism, tourism anthropology and mobility, I very much cherish the exchanges I had with Susan Frohlick, Julia Harrison, Kenneth Little,

Jackie Feldman, Naomi Leite, Michael di Giovine, Carina Ren, Quetzil Castañeda, Elizabeth Carnegie, Stan Frankland, Saskia Cousin, Chiara Cipollari, Sally Ann Ness, Claudio Minca, Pamila Gupta, Noel Salazar, Jamie Coates, Roger Norum, Edward Bruner, Nina Glick-Shiller, Heike Drotbohm, Liliana Suárez Navaz, Carsten Wergin, Kenichi Ohashi, and Mathis Stock. Among anthropologists working on Cuba with whom I have exchanged feedback over the last decade, I should mention Amalia Cabezas, Maria Padrón Hernández, Heidi Härkönen, Kristina Wirtz, Nadine Fernandez, Ingrid Kummels, Ana Alcázar Campos, Maki Tanaka, Kali Argyriadis, Silje Lundgren, Emma Gobin, Anne-Mette Hermansen, Flora Bisogno, Elena Sacchetti, Lorraine Karnoouh, Margalida Mulet Pascual, and Thomas Carter. On the themes of intimacy, gender and sexuality I profited from the insights of Adriana Piscitelli, Maïté Maskens, Rachel Spronk, Lorraine Nencel, Henrietta Moore, Christian Groes-Green, Matan Sapiro, Wim Peumans, Misty Luminais, Nathanael Homewood, Jeremy Walton, Nicole Constable, Jordi Roca, Yolanda Bodoque, Cristina García-Moreno, Verónica Anzil, Claudia Barcellos Rezende, and Anne-Linda Rebhun. Also linked to these themes were interesting discussions, centred more on anthropological approaches to ethics and morality, with Jason Throop, Jarrett Zigon, Douglas Hollan, Cheryl Mattingly, and Michael Lambeck. Finally, in the field of economic anthropology, I learned much from conversations with Susana Narotzky, Patrick Naveling, Keith Hart, and Stephen Reyna.

Besides the essays I delivered in the conferences and academic events referred to above, and often as a result of exchanges initiated there, some of the material presented in this book has appeared in earlier versions, as journal articles and book chapters. The comments of the editors of these publications certainly helped improve my texts and ideas, and I thank them all for this. Among the articles and chapters whose reworked bits and pieces can be found in this book, I should mention 'From Ethnographers to Tourists and Back Again: On Positioning Issues in the Anthropology of Tourism' (Simoni and McCabe 2008) and 'Revisiting Hosts and Guests: Ethnographic Insights on Touristic Encounters from Cuba' (Simoni 2014a), on which I elaborate in some sections of the introduction to this volume; 'L'interculturalité comme justification: Sexe "couleur locale" dans la Cuba touristique' (Simoni 2011) and 'Intimate Stereotypes: The Vicissitudes of Being *Caliente* in Touristic Cuba' (Simoni 2013), parts of which have been readapted in chapter 1; '"Riding" Diversity: Cubans'/*Jineteros*' Uses of "Nationality-Talks" in the Realm of their Informal Encounters with Tourists' (Simoni 2008a), which contains some of the examples and reflections presented in chapter 4; 'Scaling Cigars in Cuba's Tourism Economy' (Simoni 2009) and 'Tourism Materialities: Enacting Cigars in Touristic Cuba' (Simoni 2012a), most visible in chapter 5; 'The Morality of Friendship in Touristic Cuba'

(Simoni 2014b) and 'Introduction: Friendship, Morality, and Experience' (Simoni and Throop 2014a), on which I have drawn for chapter 6; 'Dancing Tourists: Tourism, Party and Seduction in Cuba' (Simoni 2012b), inspiring chapter 7; and 'Coping with Ambiguous Relationships: Sex, Tourism, and Transformation in Cuba' (Simoni 2014c), which also discussed some of the ethnographic examples employed in chapter 8.

Different research grants and fellowships have enabled me to carry out this ethnographic study, and the institutions that provided such funding deserve acknowledgement here. Sheffield Hallam University and Leeds Metropolitan University supported my investigations from 2005 until 2009. Between 2010 and 2014 a grant of the Portuguese Foundation for Science and Technology sponsored my research at the CRIA-IUL in Lisbon (SFRH/BPD/66483/2009). Finally, in the final stages of the writing process I was able to count on a research fellowship provided by the Swiss National Science Foundation (*Ambizione* Program, PZ00P1_147946), which is financing my current position at the Graduate Institute in Geneva.

I wish to thank Jackie Waldren and the editorial team at Berghahn Books for their support in the publication process: I had never imagined that relations with publishers could be so pleasant and productive. Thanks also to the two anonymous reviewers for their useful comments on an earlier version of the text; I hope they will find it much improved now. In the last stages of the publication process, I really appreciated the work of an anonymous copy editor whose timely corrections and suggestions helped enhance the overall quality of the manuscript. Nick James prepared the index with exemplary thoroughness, and I thank him for his efficiency. I am very grateful to Nelson Graburn for writing the preface, encouraging me throughout my investigation and writing, and promoting my research among colleagues. I do not think I could have found a better person to back my work.

Last but not least, I would like to acknowledge the invaluable help and support received throughout the years of my research and writing from my family: Renato, Enca, Mara, Hisako, and Lin.

I am aware that the list of people mentioned above is far from exhaustive, and I apologize to all those whom I have forgotten to mention here, but whose insights are nevertheless also reflected in this book. Any shortcomings in the text remain my sole responsibility, and I am very much looking forward to the comments and criticisms that may help improve my findings.

Introduction
Relating Through Tourism

'The problem here is that you never know why they are talking to you; if there is some hidden interest behind. Well, I guess they are always trying to gain something.'[1] This is what I retained from a conversation I had in a café in Havana with Sandra and Marta, two Swiss women in their late twenties who were travelling independently around Cuba in the summer of 2007. Their account of tourists' first encounters with Cubans in the streets of the capital was rather typical, as were the questions these relationships raised: 'Are these people sincere?' 'Can we trust them?' 'What do they want from us?'

Before my first visit to Cuba in 2005, as I thought about doing research on tourism in this country, I had several conversations with friends and acquaintances who had recently travelled there. Their encounters with Cuban men and women dominated much of our talk. What struck me most in this respect was the nuanced balancing of positive and negative aspects: 'Many Cubans just want to cheat you, but I also developed nice relationships with them', was the sort of reasoning I recalled from these early conversations. Setting off for this Caribbean island, my impression was that encounters between tourists and Cubans oscillated between two extremes. Put simply, on the one side were the positive promises of mutual understanding, hospitality and friendship, as well as romance; on the other was the daunting prospect of deceptive relationships where reciprocal manipulation and exploitation prevailed, as exemplified by notions of tourism hustling, sex tourism, and prostitution. How did tourists, in their engagements with Cuban people, discriminate between these two opposing scenarios, and what, if anything, lay in between them?

To a certain extent, these contrasting views were echoed in the writings of scholars and commentators who had attempted to evaluate the overarching nature of touristic encounters, which I had started to read. Whereas these encounters were said to be fraught with striking inequalities, highly

1

deceptive and constantly productive of misunderstanding (Krippendorf 1999 [1984]; van den Berghe 1980), they also appeared to hold the promise of cultural understanding and the establishment of positive connections between people from across the globe (Ki-Moon 2007). These contrastive narratives seemed to mirror and relationally constitute each other by way of opposition, outlining an either/or scenario not unusual in tourism literature at large, particularly when 'the big story of tourism' (Jack and Phipps 2005) is at stake.

In the conversations I had before leaving for Cuba, the contrasting tropes of mutual exchange and exploitation were hotly debated. A recurrent narrative saw people who had been warned of the potentially deceptive character of intimate relationships with Cuban men and women nonetheless being drawn into romance with locals in the course of their journey. Some had ended up marrying their Cuban partner; others looked forward to pursuing the relationship and returning to the island as soon as possible. How could expectations of cheating, deception and manipulation in relationships leave room for such gratifying and intense connections? The stories I gathered before my departure also significantly featured critiques of 'tourism apartheid', segregation between tourists and Cuban people, and an authoritarian communist regime that tried to monopolize tourists' expenditure and attention by obstructing and penalizing informal engagements between foreigners and ordinary (i.e. not employed in the tourism industry) Cubans. These critiques raised another question: how could encounters and relationships develop in spite of the alleged overwhelming control and institutionalization in the tourism industry?

In a wider sense, I was dealing here with what has been considered, for more than half a century now, a central paradox and dialectic informing the development of modern tourism, which Enzensberger (1996 [1958]: 129) phrased as 'the yearning for freedom from society' being 'harnessed by the very society it seeks to escape'. According to this interpretative model, the channelling of tourists into pre-established channels is in tensile relation with tourists' longing for freedom. To a certain extent, touristic encounters in Cuba seemed to echo this dialectic, or at least to be initially informed by it. However, these initial conversations also suggested that touristic encounters held the potential to break Enzensberger's 'vicious circle' of tourism's 'inner logic' and 'confinement' (1996 [1958]: 132), and that human relationships could not be reduced to any deterministic and ineluctable scenario. A closer look at recent anthropological debates on the matter, coupled with my ethnographic fieldwork in Cuba, progressively worked to support this view. This book shows that touristic encounters' potential to generate something new and to have effects that cannot be entirely predicted must not be underestimated and deserves all our attention. Writing about relationships

2

in tourism research, Strathern (2010: 82) recently argued that 'you can't actually read off from the characteristics – including race, gender, class – of any of the parties to a relationship just how that specific relationship is going to grow, unfold, develop a history, implicate others, expand, shrivel, die, and so forth, or what rules or expectations get put into place'. Reflecting more generally on 'the inherent ambiguity of everything human beings say and do in the presence of one another', Michael Jackson (2007: 148) observes that 'something irreducibly new is born of every human encounter, and it is the possibility of this newness that explains the perennial hope that inheres in every human relationship' (149). In the light of Jackson's remarks, we could argue that much of the ethnographic material discussed in this book draws attention to 'the energy devoted to reducing this intersubjective ambiguity and dealing with the fallout from never knowing exactly what others are feeling, thinking or intending' (148).

But there is more to it. In touristic Cuba, ambiguity could act as a key challenge to the establishment of encounters and relationships, but it was also what enabled such relationships to move forward. Jackson's (1998: 14) insight that 'intersubjectivity is inescapably ambiguous' finds echoes in Henrietta Moore's (2011: 17) consideration of 'the general underdetermination of cultural meaning, its ambiguity and indeterminacy', which 'provide the core conditions ... for self-other relations, the making of connections, cultural sharing and, ultimately, social transformation' (17). For Moore, subjectification would be impossible without ambiguity, given that 'human beings would be too overdetermined to become human subjects' (17). As I show in this book, the protagonists of touristic encounters in Cuba struggled with the potential overdetermination of their identifications as (gullible) tourists on the one hand, and as (deceitful) hustlers on the other. Highlighting asymmetries in knowledge and economic resources, these dyadic identifications called forth notions of trickery and exploitation, and were not a promising start for touristic encounters. They threatened the range of relationships and subjectivities aspired to by the tourists and Cuban men and women I engaged with, making it hard for them to establish gratifying connections. Part One of the book illustrates how these preconceptions gained shape and salience, and highlights what it took for people to meet, initiate interaction and eventually overcome such reductive framings. Following on from there, Part Two considers the different kinds of relationships that people tried to establish. Thus confronted with notions of market exchange, hospitality, friendship, festivity and sexual relations, we will follow closely how these relational idioms, about which both tourists and Cubans held a priori assumptions, acted as framing devices to qualify what was at stake in their interactions and to (re)define the agencies, subjectivities and moralities that informed them.

But while relational idioms could help people cope with intersubjective ambiguities, they could also generate new ones. It was one thing for visitors and Cubans to share some common understanding of notions of market exchange, hospitality, friendship, or festive and sexual relations; and quite another for them to enact these relationships in ways that fulfilled each other's expectations. If these forms of relationality could help soothe fears of trickery and exploitation by opening up possibilities, they also introduced their own demands and closures, calling for specific actions and behaviours. As such, they also channelled and delimited the scope of touristic encounters in certain directions, constraining their open-endedness and entailing choices and commitments that people were not always ready to make.

Investigating the formation of relationships in a tourism context, the book may be read as a journey into a real-life laboratory of human encounters, one in which relational norms and ideals were explicitly discussed, enacted, and put to test. We could argue, following Moore (2011: 15–16), that my wider interest is in 'comprehending the forms of complex relationality that characterize' 'the world we share with others'. Indeed, I wish to draw attention to the 'forms and means ... through which individuals imagine relationships ... to others' (16), uncovering how and how much any 'sharing with others' took place in an ethnographic context – that of tourism in Cuba – characterized by striking differences and inequalities. As Moore puts it, 'the recognition of diversity and difference produce particular kinds of self-other relations' (12). One of the aims of this book is precisely to specify what these forms and kinds look like, tracking their emergence, negotiation and constitution in touristic encounters in Cuba. The hope, as it were, is also to make some headway in grasping the implications of what Strathern sees as the 'Euro-Americans'' need for 'fresh ways of telling themselves about the complexities and ambiguities of relationships' (Strathern 2005: 27). This need, which contrasts with the 'huge investment ... in the language and imagery of individuals or groups' (27), hovered over the encounters addressed here, in which people strove to make sense of a multiplicity of engagements with a limited relational language, and struggled to actualize and reinvent their ways of talking about relationships.

The encounters that are the focus of this book confronted people with a range of specific, tourism-related situations that activated a set of assumptions, dispositions and expectations about roles, identities and agendas, and about the kind of relationships that could ensue. Uncovering these assumptions, dispositions and expectations is integral to my approach, which backs away from holistic views of 'the tourist' and 'the local' to focus instead on situated identifications and modes of engagement. In this sense, my goal is to shift the focus of analysis from 'tourists' and/or 'locals' to what happens between them – the practices, discourses, materialities, affects and

4

representations circulating in moments of encounter – and illustrate the insights that can be gained by reorienting research from a prevailing focus on (id-)entities towards a study of the relational processes from which (id-) entifications emerge.

Accordingly, the notions of 'tourist' and 'Cuban' employed throughout the text refer to emergent and relationally constituted identifications that take shape in precise moments of encounter, rather than analytical starting points implying the existence of two homogeneous groups of actors with clearly defined characteristics.[2] In this respect, it appears that the context of contemporary tourism in Cuba was less conducive to subsuming distinctions between insiders and outsiders, or residents and visitors, than may be the case in other tourism destinations.[3] Instead, the tourist/Cuban divide constituted the prevalent 'grammar of distinction' (Comaroff and Comaroff 1997: 25), an overarching and pervasive frame that could easily encompass other distinctions and identifications, and that allotted a key discriminating role to the asymmetry of resources between tourists and Cuban people. As I show in this book, the possibility of challenging this staunch divide by achieving other subject positions was one of the main promises of touristic encounters, fraught as they were with potentialities for redrawing lines of belonging and exclusion.

Over three decades ago Malcolm Crick (1989: 330) warned that 'the question of what sort of social relationships grow up in tourism encounters can only be answered by detailed and descriptive studies'. My aim is to provide some answers to this question, focusing on what has come to be known as the 'tourist/local' or 'host/guest' encounter. In the course of fieldwork in Cuba, when talking to tourists about their encounters with Cuban people, and vice versa, this key theme sprang immediately to the fore. How do these encounters emerge, and what are their salient qualities and features? In many ways, this text invites the reader to follow the responses that tourists and Cubans brought to these questions, as they enacted and made sense of a variety of engagements. Their common-sense understanding of touristic encounters frames the subject of my research, whose starting point was to take such understandings seriously, following how people came into contact, developed relationships, and conceptualized them.

Since Crick's (1989) review of social sciences literature on international tourism, other scholars have taken up the challenge of uncovering, via detailed ethnographic research, the kind of relationships that can emerge through tourism. Moving beyond polarizing assessments and evaluative generalizations, scholars have started to show touristic encounters' potential to regenerate the forms of relationality on which tourism relies. Thus authors have shown, for instance, how notions of friendship (Cohen 1971), reciprocity and hospitality (Adams 1992; Tucker 2003), love and partnership

(Brennan 2004; Kummels 2005), and market and commerce (Forshee 1999) are renegotiated and reshaped from within encounters. My work builds on these insights, integrating approaches that advocate for empirically informed studies to illuminate more thoroughly the complexities, ambiguities and transformative possibilities of touristic encounters and relationships.[4]

Of course, scholarly interest in contemporary forms and conceptualizations of relationships is by no means limited to research on tourism. Insightful parallels to my approach can be drawn, for instance, with recent anthropological research on love, sexuality and erotics uncovering transformations in notions and experiences of intimacy, notably in response to increased transnational connections – including tourism and migration – and changing economic conditions.[5] Current anthropological scholarship on friendship has also drawn attention to a range of different conceptions of this relational idiom in a variety of ethnographic locales,[6] encouraging anthropologists 'to be ready to observe the construction of new types of sociality in a globalizing but complex and contradictory world whose cultural and social boundaries are constantly being transformed' (Bell and Coleman 1999b: 16). My research in Cuba heeds Bell and Coleman's call, in that it tries to assess touristic encounters' potential to bring about new types of sociality and redraw lines of belonging across the North/South divide. This potential is also what explains why touristic encounters can become so absorbing for the protagonists involved. In other words, a lot may be at stake in them, given that the ways relationships take shape and develop can have profound and lasting effects on people's lives and livelihoods.

The works of Cohen (1996) in Thailand, Tucker (1997, 2001, 2003) in Turkey, and Fosado (2005) in Cuba have successfully shown how, in certain tourism contexts at least, the characterization of relationships becomes an emblematic issue constantly 'pulled into the intercourse' (Comaroff and Comaroff 1997: 29) between tourists and members of the visited population. Drawing on Comaroff and Comaroff's approach to the dialectics of the colonial encounter to illuminate touristic ones, I suggest that in such encounters too, certain discourses and practices become more central than others – including discourses and practices that inform the definition of relationships, their centrality exemplified by the fact that they are often contested and 'worked over as the dialectic unfold[s]' (Comaroff and Comaroff 1997: 29).

Once we recognize its centrality and contentious character, the characterization of relationships in tourism may be fruitfully apprehended as a 'hot' situation (Callon 1998a; Strathern 2002), in which everything (e.g. agencies, goals, motivations) is susceptible to controversy, like the 'conditions ... one might find in crises or dilemmas that seem to have many ramifications' (Strathern 2002: 54). According to Callon (1998a: 260), these controversial situations 'indicate the absence of a stabilized knowledge base', a gap that is likely in touristic encounters that bring together people from across the world. In hot situations, actors find it very hard to 'arrive at a consensus on how the situation should be described and how it is likely to develop' (Callon 1998: 263). Furthermore, the usual remedy for 'cooling down' these controversial conditions – namely, to make 'more and more elements of the situation explicit' (Strathern 2002: 254) – risks increasing the array of potentially contentious issues and can make it even harder to close the debate once and for all.

Viewed as a potentially hot situation, the definition of relationships in tourism should no longer be treated as a predictable (i.e. cold) and clear-cut issue, for such a view has often led to the dismissal of touristic encounters as superficial, commoditized versions of other, 'more real' human relationships (Krippendorf 1999 [1984]). Though tourists and members of the visited population may themselves reach these conclusions and portray their relationships as predictable, superficial and commoditized, my research suggests that this is far from being always the case. Instead, I argue, only by closely scrutinizing people's engagements can we achieve a clearer picture of the relationships that develop through tourism, of their possibilities and ramifications. It is precisely these possibilities that this book wishes to explore. By relying on 'the peculiar mileage afforded by the ethnographic method itself' (Henare, Holbraad and Wastell 2007: 2), my approach here calls on empirical evidence to dictate the terms of its own analysis, so as to unsettle taken-for-granted assumptions and generate new analytical progress. By the same token, I hope to show the usefulness of reopening a field of inquiry whose anthropological interest – three decades after the publication of *Hosts and Guests* (Smith 1978 [1977]) – is far from exhausted.

The Anthropology of Touristic Encounters and Relationships

Social Distance, Instrumentality and the Commoditization of Relationships

The study of encounters and relationships in tourism between 'hosts' and 'guests', 'tourists' and 'locals', has been capturing the anthropological imagination at least since Valene Smith's edited book *Hosts and Guests: The Anthropology of Tourism* was first published in 1977. In the conclusion to this path-breaking publication that helped establish the anthropology of tourism as a legitimate field of inquiry within the discipline, Theron Nuñez asked: 'What is the nature of the interaction between hosts and tourists?' Answering his own question, Nuñez (1978 [1977]: 212) maintained that such a relationship 'is almost always an instrumental one, rarely coloured by affective ties, and almost always marked by degrees of social distance and stereotyping that would not exist amongst neighbours, peers, or fellow countrymen'. Instrumentality, social distance, stereotyping: the anthropological literature has repeatedly highlighted all these features, as attested by the works of Pierre van den Berghe (1980, 1994, 1996), Dennison Nash (1978 [1977], 1981, 1996), Erik Cohen (1984) and Malcolm Crick (1989), which have explicitly addressed the issue of tourist-host encounters, summarizing the state of the research on the subject. In this scholarship, the nature of relationships between tourists and locals is alternately characterized as transient, manipulative and exploitative (van den Berghe 1980), impersonal (Pi-Sunyer 1978 [1977]; Nash 1978 [1977], 1981), dehumanized (Crick 1989) or 'staged as personalized' following a linear evolution towards the commoditization of hospitality (Cohen 1984).

In counterpoint to these generalizing assessments, more empirically grounded researches have shown that the type of relationships that can emerge through tourism cannot be reduced to a necessarily transient, impersonal, and commoditized affair. Studying Nepalese Sherpas' involvement in mountaineering and trekking tourism, for instance, Vicanne Adams (1992: 547–550) demonstrates how traditional patterns of wage labour are reconstituted via the 'idiom of reciprocity' and the skilful activation of strategies to create social obligations, enabling the establishment of 'long term bonds between hosts and guests' (549). Adams' insights into reconstructions of reciprocity, hospitality and friendship in tourism counter the hasty claim made by Aramberri (2001: 738) that 'the host should get lost' from the field of tourism research. Of course, we should neither idealize all touristic relationships as interactions between hosts and guests, nor consider a priori hospitality the preferred lens to illuminate them. Certainly we must examine processes of commoditization and take them into account. In doing so, however, we would benefit greatly from approaches akin to that of Adams, for as much as we strive to relocate and understand how hospitality and reciprocity regimes are brought about and re-created (see also Tucker 2003 and Sant Cassia 1999), so we should do with processes of commoditization. Under what conditions do these notions emerge? Who is using them in which situation? What do they conjure and achieve?

By refraining from categorizing a priori the types of relationships that can emerge through tourism, Amalia Cabezas (2006) has been able to show how even in the most enclavic and mass-oriented tourist environments, such as all-inclusive resorts in the Varadero Peninsula (a coastal area frequently dubbed Cuba's quintessential 'tourist bubble'), the interpretative moulds of 'staged personalized service' and 'commoditization' (Cohen 1984: 380) may obstruct subtler realities and understandings. Accordingly, Cabezas (2006: 515) shows how Cuban resort workers employed in hospitality organizations that encourage 'friendliness, subservience, and flirting' with tourist clients blur the line between the behaviour suggested by hotel management and pursuit of their own agendas. Workers seek out opportunities to cultivate various forms of relationships and intimacy with hotel guests. In this context, 'relationships that create long term obligations and commitment are, for many resort workers, more beneficial than commercialized sexuality' (516). The potential for romance and marriage with tourists, loaded with opportunities to leave the country, can thus become the most attractive prospect of employment in all-inclusive resorts. And as Cabezas shows, intimate relationships are indeed forged between Cuban employees and foreign tourists. The alleged staged personalization of service shifts into another realm that breaks down the client/worker divide, opening up other relational possibilities for the protagonists involved.

Brought together, the works of Cohen (1971), Adams (1992), Tucker (1997, 2001, 2003) and Cabezas (2006) constitute a compelling reminder of how slippery the terrain of generalizations on the nature of tourist-local relationships can be. To shed light on the very diverse scenarios that can emerge through tourism, detailed ethnography and processual, dynamic approaches to relationships like the one I advocate in this book appear to be key. Having cleared the path for the recognition of such diversity, we may now consider a realm of encounters in which issues of professionalization and commoditization are likely to become even more controversial. This realm can be fruitfully apprehended with the exploratory notion of 'informal encounter'.

From the Informal Economy to Informal Encounters in Tourism

Since Keith Hart's publication of 'Informal Income Opportunities and Urban Employment in Ghana' (1973), the concepts of the 'informal economy' and 'informal sector' have led to a number of refinements and conceptual clarifications across different disciplines. Anthropologists have been instrumental in highlighting the heterogeneity of practices that can be subsumed under these conceptual labels, and have explored the peculiar ways in which the notion of informal economy translates into different sociocultural contexts – as testified by the books edited by Clark (1988) and Smith (1990), and more recently the works of Stoller (2002) and Browne (2004), among others. In the following chapters I will also consider how in Cuba the notion of *jineterismo* – a neologism, provisionally translated as tourism 'riding', that tended to evoke tourism hustling and prostitution – pointed to a range of intersections between international tourism and the informal economy (see Cabezas 2004; Palmié 2004; Kummels 2005).

For Hart (2005: 8), 'the "formal sector" consisted of regulated economic activities and the "informal sector" of all those lying beyond the scope of regulation, both legal and illegal'. Following a similar conceptualization, Crick (1992) wrote about the 'informal' tourist sector as being 'that arena beyond the effective control of the tourism authorities – street corners, unlicensed guesthouses, cheap cafes, and so on' (136), and noted that 'through the Third World, where a tourism industry has developed, a similar "informal" sphere has grown up around its margins' (137). This sphere, in which people deploy strategies to direct any 'free floating' resource that may be available (139), has been largely neglected in tourism research, according to Timothy and Wall (1997: 336). More recently, anthropologists have devoted increased attention to the informal tourist sector, as for instance Dahles and Bras' (1999a) edited volume *Tourism and Small Entrepreneurs* testifies. These authors focus on entrepreneurship as they unpack the characteristics of tourism-oriented occupations that operate on the fringes of, but also in close connection to, the formal tourism sector.

By introducing the notion of the 'informal encounter', I aim to shift the focus from entrepreneurship and economic occupation to the qualities of encounters and relationships. The pertinence and methodological advantages of this notion become apparent once we consider that in many tourism destinations across the world, the policies being developed and implemented erect divides between formal and informal, legal and illegal interactions between tourists and members of the visited population. As I elaborate in chapters 1 and 2, this is the case in Cuba, where the authorities can selectively hinder, obstruct, and penalize informal contacts between foreigners and Cuban people. Under these conditions, the notion of 'informal' is applicable not only to economic activities and occupations, but also to interpersonal relations whose economic character remains controversial.

The existence of policies akin to those in place in Cuba has been documented in various tourist destinations and illustrates the suitability of the notion of informal encounter to address engagements that challenge what is officially prescribed and regulated, and leave the economic in a contentious place. Cohen's 1971 article on the relationships between 'Arab boys' and tourist girls' in Akko, a 'mixed Jewish Arab community' in Israel, provides a good illustration of this scenario. In that case, the local police occasionally interfered in these encounters, harassing and even arresting local youths under the accusation that they were molesting tourists (Cohen 1971: 230–231). More recently, in the tourism context of Jamaica, Mullings (1999: 78) has pointed out how 'tourism policies that seek to regulate the presence of the local population on certain public beaches ... have the potential to label encounters between local community members and tourists as punishable forms of harassment' (see also Getfield 2005).

To unpack how notions of harassment take shape in the tourism scenarios considered by Cohen (1971) and Mullings (1999), as well as in the Cuban case, I believe that the notion of the informal encounter is a more fruitful starting point than is the informal economy. As these authors show, tourism harassment is a term that can be abused in framing encounters between tourists and members of the visited population. Straight away, this notion emphasizes deception, predatory attitudes and economic instrumentality, though these are not necessarily characteristics the protagonists of such interactions would attribute to their relationships. The ease with which associations are made between the 'informal economy' and 'tourism harassment' in some tourism contexts, whereby the former can be unproblematically conflated with the latter, can become fertile ground for patronizing judgements that target 'deviant' behaviours and sustain discriminatory policies and policing of the tourism realm.

By contrast, the notion of informal encounter provides an analytical standpoint that refracts moralizing judgements that take economic agencies and instrumental rationalities for granted. This notion should at least prevent the convergence of our analytical approaches with the definition and targeting of tourism harassment, encouraging more sensitivity as to how these morally tainted constructs emerge. In this sense, the concept of informal encounter enables us to decentre and take a step back (or above, in terms of abstraction) from research on the informal tourist sector. Analytically, the step back consists in neither taking for granted nor restricting a priori the focus of investigations to the economic aspects of these touristic encounters and relationships. As our attention shifts from economic rationales to the ways people are brought together, in which economic issues may be included but also, sometimes, explicitly refuted, these issues cease to be the defining features of the process under scrutiny. By the same token, what comes to count as 'economic' in a given context becomes itself a matter for investigation, as the focus changes to how processes of 'economization' operate (Çalişkan and Callon 2009, 2010; also see chapter 5).[7]

Methodologically, however, the analytic use of this notion should not obfuscate the local conceptualizations that our ethnographies may reveal, like *jineterismo* in Cuba. In this sense, the concept of informal encounter is nothing more than an exploratory and heuristic device, geared essentially to comparative purposes. Here I follow Latour (2005: 49), who argues that 'analysts are allowed to possess only some *infra*-language whose role is simply to help them become attentive to the actors' own fully developed meta-language, a reflexive account of what they are saying'. As employed in this book, the term informal encounter – much like the terms encounter, relationship, or relational idiom (see below), for that matter – is a case of what Latour calls infra-language. Precisely because it is particularly under-determined and 'empty' (Henare, Holbraad and Wastell 2007: 20), such a notion can facilitate grasping the full extent and implications of our research participants' own conceptualizations.

The appeal of the notion and perspective outlined here becomes all the more clear once we consider the growing field of research on intimate and sexual encounters in tourism. In his review article 'The Role of Relationships in the Tourist Experience', Philip Pearce (2005: 116) sees the realm of sexual encounters as 'one marked exception to the lack of research on relationships in tourist-local encounters'. Indeed, following, among others, the pathbreaking work of Cohen (1996) in Thailand,[8] publications on the subject have flourished in the last decade.[9] Anthropologists researching the complex interface between sexual relations and compensation had long shown the pitfalls of hasty generalizations about what qualifies as 'prostitution', a term that tends to acquire negative and stigmatizing moral connotations and is often employed as a self-evident and unchanged notion (i.e. 'the oldest job in the world') (Tabet 1987: 1). In relation to tourism contexts, the works of Brennan (2004), Cabezas (2004, 2006), Fosado (2005), and Frohlick (2007) clearly show that avoiding any such aprioristic categorizations is both more respectful towards our research participants and analytically fruitful. It is worth considering Cabezas' (2004, 2009) remarks about sex and tourism in Cuba and the Dominican Republic:

> 'Prostitute,' or 'sex worker', is an identity assigned in specific situations, contingent on the social location and perceived characteristics of the participants, and lacking ambiguity in performance. In most situations, the permeable boundaries between leisure and labor, paid work and unpaid work, and private and public are difficult to discern, thus making it possible to resist the category of 'worker'. The category of 'sex worker', therefore, comes with its own disciplinary functions and … presents an either/or view of relationships and sexual practices. (Cabezas 2004: 1001–1002)

The notions of prostitute and sex worker, which presuppose fixed and stable identities (Cabezas 2004: 1002), become all the more problematic in conditions where sexual encounters between tourists and locals are not formalized and happen outside the control of institutions (e.g. brothels). Whereas in the latter case the term sex worker can become an empowering tool, leading for instance to the recognition of workers' rights, in less constrained situations the same term may seem too reductive or stigmatizing, and be rejected by the protagonists involved. Accordingly, Cabezas (2004: 1002) calls for more complex analytical frameworks that can enable us to grasp and make sense also of those situations in which 'the meanings that people attribute to actions cannot be specified in advance'.

This tends to be the case in informal touristic encounters in Cuba, as already indicated by Cabezas' (2004: 1010) remarks on the connections between 'greater economic informality' and the increasing difficulty of defining 'new social and economic ventures as labor'.[10] Building on these insights, the notion of informal encounter may help us draw attention to shifting boundaries between 'work' and 'leisure', and between what is qualified as 'social' or as 'economic'. This conceptualization can thus ensure that people's own understandings and definitions of encounters and relationships, including those interpretations which explicitly refute economic considerations, take precedence over the researcher's assumptions. As such, the notion of informal encounter is productive in highlighting the normative and potentially repressive dimensions of notions like 'tourism harassment', 'prostitution' and even 'sex work', foregrounding the processes that lead to their emergence, contestation and eventual crystallization.

The assumption that tourists are at leisure while locals work, and that this informs the nature of their relationships, has been reiterated by several leading scholars of tourism, from Nash (1978 [1977], 1981), to Krippendorf (1999), to Crick (1989). LaFlamme (1981: 473) had hinted at the possibility of interactions between tourists and locals 'in the context of mutual leisure', citing among his examples 'noneconomically motivated sexual encounters' (473), but the case made by Cabezas is an even more compelling reminder of the importance of moving beyond notions of work in certain tourism contexts, where being labelled a 'prostitute' or 'sex worker' can have very dramatic consequences for people who engage in sex with tourists, leading for instance to legal sanctions and even imprisonment.

I should make clear here that I am not suggesting downplaying or obliterating any distinction between 'tourists' and 'locals'. On the contrary, a range of key differences is likely to exist, and it is certainly our task to uncover them. The lesson we should learn is a methodological one: to be aware of the potentially contentious character of such aprioristic distinctions and categorizations. Even the seemingly unquestionable binary tourist-leisure/locals-work can, in certain situations, become a reductive, repressive framework that obstructs recognition of the whole spectrum of engagements and identifications that can emerge through tourism. By contrast, our task should be to illuminate how such divides and categorizations emerge, what controversies and struggles they give rise to, who is engaged in them, and what can they achieve.

These reflections may also help us to re-discuss recent literature emphasizing the role of 'mediators' in tourism, notably where encounters between tourists and locals are concerned (see in particular Chambers 1997, 2000; Cheong and Miller 2000; Werner 2003; and Zorn and Farthing 2007). Erve Chambers (1997: 6) points to the increasingly 'mediated' character of tourism, which means it is now 'dependent on the intervention of others who serve as neither hosts nor guests in any conventional manner'. As he puts it: 'Thinking of tourism as being predominantly a relationship between 'real' (i.e., residential) hosts and their guests has become problematic in several respects' (6). I agree that such assumptions may well be problematic and should not be taken as analytical starting points, but this should not lead us to shift from one extreme to the other and assume that no 'immediacy' can be achieved in touristic encounters.

This book reveals the efforts that both tourists and members of the visited population devoted to enact such immediacy, showing the risk of seeing immediacy simply as a lack or void of something (i.e. mediators), located at the bottom end of a linear evolution leading to increasing complexity and mediations. Instead, immediacy is approached processually as a situated achievement, as a construct that may require much investment to come about and be upheld. As Adams (1992) and Tucker (2003) have shown, the identifications of 'tourist' and 'local', of 'host' and 'guest', are themselves the result of processes in which a range of actors and agencies intervene. The chapters in this book support this view, showing that the question of determining whether tourists are dealing with 'professional tourism brokers', 'experienced tourism entrepreneurs', 'hustlers', 'prostitutes', 'ordinary Cubans', 'friends' or 'partners' is one that occupies and informs much of their engagement with members of the Cuban population, and also informs what counts for them as a genuine encounter or relationship and in what way.

Relational Idioms and Insightful Controversies

From 'hospitality' to 'commoditized relationships', 'tourism hustling', 'friendship', 'sex tourism', 'prostitution', 'love' and 'romance', the academic literature on tourism has alternatively dealt with these notions in more or less reified or processual ways. Scholars like Adams (1992), Cabezas (2004, 2006, 2009) and Tucker (2003) have shown the interest of empirical study to uncover the punctual, variegated and often contested enactments of these relational idioms in different tourism contexts. In her fascinating book on transnational desire and sexual touristic encounters in the Dominican Republic, Denise Brennan (2004: 22) also considers how 'Dominican sex workers and foreign sex tourists forge new practices and meanings of "love" that grow out of the tourist and sex-tourist trades'. Investigating local meanings of prostitution, marriage and womanhood in Cuba, Ingrid Kummels (2005: 10) argues on her end that 'in the transcultural relations between sex tourists and locals, models of womanhood, partnership and love are not merely "given" by the social structure in the context of a globalized modernity.

Instead they are to a large extent actively produced via agency or are rene-gotiated'. Working in the very different tourism context of Yogyakarta in Java (Indonesia), Jill Forshee (1999: 294) highlights how tourism in this city gives rise 'to new forms of social interaction', including a range of perpetually evolving market idioms and approaches to commerce (296–298), which the anthropologist then sets out to uncover.

The following chapters, and more particularly Part Two of the book, show how encounters that happen through tourism can constitute a privileged ethnographic case shedding light on people's investment and absorption in the conceptualization of relationships, or what may be phrased as the explicitation and (re)qualification of relational idioms. I use the notion of the 'relational idiom' to refer to various types of relationships as defined and qualified by the subjects of my investigation. This heuristic concept draws attention to the way tourists and members of the visited population conceptualize and frame their relationships, be it, to cite some possibilities, in terms of 'hospitality', 'friendship', 'commerce', or 'romance'. Working on notions of friendship in Chinese societies, Alan Smart (1999: 120; see also Bell and Coleman 1999b: 15) has shown the usefulness of considering 'friendship as an idiom of interaction: a way of talking about relationships, rather than a set of criteria which can define the term'. According to Smart, 'friendship must be seen in the context of other idioms of interaction' (120; see also Killick and Desai 2010). The notion that different relational idioms inform each other, and therefore that considering and understanding them in conjunction may be useful, can certainly illuminate the workings of relationships in other contexts and in fact guided my own investigation in touristic Cuba.

Building on these insights, I wish to show how different relational idioms mirror and acquire their meanings in relation to one another, notably by way of convergences, contrasts and opposition. I am interested in the way people formulate criteria to define and qualify what relational idioms are about, using one to criticize another, outlining continuities but also drawing boundaries and incommensurabilities between them. Indeed, I also focus on how shifts and transitions from one relational idiom to the other operate, that is, on the mechanisms of their convergence/divergence and overlap-ping/separation. Furthermore, my understanding of relational idioms is not limited to the way people talk about relationships but also includes the normative expectations, dispositions and moral ways of being that these idioms conjure. Expectations and dispositions towards different types of relationships shape people's discourses, behaviours and ways of engaging with each other, and are in turn challenged and reshaped by them. The importance of moving beyond discursive rationalizations in understanding relational idioms and their transformations becomes all the more clear once we consider 'that thought alone is not enough to bring about change' and that 'we need to take account of the way in which thought is bound up with fantasy, affect, emotion, symbols, and the distortions of space and time' (Moore 2011: 18).

Touristic encounters are likely to involve discrepancies in terms of people's expectations and dispositions towards engaging with each other, fostering the emergence of controversies about the relational idioms at play. The importance of such ambiguities and controversies is clearly revealed in the works of Cohen (1996) in Thailand, Tucker (1997, 2001, 2003) in Turkey and Fosado (2005) in Cuba, which show how deeply the issue of qualifying relationships can absorb tourists and members of the visited population. In her research on gay sex tourism, ambiguity and transnational love in Havana, Fosado (2005: 75) maintains that ethnographic work must preserve and account for the ambiguous character of these relationships, highlighting 'the need for a new theoretical framework that allows for uncertainty and ambiguity as defining factors in relationships'. In these ethnographies we find tourists and locals who, puzzled about their relationships, scrutinize each other's actions for clues that can help them make up their mind and discriminate between various types of relational engagement (e.g. 'friendship', 'hospitality', 'hustling', 'prostitution', 'love'). As we shall now see, the question of the kind of relational idioms that could be at play in touristic Cuba was also one that affected my fieldwork trajectories and possibilities.

The Ethnography: Locations, Positionings and Relationships

Fieldwork Locations

In February 2005 I went to Cuba for the first time to carry out an initial month of exploratory fieldwork and assess the feasibility of my research project. I spent most of my time in the capital, Havana, which was to remain the key location of my subsequent stays: two months in 2005 (July–September), four months in 2006–2007 (November–March), two months in 2010–2011 (December–January), two months in 2011–2012 (December–January), one month in 2013 (April–May), and one month in 2014 (July). Of the total thirteen months, about eight were spent in the city of Havana, with the remaining five divided between the beach resort of Playas del Este (a half-hour drive east from the capital) and the rural town of Viñales (about 200 km west of Havana). Most tourists visiting Cuba arrive in Havana, which proved an ideal location to carry out fieldwork on informal touristic encounters. Just strolling around tourism areas in the city quickly made clear that such encounters abounded and were highly varied in kind. Tourists travelling in groups or independently, young and old, from different countries and with different interests and agendas, mingled on the streets of the capital. This diversity of tourists and tourism practices was matched by an equally diversified array of informal tourism-oriented activities of Cuban people: befriending visitors; offering their services as guides or companions; selling cigars; proposing sexual services, private 'illegal' taxis, accommodations, food, and so on.

In Havana, I spent much time at the tourism hot spot of Old Havana (La Habana Vieja) within the circumscribed area declared a UNESCO World Heritage Site in 1982, which featured restored squares, streets and buildings dating back to Spanish colonial times. The site features the city's highest density of must-see tourist attractions. Even the shortest guided tours of the capital, lasting only a few hours, passed through the four main squares (*plazas*) of San Francisco, Armas, Catedral and Vieja (see Figures 0.1 and 0.2), giving to this area of the city the allure of an open-air museum, an 'enclavic tourist space' (Edensor 1998) visited daily by thousands of tourists[11].

Besides spending time meeting and engaging with tourists and Cubans in the touristic core of Old Havana, I frequented other, more 'heterogeneous tourist spaces' (Edensor 1998) in the capital, where informal encounters thrived. Such were the areas around the Capitolio Nacional, the Paseo del

FIGURE 0.1 • *Plaza de la Catedral, Havana*

Figure 0.2 • *Plaza de San Francisco, Havana*

Prado, the Malecón and the Barrio Chino (Chinatown, situated behind the Capitolio) (see Figures 0.3 and 0.4). Here the streets tended to be more chaotic, and few roads and buildings were restored like those in the museum-like circuit of Old Havana. Regulation and surveillance by police and CCTV cameras were also less intense, and this loosening of the control apparatus – notwithstanding the lesser density of tourists – allowed for greater scope in informal contacts (Simoni 2005a).

From the evening onwards, often until the early hours of the morning, my fieldwork locations shifted as bars and nightclubs became the foci of touristic encounters. Newer areas of the capital, particularly the area of Vedado around the Calle 23 (popularly known as La Rampa), bustled with nightlife activity as tourist and Cuban men and women gathered in and around lively bars and clubs. At night these bars and clubs, as well as those located in the more upper-class neighbourhood of Miramar, attracted many of the tourists who had spent their day relaxing at the beach in Playas del Este. My desire to know more about such 'beach tourism' – *turismo de playa*, as several of my Cuban informants put it – and the kind of encounters it fostered, prompted me to move from Havana to Playas del Este.

Stretching along several kilometres of coast east of Havana, Playas del Este has long been a leisure destination favoured by residents of the capital. Cubans flocked to these beaches during my fieldwork, especially during

18

FIGURE **0.3** • *View from the Capitolio Nacional, Havana*

FIGURE **0.4** • *The Malecón, Havana*

weekends in the summer season. By contrast, Playas del Este drew tourists all year long, since even (if not especially) in winter the Caribbean beach exerted its fascination on visitors who had left cold Europe and North America for a hot place in the sun. Playas del Este was a hot spot of international tourism throughout the 1990s, when the town of Guanabo gained a reputation for parties and 'easy' Cuban women, attracting crowds of single male tourists in search of fun and sexual adventures. By the time of my fieldwork, following several crackdowns by the Cuban authorities (see chapters 1 and 2), international tourism in Guanabo had dwindled, and the presence of foreigners was most visible on the beach of Santa Maria, a few kilometres west.

On this hundred-metre strip of sand in front of the Hotel Tropicoco (Figures 0.5, 0.6 and 0.7), tourists gathered to enjoy beach life, alternating between their deckchairs, the bar and restaurant, and a swim in the sea. The possibility of meeting these largely male tourists also lured many young Cuban women to frequent the beach. As both tourists and Cubans told me, Santa Maria was an ideal place to encounter people interested in relationships of a sexual and intimate kind, which made it an important venue for flirting and seduction, a place where couples were created and meetings arranged to continue relationships later at night in the clubs and discos of Havana.

FIGURE 0.5 • *Santa Maria Beach, Playas del Este*

FIGURE 0.6 • *Santa Maria Beach on a Summer Weekend, Playas del Este*

FIGURE 0.7 • *Tourists and Cubans at Santa Maria Beach, Playas del Este*

Besides Havana and Playas del Este, the other major tourism destination in which I conducted fieldwork was the town of Viñales, located in the western province of Pinar del Rio, a three-hour bus ride from Havana. In my first month in Cuba, I went to Viñales on the recommendation of other tourists, who had many good things to say about this countryside town and its people. One such endorsement came from my mother, who had travelled there a few years earlier and given me some gifts to bring to the family that had hosted her. Once in Viñales, I was immediately fascinated by the rural atmosphere of the town and its surroundings (Figures 0.8 and 5.4–5.8), which I found particularly refreshing after several weeks roaming the streets of the capital. More important for my research, starting on my first stay in town I managed to make a number of excellent contacts with young men – Viñaleros – and forge relationships that proved very rewarding throughout my fieldwork and kept drawing me back there. Viñales' small size facilitated daily encounters with the same people and consequently fostered the cultivation of strong ties with some of them in a way that I found more difficult to achieve in Havana due to the more dispersive nature of my fieldwork trajectories there.

The main tourism destination west of Havana, Viñales and its valley were often praised for their stunning landscapes (especially the peculiar hills called

FIGURE **0.8** • *Viñales and Its Surroundings, Viñales*

mogotes), their tobacco fields and farms, the possibility of excursions and other 'nature tourism' pursuits – the whole experience possibly enhanced by the 'friendly and hospitable' character of 'rural folks' and a familiar stay in one of Viñales' *casas particulares* (literally 'private houses', guesthouse-type accommodations that rent rooms to foreigners). Since 1999 the valley's World Heritage status has added to its popularity, and the area has attracted an increasing number of visitors, mostly independent travellers, prompting a boom in *casas particulares* and other tourism-related businesses. Provided both formally and informally, the latter included guide services for walks in the countryside, bicycle rentals, horseback riding, and visits to tobacco farms. While Viñales, in this book, appears mainly in relation to these farm visits (chapter 5), the close connections and conversations I had with several young Viñaleros proved fundamental to my overall understanding of touristic encounters.

Positioning the Tourist/Ethnographer

Anthropological debates on reflexivity and the positioning of the researcher have highlighted the challenges that can arise during fieldwork, in terms of interpretations of the researcher by the researched, competing obligations towards informants, and the various problematic negotiations involved in trying to shift perspectives and subjectivities (Hume and Mulcock 2004; Narayan 1993; Parkin 2000). In this respect, Crick (1995) and Michel (1998a) have pointed out how encompassing and resilient the identification of any foreigner as tourist can become in some tourism destinations, making it very hard to overcome such a framing (Simoni and McCabe 2008). When I first went to Cuba, I was aware of the likelihood that Cuban people would consider me first and foremost a foreigner, one of the tourists and thus also potential 'prey' for *jineteros* and *jineteras* – the 'tourist riders' whose reputation preceded my initial experience of the country. As I soon realized in the first days I spent walking around tourism areas of Havana, the locals I encountered indeed saw me mainly as a tourist.

This initial framing as tourist both enabled and restricted the scope of my research, informing the kind of access I had to Cuban people on the one hand, and to foreign visitors on the other. Being perceived as a tourist granted me plenty of opportunities to interact with Cuban men and women, notably those who actively sought to meet foreigners. Whether they were offering cigars, guide services, companionship or sex, or just hoping to exchange a few words, little effort was required from me to engage with them. These interactions provided a wealth of auto-ethnographic data on the possible functioning of touristic encounters in Cuba, and more particularly their opening moments (chapter 4). That said, I am aware of the risks of loosely employing this material to make sense of the experiences of other tourists, a pitfall recently discussed by Graburn (2002). Reflecting on the embodied nature of our fieldwork experiences in tourism ethnography, Frohlick and Harrison (2008b: 12) remark:

> The question of why particular individuals talk to us is related in part to how we inhabit these places through our bodies – whether we are young or old, female or male, how we look, what we wear, whether we go to the beach, if we go dancing, bring our children or partners with us, take our camera, and so forth.

The most obvious illustration of how my embodied self shaped fieldwork in touristic Cuba related to gender and sex. In their work on sex tourism in Amsterdam and Havana, Nancy Wonders and Raymond Michalowsky (2001: 547) noted that: 'As gendered researchers ... our access to information was also gendered. Ray could more easily fall into conversation with male sex tourists, and could enter into conversations with sex workers and pimps as a result of their initial interest in him as a possible customer'. During fieldwork I was frequently approached as a possible consumer of sex, which made it harder to establish close rapport devoid of sexual connotations with Cuban women. That was not the case with Cuban men, with whom I also had more chances to participate in moments of peer sociability.

To the wider challenge of being perceived as a foreigner, a *yuma* (a derogatory term for foreigners) and therefore also a potential source of gain, I responded with attempts to negotiate and shift my position, singularizing my persona and distinguishing myself from tourists. My position tended to change, or at least assume other shades, after an initial exchange and explanation of my research and the purpose of my stay, but for many of my Cuban research participants I think I remained essentially a rather peculiar foreign visitor spending more than the average time in their country. But here generalizations must also be tempered. Indeed, as I maintain more generally in this book, encounters with Cuban people also offered a platform for negotiating new subjectivities and achieving new relational positions (see Simoni 2014d).

Meanwhile, my access to foreign visitors presented other challenges and opportunities. Graburn (2002) and Frohlick and Harrison (2008b) show that a key difficulty of ethnography in tourism settings relates to the transitory nature of tourism and the fleeting presence of visitors in destinations. Furthermore, tourists are likely to be absorbed in pleasure-seeking leisure pursuits, which may unfavourably inflect their predisposition to 'serious talk' with researchers (Graburn 2002: 20; Frohlick and Harrison 2008b: 6). During fieldwork, I soon realized that whereas Cuban people approached me as a tourist, things were rather different with tourists: I had to make an effort to create a first connection. Knowledge of the tourists' language proved instrumental in establishing a first bond and striking up a conversation, which explains the over-representation of Italian-, French-, English- and Spanish-speaking foreigners among my research participants. Gender, age, and appearance also informed my ability to meet and establish close connections with certain kinds of tourists more than others. The tourism places I frequented are another important element to consider: from a beach patronized mainly by single male tourists relaxing and flirting with Cuban women to a folkloric show of Afro-Cuban music and performance, any such place had its own atmosphere, to which I tried to adapt, with various degrees of success, in order to establish meaningful connections with tourists on the scene.[12]

Developing Relationships

Tourists' willingness to spend time with me tended to intensify once they understood I was doing research in Cuba, had spent significant time there, and was therefore 'something more' than a 'mere tourist' having his first experience of the island. Many were eager to know about my experiences and knowledge of Cuba and Cuban people, as well as my research findings, and when asked about their own experiences were generally keen on sharing their stories. On several occasions, I became a sort of confidant for people who felt intense, contradictory emotions towards their Cuban friends and partners – especially tourists involved in sexual and romantic relationships with locals.[13] In such cases, tourists seemed to appreciate having someone to listen empathetically to their stories, to whom they could unburden their awkward feelings, and who could help them make sense of what was going on in these relationships. Interactions with Cuban research participants also resulted in such intimate moments of self-disclosure, which became the most rewarding instances of my fieldwork and may be seen as islands of intimacy in what was otherwise an emotionally draining realm of ambiguous and potentially deceptive relationships that kept reminding me of my otherness, foreignness, and privileged position.

The question of ascertaining what kind of relationship I had with Cuban people absorbed me throughout the fieldwork. How much was their interest in my company due to my privileged economic position, and how much did it depend on my 'personality' and 'human qualities'? Was it really useful to separate the two? These kinds of questions also puzzled many tourists I met. Establishing a relationship with the sort of tourist-ethnographer I was could appeal to people for reasons besides immediate economic considerations.

For instance, on several occasions I became a means of access to other visitors as 'the very good friend' that the Cuban at stake had known 'for ages', and who could reassure sceptical tourists about the Cuban's good reputation and intentions (see chapter 6).[14] Another means of reciprocity towards my Cuban research participants was to become more actively involved in their activities, acting explicitly as a collaborator, someone who could direct tourists towards them and even arrange some deals on their behalf. Here I faced the question of how far I should involve myself in my Cuban and tourist research participants' agendas, especially when these seemed incompatible.

Competing Obligations

One challenge in my collaboration with Cubans was to avoid being perceived as a *jinetero* and hustler myself. My aim was not, of course, to make money by taking advantage of tourists, nor did I want to enter into any competition for tourists with Cubans. Interestingly, numerous examples circulated of long-term tourists who had ended up playing *jineteros* themselves, bringing tourists around and doing their own informal business with them. Given my willingness to get to know foreign visitors, I could easily be identified as one such *jinetero*, and on several occasions, after telling my Cuban friends how I would frequent tourist areas trying to meet foreigners – that is, do fieldwork – I was indeed teased for being a *jinetero*. The reasoning here was that anyone who actively tried to meet tourists had to be a *jinetero*. More subtly, a friend once told me I was doing *jineterismo informacional*, that is, doing *jineterismo* to gather information. This reveals the strength of *jineterismo* as a lens through which Cuban people viewed relationships with tourists,[15] raising questions about the practice of ethnography itself and its instrumental dimensions.

Whenever I wished to help Cubans engage with tourists, I also had to decide whom to help, which could become a sensitive matter given the strong sense of competitiveness and the factionalism inherent in the struggle to 'get' foreigners and establish exclusive relationships with them. In a few instances, I became myself an object of contention as people fought over their entitlement to stay with me. Disputes over tourists as 'property' could become rather serious and put me in the awkward position of trying to redefine and clarify my relationships. There was then also the issue of the obligation I felt towards tourists. How should I react, for instance, if I thought that the cigar deal offered to the tourists I was hanging around with was not good? Whose side was I to take? My decisions were generally made on the spot, as I struggled between the responsibility I felt towards tourists on the one hand and my relationship with Cuban people on the other.

A Multiplicity of Perspectives

During fieldwork, my most obvious source of data was auto-ethnography, which derived essentially from 'what happened to me-as-a-tourist'. Alternatively, I could observe and participate in touristic encounters by accompanying tourists who then met Cuban people, or by hanging around with Cubans who encountered foreign tourists. Both these situations opened a window onto how touristic encounters emerged, and relationships developed. As I was not the main protagonist in these meetings and relations, I was able to observe and participate in encounters from within without taking a leading role. Frohlick and Harrison (2008b) discuss the anxiety that can derive from the assumption that, as ethnographers of mobile subjects, we do not spend enough time with the same people. Accordingly, it became imperative for me to be 'hyper-attuned' and 'open to the unexpected' so as not 'to miss a single opportunity' (2008b: 14) to engage for as long as possible with research participants. This meant very late nights in the company of partygoers, early mornings showing up for planned excursions, and more generally the cultivation of a flexible self that could adapt to other people's agendas. Complementing the data generated from within touristic encounters was information derived from more external vantage points, as when I observed the behaviours of tourists and Cubans interacting in proximity to me in public places, without them knowing about my research agenda. While this provided me with plenty of potentially useful data, it also made me feel uncomfortably like a voyeur, which is why I much preferred situations in which I was more overtly part of the interaction.

Finally, other important sources were the numerous occasions on which I listened to and talked with foreign tourists and Cuban people, beyond the moments when they were interacting with each other. These conversations were very diverse in register, spanning from public gossiping to more personal, intimate exchanges. As already mentioned, among Cubans I was more easily involved in situations of male sociability, for example when Cuban men conversed among peers about their encounters with foreign tourists. Similar to what Malcolm Crick (1992: 141) remarks regarding the Sri Lankan street guides he worked with, on these occasions 'myth making, exaggeration and bravado' abounded, as Cuban men boasted of their – notably sexual – exploits with foreign women.[16] In such conversations, people tended to objectify tourists, following the semantic registers of *jineterismo* and becoming 'tourist-riders' conquering foreign targets for essentially instrumental purposes.

Other, contrasting types of discourses emerged when I had the chance for more intimate discussion with my research participants. Here, other views of relationships with tourists could take shape, and emotional attachments and more vulnerable selves entered the picture. On these occasions I became a sort of confidant – a relatively neutral and complicit outsider with whom people felt comfortable discussing their more intimate feelings, doubts and anxieties about their connections with foreign tourists, without having to fear their Cuban peers' cynical remarks about being 'too soft' or sentimental. This is something that also happened with tourists, particularly men, with whom, as mentioned above, I occasionally assumed a similar role as confidant.

The variety of situations and registers of conversations in which I became involved – from the most transitory auto-ethnographic moments to the more prolonged and confidential relationships – ultimately gave me access to touristic encounters and relationships from a multitude of perspectives. Accordingly, the data I rely on in the following chapters reflects various degrees of ethnographic 'thickness', juxtaposing for instance fleeting conversations overheard in a bar with more intimate dialogues with research participants I have known for years. I would argue that this diversity of fieldwork engagements also enabled me to remain sensitive to, and understand, a wide range of enactments and interpretations of touristic encounters. As a result, I uncovered a variety of modes of being and of reflecting on these interactions that draw attention to heterogeneity within the lives of the subjects of my research and shed light on their multiple, often paradoxical, ways of experiencing touristic encounters. Understanding this variety, and drawing these different moments of interaction together without aprioristically ranking them as more or less significant or revealing of any single 'truth' of touristic encounters in Cuba, became important in my work, and I believe such an approach can offer new insights into the experience and implications of these relationships for the lives of the protagonists involved.

I should also state clearly that all in all, my research was not based on any supposedly representative sample of tourists and members of the visited population making contact in touristic Cuba. Most of my ethnographic material reflects the practices and views of young – mostly in their twenties and thirties – male, heterosexual members of the tourist and Cuban population. In the case of tourists, Italian-, French-, English- and Spanish-speaking people predominate, and visitors from Italy are clearly over-represented (particularly in chapter 8). As for Cubans, the examples discussed in the book come mainly from residents of Havana who were eager to meet and engage with foreign tourists (see chapter 2). Any related biases, however, should not detract from the overall argument, which has to do with how touristic encounters emerged and were qualified in Cuba, and aims to draw attention to common processes running across a wide range of situations of interaction. I decided to take into account an ample repertoire of encounters precisely because they illuminate each other, enabling deeper insights into their transversal mechanisms and overarching features.

Organization of the Book

The book is divided into two main parts and organized according to a rather linear narrative. Drawing on my observations, I describe how encounters between foreign tourists and members of the visited population in Cuba emerged (Part One), and how relationships were given shape and qualified (Part Two). Thus, the first part of the book mainly concerns what preceded and informed the occurrence of encounters, from the historical develop-ment of tourism in Cuba up to the first moments of contact. The second part focuses on a key range of relationships that developed from such initial contact, relationships that brought into play the idioms of commerce and hospitality, friendliness and friendship, festivity and seduction, and sexuality. Below I summarize briefly each of the chapters' main arguments.

Discussing the prevalent features of tourism development in Cuba from the turn of the nineteenth century to the present day, chapter 1 sets the stage for the remaining empirical chapters of the book. An overview of the emergence and evolution of *jineterismo*, a contentious term tending to evoke notions of 'tourism hustling' and 'prostitution' that was selectively employed to designate a range of informal engagements in the tourism realm, progres-sively paves the way for chapter 2, which focuses more thoroughly on this phenomenon, highlighting its heterogeneous character, elusive nature, and the moral controversies it generated. I therefore consider how, with the coming of age of international tourism and *jineterismo* in Cuba, tourists' and Cubans' awareness of each other's expectations also matured, raising questions about the compatibility of their agendas. Chapter 3 examines the resources, tactics and predispositions tourists and Cubans could rely on to deal with, and eventually overcome, the normative suggestions and control of the Cuban authorities, which tended to reinforce the tourist/ Cuban divide. The consideration of such prerequisites to the establishment of informal encounters highlights all the 'background work' that made them possible. Chapter 4 addresses how tourists and Cubans got in touch and ini-tiated interactions, a step that absorbed the protagonists of such encounters, who saw in it the possibility of a first assessment of each other's desires and agendas. Building on chapter 3, chapter 4 reinforces the idea that touristic encounters in Cuba activated a wide range of resources that constituted the protagonists involved as more or less competent actors in this peculiar realm of relationships.

The second part of the book explores how, from the initial moments of an encounter, various types of relationships were enacted, testing the tourists' and Cubans' proficiency in a range of relational idioms. Chapter 5 considers a realm of engagement that tended to epitomize the transient, manipulative, commoditized character of touristic encounters, as well as their most instrumental dimensions: cigar deals. Chapter 6 examines friendliness and friendship, a recurrent relational idiom informing touristic encounters in Cuba. Issues of trust take centre stage as the spotlight falls on the crucial tension between the asymmetric and instrumental character of relationships and ideals of friendship. The chapter also reveals how, in the light of their experiences and as a result of touristic encounters, the protagonists involved were led to (re)formulate what they meant by friendship, questioning taken-for-granted assumptions and voicing their hopes and aspirations on the matter. Chapter 7 is concerned with festive relationships and shows how partying brought about shifts in modes of engagement that encouraged people to follow their affective drives and desires and open up new relational possibilities. Building on these insights, chapter 8 considers in more detail a variety of narratives and justifications regarding sexual relationships between tourist men and Cuban women. The increased attention to personal stories highlights how important changes in peoples' attitudes and discourses resulted from their engagements, providing further insights on the generative potential of touristic encounters.

The conclusion reviews and elaborates on the main contributions of the book, and revisits the heuristic potential of the notions of informal encounter and relational idiom. Drawing together the insights developed in the different chapters, it outlines theoretical and methodological paths to stimulate further research on touristic encounters and, more broadly, the formation of relations across difference and inequality in the contemporary world.

Part One

ACHIEVING ENCOUNTERS

Chapter 1
TOURISM IN CUBA

This chapter aims to contextualize the emergence of informal touristic encounters within the wider picture of tourism development in Cuba by providing a selective review of the history of international tourism in this country, particularly since the 1990s. The idea is not to be exhaustive, but rather to highlight the most relevant continuities and discontinuities that further understanding of tourism's present condition and can shed light on the main promises and challenges of such encounters.

After the first half of the twentieth century, when Cuba gained the reputation of a 'tropical playground' for U.S. citizens, the success of the revolutionary movement led by Fidel Castro in 1959 marked the end of an era in Cuba's history and a turning point in its associations with international tourism. Towards the end of the 1980s, after about three decades of relative stagnation in terms of international tourist arrivals, a rapidly worsening economic crisis prompted the Cuban authorities to renew their efforts to develop tourism, which received further impetus with the beginning of the Special Period in Time of Peace (*Período especial en tiempo de paz*) in 1990 – the time of austerity and economic hardship that followed the collapse of the Soviet Union.

As Cuban people struggled to get by and ameliorate their economic conditions, the Special Period saw the explosion of an ample range of informal economic activities on the island, among which tourism-related ones played an increasingly salient role. This realm of activity has come to be known by the contentious term *jineterismo*, which tends to evoke notions of 'tourism hustling' and 'prostitution' and is employed selectively to designate various informal engagements in tourism. By the mid 1990s, Cuba had, in some tourism circles, acquired the reputation of a 'tourist paradise for sex', attracting visitors who revelled in the island's promise of sandy beaches, hedonistic parties and sensual, sexually liberated Cuban bodies. Scholars have highlighted the ambiguous character of the Cuban authorities' initial response to the issues of 'tourism-oriented prostitution' and 'sex tourism'. Later in that decade, however, the Cuban government took a less ambiguous stance, cracking down on *jineterismo* and trying to shift and diversify the tourism appeal of the country.

Far from disappearing under the new conditions of stepped-up controls and increased repression by the Cuban authorities, *jineterismo* progressively adapted itself by becoming less visible and relying on subtler tactics to approach tourists. A consideration of these latest developments in Cuban tourism paves the way for chapter 2, which focuses more thoroughly on *jineterismo*, its increasing popularity and diffusion in tourism related narratives, and how this shaped tourists' and Cubans' predispositions and expectations towards meeting each other.

Cuba and Tourism before the Revolution

Following its 'discovery' by Christopher Columbus in 1492, Cuba, much like its Caribbean neighbours, soon became the setting of a plantation society in which black slaves arriving from West Africa progressively replaced a decimated indigenous workforce in the prosperous business of sugarcane. In Cuba the Spanish did not find much in the way of resources they had coveted, such as jewels and precious metals, but the island – the biggest in the Caribbean – became a crucial stopover in the trade between Africa, the Americas and Europe. Cuba's strategic location as a crossroads of trade routes contributed to its masters' economic prosperity and also attracted many visitors (Hall 1992: 109). By 1760, with the slave trade and the sugar industry thriving, Havana was a larger city than New York (Baker 2004: 29).

Resisting pressures from other colonial powers, Spain did not abolish slavery in Cuba until 1888. By the mid nineteenth century, the struggle for independence from Spain, which continued to privilege rule by native-born Spanish in Cuba, had intensified. However, only after two wars of independence and an opportunistic military intervention by the U.S. army at the turn of the century was Cuba declared independent in 1902. The U.S. government had tried to buy Cuba from Spain since the early nineteenth century. Its military intervention late in a war against Spanish forces that Cuban rebels (known as *Mambi*) seemed bound to win legitimated the United States' claim to a considerable stake in Cuba's future. Instrumental in this were the Platt Amendment, which granted the United States the right to intervene in Cuban affairs when was deemed necessary, and the ensuing establishment of a naval base in Guantanamo Bay. Known as the era of a 'pseudo-/neocolonial' Cuban Republic, in reference to political and economic affiliations with the United States that lasted until the 1959 revolution led by Fidel Castro, this period saw the development of international tourism, predominantly from the United States, and the progressive equation of Cuba with 'Pleasure Island' (Schwartz 1999).

From the early 1900s, Cuba became an increasingly attractive recreational destination for North Americans, favoured by easy accessibility (Key West, in Florida, is only ninety miles away) and a mild climate during the winter season (Hall 1992: 109). Accordingly, in tourist fantasies the country became 'a smiling, luxuriant tropical land where romance, beautiful women, soft music-filled nights, and the enchantment of Spanish culture awaited visitors' (Schwartz 1999: xxi). Tourism development in the early twentieth century was fostered by major public works and government concessions for tourism-related facilities – notably those for gambling – that made Cuba 'the tourist hub of the Caribbean region' (Hall 1992: 109).

According to Schwartz (1999: 15), 'few travel magazine writers and brochure scribes of the 1920s failed to link Cuba to entertainment, excitement, recreation, romance, and indulgence'. From peep shows to prostitution, the sexual ingredient was key, nourishing the image of a tropical sexual paradise for pleasure seekers. Forms of prostitution had been present in Cuba well before the twentieth century, but the development of a hedonist type of tourism gave the phenomenon new dimensions and increased its visibility.[1] But tourism in the days of the neocolonial Republic should not be reduced to a concerted, linear progression towards more and more of the gambling-prostitution dyad, since tensions also existed between the more indulgent leisure pursuits and other paths tourism was taking on the island (Schwartz 1999). For instance, travel writers invited by the Cuban government lauded Cuba's interior areas and praised the country's history and culture (Schwartz 1999: 72). Tobacco farms and factories, the spectacular rock formations of Viñales, and the colonial city of Trinidad were among the sights visited by tourists, and in the 1950s, families with children started taking holidays in the newly developed Varadero Peninsula eighty-five miles west of Havana (Schwartz 1999). In spite of these efforts to cater to a diversified range of tourism fantasies, however, in the course of the 1950s Cuba's image was increasingly dominated by Havana's reputation as 'the brothel of the Caribbean', with many North Americans travelling to the capital on 'sin junkets' (Clancy 2002: 64).

By the mid 1950s, massive injections of foreign capital had led to the emergence of the 'Las Vegas–type hotel casino' in Havana (Schwartz 1999: 128). The number of hotel rooms in Havana almost doubled between 1952 and 1958, and in 1957 – the year with the highest number of foreign visitors in the decade (272,491) – the city accounted for 'twenty-one percent of *all* visitors to the Caribbean, with 86 per cent of these visitors coming from the United States' (Wonders and Michalowski 2001: 560). As Wonders and

Michalowski put it: 'In the eyes of many potential tourists in the 1950s, the estimated 270 brothels and as many as 100,000 prostitutes who operated there, defined Havana' (560). However, the lucrative tourism business was short-lived for President Fulgencio Batista and his North American allies. After the peak in 1957, the tourism stage progressively became a battleground for Cubans rebelling against Batista's dictatorship (Schwartz 1999). Opposition to the regime had grown stronger throughout the 1950s, with different rebel groups – the one that was to prevail led by Fidel Castro – taking increasingly visible military action and attracting more attention from international media. The images of gambling and prostitution, as part of a decadent tourism development controlled by a corrupt government and its foreign investors and mafiosi associates, certainly helped the rebels gain support among the Cuban population, whose large majority lived in dire poverty and saw no benefit from the dollars pouring into the country.

By 1958, the international media had started focusing 'on the underside of Cuban tourism' (Schwartz 1999: 182), highlighting president Batista's links with the mafia and the most sordid aspects of Havana's gambling industry. Throughout the year, the stories covered by major newspapers, from *Paris Match* to the *New York Times*, became more and more about Castro and an awaited revolution (192) that would change the face of the country and put an end to what was increasingly seen as a vicious and degrading tourism development. Finally, the turning point arrived. After years of campaigning against a corrupt dictatorship, thriving social inequalities and U.S. imperialism, the Rebel Army led by Fidel Castro succeeded in January 1959, and Batista fled the country. The era of the Cuban Revolution was about to begin: a time of radical social and economic reforms that transformed life in Cuba and the country's relation with international tourism.

Tourism and the Cuban Revolution

The new Cuban leadership had little understanding of tourism and tourism development policies (Schwartz 1999: 196), and the first years of the Revolution were marked by contradictory stances towards this industry, which had gained increasing importance in the country's economic balance. Thus, a few days after casinos had been ordered to close, Castro announced that they could reopen, this time operated by 'honest men' (197). Within weeks of the Rebels' victory, a tourist commission was organized with the aim 'to attract even greater numbers of visitors to a new, democratic Cuba' (198). 'Curiosity-seekers' soon started visiting the new Cuba, 'thrilled at the opportunity to survey a freshly enshrined battleground' (199). As Schwartz put it, these visitors 'poked their noses into the wreckage of once-elegant casinos, looking for war souvenirs, and clicked their camera shutters at bearded revolutionaries incongruously camped in luxurious hotel lobbies' (199).

This ambivalent fascination with the wreckage of an older era and bearded revolutionaries seemed to prefigure certain tropes that still thrive in contemporary tourism promotion of Cuba: the nostalgia elicited by the remnants of a pre-revolutionary past, and the experience of a thrilling and historic revolution. Nowadays, tourists are encouraged to indulge in Cuba's 'nostalgic appeal' (*Time Out* 2004: 2), to be 'intrigued by the heady nostalgia of its past' (Ellis 1999: endpaper) and at the same time to relish the possibility of visiting the 'last communist bastion', an island that has managed to resist the global forces of capitalism and constant pressure from its mighty neighbour, the United States.[2]

But in 1959 the Cuban Revolution was in its infancy, and new images of the island were still in the making, fuzzy and uncertain. The title of the magazine published for the American Society of Tourist Agents convention held in Havana in October 1959 continued to portray Cuba as the 'Playland of the Americas' (Schwartz 1999: 201). On that occasion, Castro 'acclaimed tourism as Cuba's salvation' (201) and told delegates that 'he hoped to establish Cuba as "the best and most important tourist center in the world"' (Wonders and Michalowsky 2001: 560). But in spite of these hopes and the travel agents' overall enthusiasm, international visitors did not flock to Cuba. Facing a political climate that many still perceived as very unstable, and marred by 'uncertainty, inconvenience, and unpleasantness', the tourism industry contracted (Schwartz 1999: 202). The influx of North American tourists that had provided the bulk of visitors in pre-revolutionary times declined sharply as of 1961, when the newly established U.S. economic blockade effectively began to work as a travel ban, preventing U.S. residents from visiting the island (Clancy 2002: 77). That year, facing the threat of a possible invasion by the United States, Cuba turned to the Soviet Union for economic and military support. Thus began a close relationship between the two countries that would last for almost three decades, shaping the future of the island up to the present day.

The steep drop in international visitors reached its nadir in 1974, when Cuba received only fifteen thousand foreign tourists (Wonders and Michalowsky 2001: 560). At this time, international tourism was no longer among the government's priorities. Instead, another mission for tourism had emerged, centred on domestic development. While casinos closed down and international tourism deserted the island, throughout the 1960s the Cuban government fostered the development of a domestic, 'social' type of tourism (Hall 1992: 11), a form of Cuban vacationing and 'tourism for the masses' that is nicely portrayed in Cabezas' (2009: 44–49) description of 'Revolutionary tourism'.

The Department of Beaches for the People (Departamento de Playas para el Pueblo), created back in February 1959 (Colantonio and Potter 2006; Cabezas 2009), made formerly private beaches open to the public (Schwartz 1999: 200). Families were encouraged to (re)discover their land and learn about the new socialist achievements of the Revolutionary government. These institutionally promoted forms of tourism emphasized education, complementing the national literacy campaign and other measures the government put in place to reduce socio-economic inequalities. Holidays were subsidized and organized by collective institutions such as trade unions. Priority was given to under-privileged groups who had never before enjoyed paid holidays, to war veterans, and to model workers (Hall 1992: 111). Some of my research participants recalled the 1970s and 1980s with palpable emotion as the 'good old days', when a stay in one of Cuba's most exclusive hotels was an affordable and much sought-after prospect, and Cabezas (2009) reports similarly poignant narratives of other 'unlikely' tourists, such as that of a Cuban farmer coming for the first time to Havana to spend his honeymoon at the famous hotel Habana Libre (formerly the Havana Hilton).

In these initial years of the Revolution, the new leadership also launched programmes to eradicate the other major 'evil' (besides gambling) associated with international tourism: prostitution. A turning point in this respect was the creation of the Federation of Cuban Women (Federación de Mujeres Cubanas, FMC) in 1960, which launched a series of programmes to redress gender inequality, and more particularly to rehabilitate prostitutes and reintegrate them into society (Trumbull 2001: 357). Literacy campaigns, training and care centres were organized to this end, with the result that many Cuban women became able to access education and formal employment as never before. Following the success of these campaigns, the Cuban government officially declared prostitution and its related hustler networks extinguished in 1965 (Kummels 2005: 15), and from this moment onwards, the regime tended to see any suggestion otherwise as problematic, at least until the 1990s (Berg 2004: 47). According to Valle (2006: 195), the government's measures to curb this phenomenon had a profound impact, and if they did not eradicate prostitution, they certainly decreased its visibility.[3]

The 1980s were an era of relative prosperity for the Cuban economy, thanks in particular to its close ties with the Soviet Union, which heavily subsidized Cuban exports (above all, cane sugar). As of the second half of the 1970s, the Cuban leadership took notice of the importance of regenerating the tourism industry and refurbishing its infrastructure (Hall 1992: 111), which lent fresh impetus to the development of international tourism. In the late 1970s and the 1980s, however, it grew only slowly, at a pace that was in no way comparable to what was happening in neighbouring

Caribbean countries, which collectively attracted seven million tourists in 1982 (Schwartz 1999: 205). Accordingly, not until 1989, when 275,000 international tourists were registered on the island, did Cuba reach a number of foreign visitors comparable to that of 1957 (Figueras Pérez 2004: 90).

In 1987, facing deteriorating economic conditions and a progressive decline in support from its Soviet allies, the Cuban government finally decided to make the development of international tourism a top economic priority (Hall 1992: 113). The Cubanacan Corporation was founded with the main objective of attracting foreign capital, generating new joint ventures, and modernizing the tourism industry (Colantonio and Potter 2006: 106; Hall 1992: 113). In 1988, a quarter of the foreign tourists visiting Cuba still came from Eastern Europe and the Soviet Union, but their numbers decreased dramatically in the following years (Hall 1992: 114). That same year Canada was the major single source of international visitors (around 17 per cent) (Hall 1992: 114), and since then it has kept its leading position almost without interruption. All the while, the numbers of tourists from the United States remained largely insignificant.[4]

At the end of the 1980s, the collapse of the Soviet Union had massive consequences for Cuba's economy, and necessitated profound reforms and policy changes, including in tourism. Aid from the Soviet ally disappeared overnight in a country that depended on the communist bloc for 80 per cent of its trade. The terrible crisis confronting Cuba at that time has been described 'as the worst economic shock faced by any Latin American country during the twentieth century' (Clancy 2002: 78). In 1990 it prompted Fidel Castro to declare the beginning of a Special Period in Time of Peace, a period of austerity, reforms, and economic restructuring that has been credited with the island's progressive but unsteady integration into a 'larger global, neoliberal framework' (Cabezas 2009: 22).[5] In the new economic context of crisis, which was further aggravated by the tightening of the U.S. economic embargo, the Cuban government attached all the more urgency to the development of international tourism as a privileged path to draw much-needed hard currency into the country.

Tourism Development and the Special Period

At the outset of the Special Period, the Cuban government's tourism development plans prioritized the island's coastal areas, with the peninsula of Varadero occupying the most prominent position. Valorization of Cuba's historical and cultural heritage was also high on the agenda, notably in the two UNESCO World Heritage sites of Old Havana and Trinidad, renowned for their colonial architecture. While some scholars have underlined the government's efforts to attract tourists who were more interested in Cuba's local history and culture than in the 'four *Ss*' of 'sea, sun, sand and sex' (Michel 1998b: 264), Quintana et al. (2005: 145), in their review of Cuban tourism, calculated that the 'product sun and beach' was still the main attraction of 68 per cent of accommodations catering for international tourists on the island. In 2003, more than half of such accommodations were found at 'all-inclusive resorts' (Quintana et al. 2005), and during my fieldwork, tourists still stayed predominantly at resorts and major hotel chains in coastal areas.

The channelling of foreign tourists into tourism enclaves, particularly all-inclusive beach resorts, is an issue that continues to be debated on the island, generating much criticism among tourists and Cubans alike. As early as 1990, members of the Cuban National Assembly started raising questions about the segregation of domestic and international tourists, citing for instance the exclusion of Cuban residents from tourist taxis and hotels (Quintana et al. 2005: 145). Many resented this discriminatory segregation, prompting the spread of the expression 'tourism apartheid' to describe Cuban tourism policies (Schwartz 1999: 210). More generally, this raises the question of what type of tourism development the Cuban leadership wished to promote from the 1990s onwards. Reviewing Cuba's official tourism plans, Colantonio and Potter (2006: 122) outline a politically tainted interpretation of the matter: 'It could be argued that the concentration of tourism development in spatially self-contained coastal areas has been carefully planned by the Cuban Leadership in order to minimize or, at least, retain control over the cultural and political exchanges between international tourists and Cubans'.

The debate on this remains open, and the nature and limits of my fieldwork leave me unable to corroborate these authors' remarks. But as I show in the coming chapters, similar interpretations thrived also among the tourists and Cuban people I encountered during fieldwork. At any rate, for Cubans not formally employed in the tourism industry the favouring of tourism enclaves and all-inclusive resorts has certainly contributed to curbing opportunity to engage with visitors.[6]

Emerging Tourism Tropes: From Che Guevara to 'Hot' Parties

By prioritizing the development of coastal areas, the Cuban government encouraged the development of a 'sea, sun and sand' type of tourism in the 1990s. Package deals for beach resorts, sold at prices that were very competitive on the Caribbean market, certainly helped attract tourists to Cuba in those years, but other tourism tropes and promises also lured visitors to the island. Examining the government's efforts to diversify its offerings in tourism along with other sectors of the economy, Babb (2011: 26) identifies several targeted travel niches, including 'sun, sand, and sea tourism and eco-, educational, heritage, cultural, and health tourism'. The possibility of experiencing Cuba's unique history was certainly amongst the marketed attractions. Cuba's tourism promoters, banking on the 'ambivalent yearnings' described by Babb (2011: 187, note 15), touted sights ranging from stunning examples of colonial architecture in Havana and Trinidad, to the relics of pre-revolutionary times, to the ubiquitous signs of the Revolution and its ongoing epic. Cigars, rum, and the increasingly successful Cuban music and dancing were also among the key features promoted, evoking the possibility of exciting parties and hedonistic pursuits. Last but not least was the 'character' of Cuban people: their hospitality, kindness and joyfulness were among the key features highlighted in tourism promotional materials in the mid 1990s (Michel 1998b: 276–277), which described Cubans as 'amiable and warm', as 'living out of smiles, dances, and music', displaying 'a lascivious and languorous joy' and a 'passion for life'.

Prolonging the semantic register of these remarks was the emphasis on the exuberant, passionate, sensual character of Cuban men and women, a way of describing the island's inhabitants that still recurs in tourism guides and publications. With Cubans' sensuality went recognition of the importance of 'love' in this country, pushed so far as to argue that 'Cubans have nothing but love' (Michel 1998b: 275). Contemporary tourist guidebooks reiterate this association between Cubans and 'love', which Michel draws from a travel supplement in the newspaper *Le Monde* published in 1992. Accordingly, in its 2007 edition, *Le Guide du Routard* (a very popular French guidebook) devotes a special section to 'Love' (*Amor*) in Cuba. Here we read that on this island, love is a 'national sport', 'an almost vital activity for Cubans' and a 'leisure conjugated in all its forms' (Gloaguen 2007: 36). Cuba is made out to be 'probably the most sensual country on earth, not to say sexual' (36). Echoed in several mainstream tourism publications on Cuba, these images willingly interlock the inclination for partying, exuberance, and diffuse sexual permissiveness that supposedly characterizes Cubans. In the *Time Out* (2004: 27) guide, Havana is thus portrayed as follows: '[A] city for music-making and spontaneous parties; a bottle of rum and a boom box is all you need and the legendary Cuban exuberance does the rest. Bodies are a free source of fun; sexual activity starts young and goes on to a full and interesting (often promiscuous) adult sex life'.

A number of scholars writing about recent developments in tourism in Cuba have underlined continuities between the sexualized images of 'hot' Cuban people and the slave and colonial past of the island (Fusco 1997; Kneese 2005; Kummels 2005; Sánchez Taylor 2000). Within this interpretative framework, reference is often made to the persistent image of the 'mulatta woman' (*la mulata*) as the 'daughter of love' and illicit lover of white men (Fusco 1997: 57). Dating back to the times of slavery, this image is found again in postcolonial Cuba, where *la mulata* has become a national symbol (Fusco 1997; Kneese 2005; Kummels 2005). These considerations converge with the more general remarks of Kempadoo (1999, 2004), O'Connell Davidson and Sánchez Taylor (1999) and Sánchez Taylor (2000) on the links between racist and colonial constructions of black women as 'naturally hot' and promiscuous, and the contemporary development of sex tourism in the Caribbean. For these authors, the reproduction of racial stereotypes explains the attraction of the Caribbean as a tourist destination where sex is deemed easy and even a natural ingredient of the holiday experience. Besides the eroticization of *mulatas* and black women, 'white stereotypes of primitive black male potency' (de Albuquerque 1998: 50) and colonial, sexualized racist fantasies of 'the "big black dick"' (Sánchez Taylor 2000: 49) are likewise said to lure female (sex) tourists to Caribbean countries like Jamaica, Barbados, Cuba and the Dominican Republic (de Albuquerque 1998; Sánchez Taylor 2000).[7]

My ethnographic material suggests that whereas there were certainly continuities in the racialization of sexuality in present-day Cuba – most notably in the (hyper)sexualization of Afro-Cubans (see Allen 2007, Fernandez 1999, 2010; Roland 2011) – the stereotype of the 'hot' Cuban was also re-actualized in a more culturalist/nationalist vein in interactions with tourists, and could apply to all Cubans regardless of racial attribution (Simoni 2011, 2013). In her study of interracial couples in contemporary Cuba, Fernandez (2010: 126) also notes that although 'racist ideology supported ample stereotypes of black males' primitive, animalistic, and uncontrollable sexuality ... notions of potent sexuality were not exclusively associated with black and mulatto Cubans'. Accordingly, 'perceptions of Cubanness, in general, were closely linked with sexuality, and there was a sort of national pride about Cuban's mythical sexuality and ardency' whereby 'Cuban men and women were seen to possess an uncontrollable "latino passion," particularly in comparison to Europeans and North Americans' (Forrest 1999 quoted in Fernandez 2010: 126).[8]

Cuba's reputation as a tropical land replete with sexual opportunity has led to controversy over the Cuban government's responsibilities regarding the promotion of such an image. Some scholars consider the Cuban government, in its efforts to attract foreign visitors and promote Cuba abroad, to have taken an ambiguous attitude at best in trying to offer an ample range of tourisms, including 'sex tourism'. Clancy (2002: 80) goes as far as portraying the Cuban state 'as pimp', highlighting instances of government inaction and 'approval through acquiescence' of the 'sex tourism' phenomenon. An episode often quoted to support these claims is the Cuban government's authorization in 1991 of *Playboy* magazine's special feature on 'the girls of Cuba', on condition that the article also covered the island's tourism facilities (Berg 2004: 52). Photographs of topless Cuban women on the beaches of Varadero appeared in this publication, nourishing debates on the Cuban state's willingness to capitalize on 'sex tourism'.

Here, perhaps, is where the *mulata* myth backfired on the Cuban authorities' efforts to promote tourism. Following Herzfeld's (2005: 57) remarks on stereotypes and the 'highly labile' 'content of cultural intimacy', we could argue that what may have been a source of pride – the beauty and hotness of Cuba's people – gradually became a source of embarrassment once this image became increasingly associated with sex tourism and prostitution. Making a visible entrance to the international tourism trade in the 1990s – the number of international tourists skyrocketed from 275,000 in 1989 to more than one million in 1996 (Figueras Pérez 2004: 90; Quintana et al. 2005: 113) – Cuba also entered the associated regimes of value and moral critique. Accordingly, its growing reputation as a pleasure destination and 'sex tourism' paradise started capturing the attention of international media and scholars.[9] The debate surrounding 'the explosion of sex tourism' in the 1990s recalled daunting images of pre-revolutionary Cuba, particularly of the 1950s. The establishment of continuities or ruptures between pre-revolutionary and contemporary Cuba progressively became fertile ground for political instrumentalization, and is still today a bone of contention between supporters and detractors of the Cuban political system (Alcázar Campos 2009, 2010; Cabezas 2009: 5; Kummels 2005: 23; Valle 2006: 230).[10]

Berg (2004) and Garcia (2010) have underlined how the official position of Cuban institutions tends to emphasize differences between a 'classic' definition of prostitution as caused by poverty (exemplified by prostitution in pre-revolutionary Cuba), and the new forms of prostitution of the 1990s, epitomized by the notion of *jineterismo*. Berg's (2004: 51) work on representations of *jineterismo* by the Cuban media and authorities since the 1990s shows the prevalence of interpretations that attribute this phenomenon to moral decadence and locate its origins in 'a desire for the satisfaction of "luxurious tastes"'. In other words, *jineterismo* was not considered a symptom of poverty or a consequence of a lack of other opportunities – a view that could point to the failures of the revolutionary project (Berg 2004: 51; see also Garcia 2010). For Palmié (2004: 243), this official view finds parallels in much popular discourse on the matter, where *jineterismo* 'speaks to morally highly ambiguous notions about commoditized exchange, luxury consumption, and the creation of social identities through processes of objectification'. The 'victims' of such objectification become the tourists, here cast as the prey of unscrupulous *jineteros* and *jineteras* who 'ride' them for purely instrumental motives, extracting cash and other desired commodities from them (imported goods, entertainment, etc.).

The mediatized debates on sex and tourism in Cuba projected the issue of tourist-oriented prostitution in this Caribbean country onto the global stage. But the Cuban authorities, who had repeatedly expressed concern about the social harms tourism could engender (Alcázar Campos 2010: 286) and often saw the sector as 'a necessary evil' (*un mal necesario*) to rescue the revolution from the economic crisis (Fernandez 1999: 83–85; Babb 2011: 30–32), were not about to let the image of Cuba as a 'tourist paradise for sex' thrive unchallenged. A report submitted to the 5th Congress of the Cuban Communist Party in 1996 pointed to a series of problems related to tourism and requiring 'political-ideological attention' (Soler 2004 quoted in Alcázar Campos 2010: 286–287). Among these were the following: changes in values prompted by legal access to the dollar, the high earnings of owners of *casas particulares*,[11] the influence of ideas coming from consumer society, the Cuban population's influence on tourists, and the need to combine openness to tourism with ideological firmness (Alcázar Campos 2010: 286–287). The report also called for alertness to phenomena associated with business and capitalism (bribes, corruption, individualism, etc.), and singled out '*jineterismo*' as the most visible and humiliating result of tourism development (286–287).[12]

From 1996 onwards, several crackdowns and waves of repression of *jineterismo* curbed its visibility, changing the course of touristic encounters in Cuba, or at least inflecting the way they operated. According to Colantonio and Potter (2006: 167), by the early 1990s the authorities had already set up 'special police units to deal with tourism-related crimes'. However, no provision in the Cuban penal code dealt explicitly with prostitution. To confront the increasingly visible phenomenon of *jineterismo*, the Cuban government had to rely on a broader provision of its penal code, updated in 1987, concerning the 'state of dangerousness' (*el estado peligroso*, also known as *índice de peligrosidad*): 'the special proclivity of a person to commit crimes, demonstrated by a conduct that is in manifested contradiction with the norms of socialist morality' (Asamblea Nacional del Poder Popular n.d.).[13] In the course of my fieldwork, Cubans also used the expression *asedio al turista* (besieging/hustling of the tourist), or simply *asedio*, when referring to the police's accusation of engaging informally with visitors. Accordingly, the police used a system of warnings ('warning of nuisance of tourism', *carta de advertencia*, or *carta de avisos de molestia al turismo* according to Tiboni 2002: 41) to chasten people accused of *asedio*. The accumulation of such *advertencias* would weigh on one's criminal record and could ultimately lead to more severe penal sanctions. Depending also on a range of other considerations and discriminatory elements – some of which will be considered more extensively in the following chapters, and whose assessment tended to leave much discretionary power to the officers involved – in the worst-case scenario the accused risked doing one to four years in prison (three, according to most people I heard talking about it).

In 1996, the Cuban authorities carried out their first major crackdown on *jineterismo*. Their intervention, focused on prime tourism locations where the presence of *jineteras* was most visible, initially took as its main target the peninsula of Varadero, Cuba's most popular beach destination. This is the picture Trumbull (2001) portrays of that (in)famous crackdown:

> By 1996, thousands of women worked as prostitutes in the 19-kilometer penin-sula. Women came from all parts of the island and rented rooms in the town of Varadero or in Matanzas, 40 kilometres away. Competition for customers was strong and men were frequently solicited and even harassed on the streets. In the first months of 1996, authorities returned 7000 women to their homes, inves-tigated over 400 houses suspected as brothels, and shut down a pornographic movie ring. (CubaInfo 1996). (2001: 363)

According to Trumbull (2001: 364), while this major crackdown helped eliminate much of the prostitution in Varadero, it also threatened the future of tourism in the area. The government made it illegal to rent rooms on the peninsula and encouraged the development of all-inclusive resorts that could appeal to honeymooners, retired couples, and families (364).

It thus seems that from 1996 onwards, once *jineterismo* had become an increasingly visible phenomenon fostering Cuba's reputation as a 'sex, drugs, and beach parties' paradise, the government took a more proactive role in reorienting the course of its tourism development. Since then, crackdowns on *jineterismo* have been a prominent feature of Cuba's tourism-related poli-cies. After the intervention in 1996, other major crackdowns took place in 1998–1999 (Clancy 2002: 80; Corbett 2002: 74–75), and police raids in selected tourism locations, particularly places where people gathered for nightlife activity, continued during the time of my fieldwork. Among my Cuban research participants, accounts of stepped-up police checks and raids (*recogidas*) nourished a widespread, albeit not generalized, narrative that depicted the Cuban authorities as constantly tightening their grip and repression through the years.[14]

Assessing the consequences of the late 1990s crackdowns, Palmié (2004: 245) reflects that what they achieved was merely to drive Cuban women 'off the streets, and into the arms of the waiters at hotel lounges and tourist discos, who often seem only too happy to protect them from the police and state security for a substantial cut'. Valle (2006: 243) also reports significant changes in *jineterismo*, particularly in the activities of *jineteras*, as a result of the Cuban authorities' stepped-up interventions in the late 1990s. For Valle, crackdowns on *jineterismo* have neither prompted its disappearance nor reduced its magnitude: instead, *jineterismo* has transformed and adapted itself to new conditions, becoming more subtle and less visible. Summarizing the changes in the modus operandi of *jineteras*, Valle (2006: 242) highlights for instance a tendency to dress as 'normal' girls, as opposed to wearing provocative outfits. Before, *jineteras* had tended to walk through tourism areas in open daylight, whereas now they operated mostly at night, waiting for tourists in specific houses to which their pimps (*chulos*) would lead them (242). The range of changes summarized by Valle suggests a general tendency in the realm of *jineterismo* to become more discreet and less visible, finding subtler ways to bypass policing. In the following chapter, I will consider more extensively some of the tactics that my Cuban informants employed to circumvent such control. What should be highlighted here is that the police crackdown on the phenomenon led not to its disappearance but rather to its transformation, and to the tailoring of subtler techniques to make contact with tourists. But how did international tourism react to these repressive endeavours and the changes they fostered?

Reconfiguring and Diversifying Tourism Promises

I talked to several tourists who, having come regularly to Cuba for over a decade, criticized the government crackdowns on *jineterismo* and the transformations they attributed to it. Such repression was often portrayed as exemplifying the Cuban authorities' will to maintain total control over tourism by segregating foreigners in all-inclusive resorts and limiting their chances to interact with Cubans. Strikingly, and I think there is no coincidence here, the number of Italian tourists visiting Cuba reached its peak (of around 200,000) in 1997 (Ginestri n.d.). At that time in Italy, Cuba was widely seen as a typical 'sea, sun, sand and sex' destination, alongside other countries like Thailand and Brazil. Testifying to this reputation, in a 2001 book on Italian tourists 'from Cuba to Brazil', Pietro Sozzari wrote: 'In Italy, in travel agencies, you feel ashamed of booking a flight to Cuba, and while doing the booking you whisper in a faint voice the name of the island: you are then immediately identified, by the kind employees, as a tourisex' (Sozzari 2001 quoted in Tiboni 2002: 54). As my conversations in Playas del Este suggested, several tourist men who had been lured to Cuba by the promise of 'hot girls' on amazing beaches, hedonistic parties and 'easy sex' were now starting to look elsewhere, and to explore other tourism destinations, such as Brazil, where similar 'treats' were on offer but control and repression by the authorities were not so stringent. Stricter surveillance and law enforcement could obstruct the smooth and carefree course of one's ideal holidaying, in which pleasures ought to be always within easy reach.[15]

In spite of the reduction in Italian tourists, the total number of visitors to Cuba continued to rise in the late 1990s and early 2000s. Foreign tourists topped 2.3 million in 2005 (Oficina Nacional de Estadísticas 2005), almost ten times the number in 1989. As the numbers grew, the types of tourism also changed and diversified. The government's efforts to curb *jineterismo*, or at least reduce its visibility, operated in conjunction with more positive measures to diversify Cuba's 'tourism product' (Quintana et al. 2005). From rehabilitation clinics and thermal treatments specifically tailored to a foreign clientele, to renewed efforts to preserve and promote Cuba's cultural heritage (architecture, museums, theatres, festivals, cultural events), the establishment of national parks and ecological reserves, the development of international events and conference facilities, the valorization of nautical and diving opportunities, and the construction of cruise terminals, the Cuban government encouraged diversification of its tourist attractions (Quintana et al. 2005). Meanwhile, the stepped-up promotion, from the mid 1990s onwards, of all-inclusive resorts, whose numbers more than doubled between 1998 and 2004 (Quintana et al. 2005: 156), could also work to reduce the scope of *jineterismo*.

All these measures seem to have affected the types of tourism Cuba attracted. Quintana et al. (2005: 125) highlight three main tendencies in the changed demographic profiles of tourists as of 1998: an increasing equilibrium between genders following the progressive increase of women tourists (from 41.7 per cent in 1998 to 45.8 per cent in 2003); an increased participation of older people; and a surge in family tourism. The same authors also recognize a growing desire among visitors in Cuba for more personalized experiences, a wish to move beyond 'massification' and mainstream forms of tourism (125), which could also explain the increasing appeal of alternative types of accommodations like *casas particulares* (139).

Most independent travellers and young backpackers I met during fieldwork were indeed looking for alternatives to the kind of mass tourism that all-inclusive resorts epitomized. Despising the four-*S* holiday scenario, some valued instead more cultural or natural pursuits, such as visits to different towns and nature areas across the island, and cherished the idea of friendly, respectful encounters with locals. Important too was to cut costs by lodging in *casas particulares* and using public transport (cycling was an increasingly popular option), and to spend at least two or three weeks in the country – between 2001 and 2005 the average tourism stay in Cuba was for ten and a half days (MINTEL 2007). This form of tourism thrived in the rural town of Viñales. The independent travellers I met there tended to dislike the world of *jineterismo*, or what many saw as hustling and tourism-oriented prostitution, which they mostly associated with tourism in Havana. Many visitors in this rural town were on a tour of the island from Havana to Viñales, and then eastwards to Cienfuegos, Trinidad, Santa Clara and Santiago before returning to Havana after a journey of three or four weeks. In the increasingly diversified landscape of international tourism in Cuba, which I have only briefly sketched here, it thus appears that different types of tourism, guided by different promises and expectations, coexisted side by side in a variety matched by an equally diversified range of informal tourism-oriented activities.

Conclusion

This chapter has reviewed some of the most significant features of international tourism in Cuba, from its beginnings at the turn of the nineteenth century to the present day. It has aimed to historically situate the emergence of the informal encounters between foreign tourists and Cuban men and women that are the focus of this book, and to highlight the main continuities and disjunctures that help to explain their present form. International tourism in Cuba changed a great deal in the course of the twentieth century. However, some of its salient tropes have proved particularly resilient, always ready to be resurrected and cast their lights and shadows on the present. Such is the 'Pleasure Island' reputation that Cuba gained in the first half of the twentieth century, a reputation recalled by tourism promoters, critics and commentators in the 1990s, particularly when debating the explosion of 'sex tourism' and *jineterismo*. However, no assumption of continuities between the past and present-day Cuba should obscure the significant changes that have affected both life on the island and international tourism.

The most relevant disjuncture in the history of tourism in Cuba resulted from the 1959 revolution led by Fidel Castro, which changed the face of both the country and its association with international tourism. The Revolution transformed the image that Cuba had acquired around the world, adding new layers to its history that still give the country a very distinctive flavour on the international tourism market. From the tourism boom of the 1950s to the revival of this industry at the end of the 1980s, more than thirty years elapsed before international tourists again visited Cuba in numbers comparable to their pre-revolutionary height. In the course of the 1990s and the Special Period in Time of Peace, the government came to see international tourism as a possible remedy for the terrible economic crisis afflicting the island. The development undertaken in those years relied heavily on the promotion of the 'sea, sun and sand' tourism product, with big hotels constructed on selected shores, and in a minor mode also on Cuba's 'nature' and 'culture'. Controversies still rage on how the fourth *S* – 'sex' – has gained a place in tourism representations of Cuba, and more particularly on the Cuban government's complicity in the matter, a government that in the 1960s had waged a strenuous battle to eradicate prostitution. The steep rise in hard currency–carrying foreign tourists, in times of extreme scarcity and economic hardship for most Cuban residents, opened up an informal realm of opportunity that many Cubans, particularly the younger generations, were keen to enter.

That realm is labelled *jineterismo*, a controversial and contested notion that could potentially refer to any activity generating income by way of association with foreigners, and that was selectively employed to evoke a range of instrumentally driven relationships, particularly forms of tourism hustling and prostitution. Informal tourism-oriented activities have undergone significant changes since the 1990s, notably in response to the Cuban authorities' shifting attitudes and intensified crackdowns on *jineterismo*. As the final part of this chapter indicates, Cuban men and women likewise updated their competences and tactics in response to such changes. The following chapter brings this reflection further, showing how, with a certain coming of age of international tourism and *jineterismo*, tourists' and Cubans' awareness of each other's expectations has also matured, raising questions about the compatibility and possible convergence of their agendas.

Chapter 2
SHAPING EXPECTATIONS

By the time I undertook my fieldwork, after over a decade of impressive growth in international tourists' arrivals, narratives of encounters between visitors and Cubans had gone beyond the images of welcoming hospitality, generous and disinterested friendships, and easy and spontaneous sexual affairs that may have prevailed in the early 1990s. An additional scenario, tainted by notions of prostitution, tourism hustling and *jineterismo*, had emerged and gained visibility on the tourism scene. *Jineterismo* had become an integral part of what Cuba was about and what tourists had to expect. It conjured notions of instrumental relationships and exploitation of tourists that had spread around the world through novels,[1] tourist guidebooks,[2] travelogues, Internet forums, newspaper articles, movies and world-of-mouth advice, a fact that is crucial to understanding visitors' doubts and scepticism as they readied themselves to meet locals.

Most of the tourists I encountered were, or quickly became, aware of the existence of *jineterismo*, or what some would simply consider prostitution and illegal business related to tourism. Avoiding cheating and deception tended to be among these tourists' major concerns. Cubans dealing with tourists were generally also aware of such fears and scepticism, and many tourists knew that Cubans 'knew they knew', so a hall of mirrors of reflexive self-presentations and reciprocal expectations sometimes informed relationships between them. In this chapter I will expand further on this key point by discussing some compelling examples of major tourism guidebooks' assessments of *jineterismo*; of the sorts of tips and warnings circulating among tourists on the matter; and of Cubans' awareness of it. But first, I will complexify the picture of *jineterismo* by highlighting its heterogeneous character and elusive nature.

Unpacking *Jineterismo*

Jineterismo *and* la Lucha *in Cuba's Special Period*

With the beginning of the Special Period, the informal practices and *jineterismo* already burgeoning on the island (Palmié 2004; Kummels 2005) acquired new dimensions and increased visibility as Cuban men and women found them important means of getting by in the face of catastrophic economic crisis and difficulty satisfying even the most elementary needs. The crisis made the distribution of state-supplied food rations in local *bodegas* (groceries) through the system of the *libreta* (ration book), introduced by the socialist government in the first years of the Revolution to cover basic products (Palmié 2004: 240), 'practically obsolete due to shortages that ravaged the delivery structure' (Cabezas 2009: 64). To access provisions, people had to resort to the underground economy or dollar stores (*tiendas de recaudación de divisas*, 'stores for the recollection of foreign currency', popularly known as *chopins*). In both cases, the prices of goods were prohibitive for all Cubans who lacked direct access to hard currency, typically obtained via a job in the tourism industry or remittances from relatives abroad (Argyriadis 2005: 32).

A key decision taken by the government in 1993 was to legalize the possession and circulation of U.S. dollars among the Cuban population (Decree Law 140). The measure officially legitimized and fostered the existence of two separate economic spheres, demarcated by the uses of two distinct media of exchange. On the one hand, most Cubans received their salaries in Cuban pesos (*pesos cubanos*, CUP) (the average salary of 180 CUP in 1995 rose to 312 CUP in 2005 [Ritter 2005: 352]). On the other hand, the U.S. dollar – the only currency accepted in *chopins* – had a black market value reaching 120–125 CUP in 1993 before gradually stabilizing around 20–25 CUP (Palmié 2004: 240), a rate that still held during my fieldwork.

The decision to legalize dollars had profound consequences on Cuban society, giving rise to a widening inequality strikingly at odds with the socialist egalitarian ethic. Following Palmié (2004: 239–240), the significance of this measure is best apprehended in conjunction with a series of other factors:

> [T]he inadequacy of state-guaranteed rations of primary goods, the legalization of the possession of U.S. dollars in 1993, and the increasing scarcity on the non-dollarized market not just of imported products, but of nonrationed goods have led to a situation where deep social rifts are opening up between emerging segments of the population with access to foreign currency, and those who remain restricted to the non-dollarized sectors of the economy to meet their daily needs.

At the time of my fieldwork, the situation Palmié (2004) described for the late 1990s seemed to have changed little. Indeed, albeit the circulation of U.S. dollars was replaced in 2004 by *pesos convertibles* (CUC),[3] Cubans receiving salaries in CUP still had to rely on CUC to buy basic items (e.g., personal hygiene products and cooking fats) at the local *chopin* or on the black market. The question was how to access the hard currency. At this point international tourism came to play a key role alongside the remittances that part of the Cuban population received from relatives living abroad (primarily in the United States).[4] Colantonio and Potter (2006: 126) estimate the monthly wage of a state employee in the tourism sector as easily reaching 100 USD (including tips) at a time when the average Cuban salary was 12 USD. Thus, even though the majority of tourism jobs in the hospitality industry were low-skilled, employment in this sector became a very attractive option for many in the course of the 1990s (126). Tourism drained workers from other, often more skill-demanding realms of activity and generated migratory flows towards tourism poles like Havana and Varadero.

While a few Cubans managed to reap the economic benefits of tourism via formal employment in the sector, others who lacked such opportunities tried to do so informally, that is, *jineteando* (doing *jineterismo*).[5] More and more Cubans, particularly among the younger generations, saw the increasing number of foreigners that visited the country in the 1990s as an opportunity to access hard currency and fulfil other desires and aspirations. In Special Period Cuba, *jineterismo* thus became part of a culture of 'struggle' (*lucha*) – a key term of revolutionary symbolism that progressively turned into a common expression indicating Cubans' day-to-day struggle to get by (Palmié 2004: 241) by looking for dollars 'in the street' (*en la calle*) (Berg 2004: 84), whether legally or not (Argyriadis 2005: 47).[6] In this new context, Palmié (2004: 241) remarks, any 'unregulated association with foreigners ... was encouraged'.

Several authors have discussed the porosity (Argyriadis 2005: 47), the ambiguities (Berg 2004; Cabezas 2004; Fernandez 1999; Palmié 2004) and the kaleidoscopic character (Kummels 2005: 24) of *jineterismo* and other related phenomena and categories in Cuba – sex work, prostitution and partnership, for instance. Scholars have emphasized that *jineterismo* is a complex phenomenon that brings issues of morality, nation, race, class and gender into play (Berg 2004; Cabezas 2004; Fernandez 1999; Simoni 2008b, and chapter 3 in this volume). According to Fernandez, who was among the first anthropologists to write on *jineterismo* in Cuba, the term was 'used to describe a broad range of activities related to tourist hustling (including selling black market cigars, rum, coral jewellery, etc.), providing private taxi services or access to "authentic" *santería* rituals, or simply serving as informal tourist guides in return for a free meal or some token gift from the tourist' (Fernandez 1999: 85). Though *jineterismo* tended to evoke notions of tourism-oriented sex work and hustling, it could potentially encompass 'any dollar-generating activity or connections with foreigners' (85). The specific meanings of *jinetero/a*, *jineterismo* or the verb *jinetear* were thus extended or constrained to include or exclude certain persons and occupations.[7] Given that the term was seldom innocuous, such categorizing moves have often been fraught with controversy, making it extremely important to consider who was using it, in what context, and to what end.

Needs and Desires

Often cast by the Cuban media and authorities as a symptom of moral failure and the desire for luxury (see chapter 1), *jineterismo* problematized the relations and divides between 'needs' and 'wants', between *las necesidades* (necessities, i.e. what is needed for survival) on the one hand, and the satisfaction of alternative aspirations on the other.[8] In interpretations of this phenomenon, the fact of privileging the importance of 'needs' over 'wants', or vice versa, could become a very delicate, ethically fraught act. Rather than trying to establish unambiguously whether *jineterismo* was motivated, alternatively and/or exclusively, by the '(real) needs' or '(superfluous) desires' of the Cubans concerned – in itself a rather challenging and questionable task – I find it more insightful to focus on whether and how divergent assessments emerged, and on the interplay of agencies and motivations attributed to and claimed from various perspectives.[9] As I realized during fieldwork, differences could for instance lie in the contrast between one's desires and someone else's survival needs, and vice versa.

Manuel,[10] a self-proclaimed ex-*jinetero* from Havana in his thirties who viewed the late 1990s as the 'golden age' of *jineterismo*, jokingly explained why he had now 'retired' from the business (i.e. *jineterismo*): nowadays there was too much competition from poor *jineteros* from the countryside (*guajiros*) who 'sold themselves cheap' (*se venden por nada*). As Manuel put it, these people were willing to walk all day long with their tourist companions, under the scorching sun, just to be able to receive a little pizza, sold on the street in Cuban pesos, at the end of the day as a present. Manuel emphasized that he was not of that kind, scornfully adding that if he wanted to buy one such pizza he just had to ask his grandmother for some pesos. By way of contrast, he told me that what he had sought from his engagements with tourists was the experience of something radically different from his everyday life, something 'strong' (*fuerte*), like a sophisticated fish dinner in one of Havana's most expensive restaurants, accompanied by a glass of good white wine. His remarks made clear that there could be important differences in what motivated one to engage with tourists.

While Manuel highlighted his desire to experience the tourist 'high life', thus distinguishing himself from *guajiros*, other research participants stressed that their engagements with tourists were driven by more essential needs, such as providing food for their extended family. That was the case of Roberto, a man from Viñales in his thirties with whom I took several tours in the countryside and developed a very close relationship throughout the years. According to this occasional informal guide, the term *jinetero* was essentially used by the authorities (*las autoridades*), people who had power (*los que tienen el poder*), as a derogatory term to discriminate and marginalize people like him by implying that their engagements with tourists were motivated by greed and fancy desires. *Jinetero* was in this sense a negative term that he would never apply to himself. Roberto emphasized that it was only the pursuit of *las necesidades* that led him to engage informally with tourists – to be in the *lucha* – since he did not have the licence that authorized a few privileged Cubans to do this openly and officially. He had to provide for his family and pay for his father's medicines, which were not subsidized by the state and cost him dearly.

These two contrasting pictures reveal how controversial and contested the notion of *jineterismo*, and its motives, could become, and how the term could point to a variety of needs, desires and aspirations while threatening to draw various personal stories and situations under the same umbrella.

Gendered Distinctions and Opportunities: Transactional Sex, Romance and Migration

One of the most tenacious and controversial lines of distinction in narratives of *jineterismo* related to gender, with women's and men's activities usually acquiring different connotations. A clear example of how this distinction could play out is the following situation, which I observed one night in Havana. I was sitting at an open-air bar in the Boulevard de San Rafael (Centro Habana), which had a reputation for being frequented by many *jineteros* and *jineteras*, when I witnessed the following argument between two young Cubans, a boy and a girl, who were having a drink at a table next to mine, oblivious to my presence. The argument was essentially about their being *jineteros* or not, and about the meaning they attributed to this term. In the course of the quarrel, the young man insulted the girl, calling her a *puta* (whore). When she angrily retorted that they were both engaging in the same kinds of activities, the man disagreed, claiming instead that he was a *jinetero*. By conflating *jinetera* with prostitute, and emphasizing the difference between a *puta* and a *jinetero*, he denied her engagements with tourists the same moral worth and positive connotation he assigned his own.

Other scholars have shown that Cuban society tends to stigmatize *jineteros* less than *jineteras* (Alcázar Campos 2009, 2010; Berg 2004; Cabezas 2004; Palmié 2004). Whereas *jineteros'* activities are considered to pertain to a relatively much more variegated and heterogeneous spectrum that can include sex and romance with foreigners but is more broadly related to tourist hustling (e.g. selling cigars or acting as brokers or tourist guides), the activities of *jineteras* are more readily equated with prostitution and transactional sex. Allen (2007: 189) pertinently points out that in Cuba, 'women and girls have less access to life *en la calle* ["in the street" but implying more largely the public sphere]'. As a consequence, 'men effectively excluded from the centre of dollar-producing activities may choose various hustles other than the sex trade, whereas women are left few choices for play-labor' (189). This, Allen continues, 'certainly impacts the differentiation in stigma against an economy of women's sex labor' (189; see also Palmié 2004: 243).[11]

Having started to consider the gendered and sexual dimensions of informal tourism-oriented activities in Cuba's Special Period, we also need to account for the emergence of another sexual identity: that of the *pinguero* (from a slang term for penis, *pinga*), a neologism designating men whose activity had to with their *pinga*. According to Cabezas (2004: 4), 'while some pingueros identify themselves as straight, they tend to provide sexual services mainly to gay tourists because male-to-male practices are more lucrative than straight sex'. Such was the case of José, a young Cuban man in his early twenties who was one of the few *pingueros* I got to know during fieldwork. Needing to provide for his wife and newborn child, after some failed attempts at seducing tourist women José had heeded a friend's advice and turned to offering sexual services to foreign men. The problem with seducing women, he told me, was that it was a more time-consuming process that required flirting skills he had not mastered, and that cash was not guaranteed because hardly any tourist women were willing to pay for sex. Besides, his pale complexion was not an asset in catching the women's attention. Expressing a view I often heard in Cuba, José maintained that tourists were more attracted to black or mulatto Cubans.[12]

While some authors portray the *pingueros'* activities as part of *jineterismo* (Couceiro Rodríguez 2006), considering them *jineteros* who work with their *pinga* and thus a sort of counterpart to *jineteras*, others underscore how *pingueros* tend to distance themselves from *jineteros*. Allen quotes one of his informants in explaining the difference: '*Jineteros* rip tourists off ... *Pingueros* work hard offering sex in return for clothes, a good night out ... or dollars' (2007: 187).[13] Allen (2007: 186) admits that the categories of *pinguero* and *jinetero* can overlap and are often imprecise, especially in Cuban common sense. But, he maintains, male sex labourers engaging with tourists should be more correctly referred to as *pingueros* and sees *jineteros* essentially as 'middlemen' who may engage sexually with tourists but only incidentally to other sort of services (187).

This picture, however, differs slightly from the one that emerged from my fieldwork, a divergence of interpretations that in itself highlights the controversial and heterogeneous character of constructions of *jineterismo* in Cuba, whereby different situated perspectives coexisted and could occasionally compete with each other. It also reflects differences in the access I had to the field, and in the groups of people I met, as compared to Allen and other authors who focused their research on *pingueros* (see Couceiro Rodríguez 2006; Fosado 2005; Hodge 2001; 2005; Sierra Madero 2013). During fieldwork, and with the notable exception of José, mentioned above, I seldom had the chance to engage and talk extensively with self-professed *pingueros*.

The perspectives I gathered by talking to young Cuban men in Havana, Viñales and Playas del Este tended to strictly associate *pingueros*' activities with homosexual relationships with tourists, rather than with a comprehensive range of sexual encounters between tourists and Cubans. Several of my Cuban informants viewed their own activities as specifically tailored to developing sexual/romantic relationships with tourist women. They were, as some put it, in the 'line of women' (*línea de mujeres*). Occasionally referring to themselves as *jinetes/jineteros*, they were generally adamant about their exclusively heterosexual proclivities and sometimes displayed rather homophobic attitudes towards *pingueros*. Their focus was to meet and seduce foreign tourist women, often with the aspiration to marry one and move abroad with her.

This was what several Cuban men who were part of a loose Rasta clique in Havana made clear to me. Those whom I got to know as 'Rasta' in tourism milieus in Havana were mainly Afro-Cuban men adopting a subculture style that may be summarily characterized as valorizing blackness and Afro-related cultural expressions, sporting dreadlocks and Rastafari-inspired accessories and clothing, and privileging a laid-back approach to tourists. These men generally self-identified, and were seen by others, as Rasta.[14] Rolando, a member of the group, once explained his motivations for courting foreign women to me. We had already met on several occasions, and each time I had seen him with a different tourist partner. Impressed by the number of intimate relationships he seemed able to sustain alongside one another, I joked that his various affairs were likely to keep him busy twenty-four hours a day. With an awkward smile, he replied that the problem was that he liked them all, these tourist women, that he felt good with all of them, and that this was probably due to the lack of contact with his mother when he was a child. More convincingly, he then added:

The point is that, when I will find one [a tourist woman] that will take me out of the country (*me saque del país*). Then, with this one … that's it (*ya*)! [Implying he would stick with her]. That's what I am looking for. But in the meanwhile, I have to be… [alert, on the move]. I don't know which is the one who is going to take me out.

Several of my Cuban research participants were similarly looking for 'the one': the tourist with whom things would work out well, until their final goal was achieved. The goal, when talking in these terms, was to be able to travel out of Cuba, to find better opportunities elsewhere and 'see the world'. However, rather than portraying relationships with tourists as exclusively instrumental, many also emphasized their aspiration to find someone they really liked, and could ultimately be in love with.

For Emilio, the prospect of being in love with a foreign woman, settling down with her and building a family together was all that mattered. In his early thirties, Emilio had been promised marriage by his German lover and had travelled to Germany only to find himself 'used for sex' for two months, as he put it, with no prospect of marriage in sight. 'I am not a sex machine!' was his outraged reaction as he complained about the tourists' misrecognition of his ability to love and need for love. In the course of our sustained conversations on these matters, Emilio repeatedly mentioned that the peak of his success with tourist women had passed. He was getting *viejo y pesado* (old and boring), had lost his freshness and appeal. In one of his soberest moods, he once told me it would now be practically impossible for him to find a partner at all, be it tourist or Cuban, unless it was some old foreign 'granny' desperately looking for a younger man. His chances with Cuban women were presently very low, he maintained, not only due to his age, but mainly because he had no interesting job or income that would make him an appealing candidate for a long-term relationship.[15] Here Emilio's reflections converged with the critique, very widespread in contemporary Cuba, of the increasing predominance of *relaciones de interés* (interested relations) among Cuban people, as opposed to 'real' relationships (Fosado 2005) and 'true love' (Lundgren 2011), and the ensuing difficulty of establishing 'normal' relationships in the current climate of economic crisis.[16]

In spite of the stereotypical views that equated *jineteras* with prostitutes and portrayed Cuban women as engaging mainly in 'sex for money' relationships with foreign tourists, a much more complex, multilayered web of drives and desires tended to inform these women's aspirations – the possibility of finding 'the one' certainly amongst them (de Sousa e Santos 2009). Researches focusing on the experiences of Cuban women support this view. As Cabezas (2004: 992) puts it: 'Liaisons with tourists provide recourse to get by and to get ahead: not just to supplement low wages but also to procure opportunities for recreation, consumption, travel, migration, and marriages'. Once again, significant differences and distinction could play out in the motivations Cuban women expressed for engaging with foreign tourists. From obtaining hard currency to provide for the needs of a family back in Cuba's countryside, indulging in expensive pleasures and commodities, or having the chance to marry a tourist and live a dreamed-of romance in a foreign country[17] – any of these could be among the motives driving Cuban women to seek intimate relationships with foreign tourists. Confronted with such a variety of needs, desires and aspirations, it is important to retain here that touristic encounters and relationships could become a privileged way to fulfil them.

Jineterismo in Tourism Narratives: Shaping Expectations, Rising Challenges

Guidebooks' Jineterismo

The Lonely Planet guidebook to Cuba, translated into several languages, was a major reference for many independent travellers I met in Cuba. Since my aim is not to provide an exhaustive review of tourist guidebooks on Cuba but just to give an idea of the narrative resources on which my tourist research participants could rely, I will draw only on this example here.[18] A specific section of the Lonely Planet, titled 'Hints on jineterismo' (Gorry 2004: 359), argues that 'if readers' letters and personal experience are an indication, *jineteros* are the number-one travel bummer in Cuba' (359). Having introduced the phenomenon as a peculiarly Cuban form of hustling – less persistent than touting 'in Moroccan medinas' and less desperate than 'Rio de Janeiro orphans' (359) – we are told that 'the point is Cubans aren't hustling to survive, and so that allows them to charm you doing what they do best: being friendly, funny and yes, helpful' (359). Several tips follow for ridding oneself of and avoiding *jineteros*; they range from ways of responding to their initial approaches and 'conversation-stopping rejoinders' to the more radical option of visiting Cuba's most secluded, less touristy, and therefore 'hustler free' provinces (359). The same guide deals with *jineteras* in a different section under the heading 'Culture' and subtitle 'Lifestyle'. Here (359) we read the following:

> That women are turning to the hustle to make some extra cash or attain baubles is disturbing. While some *jineteras* are straight-up hookers, others are just getting friendly with foreigners for the perks they provide: a ride in a car, a night out in a fancy disco or a new pair of jeans. Some are after more, others nothing at all. It's

a complicated state of affairs and can be especially confusing for male travellers who get swept up in it. As one American traveller put it: 'Although I've had many relationships with Latinas, I'm reluctant to get involved with Cubans because of the socioeconomic dynamic involved'.

Thus a rather puzzling picture is sketched here for tourists, alternatively confronted with 'straight-up hookers' or more pleasure-seeking women. To take up the last part of the quote, 'socioeconomic dynamics' indeed tended to come to the fore once the relational idioms of *jineterismo* were at stake. *Jineterismo* spoke the language of inequalities. On one side, it confronted tourists with their advantageous economic position, reiterating their status as privileged outsiders and emphasizing differences between them and the Cuban population. On the other, it also highlighted their lack of knowledge of local conditions and the possibility of being duped and deceived by *jineteros* and *jineteras*. Besides the information and 'competence-building propositions' (Latour 2005: 211)[19] provided by tourist guidebooks, it is also important to consider that with the tourism boom in Cuba and the increased flows of people moving in and out of the country, similar warnings about *jineterismo* have also circulated in the tourists' countries of residence by way of word-of-mouth tips and suggestions.

Pre-travel Warnings and Arrangements

Many of the tourists I met in Cuba had, prior to their journey, gathered practical tips and suggestions from friends or relatives who had already been there. These suggestions were likely to contain some advice on how to deal with Cubans, and more specifically with the alleged tourism hustling and prostitution. A recurrent warning was to be careful with people met on the street, particularly in Havana. Such people, alternatively referred as hustlers or *jineteros*, were reputed to be skilful cheaters and deceivers whose main goal was to get hold of the tourists' money. A frequent arrangement informing the journey of independent travellers was a list of local contacts on which one could rely: Cuban men and women that other tourists had previously met while touring the island. Arriving in Cuba with some local telephone numbers, addresses of *casas particulares* and names of trustworthy residents could reassure visitors-to-be and virtually project them into a net-work of pre-established, 'safe' connections. Similar references could come from Cuban migrants living in the tourists' countries of residence,[20] who could advise prospective tourists to visit their families and friends rather than hang around with unknown Cubans and untrustworthy *jineteros* met on the street.

Yet other stories related to the trajectories of Cuban migrants informed tourists' predispositions towards informal encounters with local people. These were the stories of relationships that had enabled Cubans to migrate, in which narratives of 'deceitful love' and 'instrumental marriages' featured heavily.[21] For those preparing to leave for a holiday in Cuba, such stories of failed relationships could exemplify the risks of getting entangled in intimate connections in which radical differences and incompatible agendas were bound to emerge. These narratives projected a gloomy, inauspicious shadow over the prospect of establishing long-term relationships with a Cuban partner met on the island.

Tips and Gossip in Cuba: 'Don't be a Dupe!'

Once in Cuba, the occasions for tourists to discuss and exchange further advice on encounters with the local population multiplied. Among the visitors I met, the underlying logic of narratives on *jineterismo* tended to go as follows: 'more or less subtle tactics, similarly instrumental drives'. This clearly appeared in discussion with Jan, a young Norwegian man in his thirties, who had visited Cuba for three consecutive years. Jan's experience of the country gave him a certain authority to instruct others about it – including less experienced foreigners, such as myself, given that I had spent only about one month on the island when we first met. As we drove to a popular disco in Havana, Jan explained 'girls' (*chicas*) in Cuba, saying there were three kinds:

> The ones that you meet and ask you straightforward for money, say forty dollars [U.S.]. The ones with whom you make love, and only afterwards ask you for some money, for a taxi to get home. And the ones who don't ask you anything, generally the most beautiful ones, and that when you come back to your country you can't stop thinking about them, about their needs and poverty, and you keep writing to them, sending them money, 100, 200 dollars, while in the meanwhile they are here in Cuba enjoying their [Cuban] boyfriends, and fucking other tourists.

Jan's grim picture of 'girls in Cuba' was informed by negative experiences he had had with two Cuban girlfriends who, he now felt, had betrayed him. In his narrative, these relationships had confronted him with the challenges and complications of 'falling in love', as a foreigner, with Cuban women: they had brought him back to earth, so to speak, disenchanting his vision of Cuba and anchoring him in the deceptive horizons of *jineterismo*. Thus he had elaborated this typology, which he was willing to share with other foreigners to teach them 'how things are in Cuba', so that they would not make the same 'mistakes'.

As I soon realized during fieldwork, the suggestions of such experienced travellers were likely to acquire a very important role in informing the dispositions of newly arrived tourists, who would value tips and recommendations coming from such elders in the location. Acting as brokers between the world of tourists and that of Cubans (see chapter 8), these veterans of Cuba abounded on the beach of Santa Maria, nourishing a flow of gossip and advice on how to engage with Cubans: where to go for what sort of encounter; how to meet the right kind of locals; how to detect their intentions and agendas; how to deal with them in order to lead relationships down a suitable path. The tips given by these experienced tourists tended to emphasize the instrumental dimensions of the tourists' encounters and relationships with Cubans, warning novices about the Machiavellian plans and economically oriented agendas of most members of the Cuban population. 'They are all looking for ways to get hold of our money!' was the type of bold statement that circulated.

The reiteration and prescriptive tone of these warnings challenged the emergence of other views on informal encounters and relationships between tourists and Cubans. Emphasis on instrumentality and deception did not favour, for instance, the emergence of narratives of friendship, love and romance. 'You must be crazy to fall in love with a Cuban girl!' was the frequent refrain in Playas del Este. In this context, tourists who were openly 'in love' with their Cuban partners could easily become objects of scorn and derision, even more so if they considered the prospect of marriage. Take the following example of a discussion I had with Alvaro and Sandro about the possibility of marrying a Cuban and moving back to Italy with her. These two Italian men, now in their sixties, had come regularly to Cuba for many years and engaged in numerous relationships with Cuban women. They made it clear that this was the worst mistake one could make. For them, to have a Cuban partner in Italy was 'like keeping a bird in a cage' (*è come tenere un uccello in gabbia*), an expression that hinted at Cubans' inexhaustible sexual appetite, a 'hotness' that sooner or later would lead them to abandon you for another man.

In tune with this line of reasoning, the proverb '*moglie e buoi dei paesi tuoi*' (wife and ox [should be] from your own land) came out in the same conversation, implying that while it was ok to enjoy sex with 'hot' Cuban women, for a serious decision like marriage it was wiser to choose someone with your own background, from your own country, someone you could trust.[22] Similar conversations with tourists in Santa Maria led to the conclusion that no matter how long you stayed with a Cuban partner, you would always remain a foreigner to them, and they would never come to treat you as they did their fellow nationals. '*La loro famiglia è una sola!*' (Their family is one and one only [i.e., the Cuban nation]). 'You'll never be able to trust them!' Such were the kinds of prescriptions that emerged in those moments of male sociability and gossip on the beach, which ended up reifying a divide between Us and Them.

The particular foci of these stories and advice could of course depend on the tourists' specific interests and agendas. Accordingly, relationships with Cuban women were the main topic of conversation among tourist men in Santa Maria, whereas discussions in Viñales tended to focus more on how to tour the countryside, whether or not to rely on a formal or informal guide, how to visit tobacco farms and fields, or how much to pay for the homemade cigars offered by farmers (see chapter 5). The point here is that tourists could quickly accumulate a wealth of information and recipes on how best to deal with the sorts of encounters that most concerned them, in tune with their particular desires and situated agendas.

From guidebooks' advice to word-of-mouth pre-travel warnings to gossip and tips once in Cuba, the examples given here have shown that narratives of instrumental and deceitful relationships with Cuban people, epitomized by the idiom of *jineterismo*, had spread widely since tourism began booming on this Caribbean island in the early 1990s. Tourists' increasing awareness of the threat of being cheated by Cubans informed their predispositions and expectations towards meeting them. Mirroring this circumspection was the Cubans' awareness of it. Much in the way they adapted *jineterismo* to cope with stepped-up control by the authorities, they refined their tactics for getting in touch with tourists in response to this awareness (see chapters 3 and 4).

Cubans' Awareness of Tourists' Scepticism

Rodrigo, a Cuban man I visited regularly throughout my fieldwork, offered a clear example of such awareness. In his late thirties, Rodrigo was an occasional street guide in Havana who always surprised me with his witty remarks on tourists and the (often hilarious) typologies he elaborated. One day, as we discussed his favourite tourists, he mentioned a few nationalities in order of preference (North Americans, Spanish, and South Americans). Then I asked him about Italian tourists, and this is what he had to say:

> The Italians, yeah, [hesitating]. But the Italians are, let's say, a bit like the Cubans already. The Italian and the Cuban are by now the same. We are in a time in which the Italian is very intelligent. Besides, in Cuba they received many blows (*han recibido muchos golpes*), much mistreatment; the women as much as the men. They [Cubans] have done things that shouldn't have been done [I understand this as evoking some sort of serious cheats]. So that's why now the Italian takes revenge for all that.

I then asked whether he still dealt with them or not, and Rodrigo adamantly clarified his stance:

> Yes, of course, I deal with the Italians, but with them, the contract [referring to his guiding fees and more generally to his monetary transactions with tourists] has to be a bit lower [than with tourist from other countries]. A little lower because they are very ... they haggle too much. They are worse than the Spanish in haggling. Even though I like Italy...

Rodrigo's remarks here focused on Italian tourists, who had been coming in big numbers since the initial upsurge in tourism in the early 1990s. According to him, Italian tourists had suffered much cheating and deception – 'many blows' – from Cuban people and had, as a result, become more astute and sceptical in dealings with Cubans. Beyond the specific reference to Italians here, on other occasions Rodrigo acknowledged that foreign tourists in general were similarly reluctant and sceptical when engaging with Cubans. He told me repeatedly that tourists were getting more and more untrustworthy (*desconfiados*) by the day. They were harder to get in touch with, and excessively worried that one would cheat them. To have any chance of developing a relationship, told me Rodrigo, you had better know how to address, soften (*ablandar*) and charm them.

Chapter 4 deals more extensively with the techniques Cuban men and women tended to deploy to overcome tourists' scepticism. For the moment, what should be retained is this sense of a critical history of informal encounters and relationships, one in which the relational idioms of *jineterismo*, of instrumentality and deception, circulate widely and progressively take centre stage. Echoing the remarks of Rodrigo, other Cubans I met during fieldwork, like the ex-*jinetero* Manuel (mentioned above), recalled with nostalgia the 'good old days' of the 1990s, when tourists were easy to deal with and left you with bags full of clothes and hundreds of dollars as presents. According to these narratives, tourists were now stingier and tougher to engage with. They wanted to use Cuban pesos instead of convertibles and show their gratitude by buying you some cheap street food. 'Now it's getting harder, they know it all; of the ways we try to get on with them, to court the girls!' complained Luis from Viñales, who, in his early thirties, saw his hopes of marrying a tourist woman slowly fading away. In the light of this state of affairs, in which tourists and Cubans drew on a vast reservoir of cumulative knowledge and competences to make sense of each other's intentions and expectations, we may argue that touristic encounters in Cuba were coming of age and leaving their more naïve, carefree, and open-ended inclinations behind.

Conclusion

With the coming of age of international tourism and *jineterismo* in Cuba, tourists' and Cubans' awareness of each other's expectations also matured, raising doubts about the compatibility and possible convergence of their needs, desires and aspirations. The steep rise in international tourist arrivals from the 1990s onwards, in times of extreme scarcity and economic hardship for most of the island's residents, opened up a realm of opportunity that many Cubans, particularly younger ones, were eager to enter. In this climate of crisis, Cuban men and women who engaged informally with foreign tourists, selectively labelled *jineteros/as*, were able to inscribe their actions within the moral framework of *la lucha* (the struggle), a key term of Revolutionary symbolism that in Special Period Cuba came to evoke people's everyday struggle to get by. Simultaneously, however, the Cuban authorities' condemnation of *jineterismo* as an immoral endeavour motivated by a lust for luxuries and capitalist consumption excluded these people's engagements from the legitimate realms of such 'struggle'. We are thus drawn here into controversies over the definition and morality of 'needs' and 'wants' that delineate processes of inclusion and exclusion into normative orders and regimes of value, of which I have provided several examples. Accordingly, Manuel portrayed his *jinetero* endeavours as driven by a legitimate quest for tourist 'high-life', while others, like Roberto, insisted their informal engagements with tourists were essentially motivated by their *necesidades* (basic needs) and refused to identify as *jineteros*.

A controversial and contested notion, *jineterismo* could refer to any income-generating activity by way of association with foreigners. It was selectively used to evoke a range of instrumentally driven relationships, in particular 'tourism hustling' and 'prostitution', and became a powerful framing tool that people also used to stigmatize, accuse and, in the case of the police (see chapter 3), even arrest targeted persons. As such, researchers should deal sensibly with this notion by paying attention to the ways in which different, sometimes conflicting actors deploy and manipulate it. Significantly, although my research informants could easily refer to their actions using the verb *jinetear* (e.g. *estaba jineteando*, I was engaging in *jineterismo*), thus denoting a situated activity and temporary engagement, they were less keen on assuming an overarching identification as *jinetero/a*. I have highlighted here the gendered dimensions of *jineterismo*, showing that whereas the *jineteros'* activities were easily inscribed and justified in a diversified realm of *la lucha* (including guiding, cigar dealing, and seducing foreign women), the *jineteras'* engagements were more often stigmatized and reduced to prostitution.

In both cases, the notion of *jineterismo* was grounded in the reification of a Us vs Them divide that objectified tourists as sources of hard currency and promoted the image of the cunning Cuban deceiving foreigners via duplicity and dissimulation. This image, which has by now gone global, informed tourists' expectations about meeting Cuban people, generating scepticism, doubt and a climate of suspicion about one another's agendas. The examples taken from conversations among tourist men at the Santa Maria beach illustrated the willingness of more experienced tourists to instruct those who had just set foot on the island about the potential pitfalls of engagements with Cuban people. Their views were rather extreme and may be located at one end of a continuum of tourists' assessments of intimate relationships with Cubans, but my ethnography suggests that most foreign visitors, women and men alike, were (or quickly became) rather sceptical of entanglement in any long-term relationship with a local. The spectre of possible deception, contrived emotions, interested marriage and other instrumental machinations at their expense often lurked at the back of their minds. The Cubans I worked with tended to be highly aware of such scepticism, and of how it could challenge their chances to get in touch and develop relationships with tourists. This was exemplified by Rodrigo's remarks on the changed attitude of Italian tourists, who had become more and more antagonistic and wary of deception, an assessment echoed in nostalgic reminiscences about the good old days of the 1990s, when tourists were more generous and easier to deal with. Tourists' and Cubans' ways of gaining access (chapter 3) and getting in touch (chapter 4) with each other must be understood and appreciated in the light of this diffuse climate of scepticism. It is to addressing these issues that I now turn.

Chapter 3
GAINING ACCESS

❦

The previous chapters have shown that for the tourist and Cuban protagonists of informal encounters, tourism held different promises. A range of needs, desires, interests and aspirations intersected, foreshadowing possible convergences but also striking discrepancies. The aim of this chapter and the next is to unpack the main challenges to making such encounters happen. The first difficulty was to gain access to each other, overcoming institutional forms of control that tended to segregate tourists from Cubans who were not formally employed in the tourism sector. For these Cubans, the main problem was bypassing the authorities' control in order to access tourism areas. On the visitors' side, different forms of tourism, and particularly their more or less enclavic, organized and scripted nature, informed the possibilities of accessing Cuban people. The second difficulty, once the issues of control and segregation had been overcome, was to establish a first connection, get in touch, initiate an interaction.

To simplify, we may argue that the first range of challenges originated from outside the encounters themselves and were directly related to an institutionally driven divide. Key agents of this divide were the Cuban police and the normative suggestions of the official tourism industry. By contrast, the second set of challenges appeared more intrinsic to encounters, in that it more directly concerned the protagonists' expectations and predispositions: tourists and Cubans had a higher degree of control over these matters and were the main agents involved.[1]

This chapter deals with how tourists and Cubans accessed each other, a question whose meaning and implications derive from the control the Cuban authorities exerted over *jineterismo*, tourism and tourists. Such control did not eliminate the possibility of informal encounters, nor was that likely its intent. Here, I consider more closely some of the fundamental lines along which it operated, as well as people's endeavours to counter segregation and make it possible to meet each other. I will discuss issues of migration, profiling and control by the Cuban police before moving on to examine the range of tactics deployed to overcome such obstacles. As for the tourists, the focus is on how different forms of tourism and different predispositions towards meeting locals shaped one's possibilities to engage with them.

Gaining Access to Tourists

Residents and Migrants

My starting point is to consider how Cuban people's place of residence – more particularly its proximity to tourism centres – could inform their opportunities to access tourists. For those already living in the city of Havana, near the beach resort of Playas del Este or in the rural town of Viñales (my three field-work locations), tourists were never too far away. But for Cubans who lived in villages, towns and cities 'off the beaten track', tourists could be much more difficult to reach. From the 1990s onwards, the prospect of engaging tourists and developing relationships with them became a powerful driver of migration to tourism centres. Havana was certainly among the most prized locations. Most visitors arrived there, so the chances of meeting them were highest in this city, and all the more so after the mid-1990s crackdowns rendered the tourist hub of Varadero largely off limits to Cuban migrants. However, movement on the island was not an easy matter for most Cubans. The journey could be a costly one, and once in the destination, people had to find a place to stay and a way to get by.

Some had relatives living in the vicinity of a tourism centre who could host them. But many who had no such connection were forced to rely on more precarious arrangements, such as the (often illegal) renting of rooms (O'Connell Davidson 1996; Kummels 2005).[2] The cost of this could vary a great deal, depending especially on the quality of the accommodation and its proximity to tourist areas. Thus, for a shared accommodation in Calle Obispo in the core of the Old Havana tourism district, Ramon, one of the many migrants I got to know during fieldwork, paid 30 CUC (convertible pesos) a month. To gather this sum, he was forced to *inventar* (lit. invent)[3] – that is, find ways to make money, a pressure he was feeling at the time of our conversation.

Even more striking for me was the case of Raquel, a girl of twenty who had come to Havana from Santiago de Cuba (almost 1,000 km east of Havana) to study. Upon moving to the capital, Raquel had stayed at her uncle's family house, a chance she felt lucky enough to have. She soon found out, however, that the uncle, his wife and their son and daughter expected her to do all the household chores and did not even reciprocate by providing her with regular meals. In Raquel's words, they had treated her 'as a slave', making her feel like an exploited stranger in their house. After a few months of this humiliating experience, Raquel followed her school friends' advice to rent a shared room in Centro Habana. The need to gather forty CUC for the rent each month was among the factors that prompted her to start going out to the Casa de la Música (a popular music venue in Centro Habana frequented by tourists, where I first met Raquel) from time to time, to try to make some money by having sex with tourists she managed to seduce there. As Raquel put it, she had always been lucky and successful in that. Even though she did not like the idea of *prostituirse* (prostituting oneself),[4] judging it morally demeaning, her concrete experiences with tourists had actually varied a great deal depending on whether or not she had liked her partners and had managed to enjoy (*pasárselo bien*) the time spent with them. When I asked her whether this was preferable to living in her uncle's house, she argued that it was and went on to explain that if she had to tarnish her dignity and self-esteem, she preferred at least to be able to decide how to do it, rather than having others, such as her uncle's family, impose it on her.

Though she feared getting into trouble with the authorities for engaging with tourists – particularly on her nights at the Casa de la Música, when she dressed up for the occasion and became an easy target of *jinetera* profiling (see below) – Raquel at least had a legitimate reason to reside in Havana: she was registered in a university course. The situation could prove more difficult for illegal migrants, who could be seen as having no proper reason to be there and thus found it harder to justify their hanging around with tourists to police officers. Conversely, Cubans who legally resided near places frequented by tourists and could prove it with the address inscribed on their ID cards could feel safer and more easily prevent trouble with the authorities. Cubans' official place of residence was thus the first crucial factor informing their chances of making contact with visitors. Still, as Raquel's example suggests, this was only part of the story, since other lines of discrimination affected their opportunities to informally engage with tourists.

Profiling: The Selective Targeting of Jineteros and Jineteras

The police profiling of the *jinetero/a* operated along several lines of discrimination, of which four interrelated ones seemed to play particularly salient roles: gender, race, style of dress, and attitude/behaviour. Let me summarize briefly here how each of these could inform the selective identification and targeting of *jineteros* and *jineteras* by the authorities.[5]

Regarding gender, a number of scholars have highlighted how Cuban men found it easier than Cuban women to hang around tourism areas undisturbed (see in particular Hodge 2001; Cabezas 2004; Allen 2007; chapter 2). Several Cuban men I met during fieldwork confirmed this. According to them, *chicas* (girls) had better walk around tourism areas accompanied (by them or other men) if they wished to mitigate police harassment. Being seen as part of a couple could deter police intervention, seemingly normalizing the presence of women in such areas. These normative views on the legitimacy of women's presence in public tourism areas could foster dependence on a male partner, with the latter claiming his stake in the woman's dealings with tourists, demanding for a share of her possible gains and thus virtually acting as a sort of protector or pimp. Raquel despised such a scenario as a manifestation of abuse of women by men who took money unduly from *luchadoras* who were already struggling to preserve some dignity in their work. As she angrily put it, if they wanted to earn some money, these men had better become *pingueros*, 'give their ass' (*darle el culo*) to foreigners, rather than seize the women's hard-earned cash. Herself, she always went around on her own, or with female friends, in spite of the increased risks this could carry.

Alongside gender, racial attribution has been highlighted as another major discriminatory tool in the Cuban police profiling of *jineteros* and *jineteras*. Fernandez (1999) spelled this out clearly in an article on women, race and tourism in Cuba, and her considerations have been further elaborated by Alcázar Campos (2010), Berg (2004), Cabezas (2009) and Roland (2011). Berg (2004: 50) pertinently points out that black Cubans, and more generally black people, were more subject to police profiling as *jineteros/as* than their white counterparts, who could more easily pass as foreigners themselves. She quotes the striking example of a black British woman and her white Swedish partner who respectively were widely perceived as a *jinetera* and a foreigner. In the course of my fieldwork I came across similar cases that led to embarrassing scenes of misplaced police questioning. They became for me irrefutable proof of the racial profiling of *jineteros/as*. As Berg (2004: 50) puts it, '*jineterismo* has been racialized to the extent that young dark-skinned Cubans have come to be seen almost automatically as *jineteros* in certain contexts' (see also Alcázar Campos 2009, 2010; Roland 2011). Conversely, tourists were generally assumed to be white, or at least non-black.

Another salient aspect in the profiling of *jineteros/as* related to the way people dressed. Raquel alluded to the risk of walking from her house to the Casa de la Música 'all dressed up' as she had been when I first met her there, in a very short leopard-print dress and high heels. That was a risk she would never take, preferring instead to get a taxi although the venue was only a few blocks away. Berg (2004) provides other clear examples of this in her discussion of representations of *jineterismo*. Accordingly, two of her informants, Afro-Cuban women in their late twenties, complained that if they dressed up as they liked to do when going to tourist areas of Havana, they were more likely to be stopped and questioned by the police, who would equate their style to that of a *jinetera* (2004: 51). For Berg, this reflects the popular assumption 'that *jineteras* dress in smart clothes, which are available only for dollars' (51). Ex-*jinetero* Fernando, one of my key Cuban informants on the world of *jineterismo*, similarly pointed out the importance of one's clothing in attracting or evading the attention of the Cuban police. To avoid being stopped by the authorities, his tactic was to 'dress as a tourist'. The many foreigners he had met in the last decade or so had left him with a good selection of different imported clothes, which he would carefully combine to give himself a tourist appearance. Being, as he put it, a *mulatico* – someone of light brown complexion – he hoped the authorities would take him for a Latin American tourist. On several occasions, he told me with a certain pride, this tactic had enabled him to enter tourist hotels at a time when Cubans were still not allowed in.[6]

Similar to the racial profiling mentioned above, what mattered here was one's visibility (*visibilidad*), Fernando explained, supporting the notion that external appearance alone could inform the police officers' identification and targeting of *jineteros*. In the previous chapter I hinted at how the police crackdown on *jineterismo* in the late 1990s brought changes in the modus operandi of *jineteras*, leading them to diminish their visibility by adopting a more 'normal' dress code (Valle 2006: 242). Among my research informants, there was widespread awareness of this discriminatory element in police profiling. However, as Raquel's example also reveals, and as I will consider more thoroughly in the following chapter, a tension could emerge here between competing efforts to diminish one's visibility to the police but also to enhance that same visibility (and a specific kind of visibility it is) so as to 'catch the eye' (Crick 1992; Dahles 1998) of foreign visitors.

While the inference of people's agendas from their external appearance seemed to play a key role in the police profiling of *jineteros/as*, other rationales that relied on less prejudicial evidence of hustling should not be dismissed altogether. This can be referred to as attitudinal/behavioural profiling. Accordingly, it could become important for officers to establish who had started the interaction in question, that is, whether it had been the Cuban or the tourist. As I will show in the next chapter, this kind of evaluation also helped tourists and Cubans map out each other's agendas and intentions. The rationale here was that if the Cuban had started the encounter, he/she was likely to be a *jinetero/a* guided by some sort of instrumental agenda. If it was instead the tourist who had first approached the Cuban, there was no apparent reason to suspect that the latter had bad intentions or was after something.

The workings of such behavioural profiling were made very clear to me by Juan, a young Cuban man in his twenties who frequented the Rasta clique in Havana, in the course of several lengthy conversations we had about trouble with the police. We discussed in some detail the case of Santa Maria, the highly surveilled beach where I had seen him a couple of days earlier, seemingly undisturbed by officers, in the company of female tourists. Juan explained that when one was already with the tourists upon arrival at Santa Maria, things were likely to go smoothly, with no police questioning. However, if he had started jumping (*brincar*) from one foreigner to the other while on the beach, obviously trying to meet new tourists, he would have caught the attention of officers who would then have been more likely to question him, check his criminal record and eventually proceed with an arrest. Juan noted that one had to learn to act discreetly, without giving the impression of hustling tourists or seeming eager to engage with as many visitors as possible. Being able to project the image of a well-established, mutual relationship with tourists, as opposed to an immediate, transient and potentially deceitful one, was indeed a very important skill when dealing with officers inclined to pay attention to such relational dynamics. Juan's remarks also reveal the importance of knowing how surveillance and control operated in tourism areas. This was indeed a key competence that people needed to cultivate if they wished to limit the risks of being stopped, questioned and arrested.

Knowing about Surveillance and Control

How did the security forces operate? How was one to deal with the different agents of control – such as police officers and closed-circuit television (CCTV) cameras – that supervised and policed tourism areas? These key issues absorbed the attention of my Cuban research informants, generating much debate among them. Valuable competences ranged from identifying plainclothes officers[7] to knowing the timing and locations of possible *recogidas* (police raids). Rumours spread quickly about these matters, and early warnings could prove essential to avoiding trouble. The location of surveillance cameras in tourism areas was important information that influenced people's movements in the touristic core of Old Havana. Some went as far as considering the whole area 'hot' (*candela*) and off limits: they would not lightly venture into this dangerous terrain and were even less inclined to try to meet tourists, given the risk of being caught on camera.[8]

Jorge, a Cuban man in his forties, clearly spelled out the difference between Old Havana and Central Havana. He himself used to come and sit every afternoon in the same spot, in one of the main squares in Old Havana, with the explicit aim of getting in touch with tourists. Showing his knowledge of the hangout, Jorge pointed discreetly to the location of surveillance cameras. He seemed to know exactly where and how to move in order to avoid trouble, but he was also aware that it was always risky to attempt to engage tourists. Though Old Havana was very hot for this type of *lucha*, it was also where more tourists could be met. Accordingly, he aimed to meet tourists there, in Old Havana's core, and then 'pull them out' (*sacar el turista*) towards Central Havana, where from the Parque Central onwards 'everything is possible' (*todo es posible*).[9]

Besides being informed about the whereabouts of surveillance and control, knowing how to deal with an officer was considered another important skill. How to explain oneself, how to get tourists involved in someone's defence, how to argue about one's right to interact with whomever one liked, how to bribe the officer concerned – all could facilitate Cubans' dealings with the authorities and increase their chances of engaging tourists. Distinctions also played out regarding one's ability to confront the police. Aurora, for instance, a Cuban woman in her thirties whom I spent much time with, told me proudly that she knew how to gain the respect of officers and what to tell them in order to be left alone. She contrasted her own skills with those of 'cheap' (*bajo costo*) girls: poorer, little educated Cuban women – 'country girls' (*guajiras*) who wore flashy cheap clothes and thus became easy targets for the police. Always ready to have sex with tourists for a trifle, these *bajo costo* girls knew nothing of their rights, according to Aurora. They were unable to argue with the authorities and so feared the police that they would easily betray their *jinetera* intentions, complying docilely with instructions.

However skilful Cubans may have been in dealing with the police, there was always the possibility that the latter would dismiss one's defensive claims and arguments and proceed authoritatively as they wished, up to an arrest. Yet in many cases there seemed to be at least some margin of negotiation. Self-assured postures, convincing explanations and justifications, the intervention of tourist companions in one's favour and, ultimately, the subtle bribing of the officer could all help one get away without being further questioned. On the other hand, arguing too much, losing one's composure and flying off the handle could further aggravate the consequences of a police check. In the course of these delicate interactions, striking the right balance was not an easy task. For instance, on some occasions I saw police maltreating and even beating up Cuban men who had been too loud and affirmative about their 'rights to engage with foreigners'.

To prevent accusations of *jineterismo*, Cubans could also instruct their tourist companions on how to deal with the police in case they were stopped. The recommendations I heard included 'Tell the police you just asked me for some information' (again, the directionality of the encounter could prove crucial); 'Tell them that we are good old friends'; 'If they want to bring me to the police station, come with me to make sure they do not keep me there'; and 'Be ready with some money to bribe them'. As I realized on a few occasions, however, some officers had grown accustomed to these scripts and could dismiss them as fabricated stories. 'Yes, of course, you have known him for years and you are very good friends – and what's his name, again?' an officer might ironically comment, downplaying the relevance of the tourist's intervention while testing the veracity of their relational claims.

Knowing how surveillance and control operated and how to deal with the police was one thing. Better still was to have contacts and resources that could enable the bypassing of such control altogether, notably as a result of personal connections.

Cultivating Connections: Relatives, Friends, Bribes

Friends or relatives who had a formal job in establishments frequented by tourists (bars, clubs, *paladares*, *casas particulares*, a stall at the handicraft market, etc.) could provide a relatively safe base from which to gain informal access to tourists.[10] Apart from these links to legal tourism businesses, connections with members of the police force could also prove extremely useful. Such was the case for Ruben, a young migrant from Guantanamo on the far east of the island, whom I met one afternoon at the beach in Santa Maria.

As we chatted on the shoreline, Ruben explained that his cousin was one of the officers patrolling the beach, which made it possible for him and the group of teenage girls he was with to come every day undisturbed. Ruben said they were all spending their summer holidays visiting relatives in Havana and had found Santa Maria to be a safe gateway to contact with tourists. While he guarded their clothes and belongings, the girls spent their time in the water, flirting with male tourists and trying to arrange dates for the evening. But whereas Ruben's cousin granted them a certain degree of protection, this also meant that Ruben was constantly indebted to him. He complained that whenever they went out together, he had to pay for everything. Ruben also explained that *las más listas* (the smartest) Cuban girls on this beach spent most of their time in the water to meet and flirt with tourists, thus reducing these interactions' visibility to the officers patrolling the shore. Other Cubans who came here to meet tourists but had no pre-existing relationship with officers had to pay a bribe in order to be left alone, Ruben told me, adding that everything on this beach was a *convenio*, a matter of arrangements with the police.

Money was indeed a key resource in the cultivation of such relational networks. In the words of a Cuban man with whom I had just a brief chat one evening in Havana, the 'good policemen' were those that you could bribe, the ones that 'let you live' (*te dejan vivir*) and do your business.[11] Similarly, my friend Humberto, an experienced Rasta in his thirties who had spent more than a decade *jineteando*, in and out of jail, told me that after all police officers were 'persons' (*son personas*), 'human beings' who also needed to provide for their families and therefore appreciated a little cash from time to time. In turn, the skilful cultivation of such relationships – a can of beer here, one convertible peso there, a little gift on the birthday of the officer's kid – granted Humberto room to manoeuvre in the tourism hotspot of Old Havana. 'Old Havana is ours!' (*la Habana Vieja es nuestra*, i.e. his and his colleague Andres'), he boasted one day, adding that '*los tenemos todos mansitos*' (we have them [the police] all tamed).

One month after this conversation with Humberto, however, all the officers patrolling Old Havana were replaced by fresh recruits, allegedly coming from *Oriente* (i.e. the East of the country), as seemed rather common for police forces in the capital. These people, as Humberto put it, still needed to learn 'how things worked' in the world of tourism, to realize that he and his friend Andres posed no threat whatsoever to tourists[12] and were rather to be seen as a possible source of benefits for the police. With the change in patrols, Old Havana had become off limits to Humberto – *candela* (hot), at least for a few weeks until things calmed down again, after the first *recogidas* (raids) carried out by overzealous, inexperienced officers. Like Humberto and Ruben, other Cubans who relied on the complicity of (a) particular officer(s) tended to know exactly when and where their contact would be on duty and adapted their own schedules and zones of activity accordingly. Those who had the means could extend their networks of tacit accomplices across a wider area, gaining safer access to an increasing number of places from which to interact with tourists. People were thus able to carve more or less ample niches of impunity.

Zonas, *Cliques, and* Ser Libre

Some areas, like Old Havana, were judged more profitable than others, and competition within them could be intense. Cliques and factions could try to monopolize certain areas by deterring potential competitors from 'stealing' tourists from within their *zona* (area, see Valle 2006: 49–50). This topic arose in the conversation I had with Juan about police control in Santa Maria, and the rationales for questioning and arresting certain Cubans and not others. On that occasion, he explained how some people's arrangements with the police led them to claim exclusive rights to engage with tourists in their *zona*:

> There are girls in this beach who have an arrangement (*han cuadrado*) with the police. They help them [the police] (*los salvan*) with something, they give them some money. Then you have others, beginners (*primerizas*), people who do not know [how things work], who come on their own. And those same girls who are [already] there, those who have an arrangement [with the police], they send them [the beginners] to slaughter (*las mandan a matar*) [i.e. they hand them over to the police]. They tell the police: 'Hey look, look at these ones who have just arrived, who have entered my area'. The [more experienced] girls themselves send them to slaughter.

According to Juan, such arrangements worked to prevent potential competitors from encroaching on a given *zona*. In his view, similar principles also operated on the Malecón, an area of Havana that at first sight could appear easily accessible and open to anyone. However, here too one had to learn not to violate unwritten rules by stepping into areas occupied by certain cliques, like that of a group of Rasta:

> Yes, the Rasta on the Malecón, they have their area. If someone arrives who is not with them; if for instance they are talking to tourists, and another guy arrives and sits beside the tourists, and starts to talk with them and they get along well, and then leaves with the tourists, well, they do not like that, they themselves will tell the police, 'look there', so they will send him to slaughter. If you take their tourists away, they'll send you to slaughter. The police have their own people, people working for them; they have their girls, their Rasta ...

I then asked Juan how one could eventually become part of such groups:

> Well, yes, if they [the members of the group] see that you vibrate (*que vibras*), as we say here in Cuba, if they see that you have a good vibration, that you know how to talk (*que sabes hablar*), that tourists stick to you (*que los turistas se te pegan*), then they may ask you 'Hey pal (*oye compadre*), stay here with us'. They let you stay there, so that you pull tourists (*pa' que hales turistas*).[13]

Whereas hanging around in a group could prove advantageous and also ensure increased protection, people like Juan, who liked to move around alone, emphasized their reluctance to join a clique and thus depend on other people. Instead, they preferred to retain full control and autonomy in their tourism-oriented activities. As mentioned above, the possibility of operating individually was not equally open to everyone, given for instance the important differences that existed between migrants and residents, or between men and women. When I asked him whether he was also part of the Rasta clique and tied to a specific area, Juan told me that he preferred to 'be free' (*ser libre*), to walk around on his own while taking care not to encroach on others' areas.

He was not the only person I met who expressed such a preference. Fernando explained the different tactics of *jineteros* in relation to their places of activity and movement. Some people, he told me, preferred to stay in a specific area and develop good connections with the officers that patrolled it, whereas others, like him, disliked the idea of having to depend on police officers or other gatekeepers (porters in tourism installations, bartenders, etc.):

> I am not of the ones who bribe the police (*sobornan los policías*). I do not want to give anything to anyone. I prefer to move around, keep moving all the time, like I am just walking around town … If you don't move, if you stay put in one place, the police will notice you.

Better still, according to Fernando, was to have some money to spend, which enabled one to independently access tourism installations like bars and clubs without having to rely on the favours of doormen and bartenders, who would then demand a cut of the profits from any tourism-related deal. This leads us to consider the degree of accessibility of tourism installations, which as Fernandez (1999) has shown, could have a serious impact on Cubans' chances of making contact with tourists.

Accessing Sitios

Tourism installations such as bars and clubs were, for many of my research participants, the ideal places to get in touch with tourists. Fernando was very clear on this point: 'If I can, I go to a place [an enclosed space, e.g. bar, club, disco] (*me voy pa' un sitio*). That's better because you don't have to worry (*puedes estar tranquilo*). Tourists come there; you don't have to worry about the police.' Without a special connection to such a place, such as a relative or friend working there, the main problem was having the cash to afford it. Indeed, even in bars without a cover charge, Fernando told me, you had to consume at least a drink, or else the waiters would start bothering you and ultimately kick you out. The costlier the admission to a place was, the greater was the chance of meeting tourists with a fair amount of money to spend. That was why it was interesting for him to go to places like La Casa de La Música, the popular venue frequented also by Raquel: 'If I go to the Casa de la Música, I can already have an idea of the budget of the tourists who are in there … I know that people had to pay ten, twenty [CUC] for the entrance.

So, even if they are backpackers (*mochileros*), I expect they have 100 [CUC] on them (*deben andar con 100 encima*)'.

Fernando was not the only one to make this kind of calculation. Many Cubans I talked to expressed their preference for tourist installations, which they saw as the most suitable, safest places to meet tourists. But again, the challenge was how to enter these sites, especially when there was a cover charge. Admission fees constituted a powerful barrier, with different prices conjuring different clienteles. Fernandez (1999) has pointed out the discriminatory implications of this, notably along the lines of class and race. Accordingly, given the continued predominance of blacks and mulattos in the poorest strata of Cuban society, they had more difficulty gaining access to popular tourism venues (Fernandez 1999). Having less access to these places meant having to engage tourists in other realms, most likely under public scrutiny, and facing increased surveillance and control (ibid.).

Fernandez's remarks lead us back to my initial considerations on how different lines of discrimination informed Cubans' opportunities to access tourists. This section has described a range of competences and resources that enabled and restrained these possibilities. Once such possibilities were created, the next challenge was to get in touch and establish a first connection with visitors (chapter 4). Before moving on to that, though, I will discuss how different forms of tourism, and the tourists' predisposition, also worked to enable or hamper informal encounters.

Gaining Access to Cubans

Which Tourism Areas? Moving beyond the 'Bubble'

Whereas gaining access to the places frequented by tourists and overcoming surveillance and control by the authorities involved much effort, investment and risk for my Cuban interlocutors, tourists, by comparison, could find meeting Cuban men and women a much easier task. Still, their experiences differed significantly depending on the type of tourism they were engaging in and more particularly on its more or less institutionalized and scripted nature. I mentioned in the introduction that the bulk of my tourist research participants were independent travellers, who were also the most likely to engage informally with Cuban people. At the opposite end of the spectrum were tourists staying in all-inclusive resorts, especially those who did not even participate in excursions outside their enclave.[14] People who took part in such excursions, like tourists on organized tours of the island, still had other windows of opportunities to meet informally with Cubans.

Travelling independently often acquired its value by way of contrast to the world of tourism resorts and the highly scripted, directed, supposedly 'bubble-like' reality of organized trips and excursions. Among independent travellers, critiques of tourists who came to Cuba 'just to stay in an all-inclusive resort' such as could be found anywhere else in the world were very common. So were condemnations of the policies that, up to 2008 at least, barred ordinary Cubans from access to tourism infrastructure like hotels and resorts. Many saw these policies as a discriminatory expression of a sort of 'tourism apartheid' (see chapter 1). Quite a few tourists emphasized their determination to avoid tourism bubbles and enclaves like Varadero, often qualified as not part of Cuba at all, at least not the 'real' one. Those who did go to Varadero tended to elaborate on the reason for doing so, justifying their a stay on the peninsula as a well-deserved few days of relaxation on a beautiful beach after a more demanding tour of the island, a sort of second-ary holiday within their primary, more valued journey across the country.

Enclaves like Varadero could epitomize tourists' failure to meet locals, to experience the real Cuba, a failure to fulfil an important promise of tourism on this Caribbean island. Bringing this reasoning to the fore, independent travellers could extend their criticism of tourism enclaves to all touristic areas of Cuba. Therefore, the city of Havana, and more particularly Old Havana's main tourism circuit, could also become tourist bubbles. The enclavic nature of these places – their highly controlled, surveilled and sanitized character – was highlighted and discredited as expressing the touristification and com-moditization of Cuba. Importantly, such critiques could also help people qualify the kinds of encounters they had, indexing them to the perceived degree of touristification of a given area. Like the alleged absence of contact with locals in the purest enclaves, most notably all-inclusive resorts, the amount of tourism hustling in touristic areas of the country was a rather common topic of conversation. This is how Havana, or at least certain areas of the city, ended up portrayed as the quintessential habitat of hustlers and *jineteros/as*, where only transient, deceptive interactions were likely to take place and where tourism harassment predominated. Among tourists travel-ling independently, a much-valued narrative saw them avoiding such tour-istic areas altogether in search of a more genuine Cuba and more genuine people and relationships (see chapter 8) elsewhere, in other regions of the country 'off the beaten track'.

Different tourism areas, in their more or less enclavic nature, were thus seen to afford different chances to engage with 'ordinary Cubans' and to inform the types of encounters tourists were likely to have. Still, other aspects need to be taken into account to move us beyond a potentially reductive view of places as predetermining the scope of touristic encounters.

Among these other dimensions was the scripted, organized and planned character of tourism practices.

Scripting, Organizing and Planning

Tourists taking part in guided tours did venture into public spaces, but they did so under the watchful eye of official guides.[15] Official guides could act to deter Cubans not employed in the formal tourism sector from approaching tourists. Furthermore, the places these groups frequented were often part of a well established, highly surveilled and policed tourism circuit, akin to the enclavic tourist spaces described by Edensor (1998), which made it more difficult for other Cubans to informally get in touch with tourists. As a result, the encounters visitors had during these tours, if any, tended to be limited to transient transactions of an essentially economic nature, such as cigar deals or charitable donations to Cubans met briefly on the street. The tourists who dared to engage in these quick interactions were generally the less disciplined ones who strayed at the margins of the group, only sporadically followed the guide's explanations and were easily distracted by what was happening around them.

During such excursions, there could also be 'free time' moments in which tourists had the chance to roam around on their own before gathering at a meeting place established by the guide. These could open up further possibilities to interact informally with Cubans. Again, though, their short duration made it difficult to establish relationships that went beyond a transient transaction, such as buying a three-peso coin with Che Guevara's effigy on it, giving away pens and candies to children or purchasing cigars. Furthermore, the guides on these excursions could explicitly discourage the participating tourists from engaging with Cubans on the streets. For instance, the guide of one official tour I took in Havana, whose participants were mainly people spending the bulk of their holidays in all-inclusive resorts, recommended not buying anything 'on the street' (*en la calle*). As she put it: 'When I say on the street, I am referring to individual persons [i.e. free-floating strangers]'. What seems to matter here is thus the question of the organization of the travel, its scripted and directed nature, and how much room for improvisation and disruption it enabled.

Organization and planning did not concern only guided tours, and major differences on the matter existed also among independent travellers. When I asked a group of Italian teenagers about their encounters with Cubans, for instance, they very clearly indicated that they tended not to respond to Cubans' calls for attention because they did not want to miss out on their tightly scheduled visits. Their determination and resolution not to be 'distracted' by unplanned events struck me especially forcefully when one of them articulated the motto: 'See the most [sights?] without wasting one's time in talk' (*Vedere il più possible senza perdersi in chiacchere*). Were they to stick to this refrain, we can well imagine the challenge facing Cubans trying to get in touch with them. At the opposite end of the planning spectrum, other tourists travelling independently took a radically different stance towards the possibility of getting involved in unplanned encounters and relationships. Accordingly, some told me, for instance, that the main aim of their holiday in Cuba was to 'meet the locals' and talk with them about life in the country (see chapter 6). Others cherished the idea of getting involved in intimate – or, more straightforwardly, sexual – relationships and therefore looked forward to the possibility of serendipitous encounters and relationships of this kind (see chapter 8). In these cases, plans and schedules tended to remain rather open-ended and adaptable to the events that might unfold during the journey.

To summarize, my ethnographic material points to the existence of significant differences in tourists' predisposition to adapt plans, schedules and agendas as a result of encounters with Cuban people. Those tourists who were open to this possibility could also take more active steps to facilitate the establishment of certain connections.

Tailoring Possibilities for Informal Encounters

An interesting case was that of tourists who rented a car to travel around the country and, dismissing the recommendations of car-rental companies, were very keen to pick up Cuban hitchhikers along the road.[16] Several tourists saw this as an ideal way to get to know Cubans while helping them reach their destination. As some put it, these were excellent opportunities to get to know ordinary folks, people who had no instrumental agendas in mind, given the lower likelihood of winding up with professional hustlers and *jineteros*. Tourists could also benefit from hitchhikers' tips and suggestions, which had led some to memorable experiences of spontaneously visiting a Cuban house, meeting a Cuban family, and even sharing a meal with them. A German couple who had had one such experience saw it as the highlight of their journey, epitomizing the unexpected moments of intimacy and close contact with ordinary Cubans they had very much hoped for.[17]

Opting for accommodation in family-owned *casas particulares* could be another way to facilitate contacts with locals. *Casas particulares* tended also to function as important nodes for other informal activities catering to tourists in Cuba. Its owners could for instance recommend other Cubans, often a member of the extended family, as guides or companions for visitors. Crick (1992: 145) has shown how in Kandi, Sri Lanka, a guesthouse proprietor could 'want to monopolise the tourist's time and expenditure to maximise his income', a desire that annoyed Kandi street guides, who saw potential clients being taken away from them. The same happened in Cuba and was particularly evident in the rural town of Viñales, where it could be very hard for Cubans who were not part of a *casa*'s network to gain access to tourists (and vice versa). Tourists could view the recommendations of their *casa particular* as a convenient, safe way to get to know Cubans they could trust, given their traceability to the accommodation.

But the owner's advice could sometimes be deemed too insistent and interpreted as an invasive attempt to channel visitors' movements, obstructing their chances of meeting locals unrelated to the *casa*. In these cases, tensions could emerge when tourists felt that their range of options and decision-making power was being restricted. How closely should one follow the suggestions given at the *casa*? Were these genuine attempts to help tourists, or interested moves to capitalize on their encounters and expenses? The ambivalence of this 'politics of hospitality' (Tucker 2003; Picard 2011) will reappear in the examination of cigar deals in chapter 5.

Always in relation to the degree of protectiveness and control in *casas particulares*, another frequent issue of concern was tourists' ability to invite Cuban partners into their accommodation. This was particularly important for those seeking intimate and sexual relationships, a case in point being the Italian men I met in Santa Maria's beach. Accordingly, for some visitors a key criterion in choosing accommodation was being allowed to bring Cubans to their room. This could inform the decision to rent a more independent apartment as opposed to a single room, or to opt for an illegal accommodation that did not require registration of all guests coming in and out. More generally, what seemed key in an accommodation was that it granted tourists much freedom of movement, opening up the possibility of their becoming hosts and entertaining whomever they liked. Tourists who had booked a hotel room, unaware of the restrictions that could keep Cubans from sharing their accommodation, could rapidly opt for alternative arrangements, such as moving to a *casa particular*.[18]

Prior to 2008, tourists who wished to invite Cuban partners to their hotel rooms generally had to bribe the hotel staff in order to do so. The 2008 legal changes that enabled Cubans to stay in hotels seem to have pushed other expressions of social control and moralizing judgements to the fore (Alcázar Campos 2010: 308–309). For instance, Cubans registering in hotel rooms with different tourism partners in a short period of time could raise the suspicion of their being *jineteros/as* and become targets of surveillance, control and questioning by the authorities: was this a case of 'sex for money' exchange or of 'romance'? In other words, the issue became to ascertain the nature of the Cubans' engagements with tourists. By the same token, this highlighted the potential for collusion between hospitality institutions, agents of disciplining and control, and supporters of normative divides between different types of relationships.

Exemplifying such collusion and its far-reaching consequences was the story of Pablo, a young Afro-Cuban man from Havana who got caught in the net linking the hospitality industry to the government's policing of touristic encounters. His friend Pedro, who was with Pablo at the time, reported the unfortunate events to me. Upon arriving with his tourist girlfriend in Baracoa (a town over 1,000 km east of the capital), Pablo had checked into a *casa* with her. The following day, once the local immigration office had processed the information on all the guests staying in *casas* in Baracoa, the authorities (who were much stricter than what Pablo was used to in Havana) came to arrest him. The rationale for the arrest was that this was one time too many for Pablo – who had collected several 'warnings' (*cartas de advertencia*) in the past – to sleep with yet another tourist. In the light of the local authorities' reputation for comparative strictness and dislike of *jineteros* who were not from Baracoa, Pedro had thought it best to sleep on the beach and avoided a similar fate. Pablo's boldness ultimately cost him three years in jail, notwithstanding his tourist partner's protests and attempts to reassure the local authorities that he was indeed her boyfriend. As this tragic example shows, strict forms of control operated not only in hotels, but also in relation to *casas particulares*. This also explained why some of my tourist informants were very careful to choose *casas* that did not require registration of all their partners, who in some cases changed on a daily basis.

The cases discussed here also draw attention to the tourists' awareness of Cuban tourism policies, notably those that could obstruct their interactions with Cubans. Such awareness seemed especially acute among independent travellers eager to establish intimate and sexual encounters with locals. Their criticism of tourism policies could foster complicity with their Cuban partners and more broadly facilitate the development of informal encounters.

Narratives of Repression: Unpacking Surveillance and Control

Several narratives circulated among visitors regarding the Cuban government's efforts to channel and control tourism on the island, and to obstruct 'ordinary Cubans'' possibilities of interacting with foreigners. A widespread criticism, viewing these policies through an economic lens, denounced the authorities' control as an expression of a typical monopolistic state that did not want its citizens to benefit directly from tourism but at the same time did not do enough to redistribute its profits. Another, more political line of reasoning explained surveillance, control and repression of informal encounters as a way for a totalitarian Cuban regime to keep non-official accounts of everyday life in Cuba from reaching tourists via the narratives of ordinary citizens who were not employed in the formal tourism industry or instructed on what should and should not be said about life on the island.[19] Such interpretations converged with those that my Cuban research informants also tended to rely on, and thus established a certain complicity, prompting alliances between tourists and Cubans to evade the authorities' control.

Indeed, among tourists too tips circulated on how to bypass such regulation. One way was to avoid major tourism areas and the most enclavic tourism spaces, where surveillance was heaviest, and frequent instead locations that enabled informal encounters to take place more freely. These could be on the margins of the main tourism routes, like the areas outside Old Havana's touristic core or, on a wider scale, provincial towns in which tourism was not so developed (see chapter 8). In the case of Havana, other advice had to do with the bars and clubs frequented by ordinary Cubans, where tourists would have greater chances of meeting and engaging with locals without being bothered by the police. Among tourists in Santa Maria, such recommendations circulated about the 'hot' discos of Havana, which were a constant subject of debate. One could not rely on old information but had to keep up to date, some argued, given that police raids regularly caused the 'death' of the targeted venues. As I familiarized myself with these tips, I learned the best places to go on Mondays, on Tuesdays, and so on, observing a meticulous form of planning that could cover all nights of the week and was specifically tailored to maximize the chances of engaging with a certain Cuban crowd, particularly women willing to engage intimately with tourists. What is more, when characterizing such venues an informant could go into great detail regarding the types of women that frequented them (e.g. more or less young or educated, *jinetera*-like).

Besides these possible ways of avoiding constraints imposed by the authorities, tourists had other means of negotiating such control, notably by taking a more active role in confronting the police.

Confronting and Benefiting from Control

In explaining tourists' determination to confront the police, one should consider the intensity of their desire to engage with Cubans, a desire that could itself generate tensions with the visitors' principles and inclinations in regards to policing more broadly, and eventually lead to their transformation. Once again, the most striking examples came from those tourists who were looking forward to intimate and sexual relationships, as they showed the strongest determination to confront the authorities. Visitors' frustration with the actions of the police reached its peak in the realm of intimate encounters. Thus Italian tourists in Santa Maria chanted the anti-police slogans '*Via! Via! La polizia!* (Out! Out! The police!). This anti-authoritarian attitude led people to assume a liberal rhetoric denouncing discriminatory and repressive policies at the hands of the Cuban state. At the same time, tourists' position could also be embraced as privileged and untouchable, deemed to float above Cuban law, securing their freedom of speech and entitling them to confront the police to free their Cuban partners. In Santa Maria, this bold attitude was often related to tourists' disappointment that Cuban women's access to the beach was restricted. Adopting a somewhat cynical take on the matter, we could argue that the reduction of the pool of potential partners hampered the tourists' quest for pleasure, prompting some of them to react with anger.[20]

Those who were familiar with this beach and came there regularly tended to have good relationships with the officers on patrol, who seldom changed throughout the years of my fieldwork. The officers greeted these veterans of Santa Maria amicably on their first day of a new tourist season, and would keenly exchange gossip, news and jokes (often of a sexual nature, and with explicit references to the sexually charged atmosphere of the beach, as it was no secret what the visitors were after), as well as favours. Such complicity with the police force granted tourists plenty of room to interact with whomever they wished, securing opportunities for any of their Cuban partners to join them on the highly surveilled beach.

Other competences had to do with the possibility of intervening in case of police questioning of a Cuban. In the course of these checks, officers tended to instruct tourists not to worry about what was happening to their Cuban companion, reassuring them that the check had nothing to do with the tourists, who should not be concerned for their own safety, and urging them to move on and continue with their doings. But at this point, the visitor might take a more proactive stance by stepping in to try to defend the Cuban partner. Several tourists I met had lived the dramatic experience of escorting their partner to a police station. Waiting there for their release, visitors might try to reassure officers about the nature of the relationship, praising their partners' behaviour in the hope this could speed up the process and facilitate their release. But the tourists' interventions could also be very selective and were not always guided by an overarching concern to get their partners out of trouble. Consider the following self-interested remarks of a group of Italian men who had recently arrived in Santa Maria, as they reported what more experienced visitors had just told them about how to deal with a police check:

If you are with a Cuban girl and the police stop you, you basically have two options. If you like the girl and would like her to stay with you, you can insist and follow them to the police station, where after a while they are likely to release her. If you don't care so much about her, then just let the police take her away.

Tourists benefited from a privileged status, and the law targeting *jineterismo* was on their side. From such a position they could activate legal vectors of power to decide whether to help, not help, or even make trouble for the Cubans who were interacting with them. On certain occasions, notably when encounters took an unpleasant turn or tourists were annoyed by Cubans gaining the upper hand in a relationship, they could draw on repressive narratives of control to reassert their privileges. 'They better behave, otherwise we just tell the police that they are bothering us, and they will get into trouble' was the common reasoning, indicating how easy it could be to keep Cubans 'docile' and 'well behaved'.[21]

This brief exploration of tourists' awareness and dispositions towards surveillance and control by the Cuban authorities shows how they could also play a role in facilitating or hampering the establishment of informal encounters. It also highlights possible fault lines between tourists' agendas and those of the Cuban authorities allegedly in charge of protecting them. Many visitors objected to the police profiling of *jineteros/as*, viewing the authorities' efforts to regulate Cubans' informal engagements with them as disproportionate and seldom relevant to tourists' actual interests or their protection from ill-intentioned locals, which officers tended to refer to justify their interventions. The visitors' evaluations of what was desirable for them and for Cubans could therefore easily diverge from the authorities' concerns, and from the rationales ascribed to their policing.[22] Instead, tourists tended to make their minds up about the suitability of encounters with Cuban men and women by other means, particularly by assessing the first moments of their interactions (chapter 4) and the way in which relationships were enacted (Part Two).

Conclusion

In this chapter I have highlighted the challenges that tourists and Cubans had to face in order to gain informal access to each other. They resulted mainly from the control the Cuban authorities exerted over *jineterismo*, and from the institutional arrangements and normative suggestions of the formal tourism industry. Their convergence fostered tourists' segregation from members of the Cuban population who were not officially employed in tourism. Confronted with these controls and normative suggestions, Cubans and tourists mobilized competences and resources to help overcome institutional barriers and thus open up space for informal encounters. Yet not everyone enjoyed the same possibilities of doing so.

Discriminatory profiling could radically inflect the Cuban's opportunities to access tourists. The extent of the challenges they faced could depend on their place of residence, gender, skin colour, attire and economic resources. It was also informed by the ability to establish profitable connections with pivotal gatekeepers in the tourism realm (especially police officers), and by the knowledge of how surveillance operated and could be dealt with. Tourists' challenges were more a matter of choice and predisposition – of the way their journey to Cuba had been scripted, organized and planned, and of their different agendas and expectations. Accordingly, opportunities to engage with locals could be restricted and minimized, or maximized and tailored to foster certain types of encounters (e.g. serendipitous interactions with 'ordinary Cubans') more than others (e.g. transient, deceptive transactions with *jineteros/as*, 'hustlers' and 'prostitutes').

Having considered the key preconditions that shaped Cubans' and tourists' possibilities of informally engaging with each other, we can now move on to examine the first instances of their encounters. As I show in the following chapter, these first moments were likely to acquire great significance for the protagonists involved, foreshadowing both the sort of relationship they would be able to develop and the tensions and ambiguities affecting them.

Chapter 4
GETTING IN TOUCH

The previous chapter discussed the challenges tourists and Cubans had to overcome to even have the possibility of meeting each other, leaving unanswered the question of how to get in touch, how to generate a first connection. The aim of this chapter is to draw attention to the assets and competences people mobilized to this end. Diverging agendas and aspirations threatened to disrupt the positive prospects of informal encounters, leading sceptical tourists to avoid any contact with Cubans for fear of being cheated and used. This grim scenario posited that the relational idioms of *jineterismo* and economic instrumentality would ultimately prevail and were better left unchallenged. To preserve the possibility of other types of encounters and relationships, tourists' and Cubans' intentions instead had to be portrayed and perceived as potentially compatible. The question then concerns how people presented and decoded their respective agendas. Part Two of the book shows a variety of ways people dealt with this issue as they negotiated different types of relationships. However, the question was likely to take centre stage as early as the initial moments of encounter – on the brink of interaction – for this was when tourists and Cubans started decoding each other's intentions.

This chapter will focus on how first connections were established. As I gathered from Cuban and tourist men and women alike, this aspect played a fundamental role in shaping prospective encounters and relationships. It contributed to place these encounters and relationships in a favourable light or, conversely, to cast a shadow of doubt and fear over them. As we shall see, the question of who made the first move in an interaction was key. The answer to this question could determine the success of an encounter and the possibility of developing a relationship further. Given that tourists tended to be rather sceptical of Cubans' approaches, I consider how the latter styled their external appearance to attract the tourists' attention, trying to 'catch their eye' (Crick 1992) and entice them to take that crucial first step in the interaction. However, Cubans could seldom rely on just the possibility of tourists coming to them, so they also deployed a range of techniques known as *entradas* (openings) in their active quest to get tourists' attention. These openings ranged from the most predictable (and least successful) to the more adventurous and improvised.

Entradas could quickly lead to 'feeling-out periods' (Murphy 2001) in which 'tactic talks' (Crick 1992) helped the protagonists involved get a picture of each other and adapt behaviours accordingly. What emerges here are the Cubans' adaptability and 'chameleon-like qualities' (Bowman 1996), as well as the tourists' responsiveness along similarly versatile lines. Linguistic competence, communicative skill and people's willingness and determination to communicate also became crucial. At this time interpersonal communication skills, wit and less tangible 'vibrations' acquired a salient role, highlighting the resourcefulness and 'cumulative knowledge' (Frohlick 2007) Cubans developed in engaging with tourists. This journey through the first steps of informal encounters between foreign tourists and Cubans highlights what it took to get in touch and generate meaningful, fruitful connections across difference and inequality. It paves the way to exploration of the relational idioms that emerged from them, which will be the subject of the second part of the book.

Attracting Tourists' Attention

As the ex-*jinetero* Fernando put it – in remarks echoed by many of my Cuban research participants – *entradas* (openings) were the most difficult part of establishing a relationship with a tourist. Once you had managed to get the tourist's attention and start an interaction on a positive note, interesting and profitable possibilities were likely to open up. For their part, tourists too tended to place great emphasis on these first moments of encounter, which enabled an initial assessment of the intentions of the Cuban person at stake. Independent travellers I met in Havana told me how, when walking the streets of the capital, they relied on a simple but apparently very efficient clue to help them draw a line between potentially interesting and worthwhile interactions on the one hand, and exchanges that were probably based on instrumental agendas and deception on the other: 'It all depends on whether you initiated the contact or they came towards you.' If the latter was the case, several tourists told me, you could be sure that the Cuban in question wanted to get something from you, which was not a good start.

As shown in the previous chapter, police officers also relied on this clue to identify *jinetero*s and *jinetera*s (which I qualified as attitudinal/behavioural profiling). At issue were the directionality of the encounter and its premeditated nature, elements that could indicate people's intentions and agendas. Were tourists dealing with a premeditated approach from a 'professional hustler', a *jinetero/a* with a clear agenda in mind who wanted to profit from them? Or were they facing an 'ordinary Cuban' who did not specialize in the tourism trade and had no intention of cheating them? Resisting the analyst's drive to differentiate those who counted as tourist brokers and mediators (Chambers 1997, 2000; Cheong and Miller 2000; Werner 2003; and Zorn and Farthing 2007, also see Introduction), it seems more interesting here to follow empirically how similar characterizations were played out by the protagonists involved, to show how this matter could become a rather contentious one to settle once and for all.

So important was the question of who made the first step that Cubans styled their outward appearance precisely with the aim of drawing the tourists' gaze and motion towards them. Before using any form of address, people started assessing each other by nonverbal means. Spatio-temporal elements such as the places frequented or the time of the day might help in this task. The previous chapter provided some insight into this, like tourists' association of the degree of 'touristification' of a place with their (inversely proportional) chances of meeting 'ordinary Cubans'. Here, I want to highlight the role that one's external appearance could play in making encounters happen, and in orienting their possible course.

After a rumba music and dance performance at Havana's Gran Palenque (also known as Sábados de la Rumba), I had the chance to meet up again with Juan, who was to become one of my key informants on the world of *jineterismo*. I had made his acquaintance a few days earlier at the Callejón de Hamel, another popular place for rumba sessions in Havana. Both the Callejón and the Gran Palenque were favoured by Afro-Cuban youth and members of the Rasta community seeking to get in touch with tourists (see also Daniel 1996; Argyriadis 2005). Juan used to hang around with other Rasta at these events, and he himself wore dreadlocks. Throughout that afternoon and evening, we extensively discussed his (and his friends') encounters with foreigners, as well as their aspirations and ways of dealing with tourists. When talking about Dennis – one of his Rasta friends and mentors, a neighbour who had first introduced him to the tourism world – our conversation touched on the issue of people's outward appearance as a way of getting tourists' attention.

Indeed, Dennis wore his dreadlocks in a quite curiously unusual manner. According to Juan, and I also became a witness to this, his eccentric hairstyle tended to captivate passers-by; tourists would often stop to stare at him. Once he got the tourists' attention, Dennis would normally put up a peaceful smile. He was happy to let them take pictures, which gave him the chance to strike up a conversation and get to know the visitors. Agreeing that

Dennis' style could be very helpful in 'catching' tourists, Juan clarified that he himself wore dreadlocks precisely because that seemed to work well with tourists and please the foreign women he targeted. Female tourists seemed to like the Rasta appearance, he told me, and felt comfortable with it. However, Juan clarified that once he had achieved his ultimate goal – to move out of Cuba with the help of a tourist lover – he would not hesitate to cut his hair and give himself a 'more decent' appearance. What emerged from our conversation was thus a highly instrumental view of the Rasta style, and more particularly of dreadlocks, as being essentially a way of tapping into the tourists' attention and fascination.

I do not want to imply here that all other members of the Rasta community shared Juan's opinion on the matter – repeated conversations with people in this circle gave me reason to suggest otherwise, as some argued strongly for attaching a much more profound meaning to their dreadlocks.[1] Juan, however, generally saw an instrumental purpose in people's adoption of this outward appearance, and that purpose was to attract tourists' (particularly women tourists') attention. The more striking the dreadlocks, as in Dennis' case, the more chances one had to excite the foreigners' curiosity. But as Juan also made clear, getting their attention and establishing a first connection did not guarantee the development of a fruitful relationship. What next became crucial was to mobilize other skills and qualities, like 'knowing how to talk' (*saber hablar*). According to Juan, Dennis, though very eye-catching, did not excel at making something good out of it and wasted a lot of opportunities. Four years after my first encounter with them, Dennis was himself led to recognize such shortcomings when comparing his own story with Juan's successful marriage and migration to Argentina. 'He was more intelligent than us' (Dennis was with another Rasta friend at the time), he remarked dejectedly as he contrasted Juan's achievement with his own failures. Dennis had been married to three different foreign women, had let all these promising relations fall through, and remained stuck in Cuba, moving in and out of jail, his dreadlocks cut as a result of his latest spell behind bars. With a glimmer of hope, though, Dennis still thought he might have one last chance to find a tourist partner and make up for his earlier missteps.

Other scholars working on tourism in Cuba have shown how Cuban people styled their looks not only to catch the tourists' attention, but also to hint at the specific nature of a prospective encounter, banking for instance on the visitor's sexual fantasies and desires (Sánchez Taylor 2000). To support her notion of 'embodied hustling', Sánchez Taylor (2000: 49) presents the example of a young black Cuban man who, on a beach in Varadero, played on tourist women's racist stereotype of the 'big black dick' to capture their attention: 'His hard sell would start from the moment he lay down beside tourist women on the beach, in his brief trunks, giving them a full centrefold pose. This pose exposed his unique selling-point which played on and "confirmed" the myth of Black male sexuality, and tapped into these women's "racialized" sexual fantasies'.

Other authors highlight Cuban women's efforts to tailor their looks to foreigners' tastes. Fusco (1997: 56) quotes two experienced *jineteras* fashioning their hairstyles to match the desires of potential tourist partners:

> 'The natural aspect has come back (*el aspecto natural ha vuelto*)', explains Margarita, 'even white girls are having a perm so that they look like mulatas'. Both admit that hairstyles are being adapted to the tastes of the clients. 'The Spanish like black girls with plaits so that now all black girls (*negritas*) have their hair in that way. The Italians they like mulatas with messy hair (*con el pelo desordenado*).

Here, typologies of tourists (in this case according to their nationality) are drawn to map out potential differences in interest and desires.[2] Fusco goes on to contrast the outward appearance of her two informants with the frequent image ascribed to *jineteras* abroad, which according to her is one of 'vulgar and uncultured chicks with platinum blonde hair and tight trousers' (Fusco 1997: 56). The latter evocation of stereotypical views of sex workers is at odds with the promise of more casual, spontaneous, non-commoditized sexual relationships with Cubans that kept luring tourists (see chapter 8) who more often favoured the kind of 'natural aspect' referred to above. This also resonates with the previous chapter's remarks about the police profiling of *jineteros/as* and the dilemma that people like Raquel faced in trying to diminish their visibility vis-à-vis the authorities on the one hand, and enhancing it to grab tourists' attention on the other. In this sense, playing on the 'natural aspect' could be a successful way to appeal to certain tourists while also keeping a low profile to avoid the police, thus responding to the stereotypical profiling of prostitutes practised by both.

Multiple examples of reflexive self-stylizations meant to captivate tourists could be mentioned here, but the overall thrust is the guiding principle of such endeavours: to awaken interest in tourists and leading them to take notice of the Cuban in question. Catching a tourist's eye could make capitalizing on this initial interest by breaking the ice and striking up a conversation much easier. This is when *saber hablar* ('knowing how to talk'), as Juan put it, could take over as the key competence to master. Moving beyond Sánchez Taylor's (2000: 49) somewhat reductive remarks on the body as a 'unique selling-point', we are led to consider other skills in Cubans' initial engagements with tourists. After all, sexual fantasies were not all that mattered in the encounters I investigated: other promises were at stake, other relational idioms in which qualities besides people's bodies were also valued.

Addressing Tourists

In his seminal article on Sri Lankan street guides, Crick remarks that 'tourists wary of being cheated in a foreign country may react gratefully to "Hello friend", a common conversational opening by the street guides' (1992: 139). In Cuba too, '*Hola amigo*' was a common way to address tourists in the streets.[3] However, visitors tended to quickly become suspicious of this rather stereotypical opening. As I reflect on more extensively in chapter 6, immediate expressions of friendliness could also raise doubts about the motives of this diffuse cordiality, as in the Turkish village of Göreme, where Tucker (2001: 880) carried out her research: tourists there were often 'suspicious of the perceived over-friendliness of salesmen and waiters'.[4] Particularly in the touristic areas of Havana, visitors easily tired of such 'over-friendly' approaches. In this context, the question of how best to address visitors called for inventiveness and subtlety. Here I will consider some of these approaches, from the most common and least successful to the more daring and original.

One way of opening an interaction with tourists was to offer them something straightaway. As I show in chapter 5, this was how informal cigar dealers tended to operate, making explicit reference to advantageous economic transactions. The instrumental character of the interactions was made obvious from the start. While these offers could appeal to people who had just set foot on the island and were looking for souvenirs in Old Havana's main tourism circuit, they were less likely to have an impact on visitors who had been around longer. As several of my Cuban informants put it, everybody in Cuba could sell cigars: it was not a very original offer and was unlikely to capture the attention of any tourist who had already spent a few hours in the streets of the capital.

Furthermore, most Cubans I got to know hoped to develop relationships with tourists that went beyond transient economic transactions. The relational idioms of friendship, seduction and romance, for example, were potentially at odds with explicit expressions of instrumental interest and immediate economic transactions (see Part Two). To preserve these relational promises and move beyond the horizon of inevitable instrumentality, other openings had to be devised. In this respect, a classic *entrada* consisted in asking tourists where they came from[5] – something of a 'pattern', according to Sudgen and Tomlinson's (1995: 164) remarks on 'hustling in Havana', dating back to 1995:

> '*Ola, senor* [sic], my friend … where are you from?'
> Not deterred by the silence, the 'find the place game' begins:
> '*Aleman* (German)? *Italiano*? *Canadese*? …'

A novice mistake is to tell him one's nationality, and get hooked:
'Ah, you are English! How long do you come to Cuba, it is beautiful, no?'... and so on and so forth.

It is an easy skill through which to get rid of *jiniteras* [sic] like Roberto and Toni – look them in the eyes, smile broadly and say kindly but firmly '*Gracias, no*' two or three times, simultaneously raising your hand palm out. This usually works, but you have to know the skill. Otherwise, you will be stuck with them for as long as you are in public and on your journey may be cajoled into making a deal to buy cigars from them, being lined up with a '*chica Cubana*' (Cuban woman), buying them beer, giving them a couple of dollars to go away, or at least giving them cigarettes.

During my time in Cuba, questions about tourists' nationality continued to be a very widespread way for Cuban people to try and initiate an interaction. Indeed, such openings were so common that they occasionally became the butt of jokes among tourists and Cubans alike as people mimicked the typical tourist-catching scene. Similarly, the *Lonely Planet* guidebook remarks, in its 'Hints on *jineterismo*' (see chapter 4): '"Where you from" is the most common opener and you'll hear it everywhere. Develop some conversation-stopping rejoinders like: Iceland, Iraq, the CIA or Marianao (a tough, respected Havana neighbourhood)' (Gorry 2004: 359).

But why was this opening so popular and diffuse? I suggest first of all that information about tourists' nationality could help Cubans tailor responses accordingly, for instance by adopting the visitors' language. Besides, such a seemingly inconsequential form of address could capture the tourists' attention with something they obviously understood: this question about a simple matter called for an answer or at least a reaction. Whether asking an acceptable question, legitimately expressing curiosity, or straightforwardly attributing tourists a nationality, this form of address did in fact tend to elicit a reaction from visitors, be it only a glance or a provocative response – *soy Cubano* (I am Cuban) was a favourite. After this first approach, a conversation could develop.

Similar forms of address took a more humorous and provocative tone, relying on stereotypes attached to tourists' geographical provenance. Thus, for example, the informal guide Rodrigo caught the attention of Mexican tourists with some typically Mexican insults: '*¡No mames cabron!*' (No bullshit bastard!), '*¡Hijo de la chingada!*' (Son of a bitch!). Rodrigo would also mimic their peculiar accent, giving his approach a light-hearted feel. He similarly surprised Spanish tourists by referring to their 'big belly' full of *jamón de pata negra* (Spanish dry cured ham), or provoked Italian tourists with ironic mentions of the Mafia. Thus, playfully employing national features and stereotypes could position the exchange on a jesting level and cast a positive, easy-going light on it. People like Rodrigo were also appealing to the complicity of visitors, who sometimes reacted with increased irony and cutting witty remarks.[6] The tone of the exchanges was playful and carefree, and the stereotypes generally hurt no one. What they did do was draw together people who, by sharing jokes and stereotypes, were also partaking of a common discourse (Rapport and Overing 2000: 347) tinged with humour and entertainment.[7]

Still, queries and remarks about someone's nationality could get rather tedious and predictable, once visitors had become too familiar with them. To counter the impression of a well-rehearsed approach, Cubans experimented with other types of openings that could give encounters a fortuitous tone. Striking parallels appear once again with Dahles' (1998) remarks on the techniques used by street guides in Yogyakarta (Indonesia), suggesting that in different parts of the world, similar solutions are devised to engage informally with tourists. Thus, Dahles (1998: 35) observes that 'from the tourist's perspective, they [street guides] seem to bump into a visitor purely by coincidence, actually being on their way to some important appointment'. According to her, 'this impression is carefully staged' (35). The same could be said of many 'fortuitous' encounters in Cuba. Jorge, whose turf of activity was in Old Havana, explained his technique for producing the effect of a 'chance meeting': he would start walking in the same direction a targeted tourist (or group of tourists) was going, as if on his way somewhere. When passing his target, he would find a pretext to say a few words and strike up a conversation.

As a frequent object of such *entradas* myself, I became more and more familiar with people's techniques and on some occasions ended up ranking their degree of inventiveness for fun. Among the most frequent, supposedly casual openings were requests for the time or a light for a smoke, which could easily provoke suspicion in more experienced tourists. Viewed as simple pretexts to get in touch, such openings often gave the impression of a premeditated encounter, hinting at the possible instrumental intentions of the Cuban concerned. On one occasion, while walking in Calle Obispo in Havana's core tourism area, a Cuban boy passing by asked my Swiss friend Bastien and me if we had a light for his cigarette. Sensing a hint of annoyance, he immediately added that this was not a *motivo* – a pretext or excuse. In response to our puzzled look, he told us that many Cubans were just asking for the time or a light as a way to get in touch with tourists. The point he wanted to make was that he was not a *jinetero*; he really just wanted a light. After this awkward exchange an officer approached, and the boy vanished.

Other authors have also reported on the prevalence of these opening techniques (see Wonders and Michalowski 2001). As they have become increasingly common and widespread, the impression of serendipity is at risk

94

of fading away, together with the promise of a genuine personal encounter with 'ordinary Cubans'.[8] To keep this promise alive, people had to devise other, more creative and original approaches that preserved a sense of something special – an encounter like no other. In general, I noticed that the more original and unusual the way of addressing tourists, the likelier the given Cuban was to capture their attention. People's ability to decode tourists' behaviour, detecting their potential interests and focus, could help tailor and personalize approaches. Fernando explained this to me upon delighting me with an instructive tour of Havana enlivened by concrete examples of the tactics used by him or any skilled *jinetero*, in his view. Passing by a tourist couple who were busy taking pictures on the Malecón, for instance, Fernando told me how he could have 'entered' them: as if on his way somewhere, he would have casually stopped by and shown some interest in the perspective the tourists had chosen for their picture, dropping a remark on the practice of photography and his fondness for this art, and eventually adding a couple of tips and suggestions. This was likely to capture the tourists' attention and make them feel they were being attended in their own specificity, which would have enabled him to move forward with a conversation. Similarly, tourists who were consulting a guidebook could be suitably approached by asking whether they needed directions or help, and so on.

More generally, Fernando's various examples clearly showed that understanding one's focus of attention and devising openings that fitted creatively into that focus was a smart, successful way of getting in touch with tourists. Again, it seemed very important to avoid any hint of premeditation or suggestion of being a full-time *jinetero*. His *entradas* were precisely designed *not* to give the impression of the well-scripted, predictable *jinetero*-type approach – exemplifying *jineterismo*'s intrinsic drive to innovate and surpass itself – and were intended to be seen as genuine expressions of interest in which he treated all tourists as particular individuals with specific personalities, interests and agendas.[9] Besides his ability to creatively grab tourists' attention, Fernando was very skilled at nourishing their interests and thus giving continuity to the encounter. 'Those [*jineteros*] who don't know' (*los que no saben*, i.e. who don't know how to 'open' properly), he told me, would, having caught the tourists' attention, let them slip away, unable to give new impetus to the encounter. Thus people's competences in kick-starting relationships come into view. The ability to sense tourists' degree of openness, interests and inclinations was once again fundamental, as was the capacity to cater to their potential desires and eventually awaken new ones.

Feeling Out Periods, Tactic Talks and Adaptability

Once a first connection was established, it was essential for Cuban people to understand what sort of tourists they were dealing with. This was often done via the kind of 'tactic talks'[10] Crick (1992: 138–139) describes in relation to street guides in Sri Lanka:

> One might acknowledge the guides' insightful, if essentially pragmatic, under-standing of human nature, their ability to read a social situation, and their skills in turning it to their advantage. Guides have a set of general conceptions about tourist motivation, national stereotypes and tourist types, which they employ in their encounters. As a guide explained, one has to 'catch the eye' and engage in 'tactic talks'.

Building on Crick's work, Dahles (1998: 35) similarly considers how street guides in Yogyakarta try to grasp tourists' needs in the first moment of interaction:

> To understand the tourists' needs, the street guides have to study their back-ground. Tourists find themselves being interviewed by these guides ... Where are you from? Where do you stay? Are you married? Do you have a boy/girlfriend? Do you have children? What's your profession? How much do you earn? This interviewing renders information that enables the guide to classify the tourist. Is he rich? Will she spend a lot of money on souvenirs? What kind of souvenirs? Is she travelling alone? Is she available as a sexual partner?

In the first moments of an informal encounter with tourists, Cuban men and women likewise tried to gather relevant information about them. How this was done reflected further differences in skills and expertise, as too many too straightforward questions could make visitors suspicious. Indeed, one should recall that tourists also valued these initial moments of interaction in making up their minds and typifying their Cuban interlocutor. Was she or he a hus-tler? What was his or her agenda? Clearly, tourists were not passive targets of Cubans' questionings but also tried hard to grasp the latter's intentions.

The wider the range of assets and competences Cubans could mobilize in dealing with tourists, the better chances they had of establishing and lending continuity to relationships with them. This moves us well beyond Sánchez Taylor's remarks on the black Cuban man's body as his 'unique selling-point', an assessment that ultimately reduces relationships with tourists to com-moditized sex alone. Embodied resources could certainly play an important role – which could be even more the case for those Cuban women whose realm of activity was mostly confined to intimate relationships with foreign tourists (see chapter 2) – but the relevance of other competences deserves to be highlighted, given also that many of my Cuban interlocutors insisted on their importance. In chapters 7 and 8, I show for instance that beyond bodies and their uses, expertise in the relational idioms of seduction and romance, and in navigating the complex interface between sex and a variety of transactional orders, could also be a fundamental asset in Cuban women's interactions with tourist men. The Cuban men I encountered, whose realms of activity tended to be more diversified, attributed an even more important role to knowing how to cater to the widest possible spectrum of tourists' interests and desires – hence their interest in cultivating a broad range of skills and abilities.[11]

In this scenario, adaptability became a considerable asset. It was precisely the importance of such 'chameleon-like qualities' (Bowman 1996: 90)[12] that Jorge made clear to me in the course of a long conversation we had one afternoon in Old Havana. Describing his informal tourism-related activities, Jorge told me that he could quickly assess what kind of person (i.e. tourist) he was dealing with, and that this informed the way he would present himself: 'If he [the tourist] is cultured, I [Jorge] am cultured. If he is delinquent, I am delinquent.' While enacting all these different characters, what mattered to Jorge was 'to do things well, to be a professional, to have ethics (*tener ética*)'. When I asked him to elaborate on having ethics – after all, he was also talking about drug dealing and pimping – he explained that this was about 'doing things well' (*hacer bien las cosas*), being serious and professional in whatever he was engaging in.

I have considered above how Cuban men and women fashioned their outward appearance to catch tourists' eye and suit their tastes, and how they adapted their verbal openings to give their approach an unpredictable, non-calculated edge. Following similar lines of reasoning, one could also (re)invent one's persona to pique visitors' interest and hold it. As Jorge suggested, the same person could become a 'university student' for certain tourists (or in his case, given his age, a 'university professor'), a 'salsa teacher' for others, and a 'cigar manufacturer' for others still. One's birthday celebration was another element Cubans typically played on to attract tourists' attention. Accordingly, I gathered plenty of stories of visitors who had met such and such a Cuban in Havana who was out celebrating his/her birthday and had invited them to come along to have some drinks and party with other friends. The uniqueness of this event was paralleled by references to unique festivals taking place only on the day, events that no tourist would want to miss. These were remarkable ways of creating special occasions, unique happenings that tourists ought to feel privileged to attend – at least until, having spent a few days in Havana, they started to notice the suspicious ubiquity of birthdays and invitations.

These examples highlight Cubans' adaptability and self-styling to captivate tourists. Meanwhile, visitors too could playfully enact different personae to give a suitable twist to their encounters. These performances also exemplify the potential tourism offers for re-creation (Graburn 1983) and self-creation.[13] To give just a few examples here, a tourist could pretend to be an expert on Cuba who had spent a lot of time on the island, in a move to show that he or she was no novice and could not easily be deceived. Some went as far as saying they were Cubans themselves, albeit such claims were generally ironic in tone and quickly unmasked. They might also pass themselves off as rich businessmen – or as poor students with no extra money to spend, enacting 'rituals of inversion' (Graburn 1983). Furthermore, they could say they were married, claim a different sexual orientation to avoid Cubans' sexual advances (see chapter 8), or become single bachelors who, without families back home to account for, thus were up for sexual experimentation.

Language Competences, Communicative Abilities and 'Vibrations'

In her pioneering article 'Eskimo Tourism: Micro-models, and Marginal Men', Valene Smith (1978 [1977]: 69) regarded bilingualism as an essential feature of tourism cultural brokers. Knowledge of foreign languages was also very important for my Cuban research participants, but the extent of it varied a great deal and was often limited to a few expressions that could serve to initiate an interaction. Most of them knew snatches of several languages rather than having extensive knowledge of one in particular. This knowledge, often the fruit of very practice-based learning processes, could depend for instance on one's personal experiences and engagements with foreign tourists. For many, spending extensive time with a non-Spanish-speaking (boy-/girl-)friend was an ideal way to learn languages. Well aware of the benefits obtainable with such knowledge, some of my research participants actively studied languages at schools or in a more autonomous fashion using (text) books, educational CDs and TV programmes.

Knowledge of foreign languages was also a source of pride and prestige. Those who knew more could be called upon to help others deal with a non-Spanish-speaking foreigner. Thus, the most fluent interpreters had increased chances to act as mediators and were able to claim stakes in other people's relationships with tourists. Such disparities and the privileges they granted seemed also to unfold along gendered lines, with Cuban men often assuming the role of translator between a Cuban woman and foreign tourists. Again, men's involvement in a more varied range of informal tourism-related activities may explain their comparatively many opportunities to develop such linguistic competence.[14]

This also raises the question of the foreign language one was dealing with. In the case of Italian, for instance – the language that predominated among male tourists in Santa Maria – its closeness to Spanish tended to facilitate communication and often resulted in ad hoc pidgins that mixed elements of several languages. Omar, a Cuban in his mid twenties with whom I spent a few days in Havana, joked for example that although he could not really speak English, he still managed to communicate in 'Spanglish'. His point, more generally, was that if one really wished to communicate with tourists who were equally willing to make the effort, a way would be found to engage in some sort of meaningful exchange.

As for the visitors, Spanish-speaking tourists certainly found it easier to develop a wide range of meaningful interactions with Cubans than did tourists who knew little of this language. They quickly got used to the peculiarities of the Spanish spoken in Cuba and even took pleasure in trying out some typical expressions. Many tourists who did not speak Spanish fluently had at least some knowledge of it and made efforts to practise it. Engaging with Cubans could in itself be recognized as a good occasion to improve one's skills. Such a prospect had even motivated some foreigners' choice to travel to Cuba in the first place.

People who knew very little Spanish generally found it much harder to engage with Cubans. Some tourists I met even dismissed altogether the possibility of establishing any meaningful relationship with locals. But even among those who knew almost no Spanish at all, the prevailing tendency was to try to overcome communicational barriers, and people often found ways of doing so. Again, new kinds of pidgin could emerge as tourists inflected their mother tongues with the bit of Spanish they knew, often with a measure of delight, in a phenomenon that, as Jack and Phipps (2005) point out, itself merits more attention. I was struck, for instance, to hear some Italian 'old timers' in Santa Maria using Cuban words and expressions even in discussion with fellow Italian tourists. More generally, Spanish speakers aside, it seemed that in most cases French-, Portuguese- and Italian-speaking visitors found it easier to communicate.

Nonverbal communication was also very helpful in drawing people together and developing meaningful interactions between them. Once again, beyond knowing the language, what seemed crucial was peoples' willingness and determination to interact. This clearly emerged in a short interview that my colleague Bastien and I filmed one evening with two young Japanese tourists on the Malecón. After Hiroshi and Kenzo told us about the intense encounters they had had in the previous days in Havana, enjoying drinking and partying with Cubans, we asked how they had managed to communicate. Their hesitant reply, which followed some embarrassed chuckles, emphasized precisely the importance of the nonverbal aspects of communication: 'Very small Spanish. Just, veeery small, and, body language [laughter]'. Had they learned any Spanish before? No, said Hiroshi, adding that they had known some words, but not much. The Cubans they had met could not speak English, he finally said, 'but it's ok. We can communicate'.

This last example points to those aspects of interpersonal communication – those 'communicative abilities' (Dahles 1998: 34) – that go beyond linguistic knowledge, and whose importance has also been recognized in other destinations.[15] Such abilities informed Cubans' capacity to capture tourists' attention and maintain the flow and intensity of the interaction. What mattered here was one's skill in bringing up possible topics of interest, finding ways of communicating that could please and charm tourists, listening empathetically and showing understanding for people's concerns, remaining sensitive to their specific needs and desires, and offering solutions and alluring prospects for the way ahead.

Beyond knowledge of foreign languages, these qualities and sensitivities are more akin to the 'personality traits' of Valene Smith's (1978 [1977]: 69) 'marginal men': 'charisma, charm, wit, gregariousness'.[16] This is how I interpreted Juan's expression *saber hablar*, 'knowing how to talk': it was not just about how to speak languages but about how to communicate with tourists, how to awaken their interest and fascination by bringing about positive feelings and emotions, suggesting enticing possibilities and thus projecting relationships forward. These qualities could be difficult to rationalize. As Juan put it (see also chapter 3), they had to do with one's ability to 'vibrate' (*vibrar*), to 'have a good vibration' that would lead tourists to enjoy your company and follow you.

For my friend Ernesto, an Afro-Cuban man in his mid twenties with whom I spent many days and nights hanging around in tourism spots in Havana, and who was also fond of the 'vibration' metaphor, what mattered most for success in this realm of activity was 'to be a mind' (*ser una mente*): to be smart and perceptive, to know about people, relationships, sentiments – 'working the truth' (*trabajar la verdad*) of these things. This was not something one could learn at school but rather the result of life experience. As Ernesto put it, the struggle (*lucha*) to get tourists in Havana's ruthless streets, pictured as a competitive world full of wickedness (*maldad*) where one could not even trust his own shadow, was a battle in which the sharpest mind would prevail, and the experience and knowledge gained *en la calle* was paramount, as it was 'street against street' (*calle contra calle*, i.e. the street's experience of one person against that of another).

'*Está en talla*' (he has stature/wit) was the kind of compliment Ernesto got from older Rasta in the trade as they discussed tourism and relationships with tourists, helping one another solve their current predicaments with foreign partners. This wit and depth of thought, which Ernesto had allegedly cultivated through the hardships of his own life, earned him respect among his more experienced peers. The problem, according to Ernesto, and the source of many of his colleagues' mistakes in dealing with tourists, was that they considered themselves superior, that they were vain (*vanos*) and looked down on tourists as if they were *bobos* (stupid, naïve). This major error in judgement, he maintained, went on to colour Cubans' ways of relating with visitors, grounding them in typifications and objectifications that the latter were bound to sense and resent. Instead, Ernesto advocated remaining open and respecting the fully fledged humanity and individuality of every tourist (see chapter 6).

The kind of intellectual dispositions, emotional attunements, and moral sensibilities addressed in these last paragraphs were, as Ernesto suggested, intimately tied to one's life experience and not necessarily easily cultivated. On some occasions, however, I noticed that a more active and reflexive pre-occupation with such matters could also be present, an explicit concern for improving one's ways of being and relating with tourists. One afternoon on the Malecón as Pedro, a Rasta in his late twenties, and I chatted about tourism, tourists and his ways of dealing with them, two of his friends stopped by. They were sweating and panting in the late afternoon sun, on their way back from the jogging they did routinely to keep their bodies fit and attractive. Confronted with this display of muscles and physical strength, I provocatively asked Pedro, 'What about you?' wondering if he also cared to enhance his appearance that way. With a knowing smile, Pedro pointed silently at his temple and then mimicked the act of talking. He went on to explain that his thing, in that very moment, had been to exercise his brain, his articulation and his relational competences by talking with me and learning new things that could prove useful in his future dealings with tourists, enriching his cosmopolitan competences. The two joggers were training their bodies; he was training his mind, speech and responsiveness to foreigners.

'I want to know if what they [tourists] are telling me is true or not', Dennis once told me, determined not to come off as a fool in conversations with foreigners. Dennis asked me specific questions about life abroad, things he wanted to know so as to be able to engage with tourists from a similar standpoint and level of knowledge. His aspiration here was to position the exchange on shared cultural competences and wisdom and be recognized as a competent citizen of the world – despite having never left Cuba – in the same way tourists were deemed to be. As I will discuss more extensively when dealing with expressions of friendship (chapter 6, see also Simoni 2014b), such aspirations and 'claims of membership' (Ferguson 2006) were a very important dimension of Cubans' engagements with tourists, and one that deserves all our attention since it carries key implications for the analysis of issues of belonging, morality and subjectivity in these Self-Other relations across striking differences and inequalities.

Ernesto, Pedro and Dennis were not the only ones to explicitly recognize the importance of communicative, argumentative and emotional sensitivities in relations with tourists. During fieldwork I was repeatedly confronted with stated efforts to improve competences and skills in these regards. Grasping multiple points of views, understanding different approaches to tourism and tourists, attending to the subtleties and sensibilities of relating to people who differed in terms of their origins, age, gender, socio-economic status, interests and more – in this sense *jineterismo*, as some of my interlocutors put it, could be seen as *un arte*: an art of communicating and dealing with people, of sparking interest and developing relationships. Theirs was arguably a portrait of *jineterismo* in its most anthropological and cosmopolitan mode: a positive body of knowledge about humans and human relationships.[17]

Conclusion

The aim of this chapter was to highlight certain key resources, competences and sensitivities that enabled Cubans and tourists to get in touch and bring about an encounter. The starting point was to acknowledge tourists' widespread scepticism towards predictable ways of addressing them, which were likely to cast the shadow of hustling over any potential interaction. The importance of 'who made the first step' explains Cubans' efforts to entice tourists with their outward appearance, styling themselves to catch the eye and appeal to the visitors' potential desires and expectations. The issue of how this first step was made then led to the examination of a range of more or less successful opening techniques, from the most predictable to the more creative. Once an initial exchange was made, feeling out periods and tactic talks helped tourists and Cubans alike to more closely assess each other's interests and agendas. Here the Cubans' ability to draw on a variety of skills, competences and personae to suit and captivate tourists was highlighted, as were tourists' playful responses along similarly imaginative lines of self-(re)-creation.

Linguistic ability, communicative skill and other qualities, such as having wit, a good 'vibration' and sensitivity, also facilitated the development of touristic encounters, improving the chances of moving beyond transient moments of interaction. In this respect, and beyond being able to speak the same language, people's willingness and determination to communicate and engage with each other seemed paramount. Several of the examples presented spotlighted Cubans' ability to understand tourists – as opposed to dealing with them as interchangeable strangers and objectified types – and view them as fully fledged persons whose potential inclinations and interests had to be respected and nourished. People's immersion in the world of tourism prompted a heightened awareness of one's responsiveness and attunement to tourists, their potential desires and the possible ways of moving relationships forward, and led some of my Cuban interlocutors to point out the 'artful' qualities of their engagements with visitors.

Part Two of the book probes further into these skills and abilities, delving deeper into the competences that both tourists and Cubans deployed while negotiating various types of relationships. We thus enter a kind of real-life laboratory of human relationships, in which the relational idioms of economic transactions, hospitality, friendship, festivity, seduction and sexuality were evoked, enacted, put to test and eventually reformulated.

Part Two

SHAPING RELATIONS

Chapter 5
MARKET EXCHANGE AND HOSPITALITY

This second part of the book is a journey into the various types of relation-ships that emerged from informal encounters between tourists and Cuban people. After the initial moments of interaction considered in chapter 4, how were relationships developed, enacted and negotiated? What sort of relational idioms were brought into play to inform and frame these interac-tions? To start addressing these questions, here I examine the case of cigar deals. The aim is to show how these deals generated various forms of eco-nomic transactions while potentially redefining what counted as 'economic' itself (Çalişkan and Callon 2009, 2010). The chapter highlights the key role of material entities (money, tobacco, legal inscriptions, rural landscapes, etc.) in informing people's characterization of relationships. In this case, what emerges is the relationships' ability to shift between 'market exchanges' and forms of 'hospitality', depending on how the various entities involved in the enactment of a certain reality were framed and qualified. By the same token, this analysis enables us to move beyond a simplistic image of touristic relations as relations between producers and consumers engaged in buying and selling commodities (see Jack and Phipps' [2005] insightful critique). Building on the work of Mauss (1969 [1925]), Thomas (1991) and Callon (2007) in economic anthropology, I show how such a reductive approach risks obscuring the actual diversity of transaction that may take shape in the realm of tourism.

The importance of recognizing such diversity becomes obvious once we start taking seriously and paying due attention to people's struggles to perform and stabilize boundaries that differentiate contrasting realities, on which a range of experiences and livelihoods also depended. In this chapter I call attention to these 'performance struggles' (Callon 2007), following cigar deals from the streets of Havana to the tobacco farms of Viñales. Instead of approaching cigar deals a priori as yet another example of com-moditization and market exchange in the tourism economy, I consider the situated emergence of various forms of transaction from the perspective of the protagonists involved, drawing attention to the different qualities of the relationships that ensued. I chose the example of cigar deals because they were ubiquitous in touristic Cuba and were often used to exemplify the transient, commoditized, deceptive character of touristic encounters. As such, they were generally seen as an emblematic turf of tourism hustling and *jineterismo*. However, a closer look at how these deals unfolded in practice helps relocate such characterizations, showing how tourists and Cubans themselves often strove to overcome these widespread narratives in order to achieve alternative realities.

Cigar deals are taken as the example here, but other types of informal exchanges between tourists and Cubans may reveal a similar oscillation and blurring between different forms of transactions and relational idioms. In his analysis of processes of commoditization, Appadurai (1986) has shown how these can affect a wide range of entities, something that tourism scholars from Greenwood (1978 [1977]) to Cohen (1988) to Bunten (2008) have been particularly apt to point out. The case of the cigar deals examined here also sheds light on processes of commoditization by attending to the ways in which things tend to become commodities, economic transactions market exchanges, and Cubans and tourists buyers and sellers. But it also shows how in certain situations a convergence of discourses, practices and materialities transformed cigar deals into something else altogether. In the course of tobacco farm visits in Viñales, for instance, tourists and Cubans alike resisted contentious processes of commoditization and marketization, and struggled to bring about other forms of transaction and relational idioms, including forms of reciprocity and hospitality. By moving beyond taken-for-granted assumptions on market exchange in tourism, this chapter takes a first important step to uncover the generative potential of the relationships that emerge from touristic encounters – in this case, their potential to redefine the nature and meaning of (economic) transactions.

Street Deals: Shaping (In)Formality, Stabilizing Market Exchanges

'Pssst, pssst... *tabaco*, Cuban cigar, Havana cigar'; 'Cohiba, Montecristo, Romeo y Julieta';[1] 'Good price'; 'Original, from the factory': walking the streets of Old Havana's main tourism circuit, tourists were regularly confronted with appeals to buy Cuban cigars.[2] The people proposing such deals often stood on street corners or at the entrances of private houses in which the transactions could then take place, should the tourists be willing to follow them. The cigar dealers were more concentrated in the proximity of cigar factories and shops, and (supposed) employees of these establishments occasionally made their own offers. It was generally men, and more seldom women, who cautiously addressed tourists in the ways listed above. Dealers advertised *Habanos*, Cuban or Havana cigars with famous brand names, emphasizing bargain prices and the good quality of products 'coming straight' from state-run factories. The cautious tone of these propositions, together with references to brands, prices and cigar factories, underlined the crucial tensions pervading these street deals due to their potentially risky nature, and the quality-price ratio of the products on offer.

Among the commonalities emerging across different situations was indeed the dealers' emphasis on the good value of their products, compared with prices in state-run shops (often referred as *tiendas del estado*). A box of Cohiba or Montecristo was offered at prices ranging from 30 to 100 CUC instead of the 180 to 300 (sometimes up to 500) CUC charged – as dealers stressed – 'for the same product' in the *tiendas del estado*. In offering their bargains, they could urge tourists 'not to trust' the official shops, implying that items there were overpriced and tourists were being cheated. By contrast, their 'correct' prices were allegedly based on the 'real' and 'objective' value of cigars, free of any discriminating surcharges targeting tourists. This inducement to distrust state-run shops integrated a widespread narrative that portrayed the Cuban government as abusing its monopolistic control of the economy, inflating prices and trying to squeeze as much as possible from tourists. This narrative could strike the right note and generate complicity with tourists, prompting alliances in which dealers helped visitors avoid being 'cheated' by the state.

The vocabulary dealers employed to emphasize the fairness of their prices could also be diversified to captivate tourists with offers of cigars at 'family prices', for instance. Standing by the entrance of one of Havana's tobacco factories, others offered cigars at 'workers' prices', thereby suggesting a direct link between the manufacturers' work and the value of the goods, once again free of the alleged price-inflating bureaucratic detours of official distribution channels. Always evoking fairness in prices, a dealer once advertised his 'socialist prices' to me, thus mobilizing the ideal of a 'socialist exchange' without hierarchies, one including both Cubans and tourists allied in an uncanny class struggle against the machinations of a bureaucratic elite.

While emphasizing good prices and contrasting them to the 'inflated' ones in official shops, street dealers strove also to reframe and reconnect their free-floating cigars with the world of cigar factories, state-supervised production and official branding, a seemingly paradoxical move from informality to formality that was geared at disentangling their products from the realm of illegality and fakes. Arguing that their cigars came straight from the factory, dealers highlighted how they (or at least a close friend or relative) worked there and therefore were legitimate experts/professionals in the field.

FIGURE 5.1 • *Partagás Cigar Factory, Havana*

The enactment of connections to the official world of cigars could also be afforded by the location of the deal, as in the case of offers made right next to factories and official selling points (see Figure 5.1), suggesting that dealers had some relation to them. Some worked as uniformed, badge-wearing door keepers of these establishments and could capitalize on their privileged position and attire to catch the attention of tourists coming in and out, offering them a better deal.

Addressing tourists before they entered the shop or the factory, dealers could suggest having a first look inside, checking out prices and then joining them to buy at a better price. 'Want to see or want to buy?' asked a man as Bastien and I were filming outside a factory. Whereas the shop was the place to see and get an idea of prices (see Figure 5.2), purchases, he assured us, were best made at the 'market of the factory workers' (*el mercado de los trabajadores*), where buying was more advantageous and 'totally legal'. The issue of legality and compliance with customs requirements was central to the later stages of many informal deals. Receipts could be given to tourists, and logos, stamps, and other legal inscriptions carefully applied to cigar boxes to reassure buyers they would be able to export the cigars without problems. Sometimes, these officialization procedures were explicitly negotiated, with holographic stamps or bills adding to the price of a box. Thus, a parallel version of the sales routines that characterized state-run shops (see

Simoni 2009) took shape, often with tourists' playful complicity. Here, the same devices (logos, bills, etc.) that worked to standardize market exchanges were manipulated to (re)enact the very same regulations.

In spite of efforts to reassure potential buyers and formalize the exchange at stake, most of these deals still lacked any direct connection with the

FIGURE 5.2 • *Cigars in the Partagás Factory Shop, Havana*

essential materialities that constituted official cigars and purchases, such as museum-like displays of cigar boxes, shop counters, cash registers and air-conditioned rooms – key elements framing 'proper' market exchanges and entangling cigars in a realm of standardized production and distribution (see Figure 5.3). But dealers could resort to another tactic to compensate for the irretrievable 'absence' of these material elements in the 'presence' of their cigars (Law and Singleton 2005) and still win tourists over in the performance struggle to enact good-quality, 'real' branded *Habanos*.[3] This consisted in channelling and restricting tourists' attention to the properties and internal features of their products.

Whereas the cigars sold in the *tiendas del estado* did not require any further test of their conformity to standards, uncertainty about quality and authenticity predominated in street deals. Relying on the rationale that even those who were suspicious of the nature of the deal would ultimately realize that what really mattered were the quality and the price of the cigars them-selves, dealers could thus proceed to test, in front of tourists, the excellence of their products based on the cigars' colour, texture, smell and flexibility in carefully performed procedures designed to prove the fineness of the goods on offer. In really tough cases of tourists' scepticism, dealers even proposed opening a cigar and jointly examining its interior in a kind of autopsy as the

FIGURE 5.3 • *Partagás Factory Shop, Havana*

ultimate proof of authenticity.[4] As a last resort, tourists were encouraged to smoke a cigar, taste its quality and judge additional indicators such as the way the cigar burnt, the colour of the ashes and their consistency.

Unlike the process of relating cigars with the factories they supposedly came from or to the status of the seller, this restriction of the focus to the cigars' own qualities helped to 'cut networks' (Strathern 1996), that is, narrow the frame of the relevant elements that potential buyers should consider in order to make up their mind. By reducing the cigars' attachments and cutting off what was external to them, dealers could claim a higher degree of control over the authentication process. Indeed, having decided which elements were to be considered pertinent, they could then go on to prove and test them directly in front of their customers. Even tourists who knew little about cigars were thereby confronted with 'competence building propositions' (Latour 2005) that enabled them to judge of the quality of the products on offer and assess the suitability of their price.

The intersection of discourses, practices and materialities that characterized these deals verged on the enactment of a commodity/market exchange as qualified by Thomas (1991) and later by Slater (2002). Accordingly, tourists and Cubans were encouraged to take on the roles of buyers and sellers engaging in an economic transaction in which objectified goods were exchanged for an agreed quantity of money, leaving the parties with no further obligation towards each other. Yet the transactions in this case at best approximated the ones that took place in official cigar shops. Indeed, no effort to reconnect cigars with regulations and conformity to standards, to stabilize them as lawfully branded goods, or to evoke and give legitimacy to the seller's role was likely to dissipate the impression that something slightly risky and illegal was going on. Perceptions of risk and illegality could put tourists off and dissuade them from accepting street dealers' propositions for fear of being cheated (the cheater/cheated dyad lurking in the background of the seller/buyer one). But sometimes risks could also lead to a much-valued experiential thrill, once visitors dared engage in the deal, as the following example suggests.

James and Mary, a young English couple travelling independently whom I met in a *casa particular*, seized my attention with the story of their adventurous cigar deal in Havana. This is how I recalled their narrative in my records:

> We were at the Capitolio, and then a guy met us. He brought us down, to this street, and we entered a huge building. [Inside the building] we went up, and down, and turned, and up again [using his hand to show the intricacies of their movements within the building]. Then we entered into a room, where there were plenty of tobacco boxes. But the boxes were a bit damaged, so we did not want to get the one he suggested us. So then we went out, turned around the Capitolio

again, just around the factory. The guy knocked at a door, he woke up a friend. He [the friend] threw us the key, we opened the door, and then we went up again. In this room, and there were always a lot of people, talking to each other. Can't get a word in Spanish, didn't know what they were saying. Anyway, we could get it, and, yeah, it was quite an exciting experience!

From the encounter with a stranger to the thrill of following him and feeling lost along the corridors of several private houses before finally arriving at a room full of people where the purchase was made: their story added to the picture of a cigar deal a whole range of elements that contributed to enhancing its value, placing it on a very different level from that of standardized market exchanges taking place in official shops. The excitement of subverting rules, the unique and challenging experience, and even the complicity established about it with the dealers had become for James and Mary a meaningful and rewarding experience of its own, with the added value of a compelling story to tell.

Though I heard other, similar narratives of adventurous deals, most of the tourists I met in Cuba rarely dared to engage in this sort of transaction, deemed too risky and too close to classic 'bad deal' scenarios. If they ever bought cigars in the informal market, it was more likely from people they already knew – such as personnel at their hotel, owners of their *casa particular* or other Cuban friends and acquaintances. Distinguishing these purchases from street deals were the traceability and reputation of the dealer involved, in contrast to the transience of exchanges *en la calle*, where tourists faced 'strangers' they knew nothing about and were likely to see them as hustlers and *jineteros*. However, a closer look at street deals shows that the rationales for any such distinction were often challenged by the dealers themselves, who struggled to re-qualify the nature of exchanges. This is when dealers put emphasis on moral commitments – recall here Jorge's *tener ética* (chapter 4) – such as traceability and reputation, rather than on their shaky connections with officialdom.

The traceability of people offering cigars was explicitly emphasized at *casas particulares* and other tourist installations. The moral framework thus negotiated entangled the exchange with the dealer's responsibility and reputation, projecting relationships in longer time frames and bringing past and future to bear on the present of the transaction. Another temporal dimension had to do with the duration of the transaction, as owners of a *casa particular* might highlight, for instance, the advantage of being able to carefully and closely examine the products at stake in a homely environment, unlike in a rushed street deal. These contrasts may have applied to certain street-deals, but they ignored the fact that street-dealers themselves often relied on very similar arguments, inviting tourists to take their time to scrupulously examine their products and eventually smoke one before any purchase. On one occasion, one such street dealer even encouraged me to take the box home first and try the cigars, making himself traceable by explaining that he always hung around the same area at that time of the day: if I did not like them, I could bring the box back and he would reimburse me. Well aware of tourists' scepticism of transient and potentially deceitful encounters, dealers offering cigars in the streets of Havana did their best to overcome their reluctance. All these sales procedures evoked professionalism, an excellent reputation, and a moral commitment to engage in proper, honest economic transactions, respecting tourists' rights as buyers and fulfilling dealers' obligations as sellers.

They could also generate a shift towards other relational idioms, grounding commitments and obligations in the normative expectation of a host-guest relationship. This way, any clear-cut divide between the idioms of economic transactions and those of hospitality was potentially blurred and eventually redefined. The following section delves deeper into these shifts and blurrings, considering exchanges that foregrounded notions of generosity, reciprocity, mutual help and hospitality.

Entangling Cigar Deals with Generosity, Reciprocity and Hospitality

In the case of *casas particulares*, a cigar proposition could be articulated as a very special, exceptional offer made by the hosts to their guests. Rather than suggesting enrolment in a transient market exchange between buyers and sellers trying to maximize profit, the transaction here evoked notions of hospitality, generosity and reciprocal help, so that haggling on the suggested price seemed less appropriate than in street deals. This brought about a transactional regime that affected, distorted and reformulated economic calculations and clear-cut equivalences between prices and cigars through the prism of mutual collaboration between parties. The relational idioms at stake helped materialize an exchange between honest, obliging guests on the one hand, and an economically privileged, generous host on the other.

As I noticed on several occasions, however, the enactment of these relational idioms could be rather short-lived, failing the test of time and subsequent trials to which it was submitted. In other words, the projection of relationships in the long term – the foundation of the moral framework of the transaction – could be disappointed. For example, tourists who had bought cigars in their *casa particular* and experienced the deal as a positive and gratifying exchange between hosts and guests, might re-qualify that same transaction as a bad commodity exchange some days later upon realizing that people on the streets were offering 'the same products' at a cheaper price. Such a scenario reveals the potential fragility and indexicality of the transactional regimes and relational idioms that emerged in informal touristic encounters, foregrounding continuous processes of reassessment in the light of the tourists' trajectories, experiences and learning.

Tourists' explorations of tobacco and cigars in the rural region of Viñales (Figure 5.4) provide further evidence of how cigar deals could move beyond commodity exchanges, materializing other forms of transaction and relational idioms. We delve deeper here into a realm of reciprocity – of relationships internalizing an increasing array of elements that became part of exchanges between tourists and farmers – where cigars themselves could hold surprises, becoming something other than what was seen theretofore. The valley of Viñales, declared a UNESCO World Heritage Site in 1999, is a well-known tourist destination in Cuba, famous for its peculiar hills (*mogotes*) and its tobacco fields (Figure 5.5). During my time there, tourism in Viñales centred on excursions through the valley. Whether tourists travelled by bus, on bicycles, by foot or on horseback, most excursions involved stops at the valley's must-see attractions: tobacco fields and farms.

In the course of these visits the handling of tobacco acquired a salient role, and cigar deals took shape. On a typical tour, tobacco farmers guided tourists through the processes of tobacco cultivation, treatment and cigar manufacture, encouraging them to experience with all their senses the rural

FIGURE 5.4 • *The Valley of Viñales, Viñales*

FIGURE 5.5 • *Tobacco Field, Viñales*

FIGURE 5.6 • Secadero, *Viñales*

environment and the qualities of tobacco fields and plants. Depending on the season, tobacco plants would be growing in the fields, enabling farmers to explain the plants' size, colour, height and quality to the visitors. Some farmers, whose fields were not in the immediate surroundings of the house where they welcomed tourists, took care to plant small samples of tobacco near the house and would use them as a sort of educational garden to illustrate the process of tobacco cultivation and growth.

From the fields, the tours moved on into the *secaderos* (see Figure 5.6) – huge, dim buildings where cut tobacco was hung to dry for several weeks. Here, explanations of the processes of collection, drying and fermentation directed tourists' attention to the smell, colours, touch and texture of the tobacco leaves. During these visits, 'locally produced' coffee or fresh fruit juices were offered to tourists while farmers demonstrated how to roll a cigar (see Figure 5.7), taking care to emphasize key motions and techniques. In some cases, the farmer would then invite tourists to roll their own. The 'natural' and 'local' character of the cigars thus made was usually highlighted, with farmers stressing the produce's direct connections with the nearby fields and environment. Tourists were then encouraged to smoke the freshly rolled cigar.

FIGURE 5.7 • *Farmer Rolling a Cigar, Viñales*

FIGURE 5.8 • *Bundles of 'Natural' Cigars, Viñales*

Recounting to fellow tourists the amazing experience he had had on one such visit, Jonas – a young independent traveller from Austria – enthused about the experience of sitting by a shack sipping coffee in the sun while learning how to roll a cigar and glue the cigar tip with honey, and then tasting the blend of honey and tobacco in the ultimate act of smoking. Before leaving, he and his friends had bought two bundles of ten cigars: 'natural cigars', 'without any chemical whatsoever', he emphasized – echoing the common narrative farmers employed to give value to their products – before concluding that, without doubt, these were 'very good cigars!' As Jonas' story suggests, on such visits the prevailing rural atmosphere easily blended with the cigar itself and the experience of smoking, thus creating a unique value grounded in the experience of having been there.

After the climax of cigar smoking, the typical visit would end with the farmer offering bundles of 8–10 'locally-produced' cigars (see Figure 5.8), carefully packed in palm leaves, for tourists to take home.[5] Not all tourists accepted the deal. Some preferred just to offer some money in exchange for the coffee they drank, the fruits they ate or the cigars they smoked. But others, like Jonas, willingly agreed to the farmers' proposals, normally without questioning the suggested price. More generally, in the course of these encounters the visibility of monetary transaction was downplayed and performed with discretion. This enabled people to dissociate these exchanges from the realm of clear-cut equivalences and commoditization. Meanwhile, most tourists lacked the competence to assess the exchange value of such a unique, non-standardized product, which made it difficult to discuss the price suggested by farmers. Instead, exchanges were framed as forms of reciprocity, as gifts and counter-gifts (Mauss 1969 [1925]). Indeed, some farmers argued that it was all about 'offering gifts' (*brindar obsequios*), supported by the guides who occasionally mediated interactions between them and the tourists.

Some of the guides I talked to, however, shattered any ideal of spontaneous reciprocity by stating another reason for farmers to refrain from straightforwardly asking for money or explicitly naming prices: they were not supposed to engage in any market transactions with tourists and could be legally sanctioned by the Cuban authorities if such deals were unveiled. However, this was a risk that several farmers seemed willing to take. Their ways of proceeding ranged from saying nothing about monetary value, to more or less veiled suggestions, to explicit pricing – something I realized was becoming more and more common every year I came back to Viñales, suggesting perhaps a progression towards increasingly commoditized forms of exchange. When farmers suggested no price and relied solely on what tourists were willing to offer them, they also incurred the risk of inappropriate reciprocation by stingy visitors, as some put it. But as it happened, they were generally very skilled at enticing tourists to reciprocate. The latter often found themselves caught in a regime of reciprocity between hosts and guests that the farmers had set in motion with their initial hospitality and 'opening gifts' (Mauss 1969 [1925]), and in which equivalences of value and appropriate ways of reciprocating could be hard to figure out.

Karl, a young Austrian independent traveller, recounted how he and his friend had visited a tobacco farmer and experienced the uneasy, awkward feeling of having inappropriately behaved in reciprocating the farmer's hospitable kindness and generosity:

This farmer, he was in the fields, working in the fields, and then he told us: 'Come, come, you want to have a look?' He showed us this place where the tobacco dries. He explained us about the fermentation of the leaves. Then he rolled one for us. He was so kind, showing and explaining us everything, so polite. We felt so bad not to buy the cigars at the end. But we didn't know if the one he made was going to be the same as the ones in the package. Yes, the one we smoked was good. But I don't know anything about cigars. So many people told us not to buy like this. It's illegal. But that's the problem here [in Cuba], it's hard, you don't know who to trust. You don't know how to trust anymore. It's a problem. We just left him something for the cigar he made – we smoked it – and the drinks. I wonder what he must have thought of us: 'Who are these guys, the two bastards who don't buy anything'. Maybe he felt sad.

Several tourists, like Karl and his friend, found it hard to judge how much money to leave, sensing that the farmers' generosity – in showing their farms and fields, explaining to tourists the processes of tobacco growing and manufacturing, and sharing the fruits of their labour – called for munificence. Thus, many visitors I met preferred to give in abundance rather than leave the impression of being mean, which was something Karl seemed to regret. In case tourists did not understand that farmers would appreciate something in return for their hospitality, this expectation could also be explicitly stated, notably by the accompanying guides, who gave tourists advice on how 'good guests' ought to behave (Sant Cassia 1999; Tucker 2001; Herzfeld 2012). Distinctions between visitors also played out along these lines: some contrasted their generosity with the attitudes of parsimonious tourists who dared not even accept farmers' invitations or were unable to let themselves go and enjoy these moments of peaceful sharing, trapped as they were in fears that farmers would cheat them or ask them to pay disproportionate amounts.

All in all, the forms of transaction and relational idioms that took shape during tourists' visits to tobacco farms in Viñales tended to embody forms of reciprocity and hospitality. These were well in tune with the view of a self-contained reality where traditional modalities and moralities of exchange held sway and where, isolated from the wider socio-economic context of Cuba, fields, plants, farmers' skills and hand/home made products traced a direct continuum of metonymic-like relations. Still, though, the forms of reciprocity and hospitality enacted remained rather unstable, subject to continuous reassessment and susceptible to contestation. This tended to happen in connection with the circulation of money, the dilemmas raised by this circulation and the ensuing intrusion of other rationales that brought notions of commoditization and market exchange back into the picture.[6] The very short time lag between the farmers' gifts and tourists' counter-gifts was another crucial aspect contributing to suspicions of instrumental calculation, breaching ideal views of relationships governed by mutual and disinterested generosity.[7] Accordingly, although farmers and visitors could converge in enactments of reciprocity and hospitality, doubts and ambiguities about calculation and exchange value were always on the brink of resurfacing. They could easily reappear after such visits took place, once tourists shared their experiences with fellow travellers and reflected retrospectively on them.

Blurring Transactions: Tensions, Ambiguities and Contestations

In Viñales, unlike in the street deals discussed earlier, no effort was generally made to relate tobacco and cigars to factories and state supervision. In the valley, the attachments of cigars consisted in immediate relations with the surrounding elements of the landscape, with the farmers' skills and with the earth and plants that also produced the coffee and fruits consumed. These connections were made clearly visible. Tourists were encouraged to experience them straightforwardly through all their senses, and thus to learn about the culture and life of rural Cuba. These occasions were a sort of celebration of locality that opposed a self-contained reality and rustic authenticity on the one hand to cigar factories' hierarchic organization and supervision, fragmentation of the work tasks and legalized authenticity on the other (see Simoni 2009). If farmers in Viñales ever evoked cigar factories and state supervision, they did so in rather negative terms, depreciating them as examples of homogeneous standardization and economic monopoly against the more valued backdrop of a realm of nature, uniqueness and skilful self-sufficient countrymen – a realm successfully mediated by the farmers' handling of tobacco, from the fields and farms to their manufacturing tables.

As described above, these two realities contrasted sharply, giving shape to very different forms of transaction and relational idioms. Nevertheless, the contrast between the two also shows how these different realities related to one another. Furthermore, the evocation of the world of official cigar brands – positively connoted in Havana and negatively connoted in Viñales – reveals imbalances and 'power geometries' (Massey 1993) between these realities in terms of their reciprocal diffusion and popularity. Brands, state control, official production and distribution were the more powerful players in the game, as exemplified by the transnational promotion and commercialization of branded *Habanos* across the world. When the normative view of 'good' and 'original' Cuban cigars as commodities controlled and managed by the Cuban government prevailed, tourists in Viñales tended to stop attributing much value to the farmers' own manufacture of cigars, or at least to be cautious about engaging in any cigar deal with them, as in the case of Karl and his friend. Other visitors told me they had seen cigar making in Havana's factories and did not want to see it again in Viñales. On excursions in the countryside they would just have a look at the farmers' work in the fields or maybe visit a drying house, urging their guides to move on when they suggested stopping to observe how farmers manufactured cigars. Following the canonical script of the official narratives about proper procedures of cigar production and distribution, Viñales was only the place where tobacco was grown and dried, whereas rigorous manufacturing took place in factories, and legal sales in *tiendas del estado*.

Besides diverging, the worlds of tobacco production and cigar deals in Havana and Viñales could also blur and impinge on one another. Some tourists immersed themselves in the picture of a coherent rural life in Vinãles, lived by wise farmers interacting skilfully with nature, crafting homemade cigars and relating hospitably towards guests. Others, though, would engage only partially in this self-contained world. Their judgements and evaluations remained informed by other kinds of scripts and scenarios, bringing into play other entities such as the wider Cuban society, the governmentally pre-scribed transformation of tobacco into cigars, and the transactional regime of market exchanges. These tourists' concerns tended to revolve around the amount of money a farmer asked – or more likely discreetly suggested – that they pay (or leave) for the bundles of homemade cigars. Indeed, even though the visibility of monetary transactions was often downplayed and exchanges were framed as forms of reciprocity in a (stereo)typical host-guest relation-ship, preoccupation with money and efforts to attribute objective exchange value to things could easily re-emerge, reframing the situation in commercial terms. For instance, Neil, a young independent traveller from England, told me and other fellow travellers about his and his partner's encounter with a farmer: 'He [the farmer] offered us ten [cigars] for ten [convertible pesos], but finally we thought it was expensive'. Sipping a mojito after the day's excursion, he reflected: 'We paid for the cigars we smoked there. Maybe we should have bought them. Of course it's only one [convertible peso] for one [cigar]. But then: he was making them there. It seemed quite easy. We thought it was a bit expensive'.

Here Jonas, the Austrian tourist who had bought the cigar bundle two days earlier, replied: 'Yeah, I bought ten. Just because ... I liked him!' Rather than arguing for calculation and attempts to establish objective equivalences, Jonas scaled explanations down to idiosyncratic, spontaneous, uncalculated feelings of generosity. Elaborating on the reasons why they had not bought the cigars, Neil voiced concern about spoiling or disrupt-ing the 'local economy' and the functioning of the overall 'social system' by paying an amount of money that seemed exaggerated when compared, for example, to average Cuban salaries. 'If a doctor is really earning twenty convertible pesos a month, how can we give ten to a farmer, just for some handmade cigars?' 'How much would a Cuban pay for that?' 'Are they manufacturing and selling cigars because we are tourists?' Questions like these came to the fore, helping to bring the unflattering scenario of staged and potentially deceptive tourism relations back into the picture. Exchange value, monetary equivalences, Cubans' salaries, the impact of tourists and their hard currency on the local economy, and the coherent functioning of Cuban society were alternately externalized, maintained outside the frame of a transaction or made into active participants to qualify cigar deals. In the latter case, any clear divide between the world of tobacco farmers and that of state control and supervision was transgressed, and with it the demarca-tion between reciprocity and hospitality on the one hand, and market exchanges on the other.

Tourists were not the only ones contesting and breaching such framings and distinctions. In this respect, it is important to note that clear-cut divides between the world of Viñales and that of cigar factories and brands, and the valorization of the former to the detriment of the latter, collided with the interests of local residents who engaged in street deals more akin to those done in Havana. A Viñalero called Carlos, for instance, saw a promising deal for a box of Cohiba cigars vanish after the tourists who were supposed to buy it ended up with a farmer, enjoyed smoking the 'natural cigars' he made for them, and bought ten each, afterward reneging on the Cohiba deal agreed on earlier. When I told Carlos that they had probably been captivated by the charm of naturally, freshly made products, he answered with disdain that those were not original cigars: they were 'shitty cigars' (*tabaco de mierda*) made in rudimentary ways, without the right twist, the nice finish or the external layer. According to him, tourists were clearly overpaying for them.

Carlos did not buy into the self-contained reality promoted by farmers. More precisely, he downplayed the disjuncture between a supposedly local-ized world of farmers and tobacco fields, and state supervision of the cigar commodity chain, in which farmers' only task was to furnish tobacco leaves and receive payment accordingly. His discourse brought the two together, entangling tobacco and cigars in a wider scale: that of official cigar produc-tion.[8] By the same token, Carlos was not partaking in the view of two dis-tinct transactional regimes at play either – a view that opposed reciprocities to market exchanges. He saw both himself and the farmers as engaged in the same *negocio* (business) of selling cigars to tourists. The tourists he had been dealing with, however, did not share his view; instead they cherished the very same disjuncture he was overlooking.

Conclusion

As this last example shows, processes of entanglement and disentanglement, that is, of framing what was to be included or excluded in a transaction, could become very contentious, given also that these characterizations could have far-reaching consequences. The success or failure of a deal could depend on the success of these framing processes, and the convergence or divergence of tourists' and Cubans' views on them, in turn impacting the livelihood of the Cuban people involved by enabling or curtailing their chances of getting a share of the resources in the tourism economy. These same convergences and divergences also informed the emergence of different relational identi-fications, such as those of cheaters and the cheated, sellers and buyers, and hosts and guests. Accordingly, I would argue that in their wake, cigar deals also materialized and reshaped what people understood as 'tourism hustling', 'market exchange', 'reciprocity' or 'hospitality'. Each deal gave rise to situated translations of these notions and the relational idioms attached to them.

This chapter has considered cigar deals to illustrate how what might be seen a priori as a unified process of market exchange could acquire diverse shapes and meanings for the various protagonists involved, and to highlight how characterizations of these process were themselves a crucial arena of struggle, controversy and contestation. As Slater (2002: 243) puts it, 'framings are political and strategic battle-lines – over liabilities, profits, ethical and political interests'. Here, I have purposefully stressed the role that materialities played in such framing processes, showing how different deployments of money, tobacco and cigars contributed to the enactment of different types of transactions and relationships. Far from being always stable and clear-cut, the boundaries between these modes of exchange and of relating to each other were regularly overstepped, blurred and renegotiated, a clear example being the tourists' questioning of homemade cigar prices in Viñales, in which notions of market exchange and hospitality came into conflict and generated tension and ambiguity. Disjunctures and differences between forms of transactions and relationships were fragile constructs, often only temporarily achieved through the felicitous conjunction of specific ideas, discourses, practices and materialities. At any rate, the significance of their effects, for instance in relation to people's livelihoods, urges us to examine such nuances and thus move beyond an overarching, clear-cut view of economic transactions in tourism, towards more finely tuned, ethnographically grounded accounts of the different shapes taken by the economic – and by what is made to count as such.

Chapter 6
FRIENDLINESS AND FRIENDSHIP

Appeals to friendship were among the favourite *entradas* Cubans deployed to get in touch with tourists. But far from receiving visitors' straightforward endorsement, (over-)friendly openings could generate scepticism and suspicion, especially when deployed too loosely, without any apparent effort to substantiate them. After examining the paradoxes of such friendliness, in this chapter I consider the entanglement of friendship with issues of trust and reputation, and examine the role that verbal reassurances could play in moving from friendliness to friendship. Generally, these reassurances were not enough to convince sceptical tourists. Often, more pragmatic proofs were needed to help ground such claims in concrete experiences and realities, thus substantiating the friendship, fleshing it out, and putting it to the test.

In touristic Cuba, narratives and practices of friendship, and the contrast often entailed between this relational idiom and notions of economic instrumentality, could serve to soothe visitors' fears of being cheated and exploited. Indeed, a closer look at the ways in which friendship was enacted highlights its antagonism to various forms of exchange, most notably monetary transactions but including also certain notions of gift giving and reciprocity. Far from depicting friendship as a rigid relational idiom, and accounting instead for 'its ambiguous character as a form of sociality' (Coleman 2010: 204), the exploration of its emergent contours shows people's ability to transform their views upon having to account for its specific expressions in the context of touristic Cuba. At the same time, analysis of the empirical material also highlights a certain resistance to such contextualizing moves, notably when they called into question Cubans' claims and aspirations to a more universal ideal of friendship. This shows that notions of friendship, however adaptable, could not be stretched too far, and that drives to make friendship 'impure' (Coleman 2010) could be countered by competing efforts to 'purify' it whose rationales, implications and 'aspirational character' (Moore 2011) demand close anthropological scrutiny. The chapter also introduces another crucial aspect of touristic encounters, namely, the way tourist-Cuban relationships could thrive despite, but also perhaps thanks to, their ambiguous character and their potential for misunderstanding. Indeed, the examination of friendship in this particular context of interaction shows that beyond the need to find common ground in relationships, tourists and Cubans could also willingly cohabit, and even profit from, the ambiguities impinging on them.

Immediate Friendliness, Fragile Friendship

We were there, sitting on the Malecón [Havana's seaside promenade], when suddenly this Cuban guy showed up. He was very nice at the beginning, and invited us to this cool bar, where we had a mojito. Then he invited us to this *paladar* [private restaurant], where we had this shitty fish: hard as a stone! And I mean; we had to pay twenty each! And then, when the bill arrived, he just stood there, holding his hands, didn't make a move. We had to pay! He certainly got his commission afterwards: just before leaving he told us that he had to go to the toilet, but then we saw him talking to the woman at the counter …I mean if he hadn't brought us there in the first place, we would never have found it. He also explained us about the history of some buildings … I mean, he was nice; he was not like the others. But then he also wanted me to give him my sunglasses – no way! … And yes, we also bought some cigars from him. We paid fifty for a box of twenty-five, but later on other Cubans told us they could have given us the same ones for twenty-five … But anyway, this was the first day. After that experience, we learned: now no one is going to cheat us anymore! There we understood how things worked … The problem here is that you never know why they are talking to you; if there is some hidden interest behind. I guess they are always trying to gain something.

The selected passages quoted above come from a conversation with Sandra and Marta, two Swiss women in their late twenties who spent one month travelling independently around Cuba. After repeated conversations with such tourists about their first encounters in Havana, I noticed a recurrent narrative that saw them venturing into the city streets and meeting 'by chance' (a) friendly Cuban(s), who would then offer to show them around. During the tour, the Cuban(s) would invite the tourists to have a drink and/ or food, which the latter were then expected to pay for. Towards the end of the encounter, some sort of deal was generally proposed: a box of cigars, an exchange of currency, a helpful bit of money, and so forth. From their evaluation of these first encounters, tourists drew cues and lessons that could orient their attitudes towards Cubans for the rest of their journey (as Sandra and Marta's example made clear). These had to do with the (un)suitability of trusting them (or at least, 'some Cuban people'), and of taking their friendly attitudes seriously.

In this respect many travellers, especially independent ones, were led to conclude that Cubans met in the streets, particularly in tourism areas, were interested in their money – 'When they look at us they see the dollar sign!' – and that this interest was often concealed behind an exaggerated, contrived friendliness. The approach adopted thus seemed to rely on a front/back opposition akin to that theorized by Goffman (1959) and further elaborated in MacCannell's (1973, 1976) notion of 'staged authenticity' in relation to tourist settings, the rationale in this case being that behind the Cubans' 'front', a superficial expression of friendliness, lay the more real 'back' of instrumental agendas.[1] Supporting these assessments was the fact that many such first-day encounters ultimately gave the tourists the impression that the Cuban friend had somehow cheated them, be it through an unfavourable currency exchange, commission-inflated bills in bars and restaurants, or an overpriced cigar deal.

Whatever answers tourists gave retrospectively to the question of ascertaining their interlocutors' (real) intentions, on the spot it was not always easy, in the course of interaction, for them to deny or discredit someone's professions of friendliness, or to refrain from reciprocating along similar lines. We are confronted here with issues of etiquette, politeness, and moral conformity in public behaviour, of the difficulty people could have in disentangling themselves from routines and implicit norms of interaction, which for this reason could also be easily manipulated in instrumental ways. A friendly attitude, in this sense, called for an equally friendly response[2] and could be seen as an 'ethical demand' (Zigon 2009, 2010), an invitation to enter into a certain kind of relationships. To refuse this invitation could generate uncomfortable feelings and a sense of unease similar to what Karl felt upon rejecting the deal with the generous farmer in Viñales (see chapter 5). Although tourists could feel compelled to reciprocate friendly calls, they could also keep some distance, playing 'as if' and getting along in a friendly way while covering their backs and not giving away too much, just in case things turned out not to be what they seemed.

Indeed, visitors' reactions to immediate professions of friendliness ranged from complete disregard for the Cuban involved (it could be more comfortable to pretend not to have heard a friendly call than to openly deny its significance) to more positive responses granting them at least the benefit of doubt. In the latter case, even sceptical tourists could playfully get along in the relationships while remaining highly guarded, keeping their engagement in check so as not to risk enough to incur much of a disappointment. Cubans, on their side, often struggled to evaluate the tourists' engagement and assess their degree of commitment. Visitors' scepticism and inability to let go, open up (*abrirse*) and trust them could prove very disheartening and disappointing, hampering the possibility of developing a more fully fledged, open-ended relationship.

In spite of widespread scepticism, many tourists I met still cherished the idea of 'meeting the locals' and getting to know 'ordinary people' (see chapter 3) with whom they could talk, for instance, about the realities of everyday life in Cuba, and develop relations that could help them move 'backstage', beyond the tautological connotations of the 'tourist bubble'. Cubans could capitalize on these expectations by quickly reminding tourists that they had come to Cuba to discover their country and its people, and therefore had to meet and make friends with the locals. The right attitude prescribed here was to *abrirse, confiar* (trust), if one wished to gain access to the *Cuba de verdad* (the real Cuba), moving beyond the glossy images of tourism brochures. Therefore typical tourism narratives of cross-cultural communication and understanding were activated to build closer connections with tourists.[3] These friendliness-/trust-arousing discourses thus constructed tourism, tourists and processes of touristification in their wake, affirming hierarchies between different tourist practices and touching on the sensitive issue of tourists' agency and freedom.

By bringing visitors' attention to the limitations of the typical tourist role and its normative dimensions – for instance, in terms of being channelled into the routes and circuits prescribed by the industry – these narratives tended to strike the right note, triggering sympathetic and consensual reactions. Suggestions that opened up new fields of possibility were a common follow-up to this encouragement to trust and make friends with ordinary Cubans. For example, they might allude to the promise of unforgettable and unique experiences 'off the beaten track' and evoke with complicity a sense of defiance of the monopolistic machinations of the state and the tourism industry. This was also when Cubans could try and take the lead in their relationship with visitors, at least with respect to decision-making. Enacting the quintessential local and displaying their insider knowledge, they encouraged tourists to follow them as friends, listen to their stories about everyday Cuba and explore places that other tourists would never see.

Several tourists I spoke to had been seduced by such narratives and positively surprised by the immediate friendliness and helpfulness of their Cuban friends. Was this a Cuban characteristic? As two French women told me, on their first approach Cubans seemed indeed to be extremely kind and welcoming, and the way one could quickly get very deep into incredibly intense and intimate relationships (*ça va très vite très profond!*) was impressive. Advising thrifty tourists on where to shop, eat and drink, sharing confidences about the shortfalls of the communist system and the hardship of everyday life on the island, inviting visitors to have food in their homes or some out-of-the-way *casa* not on any official tourist map – in doing all this Cubans could be striving to gain the tourists' amity, complicity and trust, and to flesh out their friendship claims. Cubans' emotional expressiveness and easy-going physical manifestations of affection also helped materialize this sense of closeness, intimacy and intensity in the relationship, as exemplified by the ubiquitous hugging and handshaking, the dedicated absorption in any issue of concern for their tourist companions, or the enthusiasm shown for the communal sharing of food and drink. These traits certainly fitted the Cuban population's affable and warm-hearted reputation, as reiterated for instance in much tourism promotion material (chapter 1). But was all this genuine? As the sceptical tourist might retort: What if they are just pretending to be friends while really being after our money?

Verbal Reassurances:
Entangling Friendship with Reputation and Trust

While engaging tourists, I repeatedly heard Cubans refer to the prevalence of *jineteros* and 'fake friends' in tourism contexts on the island and cast themselves, by way of contrast, as the exception, the real friend one could trust and rely on. 'As a foreigner to this place, you would not know where to go! As long as you hang around with me, you are safe … You were so lucky to find me, and not some *jinetero*: a real friend, a sincere friendship.' These are some sentences I recalled Pepe – one of the first Cubans I met on the streets of Havana – uttering as he tried to reassure me of the genuineness of his friendship. I soon realized that this kind of discourse was very widespread, so much so that it could quickly lose all its appeal to more experienced tourists. 'Be careful, not all Cubans are the same!' was the typical refrain of this 'idiom of exception' (Torresan 2011).[4] Weary of the widespread warning not to trust 'other Cubans', and increasingly suspicious of the 'how lucky you are to have found me' kind of narrative, Gilberto and Dario, two young independent travellers from Italy whom I met in Viñales, came to the conclusion that in the end, these self-proclaimed exceptions were the most likely to cheat you.

The diffusion of stories on the ubiquity of deceitful Cubans kept injecting distrust into these encounters, nourishing tourists' misgivings about relating with Cuban people. The fragility and vulnerability of trust, according to Gambetta (2000: 234), becomes all the more apparent when trust is compared with the strength and persistence of its counterpart, distrust: 'Doubt is far more insidious than certainty, and distrust may become the source of its own evidence'. Reflecting on the consequences of such a scenario, Gambetta observes that 'only accident or a third party may set up the right kind of "experiment" to prove distrust unfounded' (234). Cubans struggling to overcome tourists' distrust recognized the importance of such third-party mediation in reassuring visitors of their reputation and trustworthiness, and of the seriousness of their friendship claims. It could be the job of other Cubans, often members of the same peer group, to vouch for the person in question. Less suspicious, and therefore even better, was to place another foreigner in the role of a guarantor praising the person's honesty in front of other visitors. Using the mediation of a foreign friend to get to know other tourists and infuse trust in newly created relationships was a widespread tactic that Fernando particularly explicitly described to me:

> I used to pick up a foreign mate (*coleguita extranjero*), like you – you could be one – and things tended to get easier. It was not with him that I would do my business (*negocio*), but through him I could get to know other tourists. People [tourists] would see me with him, we would introduce each other. He would tell them 'look this is Fernando, he is a friend of mine'. He would tell them that he had been to my house to have food, that he had met my family. This makes people [other tourists] feel safer, they get more confident and trust you. Then I could sell them my cigar boxes, etc.

When such foreign friends were not present, they could also be evoked through exemplary stories of friendship, mutual trust, reciprocal help and a long-term relationship.[5] By the same token, these narratives also suggested to visitors that this was the right attitude to adopt. They exemplified, we may argue, 'the way of the good tourist', who by trusting the right person enjoyed his or her stay in Cuba and made it an unforgettable experience.[6] Such portraits of ideal friendships highlighted the mutual gratifications and advantages that could result. As a foreigner myself, I was often called to act as a sort of guarantor by my Cuban research participants, who would bank on my status of long-term outsider to boost their reputation and infuse trust in their relationship with other tourists. 'Valerio knows me well!' 'We have been friends for ages!' 'We are like brothers!' 'He can tell you what kind of person I am!' Such were the encouraging statements addressed to other tourists in my presence. These reassurances could also help reassert and reinvigorate the ties between the Cuban and the person doing the vouching, by confirming their friendship in front of an audience.

But convincing sceptical tourists of one's friendship just by professing it, as in a kind of self-fulfilling prophecy, often proved insufficient. As shown above, verbal claims could even be counterproductive when seen as superficial expression of a '(false) front'. To become more persuasive, friendliness and friendship had to be fleshed out by concrete actions that could support one's reassurances. This is the realm of 'tests' and 'trials' to which Callon's notion of 'performance struggles' (2007: 330) draws attention. In this sense, tourists were looking for practical proof of friendship to decide of the 'success or failure' of their Cuban friend's 'act of language' (330). Writing about the ethical nature of human endeavours as related to both speech and action, Lambek (2010: 63) remarks that 'every utterance entails a commitment to our words', so that 'we are continually put to test to keep, as it were, our promises'. Tourists could hope to find proof of such commitment to friendship in their companions' behaviours, to see if they really meant what they said. For their part, the self-professed Cuban friends were also generally very eager to highlight those practical instances and concrete events that could corroborate their verbal claims.

Fleshing out Friendship

To give substance to their professions of friendship, Cubans could draw attention to concrete proofs of exceptional, virtuous behaviour in their interactions with tourists. The following example clearly shows how they might flesh out the relational idiom of friendship by pointing to their exemplary conduct. I was sitting at the counter of the Bodeguita del Medio, a very popular tourism spot on Old Havana's main circuit, when I made the acquaintance of Alejandro, a Mexican man in his fifties, and his Cuban 'friend' Gerardo, who looked much younger, probably in his thirties. When we started chatting, both were drinking round after round of mojitos, which Alejandro seemed willing to sponsor. Alejandro kept talking to me about Gerardo and his relation to him, and Gerardo did the same with regards to Alejandro. In a way, they were assessing the nature of their ties via their conversation with me, which made me feel like a witness – a testifying audience – in a sort of trial of their relationship. Here are some passages I recall from the conversation:

> He is a good person, he is no thief. See this, we went to the beach; I left him my mobile phone, my iPod. When I came back, everything was there. No because, you better be careful! Because many Cubans steal you, they cheat you (*te sacan la cara, te estafan*). He doesn't steal! He helps me. For instance, he tells me the prices. He tells me how much. For a girl, for instance: he tells me 25–30 [convertible pesos], not more. For instance, a taxi to the beach: they asked me twenty-five. With him [with his intercession] ten! Because he speaks: he tells them 'I'm Cuban. This should cost ten!' I met him in the street. At the beginning I didn't believe him much. But then; he doesn't steal. He doesn't tell lies. [Whispering in my ear] Because Cubans; they steal, I mean, they are treacherous (*traicioneros*), they tell lies. He tells me everything. How prices are... And I don't pay him anything! I pay him the drinks and the food, and that's it! With the money I save with [thanks to] him, I can offer him food and drinks, and there's even money left. (Alejandro)

He [Alejandro] is my brother already; a friend of mine … It's four days we know each other, but it seems it has been like one year. I'm like this; for me the important thing is friendship. The brother-ness (*hermanidad*). That's what my father taught me: don't steal, be polite (*educado*), be sincere. They taught me to be an honest person … friendship and the heart (*amistad y corazón*) [that is what matters]. So when he comes back in April he just calls me. We meet up again … He is a friend. He comes to eat at my home. Do you remember? You are a friend aren't you? I offered you (*te brindé*) my home. I'm poor, but still [I invited you] … (Gerardo)

At some point in our conversation, the musicians playing in the bar came around to sell their CD. Alejandro had a look at it, and asked the price: ten convertible pesos. Too expensive, he argued, adding that he had already bought other CDs in Cuba for much less. Gerardo also got involved in the haggling, and finally advised against the deal: 'They want me to cheat you. No! You are my brother, my friend. Why should I cheat you. Most Cubans are treacherous, but I'm not like this. I know that this CD, you can find it in a shop for two convertibles [CUC]. So why should I suggest you buy it for ten?'

While Alejandro seldom referred to Gerardo as a friend, the latter went as far as describing their relationship in kinship terms, as brother-ness: an honest and sincere relationship, one that had a bright future ahead. The Mexican man's words show that what seemed most important to him was that his Cuban companion did not steal or lie, and that he told him everything he needed to know to avoid being cheated. After a sceptical beginning, and following some compelling proofs of Gerardo's honesty, Alejandro had now come to trust him. Still, he kept justifying their relationships in instrumental terms based on his own interests and economic calculations: for Alejandro, staying with Gerardo was very convenient; further, he felt safe and even managed to save money. Albeit he never described their relationship as friendship, neither did he contradict Gerardo's claims. His Cuban companion foregrounded the relational idiom of friendship, and he rather happily went along with that, though with a certain detachment. In this sense, we may argue that idioms of both friendship and economic rationality were simultaneously in play here. Rather than hampering the relationship, the ambiguities generated by such co-presence seemed to enable it to function and move forward.

Gerardo's projection of the relationship into the future – 'we will meet again' – points to another important dimension that could pose an obstacle to friendship in touristic Cuba, namely its temporality. 'How can they pretend that we are friends if we just met a few hours ago?' was a common question among tourists. Temporal considerations challenged the moral grounds of these friendships, giving them a spurious edge. 'Friendship needs time.

And it's not only something that you make, but something that you keep', Lukas, a Norwegian man in his fifties, told me as we discussed the issue: 'I stay here only three weeks, and then I am leaving, and won't see these people again. And here they don't have Internet, they don't have Facebook. It will be difficult to have any friendship at all.' In Lukas' words, the continuity of a relationship was a key element informing the possibility that it would become a friendship. Its moral inscription in time was clearly at stake.

Aware of possible misgivings related to these temporal ideals of friendship, Gerardo had explicitly addressed the issue, claiming that even though he and Alejandro had spent only four days together, it felt more like a year to him. Here the subjective perception of time, particularly its quality and intensity, was prioritized over any objective calculation as Gerardo amplified the moral traces and tidemarks of their relationship as well as its potential outcomes. 'So when he comes back in April...', the Cuban man predicted, going on to fantasize about the possibility of visiting Alejandro in Mexico one day. Gerardo also made a point of recalling Alejandro's visit to his house, highlighting its significance and making it a landmark event exemplifying the intimate nature of their relation. As I witnessed on similar occasions, Cubans trying to make friends with tourists liked to recall these sorts of events (see also Fernando's case above) in an effort to intensify and strengthen their bonds. Drawing on Mattingly's (2010: 51) conceptualization of 'narrative emplotments', we may argue that such events took on the qualities of 'memorable experiences' that 'demarcated a "before" and an "after"' and were acted upon to invoke 'common ground'. Though we may cynically dismiss Gerardo's claim of friendship as a rather superficial, self-interested endeavour, his discourse may also be seen as a plea to be recognized as worthy of friendship, and an aspiration to relate despite striking differences and inequalities. I shall return to this line of interpretation below.

Already apparent in Gerardo and Alejandro's example, Cubans' generosity – as manifested, for instance, in sharing with tourists the meagre resources one had – could be cast as important evidence of genuine friendship. When the more economically disadvantaged Cubans were the first to display generosity in the encounter, this could be brought up to exemplify a lack of economic interest in the relationship and to present it instead within the moral frame of friendship, beyond the sphere of calculation typically associated with *jineterismo*. We are here confronted with situations in which, in the words of Zelizer (2000, 2005), 'relational work' took place to mark boundaries between different types of relationships via the characterization of appropriate forms of transaction (e.g. money as a gift rather than a payment). In the light of Zelizer's insight, the way transactions occur and are interpreted becomes a means of contrasting different types of relationships, in this case a friendship versus an interested economic relation. In touristic encounters in Cuba, the potential unidirectionality of material exchanges and the notion that money was constantly flowing from tourists to Cubans tended to magnify inequalities between the two, easily leading to accusations of 'false friendship' (see Mains 2013) and *jineterismo*. In this context, the Cubans' expressions of generosity could help in the task of requalifying all transactions that took place by casting them in the light of friendship, downplaying the importance of inequality and calculation as drivers of a relationship.

Among those who were particularly keen to deploy and display generosity in their dealings with tourists were members of the loose Rasta circle that regularly hung around the Malecón and Parque Central. They were used to the company of young travellers and backpackers, who tended to have open-ended travel plans and looked forward to the possibility of engaging with locals and getting closer to their everyday lives. The Rasta I engaged with willingly emphasized the value of a simple lifestyle, pointing out their aversion to touristy places in Old Havana. They would criticize the commercialism of tourism installations, epitomized, for instance, by those establishments whose business was based on 'prostitution' and sales of expensive, overpriced mojitos. As an alternative to this, the Rasta might suggest gathering some money collectively and buying a bottle of rum for everyone to share, including the foreign friends. Thus the companions could sit on the wall of the Malecón and 'share, the Cuban way' (*compartir, a lo cubano*), even paying in Cuban pesos (CUP), a currency everyone could afford.

When accompanying tourists around, the Cuban friends would similarly emphasize 'the places of the Cubans' (e.g. bars, restaurants and other public establishments) as venues where visitors could save money, avoiding expensive 'tourist-only' locations. Again, these instances could be portrayed as compelling evidence of a sincere, disinterested friendship and contrasted with the behaviour of 'other', ill-intentioned Cubans who got the highest commissions by bringing tourists to expensive tourist bars and restaurants. In this sort of relationship, the handling of money was downplayed, becoming entangled in specific moralities of exchange (Bloch and Parry 1989) that avoided any hint of calculative endeavour, akin to those that prevailed on visits to farms in Viñales (see chapter 5). Ideals of reciprocity were materialized by the sharing of drinks with friends, extending relationships in time via the assumption that favours would be reciprocated in the future.

Partaking in these moments of sociability with their Rasta companions, tourists could easily accept the professed friendship – a friendship supported by concrete expressions of generosity, disinterestedness in monetary gain, and mutual sharing. Accordingly, visitors and Cubans seemed to have convergent ideals of what a friendship ought to be about, that is, the expectations, dispositions and normativities that informed this relational idiom.

Such ideals called for downplaying asymmetries between the parties and striving to place tourists and Cubans 'as friends' on a more egalitarian footing grounded in communal sharing and the projection of sociabilities into the long term. This way, the spectre of *jineterismo* and its emphasis on inequality could be kept at bay.

Particularizing Friendship: Sentiment and Interest

The examples presented above are indicative of the extensive diffusion, in the Cuban tourism context, of interpretative approaches that recognized a tension between 'interest' and 'affection', or what Zelizer (2000, 2005) phrased as a 'Hostile Worlds rhetoric' that sees 'intimacy' and 'economy' as 'separate spheres'. The spread of these normative ideals has been noted in other tourism contexts; Tucker (1997: 121), for example, considers how visitors to the Turkish village of Göreme construe money and 'instrumental economic relationships' on the one hand, and 'friendship' on the other, as dichotomous. This subject of contention has absorbed much anthropological research on friendship, at least since Paine's (1969) groundbreaking article on the topic (see Killick and Desai 2010).

In an article on friendship among young men in urban Ethiopia, Mains (2013) has recently provided a useful overview and ethnographically informed discussion of the tensions that can arise between self-interest and affection among friends. He is thus able to show that although material help and affection can often converge and be co-constitutive of friendship, 'when a friend was being too instrumental and valuing material gain over the maintenance of affection, conflicts and tensions were created' (2013: 340), prompting desires 'to separate business and friends' (341). For his argument, Mains draws on recent literature on love and transactional sex in Africa, where globalizing ideals of 'pure love' have been uncovered (see e.g. Cole 2009). However, Mains' ethnography did not reveal any discourses referring to a 'pure friendship' (2013: 343). I shall return to this point below, when addressing my Cuban participants' drive to 'purify' their relationships with tourists of any hint of economic interest in ways that depart from Mains' findings. Here, I wish to consider instead those interpretations and reformulations of friendship that opened the door to a possible 'mix' of friendship and interest, thus 'making friendship impure' – to draw on the title of Coleman's (2010) recent reflections on the anthropology of friendship.

When I first met Julien, a Canadian teenager, he had only a few days left before returning to Canada from his month-long holiday in Cuba and was very eager to talk to me about his experiences on the island, particularly his relationships with Cuban people. One of the first things he told me was that he had mismanaged his holiday budget, and after a couple of weeks of excessive spending had had to rely – to get by – on the generosity of Cuban people and friends who recognized his predicament: his 'being like them', as he put it, 'having nothing'. Of the many Cubans he had known, including several in the Rasta circle I also knew, those who had been generous to him – occasionally offering a drink or some food – and not treated him as a privileged tourist, were the ones he considered his friends. Such acts of generosity had 'warmed his heart' (*chauffé le cœur*), and made him want to give back and reciprocate.

After several disappointing encounters with 'cheaters' and *jineteros* earlier in his journey, Julien had managed to discover 'more authentic relationships' and what he called 'intimacy': the fact of 'feeling good with somebody' (*être bien avec une personne*). This, he argued, is what created friendship: affinities certainly played a role, but intimacy too, the fact of being together, of feeling 'just good' (*d'être juste bien, d'être bien dans sa peau*). Julien's view hinted at all the affective, preconceptual and therefore difficult-to-rationalize dimensions of feeling in relations with others. Such feelings and intensities of affect, hardly verbalized, certainly played a key role in the emergence of friendships between tourists and Cubans. Several visitors I met, for instance, told me they relied on their intuition, their feelings and their 'sense' of a person when deciphering the other's intentions. This in turn informed their judgement about whether it was worth getting along with them, spending time together and crediting the Cubans' professions of friendship.

As we continued discussing his friendships with Cuban people, Julien also recognized that however good and gratifying these had been, they were not like those he had back home, which were of a more 'intimate-intimate' kind. In Cuba they were slightly special friendships (*une amitié un peu spéciale*). We may recall here Santos-Granero's (2007: 10) remark that 'friendships emerge in particular circumstances or social situations' that inform their qualities. In Julien's formulation, it was precisely these (long neglected) 'situational elements of friendship' (Suttles 1970, quoted in Santos-Granero 2007: 10) that had salience. For the young Canadian, the relationships he had managed to establish with Cuban people could hardly be completely disinterested, given that even when people did appreciate you – as opposed to just being interested in your cash – they still 'had nothing' (*ils n'ont rien*), so you were expected to pay for them.

Working over his experiences and notions of friendship, and being encouraged to reflect on them in the course of our conversation, Julien progressively managed to soften the overarching tension between 'interest' and 'affection', between 'instrumental economic relationships' and 'friendship' that traversed so many of the relationships tourists had with Cuban people. From in-depth discussions like the one I had with Julien it was clear that, far from being fixed and impermeable, notions of friendship could also be reformulated in direct response to specific features of touristic encounters, more particularly their asymmetric character. Accordingly, a degree of short-term interest and economic instrumentality could be internalized in renewed views of friendship, reconciling the 'hostile worlds' of intimacy and economy even more broadly.

Mark, a British independent traveller in his thirties, reflected on the encounters that he and his brother had with Cuban people and on the role that money played in them:

> Eventually we understood that, it wasn't incompatible that someone could be trying to use you, to get money from you but also, really, genuinely were interested in trying to meet you. But by necessity they have to do both, you know ... After the initial disappointment finding that out [referring to the instrumental aspect of relationships], we began to understand that it wasn't incompatible with also wanting to be our friends.

Here, Cubans' desires to improve their economic conditions and their willingness to befriend tourists were integrated into a single dynamic. Instead of relying on a '(false) friendly front' / '(real) instrumental back' approach, Mark dissolved the dichotomy, opening up and reworking his notion of friendship. Possible overlaps between an idiom of economic instrumentality and one of friendship were thus taken into consideration. This may be apprehended as a way for Mark to preserve the impression of having built meaningful, intimate, friendly relations with Cuban people – people who had nevertheless also showed an interest in his economic resources – and therefore a way for him to keep the promise of positive touristic encounters in Cuba alive. While this may well be the case, I do not think Mark's insights on his relationships with Cubans should be reduced to this interpretation alone, a view that risks dismissing his reasoning as a simple self-delusion regarding what his relationship with Cuban people was 'really' about. Such a univocal and somewhat cynical reading neglects the possibility that new relational formations and notions of friendship emerge out of the touristic encounter, and more generally discredits their generative potential and transformative effects.

In Mark's view, the fundamental asymmetry of economic resources between him and his brother on the one hand, and their Cuban friends on the other, normalized relationships where interests and instrumentality went hand in hand with emotional involvement and even friendship. A degree of instrumentality was therefore included as a legitimate possibility within a contextualized notion of friendship that took into account the asymmetric status of the partners involved and their different socio-economic positioning in an unequal world, thus indexing, transforming and adapting this relational idiom to the local conditions of interaction and the positionalities at stake. Shifting to a slightly different line of argumentation to account for similar ambiguities in their relationships with Cuban people, Johnny and Sarah – two independent travellers from the United States who had spent a month cycling across Cuba – concluded that relationships themselves, in general, were hardly conceivable without some kind of interests moving the parties involved. With this conceptual move, the two outlined a more universalist theory of sociality.

Delimiting Friendship: Charity and Market Exchanges

Whereas notions of friendship could be stretched and reformulated to include some degree of economic interest and instrumentality, there were also instances in which more narrowly drawn limits of this relational idiom led the protagonists involved to redefine their relationship as different from friendship. For instance, this could occur when tourists felt that their Cuban friends' requests were becoming too insistent, giving the impression that this was the only motive behind their relationship. When a call for help became a persistent plea, magnifying the tourists' economic power and belittling the Cubans' agency, relationships could start to align with idioms of charity and paternalism, leading the protagonists involved to requalify the moral grounds of their connections accordingly. This seems to indicate that if people could accommodate a certain degree of asymmetry in their notions of friendship, the relation took other connotations when inequalities took centre stage.[7] Charity and paternalism stressed the very asymmetries and inequalities that friendship strove to downplay, thus anchoring obligations on a different moral ground. Beyond friendship, people could then take on the dyadic subject positions of destitute beneficiary and powerful benefactor (see Simoni 2015b).

In the moments preceding the tourists' departure, Cubans' efforts to arouse notions of help and gift giving in relationships framed as friendship could become all the more explicit, insistent and therefore also more problematic. This was when the tourists' attention might be drawn to the exceptional things they had been able to do, thanks to the help and guidance of their Cuban companion. Only with the benefit of such guidance, the story would go, had visitors discovered the secrets of a Cuba normally inaccessible to foreigners: a more real, safer, cheaper Cuba. Pushing relationships beyond the realm of friendship, these discourses could ultimately result in the objectification and commoditization of acts of assistance such as guiding, with the pricing of a service and establishment of monetary equivalence being the ultimate step in this direction. This could move people away from the relational idiom of friendship and its moral demands, and bring instead into the picture the norms and expectations governing market exchanges. In a way, and building on the previous chapter on cigar deals, we could argue that here we come full circle, as friendships transformed into deals, and friends became buyers and sellers.

Universalizing Friendship: Resistances, Aspirations and Calls for Recognition

Notwithstanding the more radical shifts from friendship to other relational idioms, such as charity and market exchange, the material analysed earlier in this chapter may suggest that what was emerging in touristic Cuba was an essentially 'hybrid' version of the allegedly Western, purified model of friendship as a voluntary, disinterested affective engagement between autonomous individuals (Carrier 1999), a mixed form in which economic interest, intimacy and emotional attachment could easily intermingle. Julien's and Mark's nuanced takes on friendship, for instance, accounted for its peculiar expressions in Cuba's tourism realm and resonate with recent anthropological writings on friendship (Simoni 2014b) that urge us to move beyond purified and idealized approaches to uncover its variegated expressions in different ethnographic locales.[8] What should be noted here, however, is that these hybrid takes on relationships – like all hybrids, for that matter (Latour 2005; Palmié 2013) – still safeguarded, and were predicated on, the idea of pure relationships, projecting the latter elsewhere (back home, in Julien's case) and securing it at least at the level of a normative ideal.[9] What is more, these 'impure' (Coleman 2010) approaches to friendship could also encounter resistance from self-professed Cuban friends who were unwilling to subscribe to any sort of hybrid 'compromise' (Nachi 2004a, 2004b; Boltanski and Thévenot 2006 [1991]).

A first illustration of resistance to an 'impure' view of friendship – the view of the ethnographer, in this case – is evident in the offended reaction of Pablo (a self-professed friend with whom I spent a couple of afternoons in Havana) to my provocative allusion to the commission he was likely to gain on the drinks I had just bought for us. On this occasion, he and his friend Augusto had insisted on drinking mojitos, the cocktail on which, I had been told, the gain was highest. Aware of the sensitivity of this issue, and of the awkwardness of discussing tricks that foreigners were not supposed to know with Pablo, I quickly added that I did not really care if making some money was part of his agenda and that this would not jeopardize our friendship, trying to show understanding and even admiration for his tactics of gaining hard currency from foreigners like me. In a quite outraged and emotional denial, Pablo retorted that he valued friendship and *el corazón* (the heart) well above money, that by so doing he now had friends all around the world, and that he would not risk ruining our friendship just for a commission of one or two pesos.

Why was Pablo's reaction so adamant? Why did he judge my intimation as such an offense? These questions kept puzzling me as I tried to make sense of this awkward moment. Part of the explanation may lie in the inextricable relation between forms of intimacy and sense of self, in which the former can easily become the measure of the latter so that, as Povinelli (2002: 231) eloquently puts it, 'challenges to intimacy seriously threaten the modes of attachment the subject has to herself and others, and thus challenge the basis of social coherence'. Following Povinelli (2006: 208), we may argue that my move to frame our relationship as a hybrid – a mix of interest and affect, informed by structural inequalities – relegated Pablo to a 'genealogical society' made of socially determined subjects, the 'mirror image' and 'contrasting evil' (199) of another, more valued way of being in the world, namely, that of the modern autological subject freed from societal constraints.[10] Demanding that he occupy such a position could therefore imply marking a 'geographical and civilizational difference' (200) between us. By frustrating his claim to a pure friendship, I was, in a sense, depicting his social status in comparison to mine as inescapably constrained by his societal context, as 'a form of bondage' (Povinelli 2006: 191) that determined his actions and the subject position available to him.

Countering this frame of legibility were the following remarks that I repeatedly heard Cubans address to their tourist friends and partners: 'For me you are not a tourist. You are a person, a human being!' (*Tú para mí no eres un turista. ¡Tú eres una persona, un ser humano!*). Here the stress was on grounding relationships in the fundamental commonality of the people involved: rather than being dichotomously catalogued, differentiated and targeted on the base of their assumed privileged status and the asymmetry of their resources, tourists deserved to be recognized, understood and treated as persons and human beings with all their peculiarities, idiosyncrasies, unique circumstances and ways of being. Here we can hear echoes of Ernesto's warning not to treat tourists as stupid rich *bobos* (see chapter 4).

This, of course, was also a call for tourists to reciprocate by doing the same with their Cuban friends, as opposed to confining them to the realm of *jineterismo* and *jinetero/a* identifications. The moral demand at stake was for tourists to step out of a world governed by structural inequalities, where interpretations of each other's behaviour were based on inescapable instrumentality, and commit themselves to fully fledged friendships that would respect the integrity and sheer complexity of the other and avoid reducing him or her to a type, a 'summative account' or 'partial representation' and illustration of a more general pattern (Throop 2014: 72, 75). The Cubans' summoning of this ideal idiom of relationality can thus be read as a call for openness, for partaking in a world yet unwritten and unscripted, full of generative potential for ways of being and doing things together.

'You don't understand Cuban people!' (*¡Tú no entiendes a los cubanos!*) was a recurrent reply to tourists' insinuations of hidden instrumental behaviours and multipurpose friendships. Tourists could see this complaint as yet another deceptive, *jinetero*-style self-victimizing manoeuvre to elicit foreigners' guilt, compassion and help. However, these dejected claims of a lack of empathy also call for a more empathetic understanding of their emotional and moral foundations (Hollan 2008; Hollan and Throop 2008). Reflecting that 'empathy is never an all or nothing affair', Throop (2010: 772) has recently argued that 'it is possible to see that, in some cases, it is precisely experiences of misunderstanding that potentiate possibilities for new horizons of mutual understanding to arise, even if fleetingly so'. Foreigners in Cuba, including myself, were encouraged to explore precisely these possibilities for new understanding, following the Cubans' resistance to our interpretations.

This led me to recognize that to imply an inevitable horizon of self-interestedness in their professed friendship, and to force this interpretation on them, was to deny them the possibility, or at least the aspiration, of becoming 'free', 'autonomous' moral subjects of a fully fledged 'pure' friendship characterized by 'spontaneous and unconstrained sentiment' (Coleman 2010: 200).[11] Several of my research participants assumed that such friendship would prevail under the 'normal' conditions of existence to which they aspired, as opposed to the context of exceptional and enduring crisis, scarcity and isolation they associated with Cuba, which many wished to overcome.[12] This was Ernesto's assumption as he reflected on the difference between friendship in touristic Cuba and friendship 'over there' (*allá*), in the tourists' countries of residence:

> It would be great if things here could be like over there, with higher salaries, and one could just go out simply to get to know people, to enjoy oneself, to make some friends just for fun and not for money, out of necessity. If one did not need to go and look for friendship (*que uno no tuviera que ir a buscar una amistad*), if it would be just like over there, normal.

During fieldwork I came across several other evocations of the normality of a friendship. For instance, when I met again with Marcos (a Rasta in his forties) a year after our first encounter in 2010, he was quick to reassure Ernesto (with whom I was hanging out at the time) that we were good friends and there was nothing to worry about: 'He is a friend of mine, normal. I am not looking for money, nor is it for interest or anything like that. I'm not in any trouble of the sort. Just friend, normal!' (*Él es amigo mío, normal. No estoy buscando dinero, ni por interés ni nada. No estoy metido en líos. ¡Amigo, normal!*). Marcos then went on to exemplify the normality of our friendship by inviting me to drink from a bottle of good rum he had just bought. 'When I have it, I give it to you. If I need something, I will just ask you. With no trouble, no complications (*Sin lío, sin cráneo*)'. Marcos was stressing that our relationship was one of total transparency and a generalized kind of reciprocity, and that nothing was hidden or suspicious: this was just how relations between friends were normally supposed to function.

Cubans who were unable to share with tourists as Marcos had done could feel uncomfortable about visitors always paying for them. Such was the case of Carlos, a man from Viñales in his late thirties, who poignantly shared with me his shame, sorrow and frustration (*me da pena*) at not being able to reciprocate tourists' invitations to dine, drink or enter a club. The awkward feeling of being seen as a burden, as yet another *jinetero*, occasionally led him to retreat into his house and avoid going out altogether. Carlos also contrasted the righteousness of his attitude with that of 'other' Cuban people who 'just wanted the tourists' money' and were only looking for 'interested friendships' (*amistad por interés*): they did not care about more noble and virtuous feelings or long-lasting relationships. Here again, as in the case of Emilio (chapter 2), was the critique of the generalization and increasing predominance of *relaciones de interés* in contemporary Cuba.

Deploring Cuba's exceptional circumstances, Ernesto, like Marcos, maintained that the aspiration to 'normal' relationships guided his very way of dealing with tourists, which he contrasted with that of other Cubans. Interesting in this respect were his considerations about *jineterismo* as a form of work, *un trabajo*, which came up as we discussed *jineteras* and the paradoxes of an activity that caused women to go out to discos and 'fun places' to meet tourists but also restrained the fun they could have had there. Ernesto explained that *jineteras* tended to resist the temptation to drink too much alcohol on nights out chasing tourists, preferring to keep control of the situation and avoid losing sight of their main objective – which, according to him, was to pick up a foreign partner and make some cash. '*Están trabajando*', they are working, he told me, 'they need to keep the control, have their objective there' (*necesitan el control, tener el objetivo allí*).

Reflecting on his own engagements with tourists, Ernesto then went on to admit that 'I could also say I am working'. However, he insisted, his way of working was based on friendship and sentiments ('*Trabajando, pero a base de la amistad, de los sentimientos*'). Outlining his own version of 'emotional labor' (Hochschild 1983; Cabezas 2006, 2009; see also Allen's [2007] 'play-labor'), Ernesto explained that for him, this way of working was more rewarding than other, *jinetero*-like methods: 'I could also work in a drier way (*de manera mas seca*), just to make money, talking rubbish (*dando muela*) about any topic, but I don't feel good doing that', he argued. On several occasions, he emphasized that he regarded feeling good, enjoying himself and being gratified in relations with tourists as essential. This was why he valued love and friendship so much, seeing them as the preferred way of bonding with foreigners.

By insisting on their commitment to – or at least their human potential and aspiration to engage in – disinterested, sentiment-based friendship, Cubans like Pablo, Ernesto, Carlos and Marcos were striving to align their moral selves with those of their tourist friends and thus lay claim to the possibility of being together in a shared social world (Ferguson 2006).[13] Criticizing Cuba as a dysfunctional place where 'normal' relationships could hardly be found, this cosmopolitan approach shifted the ideal grounds of belonging, and the related standards by which one's moral worth was to be assessed, from Cuba to the wider world, if only on a virtual level. Many of my Cuban interlocutors spent most of their days trying to interact with tourists, and it was also in relation to this foreign world that they constantly measured each other, judging, comparing and deliberating on their ability to understand and engage with foreigners on the same moral grounds, according to universal relational ideals. In some cases, expressions of dissatisfaction with everything Cuban and obsession with the foreign and with moving abroad, prompted comments that the person was already – in terms of mindset, at least – more 'there' than 'here' (Simoni 2015c).

Casting true friendship as a universally valued relational idiom and presenting it as something everyone should cherish, was also a way of inciting one's tourist companions to live up to this virtuous model and inspiring them to treat each other as this exemplary form of bonding demanded. As such, the world to be shared with foreigners was not only a sought-after ideal at a moral level, for instance in terms of one's values and emotional interiority, but was also a more concrete aspiration that friendship could address, eventually helping Cubans to get closer to the normality they associated with life abroad. In their attempts to cement strong, intense bonds with visitors, my Cuban research participants were also entangling tourists in the moral imperatives that came with fully fledged, uncompromising friendship. Itself an 'ethical demand' (Zigon 2009, 2010), friendship – much like love (Zigon 2013) – called for a certain commitment and continuity in relationships. It gave rise to a range of responsibilities that demanded adequate response from the partners involved. The responsibilities tourists felt towards their Cuban friends could ultimately help the latter realize other socio-economic aspirations too: never again having to worry about being left in need with no one to turn to, or perhaps even being able to travel abroad thanks to a foreign friend. By helping Cubans in this way, tourists could thereby effect a more tangible narrowing of inequalities too. In any case, what seemed vital to the preservation of the moral configuration on which such relationships were grounded was that these obligations and responsibilities be formulated and experienced not as friendship's defining motive, but rather as a simply 'normal', sentiment-driven outcome of it. In other words, the ideal of friendship in play here required that things be simply shared among friends, with all material exchanges escaping, and even standing in opposition to, any notion of interest and calculation.

As our friendship grew stronger through the years, Carlos also became more confident in talking explicitly about the expectation of mutual assistance between friends. He no longer worried that this explicitness would jeopardize the well-established and primarily sentimental foundations of our relationship, which called now for total transparency and openness.[14] This is how, in January 2011, five years after we first met, he introduced me to one of his Cuban acquaintances: 'Hey, no kidding. Valerio: it's ages I know him, my buddy (*mi socio*), my good friend. Look [in a more boastful tone] if I write to him, and I say: "Look, Valerio, I need such and such, this amount of money", he just sends it here, straight away, there's no messing around.' 'Sure, that's what a real friend should be there for [i.e., to help when needed]', replied the other.

Along similar lines, the refrain '*quien tiene un amigo tiene un tesoro*' (he/ she who has a friend has a treasure) was the grounds for Ernesto's explanation that even if his way of dealing with tourists did not provide him with much, all the 'true friendships' he was developing ensured he would never be left alone in need. One evening, he offered me the vintage Russian watch he always wore, as a present. I could not accept it. I told him I did not use watches and he needed it more than I did. When I enquired where it had come from, he explained that it was a present from a friend two years earlier: 'But this happens, it's okay, one can pass it on to another friend. What you cannot do, is that you give me something as a present, and I sell it. That is when you move from friendship to the economy, and therefore you move to a much lower level (*entonces allí ya pasas de la amistad a la economía, ya pasas a un nivel mucho mas bajo*)'. Here Ernesto was articulating a view much in line with Zelizer's (2005) conceptualization of a 'hostile worlds' perspective of the intimacy and economy dialectic, reasserting his opinion that a sentiment-based friendship had much more value, and was at a higher level morally, than an economic relationship.

While reflecting on friendship, people like Ernesto were therefore also working over notions of economic exchange, gift giving and reciprocity in friendship's wake. This was evident in the course of an insightful conversation with Luis, a resident of Viñales in his forties who engaged regularly with foreign visitors. While telling me about his expectations regarding tourist friends' gifts, he started complaining about foreigners leaving behind their 'leftovers' (*sobras*), such as a used, unwanted old T-shirt, as presents. Luis made it clear that for him, a friend's gift could not be an act of charity. Instead, such gifts had to come from a genuine willingness to offer and share something that the tourists themselves valued. He then stressed that unlike 'most Cuban people', he was unwilling to accept any sort of present from a visitor. As he put it, he had his own 'ethical principles', 'human qualities' and 'aspirations', to which he would never defer just for *interés*.[15]

Conclusion

In this chapter I have discussed a range of situations in which friendliness and friendship were brought into play to frame informal encounters between tourists and Cubans. A recurrent feature running through these diverse enactments was friendship's tension with notions of economic instrumentality. Friendship was thus evoked and exemplified in opposition to conceptions of self-interest, and contrasted with the 'cash-mediated forms of sociality' (Palmié 2004: 243) typical of *jineterismo*. In this sense, professions of friendliness and friendship, and the related efforts to flesh out these forms of engagement, enabled some Cubans to distance themselves from the spectre of tourism hustling that haunted most of their interactions with tourists.

The opposition between friends and hustlers led to the emergence of very loose and 'thin' enactments of friendship, relationships for which the terms acquaintance and companionship may seem preferable. This may exemplify what has been called the 'interstitiality, flexibility [and] adaptiveness' of friendship that give it the potential to domesticate 'strangerhood or potential enmity', and 'form ties where either no or radically different relations may be expected' (Coleman 2010: 202). Differences between tourists emerged, revealing how far one was willing to adapt and transform his or her assumptions about friendship. Much like the Brazilian immigrants to Portugal with whom Torresan (2011: 246) worked, several tourists I met had learned that 'as a foreigner' one 'had to be more flexible in [one's] view of what constituted friendship, of what [one] could expect from friends, and how [one] would behave as a friend', and that there could be different 'strengths' and 'levels' of friendship. Julien's remarks on his 'special', 'less intimate' friendships with Cuban people clearly bear this out.

In touristic Cuba, the idiom of friendship could promote mutual and reciprocal help in a relationship, calling for moral responsibility and commitment in ways that acquaintance and companionship did not. It encouraged continuity in relationships, projecting them in the long term and opening up further opportunities to realize one's aspirations, as hinted by Gerardo's hope that he might one day be able to visit his friend Alejandro in Mexico. Gerardo and Alejandro's example also showed that from the point of view of tourists, there was no need to adhere to Cuban's professions of friendship – or to question them. The value of getting along with a Cuban friend could also be assessed in the light of other relational idioms, like that of economic instrumentality. Loose, sketchy enactments of friendship could remain ambiguous yet still satisfy both parties, leading them to avoid controversy over the validity of the relational claims at stake.

In the light of these reflections, we may also note that what mattered most to tourists was their Cuban friend's trustworthiness. The possibility of trusting each other was a key aspect traversing the various examples discussed here. As the case of Alejandro and Gerardo suggests, trust was a quality that was not tied to a single relational idiom but easily travelled from one to another. But whereas friendship may have implied trust, trust alone was not sufficient to bring about friendship. While Alejandro was content to trust Gerardo and felt no need to articulate their relationship as friendship, other tourists I met in Cuba cherished the idea of making friends with locals. In these cases more demanding, 'thicker' enactments of friendship also had salience, and the relatively short time frame of relationships became more problematic, calling for the intensification and amplification of 'memorable experiences' (Mattingly 2010), such as invitations to the Cuban partner's home and the sharing of domestic intimacy. Beyond proofs of honesty, the generosity and selflessness of people's engagements were deemed essential to fleshing out friendship and substantiating one's claims to it. This is also what led to the reflexive unpacking of ideals of friendship, and closer scrutiny of each other's assumptions on the matter.

Accordingly, I have highlighted how tourists and Cubans (re)formulated their views of friendship in the light of the touristic encounter. Normative ideals of friendship could be worked over and adapted to account for the striking economic asymmetries that characterized this peculiar realm of interaction. Within limits that I have also pointed out – such as when relationships shifted towards charity and market exchanges – a degree of interestedness and calculation could be internalized within situated and particularized notions of friendship. Similar processes of adaptation and transformation of relational idioms appear in the following chapters, which consider partying, seducing and sexual relations, and more broadly exemplify touristic encounters' potential to transform people's views on relationships. But while notions of friendship could be made more 'impure' (Coleman 2010), I have also highlighted equally transformative moves towards 'purification' and 'normalization' that people like Pablo, Ernesto, Carlos, Marcos and Luis made when reflecting on their friendships with tourists and outlining their moral dispositions and aspirations on the matter. These calls for recognition gain critical importance when we heed Moore's (2011: 10) advice to take 'the aspirational character of our relations to others' seriously, and to pay attention to our research participants' interest 'in creating new connections, new meanings, novel forms of relation' (9). In this light, Cubans' universalist formulations of friendship may be read as attempts to open up new realms of possibility in their relationships with tourists, escape the reductive typifications of the tourist/*jinetero/a* dyad, and unlock other horizons of becoming by imagining common trajectories for the future.

Chapter 7
PARTYING AND SEDUCING

In this chapter I look at the relational idioms of partying, aiming to explore its potential to open up possibilities in touristic encounters and induce states of being whereby positive feelings, sensations and the pursuit of pleasure lead people to let go and give in to seduction. In the festive arenas that took shape in the realm of tourism in Cuba, partying and seducing could easily converge and constitute a continuum, but they could also bifurcate and diverge as boundaries between them were drawn. This examination of how these continuities and discontinuities arose will highlight their consequences for the development of relationships between tourists and Cubans.

The outline of the recent history and imaginaries of tourism in Cuba, presented in chapter 1, has already shown that partying was one of the key promises luring visitors to this Caribbean country. Partying and dancing, exuberance and passion, sensuality and sexuality: these were among the tropes and semantic continuities that helped project Cuba onto the international tourism stage. Invitations to take part in parties and festivals were also a common way for Cuban men and women to get in touch and initiate interaction with foreign tourists (see chapter 4). But what sorts of relationships would then ensue? Tourists and Cubans certainly held a variety of assumptions about what partying could and ought to be about. While such diversity is itself worthy of attention, my goal here is not to inventory partying scenarios. Instead, in what follows I consider some recurrent features that seemed to traverse a wide range of festive situations. My focus is on playful and hedonistic states of being: how these states were brought about, what they afforded, and what their limits were. I devote additional scrutiny to two of the central, often interrelated ingredients of partying in touristic Cuba, namely, indulgent consumption – especially of alcohol – and dancing.

An analysis of such festive states cannot confine itself to the realm of discourses and ideas, but needs to delve deeper into the embodied, affective, sensuous fabric of partying itself. This was indeed a realm in which experiential states – what we may refer to as party feelings, vitalities and 'vibes', for instance – were brought to the fore. Recent research on tourism (e.g. Franklin and Crang 2001, Fullagar 2001, Little 2005, Picard and Robinson 2012, Selänniemi 2003, Simoni 2012b, Veijola and Jokinen 1994) has emphasized the importance of considering aspects of the tourist experience that cannot be reduced to the verbal and the interpretive. Here I build on this body of work to probe and specify some of the experiences, expressions and implications of partying in touristic Cuba. Attending to the embodied and affective dimension of partying and seduction, I also take heed of Moore's (2011: 198) insights on contemporary theories of affect, which temper the notion of its 'absolute autonomy' and recognize that while the 'reinstatement of somatic engagement in the world' is in itself a very important analytical move, it is not one that is 'historically or culturally neutral' (203). This, in turn, requires us 'to take other people's theories of affect … into account' (203). Thus I also aim to draw attention to tourists' and Cubans' notions of, and dispositions towards, affect and feeling – to their convergences and divergences, frictions and transformations, and purposive and tactical deployments.

Methodologically, new challenges arise when we move beyond practices, discourses and rationalizations, which may be easier to follow and pinpoint, and into the exploration of states of being, feelings that, in the view of my interlocutors, often refracted and stood in open opposition to reflective reasoning and sober rationalization. To account for these feelings and 'vibes', my ethnography will have to rely also on tentative evocations, intuitive approaches, and first-hand impressions.

Opening Up Possibilities: Tourism and Cuba as Partying

Several of my Cuban interlocutors referred explicitly to the importance of getting tourists into a 'party mood'. For Fernando, *irse de fiesta* (going out to party) signalled a key turn in his interactions with tourists and was a top priority. Once partying was in the works, 'That's it (*ya*)!' he told me, implying that relationships were likely to become increasingly smooth and gratifying: tourists would leave worries behind and become more affable and easy to deal with. A range of opportunities could open up, enabling people like Fernando to have fun and develop rewarding relationships. But what did partying mean to Fernando and other Cubans engaging informally with tourists? When would they consider a *fiesta* to have materialized? Even though there was hardly any clear threshold marking a party's beginning, people nevertheless tended to equate certain conditions with a festive state of having fun and pleasure.

Countless experiences of *irse de fiesta*, particularly in the company of young Cuban men and fellow tourists, showed me that music and alcohol were key ingredients in bringing about a festive atmosphere. Cubans' exhortations to party often went hand in hand with the suggestion to 'buy a bottle' (*comprar una botella*), generally of rum. *Comprar una botella* meant that people were up for sharing drinks and getting into a party mood, leaving other agendas and preoccupations behind. A wide range of bottles were available for purchase, and their rankings in brand name and quality could indicate what sort of party we were talking about and how much cash was available for it. Explicit mention of what the party ought to be about tended to happen when Cubans noticed tourists' reluctance to go with the flow, so to speak. Prescriptive suggestions could easily emerge to confront such restraint by encouraging visitors to enjoy themselves and indulge in pleasure.

The assumption here was that tourists were in Cuba to enjoy themselves: '*¡hay que disfrutar!* (enjoy!), was the widespread encouragement. Visitors were urged to enjoy and indulge themselves, following the notion that this was what tourism was all about. This attitude called forth the trope of tourism as the pursuit of pleasure. Incitements to party and have fun also relied on implicit assumptions about what fun and pleasure were all about, and how they ought to take shape. As the refrain of a song often played for tourists put it, '*¡La vida es un carnaval!* (Life is a carnival!). Partying was dancing, indulging in pleasures, intoxication and immoderate consumption of food and drink. I became familiar with these notions, which the Cubans I met regularly drew upon and prescribed to their tourist companions.

A culturalist/nationalist flavour could also be added to these exhortations, for instance invoking Cuba as the perfect place for enjoyment and indulgence: '*¡En Cuba todo es posible!* (In Cuba everything is possible!), especially for tourists who had the means for it. Echoed here were the promises of Cuba as 'paradise island' (Schwartz 1999), a land of endless opportunities for pleasure, where music was everywhere, everyone loved to dance, people were hot and eroticism, sensuality and sexual fulfilment were at their best, always accessible and around the corner. '*¡La vida es una sola!* (There is only one life!) 'Party and enjoy since you are on holiday! Since you are in Cuba and this is what Cuba is about!' Such instigations were legion among Cubans who wanted tourists to let go. They were geared at triggering a party mood, bringing about euphoria and excitement, and opening up possibilities.

Exhortations to party, have fun and indulge in pleasure could then result in playful 'whirls' (Caillois 2001 [1958]) of hedonistic consumption and gratification. I witnessed these festive happenings during my afternoons with groups of male tourists and their Cuban partners at the beach of Santa Maria, or in evenings spent in the streets of Havana with young backpackers and their Rasta companions. In spite of their differences, such contrasting occasions could give rise to similarly euphoric and electrifying moments as people found themselves in a rapturously cheerful mood. Ludic sociabilities materialized via the telling of jokes, singing, dancing, clapping, handshaking, hugging, embracing, raising glasses, drinking a toast. The atmosphere of elation during these events could be extended and amplified by ordering new drinks, buying new bottles and making sure no one's glass was ever empty. To keep spirits high, people might start fantasizing about where to go next, which was the most promising venue that night, what drugs to obtain, and so on.

Sensuality and sexual arousal likewise played a key role in the materialization of festive happenings. In Santa Maria, for instance – and here I am referring mainly to interactions involving male tourists – conversations about where and when to meet 'girls', and how many, could help bring about a sense of building exhilaration. When a tourist was already in the company of a Cuban partner, their sensual pleasure and excitement played out in reciprocal caresses, touching and kissing. The sharing of exciting stories; the gazing, touching and feeling of bodies; the sensuality of music and dance; the consumption of food, drinks and drugs – all these elements could intertwine to arouse anticipation and desire, bringing about a party mood and what we may conceptualize as quintessential 'liminoid' states of being (see Graburn 1983, Selänniemi 2003, Turner 1977). I will revisit these embodied dimensions of festivity when turning to the specific example of dancing, its physicality and the sensuality it afforded. But first I will more closely consider indulgent consumption as a key dimension of partying in touristic Cuba and as one of its main hindrances as well. By looking at how partying and indulgent consumption could go hand in hand and co-constitute each other but also collide and generate controversy, we can unpack some of the relational implications of partying itself, as well as some of its limits.

Indulgent Consumption: Letting Go / Setting Limits

Drinks, food and, less often, other drugs like marijuana and cocaine played an important role in the materialization of festive states in touristic Cuba. Cubans who took it as their task to get tourists into a party mood commonly suggested a *sitio* (venue) where people would be able to indulge in such products. Once there, the Cubans would willingly take on the role of hosts (or second-order hosts), mediating between tourists and bartenders, waiters, cashiers and other gatekeepers of goods and services. Their mediation could help keep the tourists 'high' (Graburn 1978 [1977], 2001) and minimize potential disruptions to their good time and euphoria, such as having to consult a map to know where to go, finding out how to get a drink, queuing to place orders, checking menus, prices and bills, and so on. However, for these mediations to happen smoothly, tourists had to trust their Cuban companions and let them guide them, handle their money, and so forth. Regarding payments, for instance, tourists could provide the money while the Cubans took charge of the transactions, making sure the staff did not cheat them on the bill (a rather common scenario). The visibility of monetary transactions tended to be downplayed on these occasions; money itself ideally lost importance altogether. With the imperative of having fun, of indulging in the pleasures and enjoyments that made for a 'proper' holiday, came the idea of forgetting – at least in the extraordinary frame of such festive *communitas* (Turner 1977) – prices and calculations. There was no reason to spoil the enjoyment by being trivial and obsessed with money; one should instead be 'king for a day' (Gottlieb 1982): such were the rationales that could emerge on these occasions.

Festive happenings in full swing as tourist-sponsored drinks and food flowed, particularly in open-air settings, could also attract people from the immediate surroundings who might take a chance on joining in. The newly arrived would cheerfully stretch out glasses to be filled, drink toasts with those already involved, hugging them, shaking hands and blending into the atmosphere of fun, hedonism and playfulness. But at this point tensions could also arise and boundaries materialize, leading doubtful participants, most notably the paying tourists, to wonder about the relational idiom at stake. Who is at this party? Who is in the group? Who is in charge? Is this a happening where nothing matters but fun and pleasure, or are there other motives involved? Is someone, for instance, profiting from the tourists' generous sponsoring? Such questions could emerge and shatter the party vibe, raising doubts about people's intentionality and motives, and about the status of participants and their relationships.

People's concerns expressed a tension between instrumental and non-instrumental engagements, and seemed to rely on the ideal of partying and play as non-utilitarian activities (see Huizinga 1950 and Lett 1983). The suspicion that someone could just pretend to be cheerfully enjoying the event while actually having other agendas in mind could be particularly destabilizing for tourists. In an especially daunting scenario, Cubans could be thought to be working to intoxicate visitors with drinks or other drugs to profit from them by gaining commissions on the things purchased, inviting other Cuban friends to join in at the tourists' expense, and ultimately trying to get hold of their money and valuables. The emergence of these preoccupations could lead tourists from euphoria to anxiety and the fear of losing control in the face of mischievous, calculating hustlers – in other words, from festive *communitas* among equals to a sense of unequal instrumental relationships and exploitation. Once such doubts had arisen on these occasions, we may also argue that tourists were passing over their Cuban companions' exhortations to forget about worries and calculations. Now stepping out of a festive frame, they were outlining the very limits that notions of partying as a realm of endless possibilities strove to overcome.

Continuing my exploration of the elusive frontiers of having fun in touristic Cuba, I will now consider in detail another recurrent ingredient of these festive engagements: dancing.

Dancing Relations: Getting Into the Flow?

On the beach in Santa Maria, live music and dancing were instrumental in bringing about a festive, euphoric atmosphere. The performances of itinerant musicians helped create happenings that attracted people from the immediate surroundings, encouraging participation in the event. Mingling together, tourists and Cubans would sing along and clap their hands to the beat in a contagious festive mood. Cuban women eager to catch tourists' attention could make the most of their revealing beach outfits by engaging in sensuous dance moves that, notwithstanding the enjoyment they could provide to the women themselves, were also designed to charm, seduce and tantalize members of the foreign male audience, who were also expected to react to the cheerful smiles and piercing glances these dancers sent their way. These moments were generally short-lived, but they could lead to other festive developments and flirtatious interactions.

Apart from these kinds of occasional, spontaneous happenings, bars, clubs and discos were venues where, throughout the night, dancing became increasingly important in shaping relationships between tourists and Cubans. These places suggested dancing – indeed, almost prescribed it – as the main form of engagement, and Cubans willing to establish contact were keen on encouraging tourists to get involved and join them on the dance floor. An invitation to dance, or 'the dancing of the tourist' (*bailárselo*), whereby the tourist became the explicit object of the dance, was a favoured tactic for getting in touch with foreigners, a classic *entrada*. While some visitors would happily accept such invitations, others were more reluctant to do so but could also, feeling uneasy about declining a polite invitation, make excuses or use delaying tactics: 'I am not good at dancing', 'maybe later', 'perhaps after a few more drinks'.

Saying one did not know how to dance could easily turn out to be the worst excuse for turning down an invitation. Indeed, this lack of knowledge was often recast as further reason to get involved. The Cuban partner would take on the role of expert, occasionally the 'salsa teacher', urging the tourist to be his or her pupil, be it only for a couple of songs: 'You can't dance salsa?

No problem: I will teach you! You just follow me!' Luring tourists into the dance, Cubans could also invoke the admiration this experience would bring tourists back home: 'Imagine, once you come back [to your country], you will be able to impress all your friends with your dancing!' These remarks tapped into the ideal of tourism as a transformative experience, a learning and status-enhancing process, and could strike the right note among visitors.

Another, interrelated argument frequently employed to convince reticent tourists to dance was that tourists 'had to' give in to this quintessentially Cuban custom. Here again, we find the normative view of tourism as a process of discovering and fully experiencing the Other. Such exhortations as 'Everyone has to dance in Cuba!', 'You cannot come to Cuba and not try to dance!', or 'This is part of the Cuban experience!' predominated. The next challenge, for those Cubans who had managed to get tourists involved, was then to keep them in the flow of the dance and bring about an atmosphere of fun and enjoyment. After a hesitant beginning, some tourists would let themselves go and show a great deal of dedication, trying hard to get their moves right as they concentrated on steps prescribed by their partner. Other visitors might adopt a more ironic, self-mocking posture, akin to that of a complicit 'post-tourist' (Feifer 1985; Urry 1990), ridiculing their own moves and clumsiness. Such playful attitudes could themselves induce pleasure, fun and amusement.

Being taught to dance could be flattering, once people felt they were learning full speed – an impression enhanced by the praise of their Cuban teachers (see Herold at al. 2001 for a parallel in the Dominican Republic) – or be conducive to exhilarating experiences when adopting a 'post-tourist' stance of playful complicity. Yet it could also generate less positive states of boredom and anxiety (Csikszentmihalyi 1975). The latter could arise when people took the teaching and learning too seriously and felt they were not up for the challenge. Boredom, meanwhile, could emerge when tourists who just wanted to have fun and improvise, without thinking about steps or choreography, became annoyed by their Cuban teacher's overzealous insistence on the right moves to follow. In this case, people's modes of engagements could diverge and generate tensions, breaching the festive mood and impeding the relationship that might have ensued. Excessive emphasis on a serious teacher/pupil relationship underlined differences in competences and statuses, highlighting asymmetries, reaffirming distinctions between insiders and outsiders, and suggesting other types of agencies and relational idioms.

In relation to people's motivation and readiness to get into a dancing mood, alcohol consumption could play an important role by lowering inhibitions and facilitating involvement, and not just on the tourists' side. For Ernesto, having a few sips of rum could make all the difference, helping him move forward and overcome his insecurity:

The drink/alcohol [*la bebida*, i.e. alcoholic drinks, especially rum] gives you strength, it gives you power. I take two or three drinks (*tragos*) and that's it (*y ya*). All this that you have, the insecurity, the fear, goes away. If there is a girl there, I go for it (*ya me meto*). Doesn't matter how she looks, if you work with the mind and the strength of the alcohol, it just boosts your confidence and you can do whatever you want.

Empowered by a bit of rum, Ernesto, who did not consider himself a great dancer, felt more confident approaching tourists and asking foreign women to dance. This happened one night when we went together to a Havana club famous for salsa music and dancing. Regularly sipping from our bottle of rum, Ernesto did not let a song pass without inviting some tourist woman onto the dance floor, showing remarkable resilience in his attempts to kick-start relationships with them. For people like him who were looking for a tourist partner, salsa dancing could indeed be a great facilitator.

This leads me to address gender differences in how invitations to dance tended to proceed, an issue that often had to do with the type of music and dance in question. In the case of salsa, for instance, and in conformity with its prevalent 'dance floor etiquette' (Fairley 2006: 478), men usually took the first step. Men were also supposed to lead the dance, guiding and orient-ing their female partners' moves, and I soon realized that whereas Cuban men often asked tourist women to dance salsa, the opposite was much less common. Rarer too were male tourists who would lead and ask Cuban women to dance. Occasionally, though, visitors were willing to take such initiative, particularly those who were familiar with salsa dancing. Several tourists told me that they had come to Cuba precisely to improve their dancing skills and get a chance to practise with the locals.[1] Equipped with pre-existing competences, these travellers were particularly prone to reach 'peak experiences' through dancing and achieve 'states of flow' akin to those theorized by Csikszentmihalyi (1975), discussed by Turner (1977) in rela-tion to *communitas*, and further elaborated by Graburn (1983) in connec-tion with tourism. Graburn (1983: 14) summarizes the concept of 'flow' as

> the non-reflective state that is characteristic of a person who is totally and excit-edly engaged in some important activity, in which action and awareness merge, self-awareness gives way to attention focused on a limited field which the partici-pant is engaged in mastering, a feeling which is a reward in itself, not a means to an external end.

Experienced dancers could relatively easily enter such states of flow, but these could also take hold of less experienced visitors, particularly people who were determined to cast inhibitions aside and let go. As mentioned above, tourists who were unfamiliar with dancing moves could always get a crash course on the basic steps, do their best to follow the rhythm, or improvise their own dancing style. The considerations of anthropologist Yvonne Daniel (1996: 789), who examined rumba dance performances in a tourism context in Cuba, are particularly evocative here:

> Many tourists are drawn into participation by the amiable feelings, sociability, and the musical and kinaesthetic elements of dance performance. Often, not knowing the rules, they do not wait to be invited to dance, but spontaneously join in. They explore their rhythmic, harmonic, and physical potential and arrive at sensations of well-being, pleasure, joy, or fun, and at times, frustration as well.

Also according to Daniel (1996: 789):

> For many tourists, the dance becomes their entire world at that particular moment. Time and tensions are suspended. The discrepancies of the real world are postponed. As performing dancers, tourists access the magical world of liminality which offers spiritual and aesthetic nourishment (Daniel 1990; Turner and Bruner 1986; Turner and Turner 1978). Tourism, in moments of dance performance, opens the door to a liminal world that gives relief from day-to-day, ordinary tensions, and, for Cuban dancers and dancing tourists particularly, permits indulgence in near-ecstatic experiences (Graburn 1989).

In Havana, I too participated in happenings such as those described by Daniel, in which improvisation and spontaneity played a very important part and a contagious festive atmosphere took hold of tourists and Cubans alike. From then on, people could stick to their newly found partners and move on together to other places and events that could help them stay high, get on with the dance and prolong the party.

As the foregoing suggests, dancing and partying tended to be close allies in touristic Cuba. They called for and nourished each other, generating fun, pleasure and euphoria, and fostering ludic sociabilities and a sense of festive *communitas*. Nevertheless, there were also occasions when these intimate connections between dancing, festivity and enjoyment were breached. This brings me to address more closely the corporeality of dance, a key dimension that could open up possibilities but also lead people to delineate different types of engagement and relational idioms, notably when mutuality was felt to be lacking. My concern here is with the ways in which physical proximity could facilitate touch, sensuality and titillation, and with the more or less reflexive manipulations of that closeness, which some saw as going beyond the fun of dancing 'proper', of dancing as an intrinsically rewarding activity as opposed to a means to an end. With the materialization of contentious relational boundaries, notions of what dancing ought to be about also emerged.

From Dance to Seduction

My Cuban interlocutors repeatedly told me that dancing was an ideal path to seducing tourists and trying to build a relationship that could go beyond the dancing itself, opening up further possibilities.[2] The rationale behind dancing with visitors was often that it was a way to test their availability. This became particularly obvious when Cubans, upon realizing that a tourist already had a partner, cut short their dancing and directed their attention towards other potential targets. This is not to say that Cubans did not enjoy the dancing experience in itself, but rather that on such occasions, finding a suitable partner was the priority. In regards to gender-related differences, and notwithstanding the range of possible variations, my ethnographic material indicates that salsa dancing was mostly done by Cuban man and tourist women, while *regeton* (the Cuban rendition of *reggaeton*) was more popular between Cuban women and tourist men.[3] I will consider the first of these two scenarios before moving on to a more detailed examination of *regeton* dancing.

For Cuban men, salsa dancing with tourist women was ideal terrain for exploring the degree of reciprocal attraction. Would she agree to dance more than one song? Would she enjoy the physical proximity? How close could one get? How would she react to a sensuous touch, or even a fleeting kiss? These were the kind of questions one could hope to answer with dancing. As Ernesto put it, '*robarle un beso*' (to steal a kiss) was the ultimate achievement in one's attempt to seduce foreign women, a step that came after the initial 'talking' and the ensuing 'touching', and that he prided himself on having reached, on some occasions at least, within the first half hour of an encounter. According to Ernesto's script, one could also touch by gazing, by looking the partner straight in the eyes: 'From the eyes you can see the heart, the spirit.' My friend Humberto had similar views on the matter and considered the reciprocal look into each other's eyes as a clear sign of success. Once the foreign partner answered his intense staring, looking straight at him as he moved his body closer and closer, the moment was ripe to 'steal her a kiss'.

Dancing, and more particularly salsa dancing, was also a favoured setting for Cuban men to showcase their bodily skills and their ability to get the foreign partner involved, helping her enjoy herself, have fun and get high and into the flow. Sophie and Claudia, two young independent travellers from France on a week holiday in Cuba, had been surprisingly overwhelmed by their first dancing experiences with Cuban men. Sophie was quick to acknowledge the intimate links between dancing and seduction:

> Wow, the first person I danced with here – it was intense! (*c'était fort!*) I had to re-take some distance. Especially if you drink a bit, I mean. It depends also if the

158

other person is nice, if he looks good. But that's the danger if you drink, you may not even look at that any longer, you just let yourself go.

Such moments of dancing tended to be preceded by gallant invitations conforming to dance floor etiquette and normative gender roles, which could also positively impress tourists.

On the other hand, *regeton* dancing between Cuban women and foreign men tended to transgress such normative scripts. *Regeton*, which emerged in the 1990s, is considered a quintessential 'Latino' musical genre that blends Jamaican reggae and dancehall styles with Latin American musical influences. Ethnomusicologist Jan Fairley (2006: 472) has taken notice of the emergence, in late 1990s Cuba, 'of "new" dance/moves involving the "solo" female body', and has considered these changes in style as they intersect with the recent popularity of *regeton*. New dancing styles include 'the *despelote* (all-over-the-place) and *tembleque* (shake shudder) and the *subasta de la cintura* (waist auction)' (472). According to Fairley (472):

These moves define a solo female dance style which involves fast undulating and turning / swirling of the area from below shoulders and chest to pelvis (as if one is hula hoop-ing or belly dancing). Often accompanied by hand and body gestures mimicking self pleasuring, in the 1990s it constituted a noticeable change in dance style, of women dancing to be 'looked at' both by their partners, by their prospective partners, and by other spectators, using their body as a/their major asset. This was in striking contrast to the more normative couple dancing.

In her article, Fairley elaborates on the relationships between these new moves, *regeton*, 'back-to-front' dancing – a dancing style 'which sensualises the bottom and pelvis in fetishistic fashion' (472) and 'where the woman seems to lead' (482) – and the world of *jineteras*. According to her (483), these changes in dancing

developed in the climate of modern sexual flirtation and potential liaisons between Cubans and Cubans, and Cubans and non-Cubans in the heady atmosphere of Havana clubs in the 1990s when *jinetera* (service culture) and sexuality as 'convertible currency' was prime … The difference with *regeton* per se post 2000 is that it is notably danced out between Cubans. On occasions it is also danced out between Cuban women and foreigners, although publicly few foreigners are very good at it.

Judging from my observations in Havana's nightclubs, whether foreigners were 'good' or 'bad' at dancing *regeton* did not diminish its importance in captivating, titillating and sexually arousing them. Confronting tourist men by dancing *regeton* on one's own, displaying one's body and engaging in sensual and more overtly sexual moves, could be a very efficient way for a Cuban woman to capture their attention and make a first connection, one that could be reinforced by a beaming, sustained look, a wink or a kiss from a distance. Essential in this case was also the physical contact afforded by the dance, whereby a tourist's body could be physically aroused by the contact and friction of the woman's bottom on his crotch. As Fairley pertinently emphasized, in *regeton* the women seem to lead the dance. Therefore (and independently of foreign men being able to dance *regeton* 'properly') a tourist, simply by allowing the Cuban partner to swirl her hips against him, was in a sense already part of the dance. Normative scripts of dancing etiquette, which relied for instance on an explicit invitation to dance (as in salsa), seemed less relevant in these cases. Instead, a couple could be created in rather surreptitious and improvised ways by solo dancers suddenly getting together and starting to move their bodies and rub against one another.

Cuban women's dedication to stirring up their partners' 'fire', sustaining the dance and accentuating its most sexual moves could be part of a reflexive tactic to keep the tourists high and prompt a shift from playful 'as if' to serious engagement. Here the goal was also to avoid the emergence of second thoughts and changes of mind, upon which decreasing arousal could lead visitors to take other aspects into consideration: 'Who is this woman?' 'What's her agenda?' 'Does she really like me?' 'Am I really interested in pursuing the relationship with her?' Successful dancing, however, could take a definitive twist and open up the realms of seduction and sexual relations. Yet such seduction processes were far from always effective, and often tourists drew boundaries as to how far, and in which direction, their relational engagement would go.

For example, the sexually explicit movements in *regeton* embarrassed several of my tourist interlocutors, especially those who were unfamiliar with this dancing style. Others – especially those who were already positively predisposed and expectant regarding the matter – were quite easily drawn into its sensual and sexually evocative dimensions and relished the dancing-seducing continuum, eager to move intimate relationships forward. Others still were willing to get involved in a playful mode just for the fun of it, and to get a feel of this experience of physicality and close contact. At this stage relationships could get more serious and take unexpected turns as visitors 'got hooked' by the overwhelming sensuality and sexuality of the dance, ending up 'conquered' by a given Cuban partner.[4] As excitement grew, other considerations and moral commitments could be put aside, and a shift from playful detachment to full-blown engagement could occur. Stated intentions, agendas and planning could be taken over, bypassed or reformulated following overwhelming intensities of affect, physical sensations and sexual arousal.

The prospect of these unplanned developments unsettled several tourists I spoke to. Both women and men could worry about the possibility of 'losing control', of letting what they saw as physical urges and desires dictate the course of events. The Cuban partners, for their part, tended to be highly aware of this enabling potential of dancing, in all its sheer physicality. Striving to turn relationships decisively towards the realm of sexual engagement, and eventually also romance, their aim was precisely to conquer the tourists and make them lose control via the sensuality of the dance. Whether it was salsa between Cuban men and foreign women, or *regeton* between Cuban woman and foreign men, dancing practices thus constituted a privileged arena of seduction. I have emphasized gender differences here, even though it should be clear that these reflect tendencies rather than clear-cut distinctions. At any rate, these skilful deployments of bodily movement, and the imaginaries and desires they activated and aroused, could certainly help draw tourists into more intimate relationships that could then also be pursued off the dance floor.

But even tourists who had decided to give dancing a go could easily withdraw once they sensed that the relationship was being pushed 'too far too quickly' and morphing into 'something else' altogether, something more akin to, say, a sexual advance that bypassed the progressive stages, smooth transitions and mutual responsiveness that visitors might associate with 'proper' seduction processes. In her review of anthropological research on dance, Susan Reed (1998: 517) notes that 'because of the inherent ambiguity of bodily actions, there is often no consensus on what distinguishes "a 'legitimately' sensual and pleasing gesture from one that 'goes too far'" ... (Cowan 1990:190–191)'. Confronted with similar ambiguities, tourists struggled to draw boundaries between dancing and its intrinsic sensuous dimensions on the one hand, and instrumental and abusive sexual advances on the other. Issues related to agency, mutuality and notions of free will and consent could easily emerge, with visitors complaining that they had not given their partners any green light to justify such overtures. 'He always tried to kiss me!' was for instance the outraged reaction of a Swiss woman as she recounted her unpleasant experience of dancing with a Cuban man. 'Let's go! They start trying to kiss!' protested another young tourist woman, urging her fellow female traveller to put an end to the crash salsa course they were having with two young Cuban men. These reactions raised questions about sensuality and sexuality, their modalities and their inclusion in, or exclusion from, the realms of playfulness, festivity and partying.

Julie, a Parisian woman in her forties and expert salsa dancer, had very frequently visited Cuba in the last decade and was disappointed at the continuous misunderstandings her dancing seemed to generate. What bothered her most was that, contrary to what happened in France (where she went salsa dancing at least once a week), men in Cuba kept thinking that if she enjoyed dancing with them, then the door was open for a lot more to happen. Though she also clarified that she was no 'nun' (*belle soeur*), and that if she felt a particular affinity with her partner things could well get more intimate (most likely in a one-night stand, given her scepticism towards longer-term relationships with Cubans), Julie advocated one's right to enjoy dancing for its own sake, without any 'ulterior motive' (*arrière pensées*). For Julie, *la danse* was both a physical and moral need (*moral, pour la tête,* evoking a cognitive and transcendent dimension). She also complained that once you danced with a Cuban man, others would stop inviting you, assuming you already belonged to the man in question. But Julie was in Cuba to improve and expand her skills, and to that end she wanted to dance with as many people as possible – an objective that some Cuban men I spoke to interpreted as indication of promiscuity and 'easiness'. For Julie, such limitations and the relational assumptions they were grounded in were just an annoying hindrance. 'Every time you have to explain them', she told me, then adding: 'Luckily now things start to get better, as Cubans travel to France, see how it works there, and understand us [i.e. the way we want to dance]!'.

For other tourists who did not see dance as a priority and wished to circumvent any potential misunderstandings about their engagement, the sad conclusion was that it was better to refrain from dancing with Cubans altogether. They were concerned not to give the impression of being up for an unbounded party open to endless possibilities, particularly in terms of sexual availability. This diminished their ability to let go and prompted other interesting reactions from Cubans who tried to get them involved.

Thriving Ambiguities and the Play of Misunderstandings (I)

It is indeed interesting to follow how Cuban men and women dealt with tourists' moments of hesitation, reluctance and withdrawal from dancing. In such critical instances, when definitions of the situation hung in the balance and affects and emotions could easily bifurcate, different normative views of dance, seduction and sexual engagement – of their qualities, continuities and limits – confronted one another, prompting explicit renegotiations of agencies and subjectivities, and bringing into play prescriptive notions of Cubanness and tourism. More particularly, the divide that tourists outlined between dancing engagements on the one hand and the idioms of sexual relationships on the other could be blurred and redrawn by Cuban partners who recast their own seductive moves as integral to the dance. That is, what the tourists perceived as seduction and sexual advances could be presented as an intrinsic part of the realm of playful festive engagements, a situation that the tourists had simply misunderstood. 'This is how we dance in Cuba!' the Cuban partner could retort, relying on his or her legitimacy as an insider and expert in the field to define what pertained to Cuban dance. What tourists judged as an instrumental use of physical proximity was thus (re)qualified as a normal, desirable cultural experience, an experience of Cuban-ness itself. Such evocations of Cuban-ness could accompany equally prescriptive notions of tourism that exhorted tourists to let go, to enjoy and indulge in the extraordinary time of their holiday and to embrace wholeheartedly the eccentricities of Cuban culture and its unique take on dance and its sensuous dimensions. Once again, ideals of tourism as the pursuit of pleasure and as a process of discovering and experiencing the Other were used to inspire tourists to engage fully in the physicality of dance and let their partners lead the way.

Coupled with tourists' concrete experience of dancing, these culturalist/ nationalist takes on the relation between dance and sensuality in Cuba could ultimately motivate them to let go. Tourists I spoke to thus came to the conclusion that dance and sensual engagement in Cuba had their own peculiar qualities and articulations, that other patterns and temporalities of seduction were in place, and that being a tourist also meant being able to move beyond one's taken-for-granted assumptions and indulge in the vitality, intensity, and pleasure this could open up.

Tourists – more particularly, tourist men – could rely on similar deployments of cultural difference to try to take advantage of the ambiguities of dancing, for example when visitors mimicked an allegedly Cuban way of dancing and tried to make the most of their physical proximity to a Cuban partner. On a few occasions, I thus saw Cuban women trying to withdraw from a tourist-driven sexualized dance move that had transgressed the boundaries of the acceptable, relying more on the man's physical strength than on any mutual consent. The abusive character of this coercive physical contact was further aggravated, and seen as all the more unjustified, when the visitors showed no intention of pursuing the engagement off the dance floor, that is, of committing to the sexual/romantic relationship sought by the Cuban partner. In cases where the Cuban woman's agenda was precisely to achieve such a relationship, there was little point in enduring gratuitous abuse that led nowhere. At any rate, as I show in the following chapter, assessing the extent of the tourists' commitment to becoming (seriously) involved in an intimate relationship was not always such an easy matter. Visitors could become very skilled at playing 'as if' and stoking false hopes of long-term relationships, so getting a picture of their agendas and dedication could prove rather tricky.

Conclusion

A hallmark of festive relationships in touristic Cuba was that they encouraged people to 'go with the flow', open up, follow their feelings and desires, and set aside worries and doubts. Partying tended to be conceptualized and enacted in ways intended precisely to minimize visitors' concerns. When the main goals were fun and pleasure, the question of what kind of relationship people were having would ideally fade into the background. The underlying ideal seemed to be that in festive happenings, everyone belonged to the same egalitarian party community or *communitas*. But this scenario, so often evoked in Cubans' exhortations to party, did not thrive unchallenged. Doubts could easily emerge regarding, for instance, the genuineness of this communion, arousing worrisome questions of control and people's intentionality and agenda. With the surfacing of preoccupations with ascertaining drives and motives, reflexive problematizations moved back into the picture.

This oscillation between letting oneself go and going with the flow on the one hand and striving to make sense of relationships on the other became particularly obvious in the case of dancing. The exploration of different dancing scenarios highlighted significant gender-related divergences and inequalities, drawing attention to the affordances of dance and the possibilities it opened up – notably via physical contact – as well as its limits, which women (both tourist and Cuban) could find difficult to enforce when suffering occasional abusive advances by men. The discussion of processes of seduction as they emerged from dancing showed the importance of corporeal experiences, intensities of affect, feelings, vitalities and states of flow, and how these could bring about shifts between different relational idioms, and vice versa. In response to the sensory qualities of dancing, normative ideals of seduction could themselves be worked over and reformulated, leading to situated and purposive (re)conceptualizations of the (dis)continuities between dance, seduction and sexual/romantic engagements.

When doubts and controversies came to the fore, the imperative of justification also kicked back in. Differences in relationships became objects of contention and explicit debate, pitting contrasting views about what pertained to dance and playful engagements against ideas of what constituted proper seduction processes and sexual advances. Connections between partying and seducing were thus severed and remade, which in turn highlighted the emerging frictions and shifting tensions people could experience between embodied intensities of affect and pleasure and more reflective instances of rationalization – between playfulness and seriousness, desire and control, mutuality and abuse. This exploration of the (dis)continuities between partying and seducing also opened the way for the following chapter by giving us a first glimpse of the idioms of sexual relationships in touristic Cuba.

Chapter 8
SEDUCTION AND COMMODITIZED SEX

This chapter explores the idioms of sexual relationships between tourist men and Cuban women, focusing on how different protagonists justified each other's engagements and coped with the ambiguities that permeated these relationships. What emerges are various ways of responding to uncertainty about a relationship's instrumental and exploitative character, epitomized by notions of sex tourism and prostitution, as well as people's ability to reformulate their views on the subject. The examination of a range of entanglements between sex and money shows how differences in relationships were informed not only by the absence or presence of monetary transactions, but also by the specific functions attributed to them, which helped (re)define the nature of people's engagements.

As hinted in the previous chapter's examination of partying and seducing, the possibility of establishing smooth continuities between seduction processes and sexual relationships could help keep notions of commoditized sex at bay while emphasizing the mutual character of engagements. Another way of coping with the controversies affecting sexual relationships between tourists and Cubans was to normalize and embrace notions of commoditized sex. As we shall see, this was done following three main lines of reasoning portraying commoditized sex as the inescapable result of socio-economic asymmetries, as a Cuban typicality, or as conforming to transnational/universal configurations of gender relations and/or self-interestedness. Finally, another recurrent way of dealing with ambiguity, also highlighted in this chapter, consisted of keeping it alive and trying to make the most of it.

These different modalities of confronting uncertainty – some of which have already appeared in the previous chapters – exemplify the main approaches that the protagonists of informal touristic encounters in Cuba tended to rely on to (re)formulate relational idioms and sustain morally contentious engagements. This chapter's detailed examination of their workings, always grounded in ethnographic examples, shows people's ability to use them complementarily, shedding light on their purposeful deployment to make sense of and justify sexual relationships.

Enacting Spontaneous Sexual Relationships: Mutuality, First Contact, and the Seduction Process

It is past two in the morning in Guanabo, Playas del Este, and young Cubans are gathering at the Cupet petrol station. As the only place in the neighbourhood selling drinks and snacks twenty-four hours a day, it becomes a meeting point after the discos and clubs close for the night. Tourists, mostly young men, are also hanging around at the Cupet. Some are with a Cuban partner; others are still looking for a possible match. The Cupet seems to offer a platform for late flirting, a sort of last resort for those who have been looking for a partner throughout the night but have not found one yet. I am accompanied by Marta, a young Cuban woman I met at a local club, the Bellomonte. In the little time we spent together there, she repeatedly expressed her love for me and her willingness to be my *novia* (girlfriend). She would like us to go and find a place to stay together for the night, even though I told her from the start that I am not looking for that kind of rela-tion. I feel sorry for her, since I have the impression that she could have found other foreigners more willing to follow her plans: insofar as that is so, she has been wasting her time with me.

I am glad that some Italian men I have known for some weeks now show up. I can introduce them to Marta, and hopefully she will still find the partner I am assuming she is looking for. Luigi enquires about my relation with her, asking if we are together (i.e. a couple). I tell him that I just met her, and that we are not together in that sense. Taking this as a green light, he starts flirting with Marta, telling her she is very pretty and he is already *enamorado* (in love). Marta seems a bit embarrassed by Luigi's advances in my presence, as though she has already committed to staying with me. After all, she did just call me the love of her life, her perfect *novio*. She starts telling me maybe I should be going home soon, and I interpret this as subtle way of letting me know that she is willing to join the Italians, given my resistance to her advances. Trying to make her feel comfortable with it, I say I really do not mind if she wants to go with them, and finally she does. Luigi and his two friends, in very high spirits, encourage me to join them. They offer me a beer and sketch their plans for continuing the party: drive to a nearby beach, have a swim, all naked, enjoy tonight's full moon... I thank them for the offer and decline. I wait until they drive away before slowly making my way to my accommodation.

Besides giving some idea of the awkwardness of my positioning when interacting with Cuban women who were explicitly looking for a foreign partner, this brief vignette provides a good starting point to discuss the ideal, very much present among tourists I met, of sexual relationships as a

166

by-product of serendipitous encounters and festive engagements, an ideal that Luigi and his friends held dear. Several members in this group of Italians – which included in total about ten young men, all from the same town in Italy – had already told me on previous occasions how much they disliked Cuban women who explicitly asked for cash for sex in the first moments of an encounter. Whenever this happened, they would tell such women to 'go to hell' (*le mando a cagare*). As they put it, they were not the kind of people to engage in that sort of commoditized relationship. What they valued instead was to meet and gradually get to know potential partners while having fun in a festive atmosphere. If they met a woman who enjoyed their company, got along well and ended up spending the night together, that would be perfectly fine and normal.

The day after our encounter at the Cupet, I met Luigi and his fellows again at the beach in Santa Maria. He explained that the previous night it had taken them ages to find a suitable partner. Finally, each of the three Italians had found a Cuban girl (*chica, ragazza*) he liked, Marta being one of them, and had readied themselves for the much-anticipated 'beach party'. As they were about to reach the beach, however, they were stopped at a checkpoint, and the police had taken the girls away. Responding to my concern for Marta, Luigi complained about the 'fucking police' (*fottuta polizia*), who had ruined their plans, and told me he knew nothing more of her whereabouts. As we continued discussing the events, I could not help noticing that their story's emphasis was on the party they had missed out on – the spoiled opportunity to do something special with the Cuban women, namely, get wild on the beach and have a naked swim together. The accent was on being able to indulge in these festive pursuits. Luigi and his friends did not even mention the likelihood of having sex, but we all assumed it would have been the most predictable outcome of the night, a sort of natural by-product of their party. What was important in their narrative was rather the process of establishing a pleasant relationship, having fun, getting excited and enjoying themselves. In direct continuity from that process, and subtly included in a coalescing relational idiom, the prospect of a genuine, spontaneous sexual relation would materialize.

Luigi and his friends, some of whom were visiting Cuba for their sixth consecutive year, spent most of their stay in the town of Las Tunas in the eastern part of the country, several hours' drive from Havana. This rather unusual choice appeared to be directly related to their ideals of sociability and the chances it offered to engage in the types of relationships that they valued most. For Luigi, Las Tunas was a place 'without any tourism attraction', the quintessential town 'off the beaten track', possibly the only provincial capital to go unmentioned in tourist guidebooks. Their group was well known there, and their stories painted the locals as looking forward to their arrival year after year. In Las Tunas everything was cheaper, police control was less stringent than in other parts of the country (especially Havana), and you could still meet genuinely with Cuban people in a less commercialized atmosphere, have amazing parties with them and easily find a *novia* with whom to spend the holidays.

Luigi's enthusiastic assessment of their experiences in this 'forgotten town' echoed the views of other tourists I had met, who also regretted the commoditization of relationships, and more particularly sexual relationships, in present-day touristic Cuba. Ruggiero, another young Italian I met briefly in a disco, nostalgically recalled how six or seven years earlier, Cuban people had been much more innocent and naïve, whereas now, excluding some areas outside Havana, they were becoming more and more 'like us', 'money oriented', and in the process of 'capitalizing' [sic] (*capitalizzare*) themselves. What people like Luigi and Ruggero seemed to value was a sense of ingenuousness, spontaneity, serendipity and uncalculated relationships growing out of genuine desire to have fun, enjoy themselves, flirt and revel in pleasure. Their narratives highlighted smooth continuities between the idioms of carefree festivity, seduction and sexual relationships, and with them the possibility of conflating these relational engagements (note the resonance with some of the tourism promotion material examined in chapter 1). Much like Luigi's, Ruggero's view opposed a positively valued (albeit almost vanished) local culture of fun-loving, sexually permissive 'hot' Cubans (Simoni 2013), to the negative transformations for which tourism was held responsible, specifically its role in the commoditization of sexual relationships and the booming of prostitution. The solution was to get off the beaten track and jump into the picturesque frame of a still 'hot' Cuba. Here we are confronted with a long-standing trope of tourism, characterized by MacCannell (1976) as the quest for authenticity. In this case it took the shape of the pursuit of 'authentic social relations and sociability' (Selwyn 1996: 8), an authenticity to be found in intimacy (Harrison 2003: 90) and more particularly in intimate relations with the authentic hot Cuban (Simoni 2013).

The accrued privileges that could result from being a tourist in such 'good old days' and in marginal locations come sharply into view when the power dimension of these relations is examined. Rather than a quest for the authentic Other in order to become like it, as Cohen's (1979) existential tourists would have it, what seemed to be more often at stake here was a longing for an original first contact, a situation in which the tourists' alien status and privilege could be all the more striking and amplified. In the accounts of Manuele, another Italian man in his late thirties who had been coming regularly to Cuba since the early 1990s, the relevance of this rationale became quite obvious, bracketing any pretence of equality in the relationships at stake. Like many other long-time repeaters – veterans of Cuba, so to speak – Manuele liked to contrast the situation nowadays with that of the 1990s, when tourists started discovering the island, rumoured back then to be 'Paradise'. This was a time when Cubans looked up to you as if you were 'a God' or 'a Martian', and 'treated you well', explained the Italian. For him, Cuba could still be a paradise, but only for people 'who knew' (i.e. people like him), not for the 'just arrived suckers' who had no idea how to get around or deal with Cubans.

Many tourist men I met, however, saw relying on one's socio-economic privileges and aura of foreignness to seduce Cuban women as morally reprehensible. This view, which was explicitly critical of the 'sex tourism' phenomenon, required that sexual relationships be grounded in one's own intrinsic qualities – in personal skills rather than economic resources, and in the ability to seduce women 'the proper way'. It was expressed very clearly by Marcelo and his fellow travellers, whom I met one afternoon in Santa Maria. Mostly in their mid twenties, this group of Spanish men had spent barely a week in Cuba, travelling from Santiago de Cuba on the far east of the island towards Havana. Though brief, the journey had been very intense and had led them to reflect on the issue of tourist-Cuban relationships. Marcelo, who was studying sociology back in Spain, told me that during the journey he could not stop analysing the situations he had faced. Discussing about their encounters with Cuban people, and more particularly Cuban women, this is what he had to say:

> In our group we are all men, so you can imagine. You see so many good-looking girls (*chicas*) [here in Cuba], they seem to be taken out of a catalogue of models. But you know, when you go to a place, you already know that, the ones that look at you are *jineteras*. The ones that don't even care looking at you, they prefer to go with a Cuban [man] than to go with you. You already know that whichever relationship you will be able to establish, there will be an implicit contractual relationship. In these occasions, when you see these pretty girls, these models, you can't stop looking at them. But on one side you have reason which tells you something; on the other you have desire ...
>
> For instance, yesterday we went to the Diablo Tum Tum [a trendy disco in Havana]. Full of very beautiful girls, once we entered they were all around us. But well, you know, you know where all this may lead. We are from Spain, from Northern Spain, and there when you go to a disco, and you want to pull (*ligar*) a girl, you get a drink with her ... there is a way of doing it which is not ... you should know a bit about it, is like an art, is like a game. But well, here you cannot do that, you know that at the end you will have to pay for that. At the end, if you have to pay, you lose all this, all this ritual.

What seemed essential for Marcelo was to preserve a sense of mutuality in the relationship, which should not be driven by the tourist's privileged economic position but rather by people's intrinsic qualities and skills as gendered beings, by their ability to engage in seduction processes that conformed to their normative ideals of flirting and sexual overture. In the course of our conversation, Marcelo and his friends explained about their 'ethical barrier' (*barrera ética*) to engaging in sexual relations with Cuban women, knowing that money would come to play a role. 'If I am not going with prostitutes in Spain, how should I do it here? It's an ethical barrier', argued Marcelo, thus underscoring the importance of preserving linkages between 'everyday' and 'touristic' sexuality (Frohlick 2010) and keeping his moral way of being and relating intact, as a consistent whole.

Our discussion also led us to reflect on other lines of reasoning and justifications in the attitudes of other tourists who, as José (one of Marcelo's companions) put it, set their ethical barrier lower than they did. José took the example of their fellow traveller Ricardo, an older man who had been coming to Cuba for many years now and did not mind going out with Cuban girls:

> What Ricardo says is that these people [Cubans], what they are waiting for is that you [the tourist] go out with them, so they can earn something. He says that for her [a generalized Cuban girl], for her it's better. For them it's better someone [a tourist] that wants to go [pay for sex] with them, than one who doesn't. They live with that [what they can earn through sex], that's what they got used to.

This prompted further discussion on tourists' responsibility in the diffusion and reproduction of commoditized sexual relationships, leading Marcelo to the following considerations:

> Because, also, the ethical problem is not really here. The problem is in the First World, is with sex tourism. Because there are people who go to Thailand, Cuba, Brazil … and ninety percent, no let's say seventy percent of the people who come here come for that [for sex]. Therefore people here [Cubans], when they see you they think that's what we [tourists] all come for. People here got used to this, that tourists have this in their mind already.

Elaborating on their refusal to engage in 'sex tourism', Marcelo and his friends showed determination not to compromise their moral standards, not to lower their 'ethical barrier' and become accomplices in a commoditization of social relationships that they saw as driven by tourism and grounded in socio-economic asymmetries. This stance limited the scope of their interactions with Cuban women: they deemed all who approached them to be *jineteras* interested in them because of the money they had. In their narrative, tourism and *jineterismo* went hand in hand: tourism was responsible for transforming Cuba into a place where needy local women responded to tourists' demands by becoming prostitutes. As foreign men travelling to Cuba, Marcelo and his companions could not escape their tourist condition and suffered from the reputations of those who had preceded them.

In the course of fieldwork I had similar conversations with other foreign visitors, but my ethnographic material also points towards the possibility of ethical reformulations in the wake of 'moral breakdowns' (Zigon 2010) prompted by travel experiences in Cuba. According to Zigon (2010: 9), moral breakdowns occur 'when some event or person intrudes into the everyday life of a person and forces them to consciously reflect upon the appropriate ethical response'.[1] Such was the case when sexual engagements with Cuban women confronted tourists in Cuba with ambiguities and dilemmas. What ethical responses did these dilemmas generate? For Marcelo and his friends, the appropriate response was to stick to one's pre-existing, 'normal' moral disposition. For others, though, the travel experience itself could prompt a shift in their dispositions towards 'prostitution' and 'sex for money' exchanges, leading to the realignment of normality on a different axis of argumentation.

Changing Approaches: Normalizing 'Sex for Money' Exchanges

Aldo had been in Cuba for a couple of days when I first met him on the beach in Santa Maria. This Italian tourist in his early twenties had little experience of travelling abroad and had never been to Cuba before. Four days after our first encounter, during which he had expressed an adamant refusal to engage with 'prostitutes', I met him again on the same beach. Lying in the sand looking very tired, he explained that he had had only an hour of sleep the previous night and went on to tell me about his 'adventure' with two Cuban women.

Having sex with both women at the same time had been an amazing experience for Aldo, the first of its kind and one that had fulfilled his wildest sexual fantasy. After sex, the Italian, who had been drinking a great deal, had fallen asleep for an hour or so, whereupon one of the young women had run off with all his money. The irony was that Aldo had planned to leave them all he had anyway, around 70 euros, which he considered generous given that the women had initially agreed on getting only 5 CUC (about 3.5 euros at the time) each for the night. Furious with the one that had robbed him, and carried away in his anger, Aldo told me that from the experiences he had had in the last days, he could now say for sure that all Cuban women were 'whores' (*mignotte*): they all wanted to get hold of your money. Regaining some composure, and maybe also a bit disturbed by what he had just said, he then apologized, feeling sorry for having reached such a conclusion. He explained that in Italy he was not like this, but here in Cuba, in the light of what had happened to him (he told me he could write a book about it, so many were his adventures), this was how things were.

The change in Aldo's attitude and narrative, only a few days after our first encounter, was striking. In journeying from resolute condemnation of commoditized sex – along the lines of Marcelo and his friends – through his experiences with the alleged inescapable equation of sex and money in Cuba, he had arrived at a very harsh, generalized judgement of Cuban women. In Aldo's narrative, sexual relationships were (re)formulated the 'Cuban way', to which he had simply adapted (see Simoni 2011). Unlike Marcelo and his friends above, Aldo did not account for the transformative effects of tourism in Cuba, nor did he talk about *jineteras* as a response to sex tourists' agendas. In his discourse, this was simply how Cuba was, and any ambiguity was resolved via a normalization of sex-for-money exchanges in this country. In reaction to this state of affairs, he had changed his moral stance accordingly. Aldo's reasoning resonated with that of other male tourists who engaged in sexual relationships with Cuban women: they proclaimed the prevalence of commoditized sex a 'Cuban thing' integral to the Cuban experience itself (Simoni 2011). This contextualization of sex-for-money and the morality of engaging in it also served to mark it as something exceptional, something subordinate to people's 'normal' way of being 'at home' – 'in Italy I am not like this', insisted Aldo. 'Home' was thus cast as the place in which one's way of relating intimately with other people was ultimately judged. Aldo's exceptional behaviour could then be presented as an adaptive response and exceptional mode of action that only made sense in the 'imperfect world' (Povinelli 2006: 198) of Cuba. Insofar as the Cuban context was deemed responsible for deforming how things should normally have been, this was a discourse of exception, that is, of a 'normative politics' that did not tarnish the 'regulatory ideal' (208) of 'proper' intimacy and sexual relationships but simply displaced it elsewhere, back to one's own community and nation (see also Simoni 2015c, 2015d).

As the following example will show, other ways of articulating 'home' and 'abroad' – in which they converged rather than diverged – also featured in tourists' discourses on sex, economic compensation and gender relations, leading in turn to the emergence of other normative views of intimacy. The protagonists here were Gianluca, Marzio and Daniele, three Italian men in their thirties whom I met repeatedly on the Santa Maria beach. Their case not only illustrates how tourists' travel experiences prompted them to change their stances towards sex-for-money exchanges, but also provides further insight into the creative manipulations of ambiguity and misunderstanding that touristic encounters in Cuba could afford. As far as knowledge of Cuba and of Cubans was concerned, Gianluca and Daniele followed the lead of Marzio, who had already visited the island in 1999. The first time we talked, as I expected, the conversation quickly turned to the subject of sexual relationships with Cuban women, which by all indications was a very absorbing issue for the three Italians.

Having been disappointed by their experiences in Havana, which Gianluca described as 'full of whores, but with no beach to relax', they were happy with their first experiences in Playas del Este. They asked me about places to go out at night, and I mentioned the Bellomonte, a trendy hotspot known for the many Cuban women that frequented it daily in search of tourist partners. Enthused by the prospect, Gianluca pointed out that 'this' (i.e. women) was indeed what he had come to Cuba for and went on to summarize his holiday drives in three keywords: 'the beach, the sun, and the babes (*la gnocca*)'. 'But I mean, if we have to pay [for sex]', he was quick to add, 'like to pay twenty euros, then no way. I can do that in Italy if I want, I just pay twenty-five euros. There was no need to come all the way [to Cuba] for that'.

Wondering how they planned to solve this dilemma, I provocatively hinted at the possible complications of having sex without money being involved. Gianluca's reply emphasized the skilfulness required: 'Yes but you know, the taxi driver that brought us here told us that first you have to get to know them [Cuban women] a bit, talk with them, slowly, and you will find a solution [i.e., not to pay for sex]'. He was referring to a sort of negotiation script, according to which it was important to establish meaningful interaction first: to talk and spend some time together before getting to the point: 'I mean, ok, you pay them the food, the drinks; you go out together at night ... He [taxi driver] told us that you can do that. You just need to know how to do it [not to get any payment involved]', Gianluca added before concluding, 'Yeah, I wouldn't mind having a Cuban girlfriend, like, for five days.' This was the kind of relationship Gianluca was looking for: not a sex-for-money exchange with a prostitute, but rather the Cuban girlfriend experience. A number of skills were required to achieve the latter, including patience and know-how about the proper deployment of invitations and gifts to help normalize the boyfriend-girlfriend couple. Following up on this, Marzio explained how things had changed since 1999, when he had last visited the island: 'Yes you know, the last time, you just went out with a girl, you bought some drinks to her, you went dancing together. A bit like in Italy I mean. And then you would fuck her.' Via a parallel with Italy, Marzio normalized the process of relating with Cuban women: it was no longer exceptional, as in Aldo's case, but rather a variation on a well-known pattern of seduction.

Other tourists I met, like Luca and Andrea, two Italians in their early thirties that I encountered one night at the Bellomonte, echoed this view. I was curious to talk to the two men because I had noticed them playfully deflecting Cuban women's attempts to flirt with them by saying they were gay, and was wondering if this was just a diversionary tactic, which it turned out to be. When we started talking, they immediately justified their reluctance to get involved with the women in very personal and idiosyncratic terms, as opposed to the references to wider moral principles condemning sex tourism I had grown more accustomed to: 'You know, it's a question of disposition (*è una questione di carattere*)', said Luca. They then told me about their fellow Italian friend, who, always very keen to find a partner, had already headed to their accommodations 'in good company'. About the tricky issue of payment, which did not fail to come up in the conversation, this is what Luca had to say:

> Like, [you should calculate around] 15, 25 [CUC]. I mean, our friend for instance yesterday brought the girl home and then [only] paid her the taxi to go back home. He paid fifteen for the taxi to get her back home. But I mean, by us [in Italy], you bring her out for lunch a couple of times, and already [you have spent much more than that].

Here Luca underlined the cheapness of the deal, comparing it with what happened in Italy. His remarks saw the establishment of relations with women through the lens of economic investment as well, echoing a rather common discourse in this touristic milieu. According to such narratives, the norm in Italy, for instance, was that a man would invite a potential partner to lunch or dinner (possibly several times) before being able to have sex with her. Sex was thus cast as a way for women to reciprocate the men's invitations, a view posited on an asymmetry between men's and women's sexuality that denied the latter any equivalent autonomy (see Tabet 1987).

With sex becoming a matter of calculation and the cost of a taxi or a meal being accounted an exchange value, the transactional regime at issue here departs from that of the Maussian gift (Mauss 1969 [1925]). Rather than justifying monetary investment for sex with socio-economic (Ricardo) or culturalist (Aldo) contextualizations, these discourses normalized it with a more universalizing approach that brought intimate relationships in Cuba closer to home. They were just like those in Italy, which here represents the everyday, the normal routine. Albeit monetary equivalences were drawn, cash was not overtly exchanged for sex. Instead, transactions were entangled in an overarching gender hierarchy in which men sponsored meals, drinks and taxis as part of the order of things, and women granted their sexual availability in exchange. Any asymmetries signalled by the use of money were tied to gender relations more than to inequalities between tourists and Cubans. These rationalizations thus silenced the striking economic inequalities between foreign visitors and locals, together with their role in shaping relationships. Such discourses bypassed the moral conundrums of 'sex tourism' and 'prostitution' by reducing the partners involved to gendered beings simply conforming to their gender roles, following the scripts and norms of a relational grammar that they all knew too well, since it was the one that informed everyone's everyday life.

Going back to Gianluca and his two friends, our conversations also made it clear that even when inequalities between visitors and Cubans came into the picture, they did not necessarily inflect tourists' resolution not to pay for sex. As Gianluca put it:

No, if all [Cuban women] ask me for money, [there is] no way I will go with them. Sure, I will not go with any of them. I will rather just do a holiday here, on the beach, it doesn't matter. It's not that I do not want to give them money. That's not the point. It's not that I don't want to help them. I know they need. But not money to make love. What's that, I pay and then ... [mimicking a sex act]. No, that's sordid (*squallido*)!

Arguably, what was at stake here were issues of self-perception, self-esteem and one's moral attitude to engaging in sex. Gianluca did not like imagining himself paying for it and would not be able to do it that way. As other foreign men in Santa Maria told me, the simple notion of having to pay for sex would weaken their sexual potency by disrupting the feelings and fantasies that motivated them in the first place. To keep these alive, it seemed paramount to normalize any such transaction. Gianluca showed awareness of the needs of Cuban people and their difficult economic situation, but whereas he saw no problem with being charitable and generous, he rejected the idea of engaging in commoditized sex, a prospect that perturbed his gendered moral sense of self. In his reasoning, the morality of commercial sex between client and prostitute had little to do with that of a charitable relationship between generous benefactor/boyfriend and poor beneficiary/girlfriend. But how could such general principles and ideals translate into practice, when engaging with Cuban women? Would both participants in the relationship have convergent views on these understandings and distinctions? Put to the test of concrete moments of interaction, the boundaries between these transactional regimes and relational idioms could remain very ambiguous and opaque, fraught with misunderstanding and difficult to sustain. As the following section shows, this was indeed what happened that very same night to Gianluca and his friends.

Thriving Ambiguities and the Play of Misunderstandings (II)

The night after our chat on the beach, Gianluca, Marzio and Daniele ventured to the Bellomonte. 'Yes, it went well', Gianluca told me when we met again two days later. The three Italians had easily found what they were looking for and ended up pairing off and having sex with three Cuban women. Back in Italy, Gianluca had heard amazing stories about sex in Cuba, but the experience had not matched his expectations. 'But I mean, all in all it was nice, a nice experience', he concluded. I asked the others about it, and Marzio confirmed it had been all right, 'apart from the end', whereupon Daniele clarified his remark: 'Yes, there was a misunderstanding (*quiproquò*). Because, yes, she [the Cuban woman he met] asked for money. I mean, she did not tell me before, the evening before. I told her, "You did not tell me the night before, and I am not paying you!" And then, we gave the money for the taxi and they left.' In the course of the conversation that followed, Gianluca elaborated further:

> I mean, last night you [referring to the Cuban partner] did not tell us anything. If you had told me, maybe I would not have even gone with you. I mean, it's not that I do not want to give her the money, but, if she had told me before ... Then, I can also choose the girl I want. If I have to pay, it's me who decides, I also decide on the girl with whom I want to go.

The women, they claimed, had been the ones making the first move that evening. As I see it, the Italians had made rather cunning use of the notion of misunderstanding, banking on the scope for ambiguity afforded by these informal engagements and revealing at the same time the difficult situation in which the Cuban women had ultimately found themselves.

Two days earlier, Gianluca and his friends had expressed their aversion to engage with women who asked for money for sex. Now, if not openly contradicted, this view was at least augmented by an additional clause: a requirement of openness and transparency. Meanwhile, I had the impression that it was precisely the non-explicit, ambiguous character of the relationships that had facilitated the sexual encounters. Most likely, the women too had speculated on this ambiguity, hoping the foreigners would turn out to be generous but also exposing themselves to the risk of receiving nothing in return. Any explicit hint about payment beforehand could have made the tourists move on to other potential partners. This could seriously impact a woman's chances of finding a match in the competitive environment of the Bellomonte, where Cuban women far outnumbered tourist men. Because the request for payment had come after sex, Gianluca and his friends were able, retrospectively, to play the 'misunderstanding' card. In this sense, we may argue that ambiguity had enabled the relationship, and the tourists seemed to have gained the most from it. They had held the discretionary power of giving or not giving, and therefore retained the upper hand. Ultimately, their definition of the relationship had informed the nature of any transaction and determined the amount given. The only recourse their Cuban partners had was to try to contest their definition by arguing for an alternative reading in the hope of influencing the men's decision.

Another powerful illustration of a similar deployment of ambiguity and reflexive play with misunderstanding came from Armando, a man in his sixties, during a conversation among tourist men in Santa Maria. Having retired a couple of years earlier, Armando spent three months travelling every year, mainly to Cuba, a place he had visited regularly for more than two decades. He liked to see himself as one of the pioneers of tourism in this Caribbean country and was very proud of his know-how regarding, for instance, how to get around in the capital and, more particularly, deal with Cuban women. Drawing on his vast experience in sexual affairs in Cuba, he willingly shared his insights with fellow tourists on the beach, including the ethnographer. One morning, Manuele (see above) was giving advice to an eighteen-year-old Italian first-timer in Cuba who was largely inexperienced in the workings of relationships with Cuban women and puzzled by his first experiences in Havana. Briefing the teenager about the best discos in the capital, Manuele was telling him how much the 'girls' (*chicas*) there would ask for a night with them when Armando, who was sitting next to them, got visibly irritated and decided to step into the debate:

Don't tell him about discos and prices! They are young, they should not pay anything. Don't go to the disco, they are all hookers there, always the same ones … Better to just hang around the surroundings of the Habana Libre [a big hotel in one of the liveliest areas in Havana], the Coppelia [a very famous ice-cream parlour near the Habana Libre] where people are queuing, or better still near the University, where you are likely to find girls coming from other areas of Cuba, starving girls (*morte di fame*) who are looking for something to eat [an exaggeration to refer more broadly to people struggling to satisfy basic needs]. Just go there, but in the afternoon, around 4 o'clock, not in the evening, when everything changes. When you find someone you fancy, just tell her 'How beautiful you are' (*que linda*) … moreover, you are Neapolitan, you should know [how this works, how to seduce]. You just invite her to a restaurant, you pay for food. Then [Armando puts on a cunning smile] you tell her that you are in love, that you want to marry her, that you want to bring her to Italy … and then you'll see you won't need to pay a thing [for having sex with her]. [Addressing the wider audience] He's just 18, he needs to make his own experiences. You are young, you are good looking, and then there are also people here [in Cuba] who are just pleased to go out with you because they like you.

On other occasions too, Armando reiterated his disdain for people who just went to the disco to hook up with a Cuban girl. The approach he advocated was of a different nature:

> Well, some just go to the disco, that's not hard is it? To get a girl there, everyone can do that. No, I prefer going around with the car, on the streets. It's me who makes the first step. I go to the countryside near here, there [putting on a cheeky smile] they are more 'free range' [the girls]. Yes, sometimes I go to the disco, just for a change, if I want to have fun [*divertirmi*], I can go with a hooker.

Armando cherished the unpredictability of seduction processes and found the prospect of an easy catch in a disco and paying a prostitute a quite tedious scenario involving no challenge. On the one hand, he advised the Italian teenager to play out a 'proper' seduction process, 'Neapolitan-style'. Flatter the partner, take her to a restaurant: such actions were deemed to be in line with enactments of appropriate gendered roles for courtship in Italy. Being young and good looking, the Neapolitan should, as Armando saw it, definitely opt for this more gratifying option. On the other hand, the seduction enterprise that Armando prescribed would obviously be facilitated by the fact that the targets were women in need and the young Neapolitan could simultaneously play the tourist's card of a promise to a better life. Indeed, Armando had also hinted – with a wily look of admiration for his own wit, as if all the tricks were in his hat – at the tactical possibility of sparking false hopes of 'love and migration' to lure Cuban women into having sex for no payment at all. Thus the tourist's seduction skills would work in conjunction with his privileged status to make the coup infallible.

Old enough to be the grandfather of the Neapolitan teenager, Armando acknowledged that his age rendered him unlikely to attract Cuban women with his physical appeal and flirting skills alone. When discussing these matters, he recognized that Cuban women went with him because as a tourist, he offered the prospects of money and a ticket to a better life abroad. But rather than picking up 'hookers', what Armando liked was to engage in the sort of 'first contact' tourism described earlier: making some effort to meet locals who were still unacquainted with tourists, what he called 'free-rangers'. The shimmering mirage of a better life with a (comparatively) rich foreigner could be dangled in front of inexperienced Cubans who might not have thought of engaging with a tourist in the first place. This would enable Armando to act as their first foreign patron, enjoying the leverage peculiar to a sort of initiation of tourism 'virgins', insofar as naïve Cuban women were more likely to be impressed by the novelty of the tourist and the new world of possibilities he could open up. And Armando did indeed like to play the generous benefactor, the rich outsider who – as he put it – found himself in

178

the situation of 'doing good'. But rather than paying cash, he preferred to give presents to the Cuban women he patronized, helping them solve their economic problems and repair their derelict houses on the periphery of Havana. In his willingness to get off the beaten (sex) track, Armando opened new tourism frontiers, bringing tourism to unexpected places.

In the predominantly homosocial milieu of foreigners in Santa Maria, tourists who openly admitted to falling in love with a Cuban woman could easily be scorned for their naivety, especially by people like Armando and other more experienced veterans in the field, who might deride them as 'suckers' who failed to understand how things worked in Cuba. What was highly valued instead were tales of deceptive countermoves at the expense of *jineteros* and *jineteras*, narratives that highlighted the tourists' own cunningness in coping with the alleged 'typical Cuban trickery'. These included the stories of tourists who had outwitted Cuban women by managing to have sex with as little economic investment as possible, or even 'for free', as some boasted. The well-known script, already outlined by Armando above, advised tourists to feign love, pretend to be totally taken by the relationship, and play with the mirage of a possible long-term relationship filled with potential economic advantages for the Cuban partner, perhaps even the promise of marriage and migration to the tourist's country of residence. Everyone knew this did not imply any sort of commitment, since one could always withdraw or disappear when he pleased.

This latter scenario came up openly in a discussion I had with Manuele on yet another afternoon spent among Italian men in Santa Maria. It was the last day of his winter Cuban holiday (his flight back to Italy was leaving in a few hours), and he started recounting how he had promised to bring the presents of a TV and DVD player to the home of his current 'girlfriend' – a Cuban woman he had met a couple of weeks earlier – the following evening. 'But weren't you leaving tonight?' I asked. Manuele laughed at my naïve reaction, then explained that this was precisely the reason he had told the woman he would do it 'tomorrow'. He was never going to do it and would never see that woman again. There was no way for her to track him down in Italy anyway, so that was it. In the meantime, he had spent a nice two weeks in her company and had a lot of sex, all very cheaply thanks to his cunning play with the ambiguities of their relationship.

Going back to the case of Gianluca and his two friends, the change in their stance towards the idea of paying for sex is also noteworthy. If they had to pay, the reasoning had become, they wanted at least to be able to choose their partner. Payment thus seemed to have entered their range of possibilities, perhaps after realizing the challenges of having sex otherwise. 'Shit! Look at this one! What a beauty! This one … I would even give her fifteen. For this one, I would even pay fifteen euros', was for instance

Marzio's comment when a young Cuban woman passed us on that second day we spent together at the beach. Ironic or not, his remarks suggested a new openness and moral disposition regarding payment for sex. As in Aldo's case, Marzio, Gianluca and Daniele seemed to have bought into the notion that there was no getting around giving money, if one was to have sex in Cuba. Having subscribed to this state of affairs, a tourist's skilfulness would then be applied to the best way of dealing with it. Playing with ambiguity and misunderstandings seemed a favoured way of doing so.

Asserting and Stabilizing Privilege: 'I'm A Sex Tourist!'

The sections above have shown how tourists could alternatively condemn giving money for sex (Marcelo) or justify it as a help to the poor (Ricardo), an adaptation to a Cuban typicality (Aldo) or an outcome of typical gender roles (Marzio and Luca). Here I consider another way of settling tensions between sex and economic compensation. In this case, the issues of instrumentality and of commoditized sexual relationships were neither circumvented, nor criticized, nor reformulated in relativist terms, but rather embraced more straightforwardly. The stance of the 'sex tourist' brought a world of self-interested, cynical characters to life, giving shape to commoditized sexual relationships in their purest form.

On only one occasion in the course of my fieldwork did I hear someone refer to himself as sex tourist, a designation more often used derogatorily to criticize and condemn other people. It was in the course of a very long night in Havana with Gabriel – a Canadian in his late forties, long-term tourist and regular visitor to Cuba for more than a decade – that the notion of the sex tourist came up in conversation. Gabriel was quite tipsy at the time. Strolling along the Malecón we met Malcolm, a Briton in his twenties who had just arrived in Havana. This is what I recalled of the heated debate that took place between the two once Malcolm realized how much time Gabriel had already spent on the island.

Malcolm (M): Ah, so you are a traveller or…?

Gabriel (G): I am a tourist!

M: No, because you know, I was in India one year for my gap year, and … after the first three months, you would become a traveller … wearing dreadlocks …

G: Ah come on! That's bullshit! … 'I am a traveller, I am a tourist' – I am a tourist! I am not a traveller! I am a fucking tourist! What's all this bullshit about travellers! Frankly, tell me!

M: Yeah, come on, you are a traveller!

180

G: What the fuck is a traveller, I mean! We are all tourists! Shit: 'Oh yeah, I
am a traveller.' Does that mean we don't give tips or ... Is a traveller just a tourist
who doesn't give tips or what? Yeah, ok, I have been here for a long time but ...
I mean, today, this morning I was in Cancun [a quintessential 'mass tourism'
destination in Yucatan, Mexico]. You know; the big party. I had a big hotel on
the beach. I had breakfast, and I gave a tip ... I know, a traveller, shouldn't give a
tip, no?

   Yeah, you know, the backpackers, they go to a place and they don't mix,
they stay on their own and they say: 'Yeah, we are travellers' ... Because, if you
go to a resort, and have your trolley to carry around, I mean, are you of less value
than if you went around with your backpack? Are you less important? I mean,
what's this shit!

At this moment I tried to intervene in the conversation. I was getting
quite excited about Gabriel's impromptu lecture and wished to bring my
contribution to his deconstruction of the traveller-tourist hierarchy. Pointing
to the relative nature and evaluation of this widespread trope, I took the
example of conversations I had heard among my Cuban interlocutors, who
occasionally mocked backpackers, complaining for instance about their stin-
giness. But my remarks did not have the intended effect. 'No no no! Don't
misinterpret me!' retorted an increasingly exasperated Gabriel, 'I am not
saying that the backpacker is worse and the tourist is better. I mean ... I was
also a backpacker, going around with my backpack'. Gabriel then continued
praising the fact of being a tourist, becoming more and more provocative
and cynical in his remarks:

G: I am a fucking tourist I mean. I come here. I just use the people, I exploit
them ... Yeah, I mean, it's good to be a tourist ...

   And yeah, that's a good life. I don't care. I have a woman who cares for me,
who washes my clothes ... I'm glad to be a tourist.

   Yeah, actually, I'm a sex tourist! I mean, I go to a place, not for the water-
falls or that shit [referring to tourist destinations and must-see attractions]. I go
to have sex and ... I mean, I like sex! I go where there is cheap sex and ... Now,
if I am here is because there is cheap sex.

   And now, you know, I plan to move to Brazil. I mean for 80 [pesos convertibles?] I can get the woman [a woman to clean and take care of his house, like
the one he had in Cuba].

M: How was it here before? [Enquiring about life in Cuba]

G: I don't know for them [the Cubans]. I mean I don't give a shit. But for us
[tourists] I can say it's getting worse. I mean, here is good, but you can't buy a
house. I think I would buy a house in Brazil and ... I will go there. I am starting
to feel tired of here [by now, he had spent about twelve years going in and out of
Cuba].

Malcolm had clearly touched a nerve by raising the issue of the traveller-tourist distinction. I believe Gabriel's irritation with this distinction and the implicit moral hierarchy it evoked progressively led him to outline and embrace the caricature of the tourist as a privileged, self-centred individual, with whom he decided to identify. In this narrative, Gabriel revelled in the pleasures his tourist status granted him, 'happy to be just a tourist' (McCabe 2005: 99; see also Brown 1996; Selwyn 1996), and scorned the self-righteousness of other travellers.[2] His vision of tourism here contrasted sharply with any notion of intercultural communication or mutual discovery, having more to do with the self-interested pursuit of pleasure, disregarding any moral convention. In other words, and unlike the trope of the festive and egalitarian *communitas* addressed in the previous chapter, in his depiction the pleasure was for tourists alone, not for the locals.

Gabriel's inflamed discourse emphasized the privileges afforded by being such a tourist. He dismissed moral concern for other people or for inequalities between tourists and Cubans, implying that such a sentiment was out of place and plainly hypocritical, like the hierarchy established between travellers and tourists. By way of contrast with this supposedly hypocritical discourse, he legitimized his views via a rhetoric of frankness, of brutal honesty, that implied he was the one who finally dared to call things by their name. As the self-professed sex tourist, he portrayed himself as the consistent guy bold enough to assume his stance fully, on solid footing, firm in the unavoidable position that pertained to so many other (sex) tourists who were unwilling to face it. Accordingly, he was not hiding behind ambiguities but rather critiquing self-deceptive argumentation and justifications. His was not an altruistic moral concern but rather a moral stance based on honesty and uncompromising sincerity – and a very cynical world view. Carried away in his provocative speech, Gabriel had finally pushed his arguments as far towards self-congratulatory hedonism and lack of moral concern for others as I had ever heard.

This posture had extreme connotations in this specific case, but other tourists I met during fieldwork adopted it in different shades and degrees, especially the most experienced veterans, who came to Cuba regularly and year after year. One line of interpretation that may help explain this radical, uncompromising, cynical view of tourism and of tourists' privileges has precisely to do with the long-term and repeated nature of these people's engagement in sexual encounters with Cuban women, and with the contentious and ambiguous character of such relationships: the sex tourist stance had the advantage of putting doubts and ambiguities to rest once and for all, paving the way to more stable and easier to manage engagements. 'We want sex – sex is being sold – we have the money to buy it – we buy it': in the terms of this simple equation, the only thing left to negotiate was the price.

Armando echoed Gabriel's reasoning one afternoon in Santa Maria as he recalled with nostalgia the good old days of tourism in 1990s Cuba, when you could just buy Cuban women a drink or a little sandwich and go to bed with them. Now everyone was asking for something, he complained; it was always about 'I need this, I need that':

> They always ask you [for something], it's always the same story. They [Cuban women] tell me, '*yo tengo un problema* [I have a problem, Spanish in the original]... *necesito*' [I need]'. Well, now I got to the point where I also tell them: 'Me too, *tengo un problema, io necesito* pussy [*la figa*]'. So you have a problem, I have a problem. What do you want? What I want, you know. So, if we can agree, we make a deal and then we make an exchange, we solve the situation. Here everything works like this, everything works with free trade. Myself, I act like this by now.

The idea here, as Manuele put it on another occasion, was that one had to rely on the same 'weapons' Cubans used and play according to their rules – the rules of self-interestedness and instrumentality, in this case. Now we can revisit the notion of adaptation to a Cuban context where human relationships were governed by trade principles, and sex and economic compensation were closely and inexorably intertwined. The need for money and the need for sex thus became two variables to be exchanged on an equal footing. There was no ambiguity here: relationships took the shape of a calculated economic exchange. When deploying this grid of legibility, Armando and Manuele came to embody a typical *Homo economicus*, a calculative agent reasoning in terms of offer and demand, trying to satisfy his needs and maximize his profits. For instance, he had no need to get involved in time-consuming seduction processes, ambiguous regimes of reciprocity or intricate webs of unclear expectations and obligations. These relationships were akin to transient market transactions between buyers and sellers: after some bargaining, both gave what was expected from them, and then they parted company.

No anxiety, no need to sustain relationships, no medium-term commitments, no worries. For tourists who spent a significant part of their holidays in Cuba engaging sexually with different Cuban women and arguably were striving to achieve 'existentially comfortable' (Zigon 2010: 5) ways of living this reality, these absences – rather than any supposed failure to understand intrinsic 'ambiguities of love and money' or 'the native point of view', as Cohen (1996) argued in his 'cross-cultural mapping of prostitution'[3] – were perhaps incentive enough to adopt a cynical stance.[4] Confronting ambiguities and moral dilemmas on a daily basis could indeed become existentially uncomfortable and exhausting. Moreover, the clear demarcation and embrace of a commoditized relationship was also a way to reassert power, making clear which side of the tourist-Cuban divide power lay on: the side that had the money (Simoni 2008b).

These considerations may also lead us to temper Jack and Phipps' (2005: 166) remarks about the positive potential of tourism as a destabilizing force, and about tourists' discomfort and lived in-between-ness as pathways to self-discovery and reflexivity that can lead to questioning conformity and 'jolt us out of the tacit commodified forms and taken-for-granted routines that often frame our relations to others'. For people like Armando and Gabriel, the potential discomfort of being constantly confronted with relational ambiguities and uncertainties seemed instead to call for conservative reactions and a reification of the divide between Us and Them. By now it should also be clear that from the perspective of these tourists, more time spent on the island did not necessarily equate with increasing closeness to the locals. In no way did tourists' standpoint morph into a 'going native' stance or more equal power relations. Instead, they could easily strategically reassert their privileged status to establish clear-cut, advantageous principles of interaction and dismiss any sort of ambiguity.

Up till now, I have considered male tourists' narratives on sexual relationships with Cuban women, discussing various ways of dealing with the contentious entanglements between sex and money. To shed some light on perspectives from the other side of the relational tourist-Cuban divide, I now examine a case of Cuban women debating and formulating their views on these engagements. In the course of fieldwork, I had only limited occasion to access such perspectives. The following case constituted a notable exception, so I present it in some detail.

Working with and Unpacking Ambiguity

The example considered here saw Aurora (see chapter 3) and her older neighbour Ramona talking with me about the relationships Aurora and her eighteen-year-old cousin Jennifer were having with a group of Italian male tourists. As soon as the topic came up, the issue of money immediately came to the fore:

Ramona (R): How much did they give you?

Aurora (A): Twenty [convertible pesos], for both of us. No because, they know (*ellos saben*). They don't pay for whores (*ellos no pagan por putas*).

Aurora had already made it clear from the start that she had not had sex with any of the tourists, whereas Jennifer had. She justified the smallness of the amount received by saying that the tourists 'knew': they knew how these relationships could be dealt with in Cuba, how to play it so as not to pay for sex. By emphasizing the fact that the tourists did not 'pay for whores', Aurora also avoided casting herself and Jennifer as such.[5] Indeed, Aurora would have strongly argued against any identification of herself as a prostitute. The money the tourists left was for a taxi to get back home in the morning, after having spent the night with them. However, we all knew the twenty CUC had not been used for that purpose and that the two had most likely hitch-hiked their way home and kept the cash for other uses.

As the conversation went on, Aurora revealed her determination to get the most out of this relationship with the Italians. Her approach to the matter seemed clearly driven by economic instrumentality. For instance, she planned to lead the tourists to an expensive *paladar* (private restaurant) in the neighbourhood, where she had heard you could get a commission of ten convertible pesos for each tourist you managed to lead in. Should this plan fail, she added teasingly, she would drink as many mojitos as possible while in their company in order to collect at least the commissions on those drinks. Two days later, she related new details as we continued our conversation about developments in her ongoing relationship with the Italians. Again, money quickly took centre stage. As she put it, the Italians had finally 'dropped' (*la botaron*) her younger cousin. The reason they had put forward was that she was 'cold' during intercourse.

A: They say that she laughs when they make love!

R: But how can that be?

A: Yes yes, that's what they say; they say that she laughs, that she is a bit cold.

R: Ahhh, [sardonically] what these ones [the tourists] want is something hot isn't it? The cold ones they have them in their countries, or what?

A: They already told me not to bring her anymore … They gave her for the taxi, and that's it. I had warned her already the night before: 'You should work well'. To see if [hoping that] they would keep calling her.

R: But you know that it's not good from you [to get her cousin involved in this]. She is still a young girl (*una muchachita*).

A: What about a young girl!? With what she has seen in the street already! (*Con lo que ha visto en la calle ya!*). She told me that she is [going out] with a black from the neighbourhood. What for, that big black (*Pa' que, el negrón ese*)? So that he can beat her up for nothing? So that he can fuck her? And he has nothing [in economic terms]. He doesn't give her anything … This way [by going with the Italian tourists] she gained her sixty pesos [CUC].

R: But you know that it's not good…

A: She told me that her mother [back in Santiago de Cuba, on the far east of the island] was so happy about it (*estaba de lo mas contenta*)! You tell me I'm abusive (*que soy abusadora*), while her mother was as happy as ever (*de lo más contenta*)!

R: What do you mean 'happy as ever'? That's because her mother is crazy, she must be abnormal!

A: Looking at her pocket. When she has got the pocket full of dollars [i.e. CUC], sixty dollars! She would have liked to [be able to] get that again! She already bought some flip-flops, a cream, a perfume ... Yeah; she got sixty dollars [making some calculations]. Three nights, twenty pesos [CUC] ... Well, they gave her twenty pesos because they say they do not pay for whores. The old ones yes [among the Italians there was a group of younger tourists – the ones they engaged with – and another of older ones who joined them occasionally for dinners, nights out, etc.]. The old ones yes, they pay for whores, their fifty dollars [each night].

R: Does it cost 50 dollars? [Amazed at the smallness of the amount]

A: Yeah yeah. And I mean, [adopting the tourists' perspective] you haggle it down to thirty ... The other ones [the older tourists] yes they go/pay for whores. Every day they have a different one. But the others not. They say they do not go for whores.

R: [With a disapproving and disgusted tone] But they [the younger ones] are even more shameless (*son más descarados todavía*)! How shameless they are! They do not go for whores, but they catch the young girls, they fuck them, and then they give them twenty dollars. I then prefer the other ones; at least they give you fifty dollars!

A: [Supporting Ramona on the same line of reasoning] If you do not want to pay for whores, then you [should] just go to the disco, you dance, and then you just say goodbye to her [any girl in question], and you come back alone.

R: Look how they know! (*¡Mira como saben!*). Yes, they are shameless. At least the others they pay you 50 dollars.

At this point, encouraging further discussion on this apparent paradox, I chipped in:

Valerio: They say they do not pay for whores, but they give her twenty dollars ...

A: Well yes. This [money], they give it to her [an impersonal and generalized woman] in the morning, and they tell her: 'Look, for the taxi'. That's what they say. Instead of saying 'Take, this is for the taxi', they could well say 'this is for the one [we did] before (*lo de antes*)' [i.e. sex]. No. They give her twenty 'for the taxi' [and as she says this she winks at me to mimic the tourists and evoke the complicity between the two partners]. As if they did not know already [what the payment is really for] ... But I mean, the girls they already know that it [the money] is for what they did earlier. Well, and they [the tourists] know it too, but ...

R: If it was me, I would tell them to fuck off: if you want to sleep with me, you pay what you should be paying. No taxi, no bullshit (*ni pinga*)! [i.e. no nonsense]

A: Yes. But for them, when you need it ... Twenty dollars is always some money ...

Our conversation went on longer that evening, but the sections above most clearly address the issues of money, sex and ambiguity generated by competing rationales and different ways of relating. Opacity about the purpose of the money given by the young Italian tourists ultimately cleared up, leading us to take a rather sceptical view in which such money, far from expressing charitable generosity or gallant paternalism, was but mean compensation for the sexual services that had been provided. Our deconstructive endeavour of conversation geared at revealing the real meanings and intentions lying behind superficial appearances and staged behaviours (see the parallel with MacCannell 1973) finally uncovered a reality peopled by cynical characters – smart, self-interested, deceptive tourists who played with ambiguity in order to exploit Cuban women. The latter were driven by their needs to accept whatever sum of money the tourists were willing to give. Aurora and Ramona expressed a mix of anger and disgust but in a way also a grudging appreciation of the skilfulness of 'those who knew', of these tourists playing the smart guys who did not pay for prostitutes.

In our first conversation two days earlier, no one had addressed the rationales behind such monetary arrangements. The meaning of transactions had been left unquestioned, preserving the image of assistance (*una ayuda*) for the women to get back home safely. The biggest contributor to the adoption of a more sceptical stance and the resultant world of cynical, Machiavellian characters had most likely been the contrast detailed between the behaviour of the younger tourists and that of the older ones. The latter openly paid for prostitutes – signalled also by the fact that they had a new partner each day – and were ready to shell out up to 50 CUC for it. Here ambiguity was absent, and straightforward equivalences prevailed. At this point our conversation had focused on gains, profits and economic end results, making it difficult to justify giving different amounts of money for what seemed to be the same thing (i.e., sex). Aurora had brought a generalized Cuban woman into the picture as our reasoning shifted from her and her cousin's own experience to the broader workings of these relationships. What emerged was an impersonal character who, according to Ramona, should have striven to maximize her profits.

Via this depersonalization, we sidestepped the question of being identified as a prostitute, and the difference this could make for Aurora's self-esteem and moral sense of self. The anonymous vignette instead became an ideal and abstract case, an exercise that extrapolated the thoughts and actions of a rational economic agent ('If you want to sleep with me, you pay what you should be paying!'). Sex and money were treated as two variables in a straightforward equation, without regard for any other nuance or the possibility of other relational idioms coming into play. Having unmasked superficial appearances, we were left with the idiom of commoditized sex and ended up assessing the logics and rationales that made most sense within this relational frame. Relations were thus portrayed as transient economic transactions from which Cuban women should at least gain the fair market value for sex. That was as far as our conversation went that day. However, the story did not end there, and more lessons were to be drawn from it.

Indeed, our deconstructivist and sceptical endeavour seemed to neglect other important implications and alternative possibilities that we came to reconsider a few days later, when Aurora told us how the relationship with the Italian tourists had (perhaps only provisionally) ended. The issue we had overlooked, highlighted also in Cabezas' (2004, 2009) work, was that any explicit payment of cash for sex tended to foreclose other potential modes of engagement and the establishment of longer-term relationships. Indeed, the older Italians seemed to end relationships with Cuban women each time they entered into one, settling things with payment. This market-like arrangement allowed the partners to quit each other without any sense of further commitment or obligation towards one another.

Through the lens of this type of rationalization, and in contrast to this clear-cut form of payment, 'taxi money' could look like a shameless expression of hypocrisy, a manipulative trick whose main purpose was to bring down the price of sex. It could well be that in these moments all the protagonists involved had been aware, or at least entertained the thought, that the money exchanged was related to the sex they just had, as Aurora's complicit wink had suggested at that point in her story. However, the facts that no one explicitly stated any sex-money equivalence, and that the transaction was instead enacted (openly at least) as assistance, a generous offer, left room to cast the relationship as something other than a prostitute/client one. This could facilitate the establishment of other types of attachments, projecting the relationship into the future and beyond the idiom of the transient commoditized exchange. In the specific case examined here, the possibility of such an extension in time, and the chance it offered to diversify and strengthen connections, complicate relationships and bring about other relational idioms – which in turn called for other responsibilities and moral commitments – had ultimately ended up benefiting Aurora.

Her relationship with the young Italians had continued for more than a week and proved rewarding well beyond the taxi money she had received daily. By establishing relationships that (be it only apparently and superficially from a sceptical viewpoint) differed qualitatively from those between prostitutes and clients, people certainly missed out on 'fairer' direct payments for sex. However, they could also achieve more gratifying identifications that enabled them to access resources by other means, according to other transactional regimes and relational idioms, and the moral demands that went with them. By spending time with the Italian tourists, being able to tell them stories about the difficulties of her daily life, establishing a range of affective ties and infusing their relationship with empathy and notions of reciprocity and generosity, Aurora had finally managed, before their departure, to convince them to put together enough money to enable her to finally buy herself a much needed washing machine. She had also grown quite fond of the men and was now hoping that their relationship could continue in the future, on their next visit to Cuba. In the end, the Italians left her with 190 CUC, plus the taxi money and different commissions she had collected in the various places they had frequented together. Playing with ambiguity was no doubt a risky business with no guarantees of clear-cut outcomes, and previous examples illuminated its pitfalls for Cuban women. But in this case at least, all things considered, Aurora's assessment of her relationship with the Italian tourists ended up being rather favourable.[6]

Conclusion

This chapter has shown a range of ways in which tourist men and Cuban women dealt with frictions that emerged between sex and money, between intimacy and economy. From Marcelo's 'ethical barrier' to Gabriel's self-professed 'sex tourist' stance, the modalities of coping with the ambiguities permeating these relationships were very diverse. A variety of narratives and justifications criss-crossed and relationally informed each other, and we need to account for this diversity if we are to move beyond aprioristic overarching definitions of 'sex tourism' and 'prostitution' and fully grasp the significance and implications of sexual relationships in this tourism realm.

Following on from the previous chapter, we have seen the importance of seduction processes, and of maintaining a sense of mutuality in relationships in order to normalize the sexual engagements for the tourists. The ideal picture of spontaneous and naturally flowing intimacy was contrasted with a vision of prostitution and commoditized sexual relationships in which everything was biased and corrupted by money. Marcelo and his friends were clear about their ethical barriers on the matter and were determined not to abandon these self-imposed limitations just to follow their desires. Striving to align everyday and touristic sexuality (Frohlick 2010), and the moral dispositions on which both ought to be grounded, they preferred to stay on the side of reason, as they put it, stressing their allegiance to proper seduction processes with their prescribed temporalities and techniques of flirting. What was valued here was mutuality based on one's intrinsic qualities and abilities as a gendered being, rather than the asymmetries that resulted from being a tourist. In other cases, similar idealizations of a naturally flowing relationship went hand in hand with nostalgic references to the 'good old days' of 1990s Cuba and the marginal tourism locations in which (sexual) relations with Cubans could still be of a genuine and authentic kind (Luigi's case). Unlike in Marcelo's case, however, such narratives could also express a longing for 'first contact' situations that further magnified the privileged status of the foreigner and the tourist/Cuban divide, making it easier for a tourist to have his way and play the generous patron while at the same time downplaying any signs of a commoditized form of intimacy.

The chapter's examination of adaptations and reformulations of moral principles, which tourists justified by the notion that they were learning from experience, showed their ability to engage, with a renewed measure of confidence and comfort, in commoditized sexual relationships purported to be 'typical' of Cuba and therefore integral to the Cuban experience itself. But monetary transactions could also be kept separate from sexual activity and portrayed as generous, charitable offers rather than payments. Ambiguities could then easily thrive, and misunderstandings be played with, in regards to the expected payment (or not) for sex. Economic investment in intimacy could also be normalized by resorting to stereotypical narratives on gender roles and norms, outlining a transcultural/universalizing scenario of men in charge of women. In this view, asymmetries between the parties were tied to normative gender scripts rather than to the economic divide between tourists and Cubans. All these different approaches had in common their tendency to justify and normalize certain takes on sexual relationships, while downplaying the way tourism influenced those same relationships by informing their key stakes and the different agendas that could converge in them.

That was not the case in Gabriel's 'sex tourist' stance or in similar perspectives taken by other veterans of Cuba like him. Here the privileges of the tourist position were highlighted, wilfully endorsed and cast as liberating. Economic asymmetries were emphasized and exploited in the favour of tourists who valued sexual relationships with locals as cheap deals. These postures did not attempt to circumvent or move beyond the idiom of economic instrumentality and *jineterismo* but instead straightforwardly and cynically adapted to it, relying on the bargaining power of the tourists' hard currency. Accordingly, we may argue, Gabriel, Armando and Manuele related to an alleged irreducible Other in the same way they perceived this Other relating to them, following free trade principles in a sort of basic *jineterismo* in reverse. Here it was clear that with the passing of time the tourist's position did not fade to a 'going native' stance or more equal power relations. Rather, the reiterated privileged tourist status could become a stronghold from which to operate, following clear trade principles and keeping moral dilemmas and ambiguities at bay.

Also significant about Gabriel, Armando or Manuele was that no matter how striking and provocative their views were, no matter how changeable and contradictory, they could defend them in discussions with other visitors precisely by emphasizing their long-term experience of Cuba. As suggested for instance by Malcolm's initial admiration for Gabriel as a traveller and connoisseur of Cuba, visitors seemed to assume that these veterans, by virtue of the long time spent on the island, were experts on tourism and its related transformations, knowledgeable about recent developments in the country and its people, and held the key to optimal dealings with locals. Accordingly, inexperienced visitors could look up to these potential mentors who, from their authoritative position, could in turn dismiss moral critiques of their commoditized sexual relationships as 'the beginner's view' held by 'naïve suckers' who did not know how life really was in Cuba and could come to understand only with time. Having an opinion that shocked others, an original and uncompromising view, could in itself become an element of distinction that helped recast hierarchies between tourists.

The expertise of these veterans of tourism in Cuba, it must be noted, also lay in their ability to shift between different lines of argumentation and justification, depending for instance on the context of interaction. This was also what made them more capable than other tourists in dealing with the ambiguities of sexual encounters with Cuban women and the moral dilemmas these raised. Thus Armando could shift from attaching value to skilful seduction processes at one moment to a more cynical view of free-trade intimacy at another. The time he had spent in Cuba, along with his familiarity with a wealth of discourses and critiques of tourist-Cuban relationships, had made him very competent in deploying all these different arguments in his own situated engagements. Proficient in a range of moral dispositions, he was ultimately able to feel comfortable with different ways of relating with Cuban women, and of talking about and justifying such relationships.

The ability to deploy a variety of approaches to make sense of intimate tourist-Cuban relationships also appeared in Aurora's account of her experiences with a group of Italian visitors, a source of important insight on how these engagements can look from the other side of the tourist-Cuban divide. Again, the relationships' ambiguity, fostered by the circulation and unclear role of money, emerged as a fundamental issue of debate. This ambiguity could be unpacked and deconstructed adopting a sceptical approach in terms of (false) appearances and (real) agendas. In this perspective, money-as-help was recast as deceitful, stingy payment for sexual services. But this example also showed Aurora's proficiency in keeping a range of lines of action and interpretation open and shifting from one to the other depending on the situation and its possible developments. Not only could the sceptical posture lead to identification of the protagonists involved as client and prostitute, designations that both Aurora and the Italians seemed determined to avoid, but it also limited the range of achievable relational bonds and gratifications.

Here we are confronted again with the challenge of transcending the idiom of economic instrumentality and overcoming mistrust and radical asymmetries as the predominant grounds for action, and with the implications that these moves could have for both tourists and Cubans. The ability to move beyond the limiting horizons of *jineterismo*, prostitution and reciprocal exploitation also opened the way to the possibility of extending relationships in time and achieving more satisfactory relational idioms and identifications. It could also enable relationships between tourists and Cubans to eventually lead to romance, love and, in some cases, marriage and the Cuban partner's migration to the tourist's country of residence – a life-changing scenario to which many of my research participants aspired.[7]

Conclusion
TREASURING FRAGILE RELATIONS

As tourism grows and expands across the world, models and formats on how to structure and implement it proliferate. The engagements tourists have with a destination and its people are studied and scripted, not least so they can be channelled and catered for. This is arguably part of what Enzensberger described, more than half a century ago, as the process of standardization, packaging and serial production of tourism (1996 [1958]). Yet in spite of endeavours to harness, institutionalize and format tourism and the multiple processes and relationships it generates, other realms of possibility keep opening up. Among them is the realm of informal encounters, to which this book wished to draw attention. One might argue that I have done my part here in framing and formatting such encounters, reducing their complexity by delineating some of their key mechanisms and features. While this may well be the case, my primary aim was to follow how my research participants themselves gave shape, made sense of and ordered this messy field of interactions. How do touristic encounters emerge, and what are their salient qualities? These questions guided my research. My narrative was structured so that the different chapters, by building on each other, would lead to a cumulative understanding of touristic encounters, one that could progressively deepen our analytical insights on the subject. In this conclusion, I wish to draw these insights together and elaborate on the main analytical threads woven throughout the book.

Informal Touristic Encounters in Cuba

The discussion of international tourism development in Cuba (Chapter 1) highlighted the importance that informal touristic encounters have acquired there, flourishing at the intersection of the heterogeneous needs, desires and aspirations of foreign tourists and members of the visited population, and helping to (re)shape them. Before tourists and Cubans meet each other, their imaginations have already been nourished by powerful tropes and narratives that inform their expectations and agendas, and whose history and diffusion can be retraced. In other words, informal encounters – albeit beyond the scope of the official tourism industry and formally unscripted and un-directed – did not happen in an imaginative void, as if complete strangers were confronting each other. Present at their outset, and acting as their preponderant driving force, were people's asymmetric resources, most notably knowledge and economic assets: hence also the threat of reciprocal exploitation and manipulation, and of instrumental and abusive behaviours. Such threats justified tourism policies geared to protect tourists from harassment by hustlers. They also alerted tourists to the possibility of being cheated by deceptive Cubans, epitomized by the personae of *jineteros* and *jineteras*.

The promises and challenges of informal touristic encounters may be viewed as two sides of the same coin, two major sets of contrasting meta-narratives that relationally constitute each other by way of opposition. As suggested in the Introduction, these two narratives tend to parallel the characterizations of tourist-local relationships that predominate in tourism promotion material (generally emphasizing the positives) and scholarly generalizations on the matter (more likely to highlight the negatives). Empirically grounded research, however, indicates that while these tropes could inform tourists' and Cubans' expectations regarding the prospect of meeting each other, their contact was itself full of unscripted potentialities and could not be reduced to a predictable confirmation.

Accordingly, these meta-narratives should be viewed more accurately as commonsensical starting points than end results, in that they were likely to be worked over, reformulated and possibly transformed in the course of touristic encounters. This is to take seriously what happens in the engagements between tourists and members of the visited population, and to recognize their generative potential. Other scholars have already highlighted how notions of friendship (Cohen 1971), reciprocity and hospitality (Adams 1992; Tucker 1997, 2001, 2003), love and partnership (Brennan 2004; Kummels 2005), and market and commerce (Forshee 1999) are renegotiated and reshaped from within touristic encounters. The key is to treat these notions not as stable and reified constructs, but as relational idioms grounded and acted upon in concrete moments of tourist-local interaction. Adoption of this methodological stance not only encourages an empathetic understanding of the protagonists' perspectives in such encounters – one that is not based on naïve or cynical assumptions, or on patronizing condescension – but also parts company with the normative and reductive views that tourism authorities and other tourism-related institutions may put forward.

In Cuba, specialized tourism police could portray informal encounters between tourists and members of the Cuban population as cases of *asedio al turista*, or tourism hustling, a predatory, economically motivated behaviour and punishable form of harassment. *Jineterismo* and harassment could indeed be how tourists and Cubans themselves perceived a given relationship, though not necessarily. Furthermore, and in line with the considerations of other authors who have dealt with these issues (notably Fernandez 1999, Berg 2004 and Cabezas 2004), I have shown (Chapter 3) how the authorities' charges of tourism harassment and prostitution tended to rely more on discriminatory, prejudice-based profiling (in which socio-economic status, gender and race played pivotal roles) than a clear understanding of how the protagonists themselves perceived their relationship. The latter, I would argue, should be what matters most, and this is also where anthropology can make its contribution.

My ethnography of the expectations that informed engagements between tourists and Cubans (Chapter 2) emphasized the widespread diffusion of narratives of *jineterismo*, tourism hustling and prostitution, and the challenges this posed. Conversations with tourists indicated that most people travelling to Cuba were sceptical about the suitability of getting (too) involved in relationships with Cuban people. The spectre of possible deception, contrived emotions, interested friendship, false professions of love and other instrumental machinations at their expense often lurked at the back of their minds. Throughout the book I have shown several examples and instantiations of such lines of reasoning, which tended to reify a divide between Cubans' self-presentation to outsiders and their actual motivations and agendas, which were deemed ineluctably strategic.

As I have argued elsewhere (Simoni 2013; Simoni 2014a), this interpretive logic is extremely widespread in the increasingly globalizing field of tourism discourse and critique, and needs to be understood in relation to tourism's drive to reach into the most intimate realms of the places and lives it touches, and to the tourists' preoccupation with being deceived by 'fake' touristic displays (MacCannell 1973, 1976). Most tourists I met during fieldwork despised the idea of being cheated and constantly puzzled over the 'real' intentions and motivations of the Cubans interacting with them. Here, narratives of *jineterismo* could act as a key interpretative resource to 'unmask' the allegedly covert motivations of the locals. In terms of social scientists' approaches, such frames of legibility still retain much analytical purchase when used in assessing touristic encounters from a critical(-cum-cynical) perspective (Simoni 2014a).

Such interpretive grids may appear all the more compelling, operative and theoretically limitless when combined with a strong focus on structural inequalities, an emphasis on local resistance to global forces, and a conceptualization of the individual that foregrounds economic agency and rationality. I should clarify that whereas I have nothing against critical analysis per se and view it as integral to the anthropological project, in this case I see a risk in adopting such a framework a priori (Fassin 2008) – more specifically, in 'romanticizing resistance' (Abu-Lughod 1990; Piot 2010) and with it the image of cunning locals who, despite their subaltern position, are able to trick and deceive the structurally advantaged tourists, a category of people for which academics have traditionally displayed little sympathy (see Crick 1995). Going a step further, I would argue that we may easily be tempted to suppose that the disadvantaged inhabitants of tourism destinations in the South are not only able to take advantage of tourists but should legitimately do so, and that we – as critical researchers sensitive to domination and ways of resisting it, and eager to highlight the economic agencies and rationalities of the 'weak' – expect them to and like to see it. This interpretation may become even more appealing and self-evident – therefore making its moral underpinnings less likely to be reflexively acknowledged – in a Caribbean context where cunning responses to colonial domination have captured much anthropological attention (Browne 2004; Freeman 2007). The image of disadvantaged people who deploy subtle tactics and 'economic guile' to get by in unfavourable circumstances is indeed long-standing in anthropologies of the Caribbean region, an image that has been held 'to embody the most authentic in Caribbean culture' (Wilson 1964, cited in Freeman 2007: 5).[1]

Thinking about the 'romance of resistance', it is also important to consider that in Cuba, the socialist government itself rests on a long tradition of nationalist rhetoric of resistance to colonial and imperialist powers. In this context, I have shown that in the 1990s the notion of *la lucha* (the struggle) – one of the key terms of revolutionary symbolism – gradually turned into a common expression referring to Cubans' day-to-day struggle to get by. In the generalized climate of crisis that characterized post-Soviet Cuba, Cuban men and women who engaged informally with foreign tourists were able to inscribe their actions within the moral framework of *la lucha*. This is when *jineterismo*'s justificatory logic and moral footing could be brought forward. Grounded in the reification of a radical asymmetry of resources, *jineterismo* could embody a just struggle, a redistributive tactic in an unequal world where wealthy tourists visited poorer countries, like Cuba. In line with what many of my research participants believed the government was itself doing – 'squeezing' foreign visitors to bring in as much hard currency as possible – *jineterismo* could be defended by them as a rightful way to get their slice of the tourism cake, part of a nation's cunning tactics to siphon off capitalist wealth. If this involved some deception at tourists' expense, it could be easily justified by taking an Us-Cubans vs. Them-tourists approach.

The Cuban authorities' condemnations of *jineterismo*, however, did not operate along these lines of interpretation and misrecognized any such justifications and moral underpinnings. As the researches of Berg (2004) and Garcia (2010) have shown, official views of *jineterismo* did not see it as a justifiable economic endeavour and a legitimate realm of *la lucha*, but rather as a sign of moral corruption marking decadent selves guided by a lust for luxuries and capitalist consumption. In a research context where the moralities of economic and intimate engagements and their boundaries are themselves politically and ethically fraught objects of struggle, there seems to be all the more reason for researchers to become acutely sensitive and reflexive regarding their own moral assumptions and desires (Fassin 2008; Zigon 2010), and to pay attention to the competing moral claims they encounter during fieldwork (Simoni 2013). Not doing so may reduce the interpretative possibilities explored, obscuring practices that seem to go against our most cherished views of tactical resistance and strategic essentialism, such as Cubans' profession of 'true', non-instrumental friendship (Chapter 6). The findings on friendship showed the importance of taking these universalist claims seriously, especially Cubans' longing for 'normalcy' and aspiration to be recognized as 'free', 'autological subjects' who share with tourists similar moral and emotional interiorities as fully fledged members of a same 'humanity' (Povinelli 2006).

This is not to dismiss the fact that the very same Cubans could also, in other contexts of interaction where other moral imperatives prevailed, brag about *jinetero*-like feats at the expense of foreign visitors (Simoni 2013). Moments of peer sociability among Cuban men, for instance, were particularly conducive to the appearance of the instrumental idiom of *jineterismo*. Such conversations tended markedly to objectify tourists, and the people talking avoided dwelling on any emotions they felt for their foreign 'friends' and 'partners', as this attitude could give the impression of being too vulnerable and naïve. More often, they would instead align their talk with the semantic registers and moral discourse of *jineterismo*, becoming 'tourist riders' guided by instrumental purposes of securing their socio-economic needs and desires, and those of their families.[2]

Instead of trying to resolve the contradiction inherent in the possible coexistence of these competing forms of engagement – such as 'true' versus 'cunning' friendship (Simoni 2015c) – which often seemed to negate each other, or aprioristically rank them as more or less real, it seems both more sensitive and analytically fruitful to engage in the sort of 'ethnography of moral reason' that Sykes (2009: 15) has recently called for, which aims at providing 'specific accounts of how people negotiate paradoxes in their daily lives'.[3] In the light of the ethnography discussed in the previous chapters, I would argue that the productive and persistent ambiguity of touristic encounters in Cuba was precisely what facilitated such radical shifts between different modes of engagement and moral dispositions. Anthropologists striving to understand their research participants (and heed their calls for understanding) will benefit greatly from seriously, and without condescension, considering the competing claims of truthfulness of these different ways of relating to others. This, in turn, will help us move beyond the simple view of visitors and visited, each having different takes on their relationships, to support a notion of multiplicity as intrinsic to persons and relationships, drawing attention to the key processes and 'events' through which these subjects and relationships emerge, eventually, as singular and discrete (Humphrey 2008; see also Simoni 2015c).

It should be clear by now that I do not mean to underestimate the tactical and instrumental dimensions of touristic encounters, especially when these are self-professed by our research participants. Rather, I encourage an approach that devotes attention to the frames of legibility and moral horizons that underpin such endeavours, and to remain open to other possibilities and alternative endings, so as to recognize, and take seriously, also those situations in which ascriptions of tactical and instrumental behaviours are explicitly refuted and perceived as hampering the range of subjectivities to which our informants aspire. In Cuba, the image of the cunning *jinetero/a* deceiving tourists via duplicity and dissimulation is becoming a reified construct from which my research participants – key actors in its propagation – found it difficult to extricate themselves. As I have shown throughout the book, and particularly in Chapters 6 and 8, there were indeed instances in which the 'hypothesis' of 'duplicity and dissimulation' as the quintessential 'arms' 'of the dominated' (Callon and Rabeharisoa 2004: 20) became a conceptual prism (and prison) that was extremely hard to refute and disentangle. The government selectively mobilized this image (perhaps replacing 'dominated' with 'luxury-seeking marginals') to condemn *jineterismo* and justify its repression, and it was reiterated in tourism guidebooks and other international media on tourism in Cuba, activated by my Cuban research informants as they bragged about their *jinetero*-like exploits at tourists' expense, and also evoked by tourists to justify their cynical counteractive responses to *jineterismo* and erect insurmountable boundaries between 'Us' and 'Them'.[4]

To facilitate the recognition of alternative claims and scenarios, and avoid the risk of falling into overly reductive interpretations, I proposed the heuristic notion of the 'informal encounter', inspired by, but diverging in focus from, the more established concept of the 'informal economy'. Even as it calls attention to a formal/informal divide emanating from tourism policies and policing in certain destinations, and to that divide's potential effects on touristic encounters, this notion has the advantage of under-determining what these interactions are about. It thus departs from aprioristic assumptions on the (inevitable) prevalence of economic reasoning and instrumental rationality as their key drivers. Instead of reducing touristic encounters and relationships to 'cold' and ineluctable expressions of reciprocal manipulation, I have argued that their characterization may be fruitfully approached as a 'hot' situation (Callon 1998a; Strathern 2002): an unpredictable situation akin to a crisis, fraught with many potential ramifications and replete with possibilities of redefining 'what is going on' and 'who is doing what'.

Gaining Access and Getting in Touch

In order to engage informally with each other, tourists and Cubans had to first overcome a range of potential challenges cast as external and independent of their own will, challenges stemming from the normative suggestions and control of the tourism authorities and tending to push the tourists and locals apart. Scrutiny of how people coped with these obstacles and difficulties revealed significant differences between and among tourists and Cuban people that dramatically inflected their possibilities of interacting. For the former, these differences were more a matter of choice in modes of holidaying, whereas the latter suffered the impact of the discriminatory profiling of *jineteros/as*.

Facilitating informal encounters for tourists was the possibility of moving beyond 'tourism bubbles' like all-inclusive resorts and guided tours. These rather 'enclavic' (Edensor 1998) forms of tourism appeared less conducive to unscripted, unplanned, and unexpected connections. But the visitors' predisposition and expectations towards such encounters also mattered, as did their determination and ability to confront the authorities if needed. Meanwhile, Cubans' tactics were informed by their knowledge of how the policing of tourism operated. Aware of their unequal opportunities to engage with foreigners, which depended particularly on place of residence, socio-economic status, gender and racial attribution, they could cultivate connections with the gatekeepers of the formal tourism industry (e.g. police officers, waiters, porters in tourism installations), integrate cliques and factions for protection and reciprocal support, and more generally devise ways to bypass the control of the authorities and thus access tourists. Far from being always straightforward and immediate, engaging in touristic encounters could involve huge and risky investments (in time, in money, in relationships), and a wide range of competences and resources.

This book's consideration of how tourists and Cubans got in touch and initiated an encounter (Chapter 4) foregrounded the more 'internal' hows and whats of these engagements. How did people deal with, and eventually move beyond, the threat of deception and reciprocal exploitation? This was when the protagonists of interactions actualized the two-sided view mentioned above – epitomizing both the positive and negative potential of such encounters – as they tried to map out each other's intentions and motivations. The main challenge was to overcome suspicion of deceptive and instrumental behaviours, as this suspicion could work against a more fully fledged involvement in interactions with Cuban people.

It was precisely in such initial moments of encounter that visitors often began assessing the risk and likelihood of engaging in the kind of 'transient and exploitative' (van den Berghe 1980), 'impersonal' (Pi-Sunyer 1978 [1977]; Nash 1978 [1977], 1981), 'de-humanized' (Crick 1989), or 'commoditized' (Cohen 1984) touristic encounter described in early social science literature and in contemporary, increasingly popularized, critical assessments of tourism. Here is also where the question of determining whether they were dealing with 'professional tourism brokers', 'experienced entrepreneurs', 'hustlers', 'prostitutes' or 'ordinary Cubans' started to be addressed. For our analyses, the lesson here is that notions like 'middleman', 'broker' and 'mediator' can carry their own implications as to whether and how touristic encounters may occur and unfold. In some touristic contexts at least, we should therefore be particularly careful not to use them too hastily and unreflexively. Adopting such concepts a priori as analytics holds a risk of obfuscating our research participants' active engagements in, as well as resistance to, processes of categorization.

For their part, Cuban men and women showed great awareness of how the tourists' evaluation of the initial moments of getting in touch could inflect the chances of engaging with them. To avoid giving the impression of opening the interaction in the kind of premeditated, predictable way that tourists tended to equate with instrumental agendas, they devised a range of more or less creative tactics that deserve our attention, given also that they find striking parallels in other tourism destinations across the world (Crick 1992; Dahles 1998). This supports the notion that the protagonists of these engagements develop similar competences and abilities because very similar challenges affect the development of informal encounters in different international tourism destinations.

Several of my Cuban research participants explicitly recognized the importance of such competences as catching the tourists' attention, striking up a conversation, being attuned to their language and interests. Some of them even went so far as to consider *jineterismo* '*un arte*' – an art of communicating and dealing with people, of enticing interest and developing relationships, in which having a sharp mind (*una mente*) and a good vibration (*vibra*) also played a role. These positive assessments of *jineterismo* highlighted its most cosmopolitan features and gave it the allure of a discipline with its own value system and best practice criteria – a positive body of knowledge about humans and human relationships. Precisely this competence in human relationships, in bringing about and enacting an ample range of relational idioms, was considered in more detail in Part Two of the book, which focused on engagements that brought into play notions of market exchange and hospitality (Chapter 5), friendliness and friendship (Chapter 6), festivity and seduction (Chapter 7), and (commoditized) sex (Chapter 8).[5]

(Dis)Trust and (In)Equality

(Dis)trust and (in)equality – two key features that scholars have singled out as typical of tourist-local relationships (see in particular van den Berghe 1980 and Cohen 1984) – were among the most absorbing and controversial issues in the range of relationships addressed in Part Two of the book. Asymmetries were arguably the driving force of *jineterismo*, a relational idiom that emphasized economic inequality between tourists and Cubans. They also justified manipulative and deceptive behaviours intended to extract resources from privileged foreigners, but given the tourists' alertness to deception, any hint of such behaviours posed serious challenges to the development of relationships. Instead, other relational idioms tended to come to the fore, often in direct opposition to tourism hustling, prostitution and *jineterismo*. These idioms tended to downplay inequalities, or at least keep at bay the idea that they were the predominant force behind a relationship. What characterized the enactments of market exchange, hospitality, friendship, festivity, seduction and sexual relationships examined in the previous chapters was rather their potential to infuse a sense of mutuality and reciprocity between the protagonists involved.[6]

These seemed to be the main normative ideals on which tourists and Cubans could converge. Market exchanges between buyers and sellers rely on the ideal of the balanced economic transaction. Hospitality is between hosts and guests, each with his or her sense of duty and reciprocal obligation. Friends can certainly help each other out, but the primary drive should not be to profit from a friend's resources. Festive engagements cast participants as members of an egalitarian *communitas*, whereupon major differences and asymmetries are set aside. Finally, the partners in 'genuine' sexual relationships are expected to complement and satisfy each other in mutual ways. One might of course object that these are highly idealized, purified, stereotypical views of social relationships. However, I argue that it was precisely their simplistic and widely shared, commonsensical character that enabled them to act as a sort of 'lingua franca' in the 'cultural borderland' (Mattingly 2006) of informal touristic encounters, as this minimal, common view of relationships was a ground on which the protagonists involved could initially converge.

My ethnographic material seems thus to point at the widely shared character of some basic assumptions and normative ideals of different types of relationships. However vague and 'thin', and perhaps also because they were, these ideals offered people with very different backgrounds who were unacquainted with each other some initial clues on how a given relationship might be conceived and brought about, providing some elementary indication of its core features and implications. The role played by international tourism, and more particularly by the kind of encounters considered in this book, in the global diffusion, actualization and negotiation of such ideals certainly deserves closer examination. As I have shown here, informal touristic encounters fostered people's engagement with, and reflection on, different relational idioms. They led to the explicit confrontation and negotiation of normative assumptions and expectations on the matter that are perhaps less likely to become explicit in other interactional realms, especially once the characterization of relationships (i.e. as 'cold') is taken for granted and does not generate controversy.

Following Glick Schiller (2006: 10), we may want to pay attention to how these 'globally circulating ideas' – about relational idioms, in this case – may both 'normalize oppressive regimes or provide charters for struggle'. I would argue that the nature of their impacts on people's lives can ultimately be assessed only through ethnography of how these relationships operate, and of the challenges and opportunities they present for the protagonists involved. When confronted with the lingua franca of idealized relational idioms, it is also important to consider these ideals as carrying their own connotations, scalar imaginings, and relative power – that themselves tend to resonate with the balance of power between the parties involved. Current anthropological scholarship on love and intimacy shows, for instance, that in certain ethnographic contexts the ability to engage in 'romantic', 'selfless', 'pure' love becomes a marker of modernization, of being an autonomous and self-determined subject.[7] The case of friendship provided a good example of similar dynamics, in that its purified ideal (the typical 'Western model' described in the literature) was precisely the one my Cuban research participants tended to aspire to. This is what emerged in Ernesto's narrative, for instance (Chapter 6): his willingness to be recognized as capable of the kind of true friendship that he liked to project beyond Cuba's shores to the tourists' countries of residence, where life was 'normal' and relationships were not guided by the need to respond to economic scarcity and material necessities.

This leads again to the issue of equality. Accordingly, Cubans' declarations of friendship – at least some, that is – could be read as a claim for equal moral status, for equal treatment as human beings (Rezende 1999) sharing similar emotional interiorities (Faier 2007). Their ethical demand was to be recognized as autonomous individuals who were not solely, or primarily, governed by material needs and concerns. It is important to note that this aspiration to equality at a moral level then had the potential, by way of the true friendship it strove to conjure, to bring about concrete changes also at a more practical and material level. In this way a true friendship with tourists could provide not only moral gratification and satisfaction but also opportunities to improve one's material conditions. Ultimately, the enactment of this relational ideal therefore held the potential to reduce perceived inequalities at both a moral and a material level.

By highlighting the importance of recognizing people's aspirations and claims to recognition, this line of reasoning warns against any exclusive emphasis on 'contextualization' and 'localization' – what, in the anthropology of friendship, has been referred to as the need for 'making friendship impure' (Coleman 2010). While it is no doubt essential to account for local contexts and the way these inform the imagining and enacting of relationships, we also need to attend to the 'virtualities' (Willerslev in Venkatesan et al. 2011),[8] aspirations and efforts to achieve certain ideals that such contexts engender. Contextualization should also lead us to recognize the concrete issues that lie behind, and help understand, the reasons for any such idealized claim. Contexts of striking inequality like those examined here, I would suggest, may be particularly conducive to this kind of eagerness and anticipation for universalist models of relationships signalling equal membership in an imagined global community (Ferguson 2006). Following Piot's (2010) insights along Ferguson's lines, the idealization of relationships and the kinds of subject formations it brought about may then be read as a way for Cubans to reach towards the future, engaging mimetically with what they desired by being at one with tourists and urging them to take this seriously, reciprocate accordingly and thus fulfil these ideals.[9] This frame of legibility, in turn, may open up promising paths for study of the making of relationships across the North-South divide, reflecting on how processes of globalization operate at the intimate and subjective level, and shedding light on related issues of membership, exclusion, power and belonging in the contemporary world.

Besides (in)equality, and also in close connection to it, (dis)trust was the other key issue that came up in the various types of relationships considered in Part Two. Once again, idealized views of market exchange, hospitality, friendship, festivity, seduction and sexual relations helped actualize certain normative expectations related to trust. What follows is a review of their most striking implications.

In the case of cigar deals, I highlighted the dealers' efforts to officialize their status and mimic official market exchanges. Alternatively, or complementing this, dealers tried to authenticate the products on offer. Reputation and traceability were also emphasized, always with the aim of reassuring tourists and infusing trust into the transactions. On excursions to farms in Viñales, tobacco and the manufacture of cigars were deployed to dispel mistrust regarding the 'genuine' nature of what was being offered. The ways the relational idiom of friendship was enacted relied on the implicit assumption that friends would trust each other, with trust thus taken as a by-product of friendship. Even when the establishment of a 'normal' friendship was deemed too far-fetched, demonstrations of good behaviour proving one's friendly intentions could at least reassure distrustful tourists. Partying had other implications, as its relational idioms strove to silence absorbing worries altogether. Ideally, the question of trust was bypassed by encouraging people to leave worries behind, 'let go' and go with the flow. Conjuring a move from reason to feelings and emotions could help put trust on hold, releasing people from such preoccupations. To a large extent, seduction and sexual relationships ultimately sought to keep up such a move.

For tourist and Cuban men and women to evoke idioms of market exchange, hospitality, friendship, festivity, seduction and sex and share a vague notion of these relational ideals and their normative implications was one thing. Quite another was to convince each other that relationships conformed to such ideals and norms. Verbal claims may entail commitments to one's words (Lambeck 2010) and prompt 'performance struggles' to determine the 'success or failure of [one's]... act of language' (Callon 2007: 330), but they do not act straightforwardly as self-fulfilling prophecies and may have hardly any purchase on the reality people experience, when not supported by more concrete proofs. In touristic encounters, lack of the latter fostered the emergence of sceptical postures, notably the adoption of the MacCannellian stance of 'staged authenticity' (1973, 1976, 2008) predicated on the disjuncture and divide between (superficial) claims and (real) hidden motives.

Such stances clearly appeared in the case of declarations of friendship. When proffered too loosely, these tended to make tourists alert to potentially deceptive and manipulative behaviours. More generally, when relational claims appeared void of substance, they ran the risk of being discredited as staged, superficial allegations. Alternatively, people could decide to go along with them while playing 'as if', maintaining a certain distance from their role – a stance that also became apparent when considering the case of friendship. This perspective finds a parallel in the 'post-tourist' (Feifer 1985; Urry 1990) mode of engagement, in which acutely self-reflexive tourists play with normative scripts and roles and go along with tourism-related *mises en scène* with complicity. This attitude also came up in the teaching and learning of dance when tourists adopted an ironic, self-mocking stance by caricaturizing their dance moves.

Both the approaches of staged authenticity and the more playful ones of the post-tourist could hamper people's involvement and dedication in a relationship. Trying to move beyond this lack of commitment and give relational claims more purchase on the realities they wished to bring about, tourists and their Cuban partners engaged in performance struggles focused on people's practical achievements. Accordingly, the various chapters in Part Two of the book highlighted the interweaving of discourses, practices, affects and materialities through which the protagonists of touristic encounters gave substance to relational idioms. From the unpacking of cigars by dealers, to the proofs of good behaviour between friends, to the embodied nature and affective intensities of dancing, to deployments of money between sexual partners – things and discourses, affects and fantasies, abstract ideals and materialities could all converge to give shape to different types of relationship. This way, the protagonists at stake were not only confronted with hypothetical discourses on relationships, but also with pragmatic tests and trials geared at supporting and substantiating them.

Although discourses, practices, affects and materialities could all work together to shape relationships in certain ways, they could also work against each other, fostering tensions and ambiguities. Indeed, rather than remaining stable, 'cool' and predictable for long, relationships constantly came up against challenging moments and events that reconstituted them into 'hot', controversial issues. As doubts and ambiguities (re-)emerged, the protagonists involved had to renew their efforts to figure out and make sense of what was (really) going on. This often called for more explicit statements and reassurances, providing the ethnographer with further opportunities to follow how people debated and reformulated their assumptions on relationships.

Two of the typical sources of controversy merit emphasis, given their ubiquity in different situations of encounter: the short time frame of interactions, and the circulation of money. These two elements have been repeatedly singled out to characterize the nature of tourist-local relationships as 'transient' (and consequently more open to deception and manipulation) and 'commoditized' (see in particular van den Berghe 1980 and Cohen 1984). Throughout the book, I have shown that tourists and Cubans did not necessarily surrender to this characterization or let it deterministically reduce the range of relationships they could achieve. The following summarizes how money and time challenged and (re)opened debates on the idioms of market exchange, hospitality, friendship, festivity, seduction and sexual relations.

Lack of time was a constant obstacle to the establishment of relationships, breaching normative assumptions about their proper development and raising questions on the kind of engagements at stake. 'How can you say we are friends if we just met a few hours ago?', for instance, was a frequent objection voiced by tourists, enough to shed doubt on the Cubans' claims. More perplexities of this sort arose in relation to seduction processes: 'If Cuban women come straight towards you, you know what they will be expecting: money', went a popular saying among tourist men. Overly immediate claims of friendship or expressions of sexual interest tended to raise suspicion and be cast as superficial and potentially deceptive, or as a sign of commoditization. The norm that emerges here was that these types of relationships required not just effort but time, which most tourists did not have. Similarly, in the case of farm visits in Viñales, gifts and counter-gifts could follow each other too closely to be appreciated as expressions of disinterested generosity. This unsettled some tourists' assumptions about reciprocity and its temporal dimensions, leading calculative agencies and notions of the correct exchange value of things to interfere with ideals of hospitality.

To overcome the disruptive effect that transience had on relational ideals, the protagonists of touristic encounters could work over temporality itself and emphasize its subjective dimension, intensifying and amplifying the moral traces, tidemarks and legacies of their relationships. As shown for the case of friendship, memorable experiences could be foregrounded via 'narrative emplotments' demarcating a 'before' and an 'after' in relationships (Mattingly 2010), with the after being fully fledged friendship. People could also project their ties into the future by exchanging contact information and promises to keep in touch: 'We will meet again!' This was how they kept connections open while also preserving normative ideals on how relationships ought to proceed.

Money and its circulation were likely to become the most troublesome ingredient of touristic encounters in Cuba. Their intrusion into the scene threatened to push people back into negative preconceptions and expectations, underline profound asymmetries and inequalities, and impede efforts to move beyond the prospect of instrumentality and exploitation to realize other kinds of relationships. However, as Bloch and Parry (1989) have pointed out, and as the work of Zelizer (2000, 2005) urges, social scientists need to overcome the 'hostile worlds' perspective that sees money as necessarily 'corrupting' relationships and intimacy. Money gets entangled in different transactional regimes; its purposes and functions change. This indexical and pragmatic character (Maurer 2006) must not be lost in the analysis. Indeed, from 'money-as-gift' to 'money-as-payment', I have shown that different transactional regimes allowed different relational idioms to emerge and be sustained.

In informal touristic encounters in Cuba, expressions of asymmetry and inequality were arguably always on the brink of surfacing. The tourists' ascendancy tended to rest on their possession of hard currency and other coveted goods (e.g. branded clothes and accessories, electronic equipment), and on their privileged legal status and ability to move across borders. Cubans, on the other hand, often relied on less tangible affirmations of their insider knowledge (e.g. of cigars, potential dangers, places to go and more generally of Cuba) to try and take the lead in the relationship. As suggested by the words of Armando and Gabriel (Chapter 8), and by other visitors' assertion of the advantages of being a foreigner in Cuba (Chapter 3), tourists' marks of privilege were embodied 'in durable materials' (Law 1991: 174) – cash, credit cards, visas, passports – that could ultimately grant them leverage superior to that of their Cuban counterparts, helping stabilize a position of superiority (Simoni 2008b).[10] Meanwhile, to sustain one or more of the relational ideals considered above and keep notions of exploitation at bay, any such expressions of asymmetry had to be managed carefully. Moving beyond a static 'victim-oppressor' dualism (see Bowman 1996), the subtler deployments of power in these relationships call for empirically grounded exploration of their concrete vectors and materializations, so as to explain how privileged positions were brought about, secured and challenged.

Reformulating Relational Idioms

The second part of the book also discussed how ideals of hospitality, market exchange, friendship, and festive and sexual relationships could be transformed, adapted and worked over from within touristic encounters. Boundaries between relational idioms could blur and fade away, or be redrawn and reinforced along different lines, widening or reducing the range of entities that could be included within their frame and re-qualifying those entities' meaning and implications. Highlighting some of these adaptations and transformations here will in turn enable me to elaborate on the main lines of reasoning behind these transformations' articulation and justification.

Consider for instance the idiom of hospitality in the course of tourists' visits to farms in Viñales. Given the short duration of the exchange and the circulation of hard currency on such occasions, some visitors felt that a boundary between gift and market exchange was being transgressed, which raised doubts about the genuineness of the hospitality at stake. Other tourists, however, willingly engaged in what they saw as appropriate forms of gift giving and reciprocity. Their relationships with farmers materialized a world of genuine and traditional hospitality. In this case, the short span of time between gifts and counter-gifts did not prompt a shift from hospitality to market exchange but rather produced a situated rendition of a host-guest relationship that made room for transience and money-as-gift.

Formulations of friendship that managed to make room, explicitly, for expressions of asymmetry and self-interest constitute another striking case.

In the realm of informal touristic encounters in Cuba, as in other similar situations of tourist-local interaction elsewhere (see Tucker 1997), the idiom of friendship tended to be seen in opposition to notions of interestedness and calculation. Friends were ideally portrayed as equal and disinterested partners. However, I have also considered instances when people came up with a different version of friendship that accounted for the partners' asymmetric resources and economically motivated agendas. This is not to say that notions of friendship could be stretched indiscriminately; limits also appeared as to how far such adaptations could go. An overemphasis on asymmetries could for instance lead to reformulation of relationships as charitable, one-sided exchanges between powerful benefactors and powerless beneficiaries.

The chapter on partying highlighted continuities and discontinuities between festive relationships and seduction processes. The discussion of dancing showed how sensual movements and physical arousal could be internalized in a festive engagement or ad hoc formulations of dancing styles. However, they could also be positioned outside the festive frame, leading to the materialization of boundaries between the idiom of partying and those of sensuality, seduction and sexual relations. In other cases, following normative ideals of flirting and getting intimate, partying could act as a privileged platform for seduction: it helped infuse spontaneity into relationships, reassuring people of their genuine (as opposed to commoditized) character, of their organic growth in serendipitous moments of vitality and uncontrolled excitement. At this point continuities and smooth transitions between partying and seducing, rather than clear-cut boundaries, became important for the protagonists involved.

Chapter 8 also highlighted various possibilities of inclusion or exclusion of monetary transactions within sexual relationships. The circulation of money could be considered completely at odds with 'normal' seduction processes, and be straightforwardly associated with exploitation and prostitution. But it could also be integrated and normalized within a 'Cubanized' frame of sexual relationships, one that portrayed commoditization as the norm in this country. Following yet another rationale in which gender asymmetry was the key explanans, monetary considerations could lead to a general reassessment of sexual relations and normalization of economic investment in sex.

These different scenarios offer a glimpse of three main approaches people relied on to work over relational idioms, which I would term socio-economic contextualization, culturalism/relativism and universalism. In spite of their autonomy, these approaches could complement each other and tourists and Cubans alternatively or even simultaneously drew on one or another to frame and stabilize the meaning of their relationships. Several of the examples I considered in this book, particularly in chapter 8, highlighted this possibility of moving from one stance to another, and of (re)conceptualizing relational idioms according to different lines of reasoning and justification.

Socio-economic contextualization enabled tourists and Cubans to account for their asymmetric resources. Normative ideals of friendship, for instance, were contextualized, inflected and adapted to take into account people's unequal economic assets and try to harmonize economic interest with affective drives. In the case of sexual relations, even practices that could easily be seen as exploitative could be recast as just, redistributive exchanges of money for sex in the unequal context of tourist-Cuban interactions. Accordingly, commoditized sex was normalized and stripped of its moral conundrums via its contextualization in a world of unavoidable socio-economic inequality.[11] In all these cases, asymmetries between tourists and Cubans were accounted for without surrendering to the views of *jineterismo* and reciprocal exploitation.

The relativist/culturalist perspective was encapsulated in the expression 'this is (how things are in) Cuba'. Such statements, ubiquitous in tourist-Cuban interactions, encouraged people to simply 'adapt', that is, go along with the cultural idiosyncrasies of this peculiar island and wholeheartedly experience them without even trying to understand their rationales. When applied to sexual relationships involving monetary compensation, this approach provided an alternative path to normalize their commoditized character. In the realm of dancing, it could help portray physical contact and sensuality as integral to dance moves and festive relationships. More generally, as I have pointed out elsewhere (Simoni 2008a, 2011), the 'Cubanization' of relational idioms, with its seemingly limitless applicability, could enable the reformulation and justification of a great many engagements. To explain this success, we may regard the culturalist/relativist approach as perfectly attuned to the current 'ethic of interculturality' as a key legitimizing discourse of tourism (Cousin 2008), and to aprioristic valorizations of tourism as a journey towards the Other, towards experiencing another culture, other customs and other ways of relating to people (Simoni 2011). In contrast to the socio-economic contextualization perspective, the relativist/culturalist approach was likely to silence questions about the unequal foundations of touristic encounters and their role in shaping the realities people were experiencing.

Based on universalist assumptions and argumentations, the third approach found evident expression in the persona of *Homo economicus*: the calculative individual guided by instrumental rationality to maximize his or her profits. In this perspective, evoked by Gabriel and Armando (Chapter 8), *jineterismo* and exploitation no longer looked like an immoral, unjustifiable flipside of touristic encounters, but like simple instantiations of a fundamental horizon of human relationships governed by free trade, self-interest and predatory instincts. *Homo economicus* also showed his face in the conversation with

Aurora and Ramona, when sexual relationships were reduced to a manipulative exchange between calculating individuals. A slightly more hybrid and nuanced but equally universalizing idea was that human relationships, in general, were always to a certain extent motivated by some kind of interest, a view expressed by tourists striving to harmonize the instrumental and affective dimension of Cubans' friendship.

In relation to friendship, I also highlighted the significance of its more universalist purifications, expressed most clearly in Cubans' aspirations to establish 'normal' friendships with tourists. The call here was to recognize the given Cuban as a fully fledged *ser humano* (human being), capable of loving and making friends like any other. Such a call encouraged tourists to live up to these ideals, and realize them together. The contrast between this picture of human beings and *Homo economicus* becomes less striking if we follow Povinelli's (2006: 17) argument that love – and purified models of friendship, we may add – are precisely where one may 'locate the hegemonic home of liberal logics and aspirations'. According to this view, 'the ability to "love" in an "enlightened" way becomes the basis (the "foundational event") for constituting free and self-governing subjects and, thus, "humanity"' (Povinelli 2004 cited in Faier 2007: 153).

Socio-economic contextualization, culturalism/relativism, and universalism: in my view, these are the main approaches that tourists and Cubans tended to rely on to (re)formulate relational idioms and to settle and justify their relationships. One person could use any of these approaches at different moments, and people's ability to alternatively deploy one or the other was also what could enable them to feel comfortable in a wide range of situations, confronting different audiences and responding to a variety of ethical demands and expectations. The way these approaches were mobilized, often in a rather exclusive and autonomous manner, also points towards their totalizing qualities and effects. Each effectively foregrounded different subjectivities and moralities, and outlined different configurations of power in tourist-Cuban and North-South relations. My focus here was on how these three grids of legibility were applied to work over, justify, underpin and give strength and credibility to relational idioms. Their scope, versatility and far-reaching applicability, however, suggest that an ample range of entities and situations, besides relational idioms, could be productively approached through any one of these lenses to reduce intersubjective ambiguities and settle controversies, making perhaps the study of their uses, circulations, popularity and measure of success and failure an interesting venue for further research.

The relational idioms examined in Part Two of the book could provide some stable ground and moral foundations to informal tourist-Cuban interactions. They could open up possibilities for extending these engagements in time, for instance, and bring various forms of gratification to the protagonists involved. Relational claims, however, also tended to kick-start a whole set of processes of scrutiny and verification to substantiate them and assess their validity. Given the diffuse mistrust and scepticism that affected touristic encounters, calls for consistency and clarity in one's behaviour could be all the more testing, perhaps leaving less room for the sort of ambiguity that inheres in intersubjective endeavours (Jackson 1998, 2007) and facilitates 'self-other relations' and 'the making of connections' (Moore 2011: 17), ensuring their vitality and plasticity (versus their predictability and 'coolness'). The paradox of tourists and Cubans monitoring too closely their enactments of hospitality, market exchange, friendship, and festive and sexual relationships – relationships that stemmed also from the widespread drive to reach beyond the instrumental horizons of *jineterismo* and the over-determined identifications of (deceitful) tourist hustlers and (gullible) tourists – was that this drew them into other stereotypical, overdetermined scripts that narrowly prescribed and demarcated what these relational idioms were to be about. The range of notions on which the protagonists of touristic encounters relied to name and frame their relationships – from friendship to hospitality to prostitution – was in itself quite limited (see Strathern 2005), and the complexities, ambiguities and multilayered dimensions of their engagements could hardly find a perfect match in such a finite vocabulary of relationality or in the kinds of commitments, choices and demands it called forth. In this sense, we may argue that once they were made explicit, acted upon and monitored closely, these relational idioms also brought some measure of closure to the tourists' and Cubans' engagements, channelling and constraining their scope and open-endedness. An alternative to such framing and making things explicit, and the challenges they posed, was to let ambiguities thrive and to reflexively play with them. Here ambiguity took on a life of its own, so to speak, as indeterminacy was purposefully pushed to its limits, bringing other challenges to the relationships at stake.

Ambiguity's Play: Treasuring Fragile Relationships

To avoid certain tough choices, commitments, controversies and closures that the explicit disclosure and negotiation of relational idioms could bring about, tourists and their Cuban partners could also prefer to leave the meanings of their relationships unsettled. In these cases, the issue of defining the relationship tended to remain all the more 'hot' and immanent, but rather than dealing with it upfront 'through the usual remedy' of 'making more and more elements of the situation explicit' (Strathern 2002: 254), people seemed to opt for a subtler manoeuvring of implicit assumptions, while also readying themselves for the possible dénouements and misunderstandings.

The adoption of such a stance – a sort of dwelling in ambiguity – could also indicate an awareness of the risks that clarifying and making things explicit could carry. As Callon (1998) and Strathern (2002) suggest, the risk is that the range of potentially controversial elements at play in the definition of a situation could increase, thus making things even 'hotter' and harder to cope with.

In Part Two, and more clearly in Chapter 8, I discussed a range of examples in which tourists and Cubans preferred to keep ambiguities alive, rather than draw clear-cut boundaries between different relational idioms. This equivocal approach opened up realms of possibility for different manipulations, interpretations and appropriations to take place. Indeed, by avoiding explicit definition of the qualities of their relationship, the protagonists could – provisionally at least – interpret the relationship in their own ways, in line with their own agendas and normative assumptions. This was also a way for potentially divergent and conflicting relational idioms to remain simultaneously in play.

Aurora's story (Chapter 8) exemplified this stance, highlighting a shifting approach to a relationship and its rationales – from ambiguous mutuality to deceptive commoditization and back again. In the end, and despite the risk of missing out on retribution, Aurora's playing with ambiguity proved rather successful. But other examples pointed to the more perilous edge of such endeavours, showing how uncertainty and lack of definition in relationships was far from always benefiting the Cuban side of the encounter. Leaving relationships unsettled and commitments unresolved was a risky business with unpredictable outcomes. The case of Gianluca, Marzio and Daniele (Chapter 8) showed how keeping the terms of their sexual engagement vague left the Cuban partners dependent on the meagre generosity of the three Italians. When ambiguity and misunderstandings were deployed this way, tourists tended to retain the privilege of discretion. How best to navigate the frontiers between implicit and explicit assumptions on relationships was therefore no easy matter, and could be fraught with serious consequences for people's livelihoods and self-esteem.

Notwithstanding the nature and signs of their effects, on a broader analytical level these cases of play with uncertainty point to the generative potential of ambiguity and misunderstanding in informal touristic encounters. Here we may follow Tsing's (2005) remarks on 'the awkward, unequal, unstable, and creative qualities of interconnections across difference', or what she evocatively calls 'friction' (4), as well as her call to consider the productive qualities of misunderstandings and acknowledge that these do not necessarily generate conflicts, but can also enable people to work together (x, 4). In the touristic encounters I examined, connections between tourists and Cubans could indeed feed on ambiguities and misunderstandings. The latter offered a viable path for sustaining a plurality of interpretations and moving relationships forward in spite of shaky foundations. This way, tourists and Cubans did not need to agree on the relational idiom informing their interactions, or could do so only at a very superficial or implicit level. However viable, this path was more seldom a sustainable one, as the relationships faced a chronic threat of discordant unravelling and a (re)assertion of the protagonists' asymmetric positions and diverging agendas.

Arguably, these situations test the limits of ambiguity in Self-Other relations. If we juxtapose these considerations with the above remarks on the overdetermined, stereotypical, predictable character of certain relational scripts and subject positions in touristic encounters, we see how these interactions can confront people with extremes of ambiguity. How little or much ambiguity can a relation sustain, and with what kind of consequences? A lack of ambiguity could make relationships excessively predictable and 'cool', but an excess of it, especially over time, could also become a source of unease and anxiety for some. Speculating further on the matter, we may argue that more balanced measures of ambiguity could make it easier to retain a manageable sense of vitality, liveliness, mutuality and freedom in relations. On the other hand, the ethnography also revealed that the extent of ambiguity in a relationship did not directly determine its outcomes: comparing the case of Aurora with that of Gianluca, Marzio and Daniele, for instance, we may argue that what mattered most, in making ambiguity work more fairly as a possible facilitator of relationships, was people's willingness and ability to maintain an open, empathetic and collaborative disposition towards one another, rather than a penchant for confrontation and manipulation, and a need to prevail.

Once again, and more fundamentally, ambiguity and the play it afforded highlighted the fragile character of touristic encounters in Cuba: the constant need to nurture and cherish them if they were to be mutually sustained and agreed upon in the long run, surmounting the challenges that loomed over them. Rather than deconstructing people's endeavours to relate, this book stands for a constructivist account of their efforts. Thus reopened, the question of what kind of relationships can emerge from touristic encounters deserves to be put afresh at the forefront of anthropological research. The paths outlined here will, I hope, inspire more research on how people engage across difference and inequality in the contemporary world and ultimately come to confront the very question of what it means to relate – what its limits and possibilities are, and what it may take to realize them.

ENDNOTES

Introduction

1 My translation from the original Italian. Most direct quotes from research participants appearing in the book are based on recollections after the events took place. All citations not originally in English, whether from written sources or from conversations with informants, have been translated by the author.

2 Parallels in this approach can be found in recent scholarship on the relational (Abram and Waldren 1997), purposeful (McCabe 2005) and locally situated (Frohlick and Harrison 2008b) nature of tourism-related identifications. We may similarly draw on the '"contact" perspective' outlined by Pratt (1992) in her writings on transculturation and the colonial encounter, which emphasizes 'how subjects are constituted in and by their relations to each other' (7). While I agree with Abram that tourism should not be too hastily equated to 'a replaying of the colonial encounter' (1997: 32), the theoretical reflections of Comaroff and Comaroff (1997) can also offer valuable insights into the workings of such processes of categorization. On the one hand, these authors underline the heterogeneity of colonial societies and emphasize the complicated and constitutive relationships between 'colonizers' and 'colonized'. On the other, they also point to the crucial dynamics of objectification, i.e. the poetics of contrast integral to the colonizing enterprise itself, highlighting 'the general tendency of colonial encounters to force even deeper conceptual wedges into ever more articulated, indivisible orders of relations' (1997: 26). In their work, these authors show the usefulness of investigating how such processes of division and simplification – what they refer as 'grammar of distinctions' – operate. I contend that a similar perspective can fruitfully inform approaches to tourism-related categorizations, at least in destinations like Cuba, where developments in the industry have relied on, and thus reiterated and magnified, differences and separations between visitors and residents (see chapters 1 and 2).

3 See e.g. Abram's (1997) research on tourism in the Auvergne region of France, where any clear-cut divide between 'us' and 'them' becomes highly problematic. For a more thorough examination of how the categories of 'insider' and 'outsider' can be sustained, reinterpreted, and assigned different meanings in response to the changing realities of a society in which tourism has come to play a very important role, see the work of Waldren (1996) in Mallorca.

4 With the notion of 'empty meeting grounds', Dean MacCannell (1992) evoked this generative potential: the 'theoretically free space between interlocutors' that may characterize
   touristic encounters – a 'realm of possibility for the future of human relationships emerging in and between diasporas' (7). However, as pointed out by Graburn and Mazzarella
   (1994), MacCannell's work remains embedded in a dualism between 'reality' and 'illusion', thus restating a questionable divide between 'genuine, authentic dialogue' and 'false
   exchange and communication'.

5 See in particular the works of Appadurai (1997), Bernstein (2007), Constable (2009),
   Cole and Thomas (2009), Faier (2007), Hirsch and Wardlow (2006), Hunter (2010),
   Illouz (1997), Kelski (1999, 2001), Manderson and Jolly (1997), Mankekar and Shein
   (2004), Mody (2008), Nagel (2000, 2003), Ortner (1996), Padilla et al. (2007), Patico
   (2009), Piscitelli (2013), Povinelli (2006), Rebhun (1999), Spronk (2012), Venkatesan et
   al. (2011), and Zelizer (2000, 2005).

6 See the edited collections of Bell and Coleman (1999a), Desai and Killick (2010), Simoni
   and Throop (2014b), and the articles of Dyson (2010), Mains (2013), Nisbett (2007),
   Santos-Granero (2007), and Torresan (2011).

7 My reflections draw here on Çalişkan and Callon's (2009, 2010) recent work on processes
   of 'economization', a 'term … used to denote the processes that constitute the behaviours, organizations, institutions and, more generally, the objects in a particular society
   which are tentatively and often controversially qualified, by scholars and/or lay people,
   as "economic"' (2009: 370). The performativity approach to economization outlined by
   Callon (1998b, 2007) builds on anthropological scholarship on value and processes of
   valuation, from the early works of Mauss (1969 [1925]) and Bohannan (1955); to those
   of Appadurai (1986), Strathern (1988) and Thomas (1991); to the more recent writings
   of Elyachar (2005), Guyer (2004), Maurer (2006), Mitchell (2002), and Roitman (2005).
   Such an approach highlights the fact that 'what is to be included in the economy is divergent and often controversial' (Çalişkan and Callon 2010: 22).

8 Cohen's 1996 book *Thai Tourism: Hill Tribes, Islands, and Open-Ended Prostitution* contains a collection of articles on 'open-ended prostitution' in Thailand's tourism context
   published in academic journals from 1982 onwards.

9 See in particular the works of Bauer and McKercher (2003), Bowman (1996), Brennan
   (2004), Clift and Carter (2000), Cohen (1996), Dahles and Bras (1999b), de Albuquerque
   (1998), Formoso (2001), Frohlick (2007, 2008, 2010), Herold, Garcia and DeMoya
   (2001), Jeffreys (2003), Kempadoo (1999, 2004), Kruhse-MountBurton (1995), Lévy,
   Laporte and El Feki (2001), Mullings (2000), Opperman (1999), Phillips (2002), Piscitelli
   (2007, 2013), Pruitt and LaFont (1995), Roux (2007, 2010), Ryan and Hall (2001),
   Ryan and Martin (2001), Salomon (2009). Several authors have examined these issues
   in relation to the Cuban case; publications include Allen (2007), Berg (2004), Cabezas
   (2004, 2006, 2009), Clancy (2002), Fusco (1997), Couceiro Rodríguez (2006), Daigle
   (2013), de Sousa e Santos (2009), Fosado (2005), Garcia (2010), Hodge (2001, 2005),
   Kummels (2005), O'Connell Davidson (1996), Roland (2011), Sánchez Taylor (2000),
   Sierra Madero (2013), Stout (2007), Tchak (1999), Tiboni (2002), Trumbull (2001) and
   Wonders and Michalowski (2001).

10 Cohen (1996) similarly considers how in Thailand, the illegalization of prostitution from
   the 1960s onwards, and a consequent lack of institutionalization, helped 'eradicate the

crisp line dividing those women who are marked as "prostitutes" from those who are not, and to create a fuzzily delimited grey area, located between the full-fledged prostitution of brothels and teahouses ... and "straight" sexual relations' (295).

11 All the photos that appear in the book were taken by the author during fieldwork in Cuba.

12 I generally felt uneasy during conversations that magnified the stark inequalities between tourists and Cuban people, and which depicted the former as taking advantage of their privileged status, notably in sexual engagements with local women. This leads me to concur with Frohlick and Harrison's (2008b) considerations: 'Grappling with the trenchant inequalities between tourists and local people that are exacerbated through global tourism processes, the complexities of tourists' (and locals') subjectivities, and paying credence to our imperative as anthropologists to protect and represent fairly our research participants continually unsettled our research' (15).

13 As Frohlick and Harrison put it, tourists often 'seek others who might sympathetically respond to their questions, acknowledge their fears and concerns, or be able to provide needed information about local communities' (2008b: 11). A parallel can also be drawn here with Frohlick's (2008) reflections on the role she acquired in discussions with female tourists in Caribbean Costa Rica about their sexual experiences with local men.

14 In his fieldwork among foreign tourists and informal guides in Luxor, Schmid (2008) was involved in very similar situations. This led him to recognize that the guides 'could use my mere visual presence as a kind of social capital when they were trying to "fish for tourists" (as they called it) and gain trust during an initial encounter. As a Westerner', adds Schmid, 'I was a marker that they were trustworthy individuals' (115).

15 An interesting parallel can be drawn here with Venkatesh's (2002) remarks on the importance of 'hustling' as a governing principle shaping and mediating social relations in a U.S. ghetto (96).

16 See also Bowman (1996) for a parallel in the ways Palestinian merchants in a Jerusalem tourist market talk with peers about their relationships and affairs with foreign tourist women.

Chapter One

1 Valle's (2006) research on the world of *jineteras* in contemporary Cuba draws a well-documented portrait of various forms of prostitution on the island since the arrival of the Spanish *conquistadores*, from the sexual exploitation of indigenous women to that of black women at the height of the slave trade. In her article on *jineteras*, Fusco (1997: 54) considers how brothels, in a colonial society dominated by a Latin Catholic tradition of discouraging public contact between men and women, were among the few places where casual encounters could take place openly, particularly encounters between white males and women of colour.

2 In her examination of 'Cuba's diverse tourism package', which allows 'prerevolutionary capitalist attractions to coexist with socialist revolutionary ones' (Babb 2011: 20), anthropologist Florence Babb remarks that 'nostalgia for the way things were before as well as after the revolution (and even, perhaps, after an awaited "transition" in the future) has been a stock trade in Cuba and represents the biggest calling card for tourism development'

(20). Moreover, 'the improbable interlinkage of yearnings for both socialist and capitalist (prerevolutionary) Cuba has been manifest for some time on the island' (30). Babb's interesting analysis ultimately leads her to suggest that 'these two faces of tourism are not always separable … and are really two versions of the same nostalgia' (30).

3   However, according to Valle (2006), there emerged other forms of prostitution, particularly from the 1970s, that were not directly linked to tourism. Here the relation between sex and money acquired increasingly complex characteristics, becoming more sophisticated and adapted to the new idioms and ethical codes of socialist Cuba (195–196). Thus, in a phenomenon known as *titimanía*, typically young girls (called *titis*) sought the company and favours of old, affluent professionals with privileged positions in the official establishment (Valle 2006: 197–199; Kummels 2005: 15–16). According to Kummels (2005: 15), these may be seen as the first manifestations of forms of *jineterismo*, a phenomenon more often linked to the international tourism boom of the 1990s but whose emergence Kummels traces back to the 1980s.

4   According to Cuban economists' estimates, in about forty years the U.S. travel ban has cost their country sixteen billion dollars in lost income (Figueras Pérez 2004: 90).

5   The key implications of this period of economic restructuring and its relation with the development of international tourism have been recently assessed by Cabezas (2009), who emphasizes how the crisis and the way the Cuban government coped with it ultimately amplified gender and racial inequalities and gave rise to new sexual formations that found expression in the realm of tourism (see also chapter 2).

6   Alcázar Campos (2010: 318) sees the authorities' efforts to regulate contact between Cubans and foreign tourists as responding not only to concerns to safeguard socialist mechanisms of economic redistribution and pre-empt growing inequalities, but also to fears of 'ideological contamination'. In 2005, the government passed a new resolution (No. 10-2005) regulating the relationships that tourism employees could have with foreign people. It invoked ethical, moral and professional principles, encouraging workers to conduct themselves with fidelity to the country and respect for the constitution, socialist legality and governmental policy (318). Workers in the state-led tourism installation where Alcázar Campos carried out fieldwork called these new regulations *Ley 10* (Law 10), alluding to a provision that limited the time one could spend talking to customers to a maximum of ten minutes.

7   Although several authors emphasize continuities in the persistence of racial stereotypes from colonial times to the present, the importance of nuances and transformations in the imagination of Self and Other sexuality should not be neglected (Jolly and Manderson 1997). In this sense, what seems essential is a thorough understanding of the conditions under which such representations emerge and the specific uses they are put to. Introducing a collection of articles dealing precisely with these issues, Jolly and Manderson (1997) observe that similar representations of sexuality may indeed give rise to very different interpretations and effects, depending on the contexts in which they take shape.

8   As Fernandez (1999: 86–87) points out, racial attribution in Cuba remains very fluid and contextual, and can frequently intersect with considerations of one's 'education, class, refinement, or what Cubans call "*nivel de cultura*" or "cultural level"'. In addition, according to this author, 'the use of racial terms is always dependent on the intention of the speaker, comparative assessments, and shifting contexts' (87), which leads her to argue that

'black, mulatto, and white are not self-evident categories as much as they are negotiable and malleable identities constructed in social interaction' (87). Issues of race and racialization in Cuba have attracted much anthropological attention, as attested for instance by the works of de la Fuente (2001), Fernandez (2010), Rodríguez Ruiz (1997, 2008), and Roland (2011).

9   The focus on the phenomenon of 'touristic prostitution' on this Caribbean island is paralleled in other tourism destinations, and must be placed in this wider context of tourism development and critique. As the works of Roux (2007, 2010) in Thailand and Salomon (2009) in Senegal have shown, this period indeed saw increased mediatization of 'sex tourism' on an international scale, which led this phenomenon to be framed as a new social problem, a dysfunction of society calling for moral and political action (Roux 2010: 1).

10 As Valle (2006: 230) remarks, critics of the Cuban government tend to put the responsibility for the 'resurgence of prostitution' and the explosion of 'sex tourism' squarely on the socialist state. Striving for a more balanced position on the matter, Valle (2006: 231) notes that albeit the government has certainly shown signs of indolence and blindness towards the phenomenon, it is going a step too far to argue that the Cuban state has directly promoted and fomented 'sex tourism' and 'prostitution' on the island, as maintained for instance by U.S. President George W. Bush's administration (Cabezas 2009: 5).

11 Renting rooms to foreigners in private houses was among the self-entrepreneurial possibilities legalized in the Cuban government's economic restructuring in the 1990s. In September 1993 the government authorized self-employment in 117 occupations (expanded to 157 by 1997) (Enken 2004: 220), thereby opening up new opportunities for tourism-related businesses. In 1995 a governmental resolution enabled Cubans to formally open small, privately owned restaurants catering for international visitors and operating in U.S. dollars, which became known as *paladares* (Ritter 1998: 77; Sacchetti 2004: 6). In 1997, another important domain of tourism-related self-employment was officially authorized with a new type of licence that enabled Cubans to accommodate foreign tourists in private houses (*casas particulares*). Since then, the number of *casas particulares* has kept increasing on the island, reaching more than five thousand in the year 2000 (Colantonio and Potter 2006: 129). Colantonio and Potter (2006: 231) note that in 1995, before even the government legalized *casas particulares*, over 7 per cent of international individual tourists visiting Havana chose this type of accommodation, a proportion that increased to 23 per cent in 2002, and stood at 18.9 per cent in 2008 (Alcázar Campos 2010: 208). After a period of relative stagnation in which fewer licenses were granted and private enterprise was discouraged, the Cuban government, under the new leadership of Raul Castro (who took over as president from his brother Fidel in 2008), enacted new measures to foster self-entrepreneurship. In spite of the tax burden the government imposed on these private initiatives, the last few years have seen a new boom in *paladares* and *casas particulares*. During my most recent stays on the island, however, owners of these private enterprises also expressed concern for the possible saturation of the market and the high level of competition in the sector.

12 According to Alcázar Campos (2010: 288), in the early 1990s tourism became a relatively easy target, a scapegoat on which to blame the emergence of phenomena – e.g. prostitution and the proliferation of illegal drugs – that contradicted the revolutionary ethic and threatened the supposedly unified moral fabric of the Cuban nation. See also Carter (2008: 252)

for a similar take on the matter, in which the tourist comes to be seen as a 'disease-ridden carrier that "infects" Cuban citizens'.

13 See Saney's (2004: 132) discussion of the law for more details. García Moreno and Pujadas Muñoz (2011: 469–470) also refer to Decree Law 175, promulgated in 1997 by the Cuban government, as a measure that modified the penal code and toughened the penalties for *jineterismo*.

14 This impression is supported by Hodge (2005: 14), who has worked with *pingueros* – men who provide sexual services, mainly to foreign men, often in exchange for cash (but see chapter 2 for a more detailed discussion of this contentious identification) – in Havana since 1999:

> According to every pinguero with whom I have spoken in recent years, police repression has worsened markedly over the past five or six years. Officers of the Specialized Police – created to protect tourists from jineteros, jineteras, and the pingueros – assume that any young Cuban walking alone in a tourist neighbourhood must be up to no good. They see it as their duty to harass and detain such youths ('for your protection', a policeman tells me). My own observations confirm that the Specialized Police are far more aggressive than they were just a few years ago.

Some of my informants, however, mentioned that control had loosened in the last few years. Dealing with these accounts of increased or decreased control and repression, it seems always important to grasp their purposiveness in a given context of interaction, as they could easily become entangled in, e.g., wider anti-establishment and/or self-victimizing narratives (see chapter 3 for more on this).

15 In the last couple of years, however, I also noticed that tourists who had shifted from Cuba to Brazil were again preferring the Caribbean island. Their choice, several research informants explained, was motivated by Brazil's becoming much more expensive; they also said that in Cuba, interactions with the local population, especially Cuban women, were less dangerous. The more 'docile character' of Cubans and the high degree of surveillance and control by the authorities could thus also nurture tourists' sense of safety (see chapter 3 for more on surveillance policies and alternative assessments of these matters by visitors).

Chapter Two

1 Several novels published in the last decade have dealt extensively with *jineterismo*, more particularly with the relationships between *jineteras* and tourists in Cuba. See e.g. the books of Montes (2001), Sierra i Fabra (2001), and Bustamante (2003), devoted entirely to this issue, and the review of Cowie (2002).

2 Any major contemporary guidebook on Cuba is likely to have at least a small section devoted to the phenomenon of *jineterismo*, as is the case in the very popular *Guide du Routard* (Gloaguen 2007) and *Lonely Planet* (Gorry 2004).

3 The use of U.S. dollars was officially banned in November 2004, when convertible pesos (*pesos convertibles*, CUC) replaced them in a measure designed to counteract what Fidel Castro saw as a U.S. attempt to obstruct the sending of dollars to Cuba (Brotherton 2008:

268). To curb the circulation of dollars, any exchange was originally charged a 10 per cent commission. In April 2005, the dollar-to-CUC rate stabilized at 1:1.18, following an additional 8 per cent revaluation of the CUC (268).

4 Brotherton (2008: 261) describes how remittances to Cuba increased 'from a reported $50 million in 1990 to over $750 million in 2000'. In 2013, they have been estimated to be above two and a half billion dollars (Morales 2013). According to Brotherton (2008: 261), this 'significantly contributed to the growing income disparity among different groups in the population'.

5 As argued by Cabezas (2009: 16): 'Informality, however, is not just about exclusion from formal jobs. It is also a counter-economy to wage labor' and 'a structure that allows for oppositional resistance to the hierarchy of race and class that constitute labor markets'. Several authors emphasize how growing inequality in Special Period Cuba resulted in differentiated access to labour markets (notably tourism jobs), tending to operate along pre-existing lines of gender, racial and class discrimination (see in particular Alcázar Campos 2010, Cabezas 2009, de la Fuente 2001, Roland 2011). In this context, informal realms of activity could open up new possibilities for disadvantaged groups. For more on this, and on the differential risks these informal engagements could carry, depending again on discriminatory patterns, see chapter 3, which considers the issue of the profiling of *jineteros/as*.

6 For a thought-provoking exploration of the nexus between practices and notions of *lucha* and informality, and transformations in subjectivity in contemporary Cuba, see the work of Bisogno (2010), which builds and expands on the seminal reflections of Fernández (2000) on informality and the 'politics of passion' on this Caribbean island.

7 Within the religious realm, for instance, Argyriadis (2005: 47) refers to a continuum going from the basic *jinetero* to more nuanced categories of pseudo-religious *jineteros* or intellectual *jineteros*. See also Palmié (2004) for an analysis of *jineterismo* in a religious context.

8 Palmié (2004: 241) notes more generally that by legalizing the dollar and creating two economic spheres, 'the state radically redefined the meanings of "scarcity" from a failure of effective supply into a failure of effective – i.e., dollar-backed – demand'. As he puts it: 'The unintended but logical consequence was a fundamental unsettling of definitions of the legitimacy of wants' (241).

9 Stout's (2007: 724) work on gay Cuban critiques of the tourist sex trade is a further reminder that these different interpretations were an issue of struggle at various levels of Cuban society, itself a complex reality that should not be reduced 'to the government or a ruling elite on the one hand and a passive multitude on the other'. On this latter aspect, see also Brotherton (2008: 260), whose work on 'new configurations of statecraft and subjectivity in 21st-century Cuba' urges scholars to 'address state power not as a monolithic function but as a proliferation of strategies that shape individual experiences'.

10 All the personal names of research participants are fictional. People who appear in more than one example are listed by name in the index to enable the reader to follow their narratives throughout the book.

11 Alcázar Campos (2009) similarly elaborates on how gendered normativities shape Cuban men's and women's differential possibilities and stigmatization in engaging with foreign tourists. Thus, *jineteros* are easily seen as *luchadores* (fighters) who engage in a varied range of tourism-related activities taking place in the street, their 'proper' realm of activity. Any

provision of sexual services to foreign women may be framed and normalized within a hegemonic view of masculinity that values sexual exploits and promiscuity as markers of virility (Alcázar Campos [2009], but see Simoni [2015a] for a more detailed examination of different enactments of masculinity in touristic Cuba and the tensions and paradoxes they generated). For Cuban women, however, the notion of *jinetera* often equates to that of prostitute. Women's tourism-related activities are less diversified and their public presence and sexual engagements with foreigners more stigmatized (Alcázar Campos 2009).

12 The narrative that foreign tourists prefer to engage (sexually in particular) with blacks and mulattos circulates widely in touristic Cuba and applies to both men and women. Several authors have shown that this may be linked to the hypersexualization of Afro-Cubans, and more generally to the valorization of an exoticized and eroticized Other in international tourism (see Alcázar Campos 2009, Cabezas 2009, Carter 2008, de la Fuente 2001, Roland 2011). Several Afro-Cuban men I worked with capitalized on this reputation and stereotype, willingly displaying markers of their Africanness as a way to catch the eye and seduce foreigners (see chapter 4).

13 According to Allen (2007: 188), *pinguero*s also clearly distinguish their activities from those of *jinetera*s: 'Although not denying that they have sex for some form of remuneration, male sex laborers in Cuba hold that it is "the way (they) do it … friendship … showing the island … not just sex" that sets them apart from "prostitutes", who they think of as full-time (female) professionals who trade only sex for a set amount of money'. Again, the words of the *pinguero* reflect the simplistic equation between *jinetera*s and prostitutes (see above), an equation that Cuban women themselves tended to challenge (see Daigle 2013).

14 See the work of Hansing (2006) for more on the Rastafari movement in socialist Cuba and also on what this author refers to as 'Rasta *jineteros*'. In chapter 4, I will touch again on the issue of tactical and instrumental uses of Rastafari imagery in touristic encounters.

15 On some occasions, Emilio mobilized a certain 'prestige' that came with his association with me, an economically privileged foreigner, to flirt with younger Cuban girls in a move resembling those described by Alcázar Campos (2010: 298–299) among her informants in Santiago de Cuba.

16 Alcázar Campos (2009) and Lundgren (2011) discuss this issue further, showing how gendered normativities and couples' relationships are affected by economic instability and crisis in contemporary Cuba.

17 Here again we may want to consider the challenges to normative constructions of gender and couplehood prompted by strained economic conditions on the island, and the ensuing difficulties Cuban women faced in finding what they believed was a suitable Cuban partner with whom to live a 'true love marriage'. I refer to the work of de Sousa e Santos (2009), Alcázar Campos (2009, 2010) and Lundgren (2011) for more on the matter. In her work on the migratory trajectories of Cuban women, García Moreno provides a useful account of the expectations and motivations of women who migrated to Spain via connections with a tourist partner (García Moreno 2010, García Moreno and Pujadas Muñoz 2011), issues that are also addressed in the book edited by Roca (2013) on 'love migration' to Spain.

18 I have considered in greater detail elsewhere (Simoni 2011) how tourist guidebooks deal with notions of *jineterismo*, 'sex tourism' and 'prostitution', and on the contrast that these

publications often entail between such tourism-generated 'evils' and a supposedly unified, genuine Cuban sexuality.

19 Relying on the metaphor of 'plug-ins' that people 'download' to become competent actors, and tracing parallels with recent developments in the field of distributed cognition, Latour (2005: 211–212) develops the notion of 'competence-building propositions' to underline the co-constructed and situated nature of cognitive abilities. This notion may be particularly productive when thinking about tourism, tourists and the development of competences to make sense of a destination via a range of tourism mediators (from travel agents to guides and other media resources).

20 In the last couple of decades, connections with tourists have been an important vehicle for migration from the island, mainly via tourist-sponsored invitations and marriage. The steep increase in marriages between Cubans and foreigners since the 1990s is discussed in the writings of Berg (2011), García Moreno (2010), García Moreno and Pujadas Muñoz (2011) and Roca (2013), which deal specifically with Cuban migration to Spain, and provide interesting insights on the relations between tourism and migration. See also Fernandez' (2013) work on Cuban-Danish couples for more on this latter aspect.

21 I refer again to the recent work by Berg (2011), García Moreno (2010), García Moreno and Pujadas Muñoz (2011), and Roca (2013) on Cuban migration to Spain, which shows the widespread diffusion in this country of tourism-related stereotypes regarding Cuba and its people, and of suspicions of arranged and economically motivated marriages between Cubans and Spanish citizens. My own fieldwork in Cuba suggests that similar suspicions thrived in most tourist-sending countries, particularly Italy (see below). For another thought-provoking, more auto-ethnographic account of the meanings and challenges of marriage between foreigners and members of the Cuban population, see Pertierra's (2007) article on 'being a bride in the field'.

22 Here there is a striking parallel with Coco Fusco's considerations on the *mulata*'s long-standing association with illicit sex, and with the adage that circulated on Caribbean plantations: white women for marriage, black women for work, and *mulatas* for making love (1997: 57). In this case, Cuban women as a whole took on the role ascribed to *mulatas* in the colonial proverb.

Chapter Three

1 The external and internal dimensions I evoke here are intuitively drawn from fieldwork rather than analytical, and are meant to reflect my research participants' understandings. In this sense, I also take stock of Latour's (2005: 191–218) call to 'redistribute the local' and his compelling critique of approaches to the 'social' that reify oppositions between 'face-to-face interaction' and 'context'. Challenging the taken-for-grantedness of such divides, he argues, 'ins and outs, like ups and downs, are results not causes', and 'the sociologist's job is not to fix the limits in advance' (215). Our task, instead, is to recognize where and how the subjects of our investigations themselves fix those limits, something on which Strathern (1996), Latour (2005), and Humphrey (2008) also insist.

2 O'Connell Davidson (1996) and Kummels (2005) have highlighted the importance of differences between migrants and legal residents of tourism poles, distinguishing two main groups of *jineteras* in Cuba. As Kummels (2005: 21) puts it:

> One the one hand there are those who are legitimate inhabitants of a tourism centre, which allows them to exercise greater control over sex work. Then there are the migrants from inland villages and towns, who are at a disadvantage, since they live far away from profitable sex commerce and are prevented by internal migration laws from legally residing and obtaining a job in these centres or cities. There they are to a larger extent victims of exploitation by third parties. When discovered by the police, migrants are returned to their place of residence. Accordingly, they depend to a degree on bribery to overcome their illegal status.

At the time of my fieldwork, exploitation by third parties – primarily illegal renters and pimps – seemed to affect mostly Cuban women who had migrated illegally to tourism centres and lacked any secure connection there. They appeared to be the most vulnerable actors in the world of *jineterismo*, and their circumstances differed significantly from those of their male counterparts, who tended to operate more independently. In more dramatic cases, dependencies could lead to bondage situations in which people from outside the capital became permanently indebted to accommodation providers and ended up having to work for them, as O'Connell Davidson (1996: 41) observed about Varadero in the mid 1990s.

3 Along with *lucha*, Cubans increasingly use terms like *conseguir* (obtain), *resolver* (resolve) or *inventar* (invent), each with various shades of meaning (Palmié 2004: 242), to refer to everyday strategies for obtaining goods and commodities. Palmié (242) discusses the meaning acquired by the term *inventar* in Special Period Cuba: 'it designates acts of obtaining goods and commodities otherwise out of reach by means most likely to be judged devious'.

4 Tellingly, Raquel refused to see herself as a prostitute or *jinetera* (*términos feos*, ugly words), preferring instead to talk about being a *luchadora* (see Daigle 2013) but admitted to *prostituirse* from time to time to solve a given problem or help her family back in Santiago (see the parallel with the remarks in Chapter 2 on the preference for the verb *jinetear* over the overarching identification of *jinetero/a*).

5 The following considerations are based on personal observations and conversations with Cuban research participants and supported by secondary literature touching this issue. I did not discuss the matter with the agents of such profiling, i.e. police officers, because I sensed that any prolonged interaction with them (or even just the suspicion of it) could harm my relationships with the subjects of such profiling, i.e. the Cuban men and women with whom I interacted daily, who, given the informal nature of their tourism-oriented activities, were likely to be suspicious of any direct involvement with the authorities on my part.

6 As of March 2008, Cubans can legally access hotels – if they can afford them. But as Alcázar Campos (2010) remarks, in spite of this change in the law, and notwithstanding its symbolic significance, paying for accommodation in a hotel remains out of the reach of most Cubans. As one of Alcázar Campos's informants put it, if you start going to hotels without having any justified earnings that would enable you to do so, this may raise the suspicious question: where does all this money come from? (Alcázar Campos 2010: 308).

7 These were members of the Departamento 'Lacra Social' (Department for Social Misfits) of the Cuban Ministry of Interior, popularly called *lacra*: a specialized police unit that my Cuban research participants particularly feared, given that it was considered incorruptible and very hard to spot.

8 See Simoni (2005a) for a more detailed description of the correlations between different tourism spaces in Havana, their degree of surveillance and Cubans' ways of approaching tourists.

9 I had this talk with Jorge in 2006. In more recent years, however, new CCTV cameras have been installed in Central Havana, tempering earlier cleavages between these two areas of the capital.

10 Getfield (2005: 107) remarks that in Jamaica, 'itinerant street vendors and hustlers use the craft markets as their base of operations, often claiming that they are assistants to owners of stalls within the market.' This seemed to be a widespread practice also in Cuba, where people could hang around or give a helping hand in legally established businesses while also using these privileged access points to establish personal connections with tourists. The mechanism in play here is not that different from the one Cabezas (2006, 2009) outlines in relation to all-inclusive tourism resort workers in Cuba, whose employees could use their formal job as a platform to further more personal agendas.

11 Not every member of the police force was equally corruptible, of course, and my data do not enable me to quantify this phenomenon. However, as I came to realize during field-work, and as clearly emerges from the work of other authors, many officers were willing to turn a blind eye, or at least forbear to harass Cubans, in exchange for cash or other favours, including sexual ones (see Cabezas 2004 and Valle 2006).

12 Several of my Cuban informants pointed to the fact that officers had to answer to higher-ranking colleagues for any tourism-related offence happening in areas under their supervision, which also explained their apprehension upon coming across tourists accompanied by suspected *jineteros/as*. 'If something happens to the tourist you will all be held responsible' was a typical police warning addressed to Cubans I was hanging around with.

13 A parallel can be traced here with Dahles' (1998: 34) remarks on street guides in Yogyakarta, Indonesia: 'Some street guides operate in small, loosely structured groups of friends sharing and controlling a hangout'. According to Dahles, 'a newcomer requires the introduction of an already-established friend or relative; otherwise, he will not be accepted at the hangout' (34). That could certainly be the case in Cuba too. Juan's remarks, however, indicate that acceptance within a group could depend on one's qualities and ability to attract tourists. Besides referring to such dynamics, Dahles also observes that many street guides in Yogyakarta operate on their own, a situation more akin to that described by Crick (1992: 140) in Kandi, Sri Lanka, where 'street guiding … is normally a highly individualistic occupation'. As I show below, this scenario was also common in Cuba.

14 To temper these generalizations, I refer to Cabezas' (2004, 2006, 2009) work in Cuba's all-inclusive resorts, which shows that even within such enclavic spaces, encounters between tourists and hotel personnel could take a twist towards the informal and the intimate.

15 In an interesting account of a guided tour she took in Havana, Babb (2011: 34) highlights the guide's facility in 'conveying a sense that we were getting an inside story'. For a more thorough analysis of tour guiding and the related circulation of tourism discourses and imaginaries, see the recent monographs of Salazar (2010) and Picard (2011). The works

of Edensor (1998) and Jack and Phipps (2005) also offer insights into how guided or non-guided forms of travel can result in different tourist experiences of a place and of interactions with local residents.

16 Besides the many positive stories I gathered from tourists on this practice (see below), I should mention that there were also instances in which supposedly fortuitous encounters with hitchhikers turned out to be part of carefully scripted plans to profit from tourists by leading them to visit and buy souvenirs in selected places (tobacco farms selling cigars near Viñales being a classic), gaining commissions by recommending price-inflated restaurants and accommodations and, more seldom, stealing cash and other valuables.

17 We can rejoin here Harrison's (2003) wider reflections on the importance of 'touristic intimacy', which lead her to suggest that human connection can act as a key driver of people's travel. In her insightful analysis of the various forms that such intimacy may take, she encourages us to reconsider MacCannell's view of the tourist as seeking the authentic in the places visited by shifting the emphasis from places to 'the sociability, perchance the intimacy, that one encounters while travelling' (Harrison 2003: 90). Though much of her focus is on the connections tourists make with fellow travellers, Harrison also reflects on tourists' expectations of 'meeting the local people' (2003: 61–66) and their desire to engage, however briefly and incidentally, with residents of the visited destination, a desire that was very much present among the tourists I encountered in Cuba (see Simoni 2014d).

18 Conversely, cheap holiday package deals including hotel accommodations and the flight to Cuba had led Manuele, an Italian man in his late thirties who had regularly visited Cuba since the 1990s, to contemplate the possibility of having a room in a comfortable hotel with international standards, 'where I can have at least a good, properly working shower!' while also keeping his usual *casa* for intimate affairs with Cuban women.

19 See the parallel with the political interpretation of Cuba's tourism plans advanced by Colantonio and Potter (2006) and their assessment of the government's emphasis in developing tourism in 'spatially self-contained coastal areas' (see chapter 1).

20 The influence of visitors' pre-existing political views on their ways of being a tourist, and the transformative effects of travel on such views, is itself an issue that deserves to be investigated further, particularly in relation to Cuba, where political imaginaries and notions of 'capitalism', 'communism', 'democracy' or 'totalitarianism' often became hot topics of debate among visitors. Scholars have addressed the question of tourism's entanglements with and effects on Cuba's political configuration (see in particular Babb 2011 and Sanchez and Adams 2008), the 'impact of tourism on tourists' (Stronza 2001) regarding political matters seems to have captured less attention.

21 Alcázar Campos (2010: 287) deals extensively with various manifestations of this 'Us vs. Them' divide in touristic Cuba, the ambivalent positionings and hierarchies it brought about and the various axes of solidarity, resistance and conflict that related to it (287–338).

22 In some interesting cases, the authorities' intelligence became a more positive reference point for tourists when police checks on a Cuban companion showed the latter to be 'clean', i.e. to have no *jineterismo*-related criminal record whatsoever. These positive happenings could become particularly important when the prospects of long-term relationships and romance were at stake. They were then trumpeted by the tourist in question, e.g. when trying to convince their (often sceptical) peers of the 'decent' character of their partner, cast here as a 'tourism-virgin', so to speak.

Chapter Four

1 Distinctions between 'true Rasta' and 'false Rasta / *jinetero*' played out frequently in this circle and certainly deserve closer attention (see also Hansing 2006). Simon, who considered himself a full-fledged Rastafarian and had devoted much of his adult life to researching and supporting the Jamaican-born movement, pointed out that many Cuban people who attended the reggae parties he promoted wore dreadlocks simply because they knew tourist women liked them. Not being of that sort, he preferred to refer to those people as *drelas* (people wearing dreadlocks), rather than Rasta. Conversations with other members of this loose community suggest that in some cases at least, people who started wearing dreadlocks because of the '*vibra*' (vibration) this hairstyle gave them with foreign tourists ended up learning more and becoming fascinated by a 'Rasta culture' they had not previously been aware of, winding up fervent supporters and participants of it. For more scholarly considerations on the success, and the controversial adoption, of Rasta style by local men willing to seduce foreign women in tourism destinations – from Jamaica's 'rent-a-dread' to Indonesia's 'Kuta cowboys' – see in particular the works of Pruitt and Lafont (1995) and Dahles (1997).

2 The establishment of tourist typologies was very common among my Cuban research participants (see Simoni 2008a for a more extensive discussion of this aspect). Authors working in other tourism destinations (Boissevain 1996, Crick 1989, Dahles 1998, Evans-Pritchard 1989, Hitchcock 1999, Pi-Sunyer 1978 [1977], Sweet 1989) have also pointed out the importance of such categorizations, especially as a way for members of a visited population to adapt their behaviors to different tourist audiences. Dahles (1998: 38), for instance, shows how street guides in Indonesia 'cultivate different styles to cater to specific target groups' ranging from the 'cool and deadly' to 'more sophisticated appearances'.

3 Elsewhere (see Simoni 2005b), I have elaborated on the implications of similar forms of address by merchants in Ladakh, India.

4 For Tucker (2001: 880), such scepticism of 'the behavior and motives' of local men placed them 'on something of a knife-edge, caught between being too friendly and being not friendly and helpful enough and between the positions of host and tourism entrepreneur'. A similarly delicate balancing effort was perceptible in Cubans' openings to tourists.

5 This kind of opening seems very common in many tourism destinations; see in particular Dahles for Indonesia (1998) and my own research in Ladakh (Simoni 2005b).

6 As argued by Abdallah-Pretceille (1997: 380), the modalities by which communication is entered into become the crucial elements to consider when trying to understand the role played by cultural categorizations (national stereotypes in this case). A similar stance is taken by Herzfeld (2005: 16), who remarks that what gives stereotypes significance 'is not so much their actual form ... as the social uses to which they are put'. For a more thorough reflection on the multiple and controversial uses of cultural categorization and stereotypes in touristic Cuba, see Simoni (2008a, 2011, 2013).

7 See Picard's (2011: 42) work on tourism in La Reunion for an interesting reflection on how jokes and 'forms of tragedy or comedy' could help 'dissolve ... uncomfortable situations' between foreign visitors and tourist guides, putting 'everyone at the same level – a member of a common contemporary humanity'.

8 Cary (2004) elaborates a very thought-provoking reflection on the importance of serendip-ity in tourism. Her focus is on the serendipity of 'tourist moments' in which the tourists' search for authenticity is temporarily fulfilled (2004: 66). See Simoni (2014d) for a discus-sion of this point and its relation with the valorization of intimacy and individuality in tourist-Cuban interactions.

9 As I have detailed elsewhere (2014d), interesting parallels are evident here with Sant Cassia's (1999: 253) reflections on tourists in Malta striving to 'personalize their interac-tion' with hosts and 'transform their role' so as to become 'more individuals and less "mere tourists"', an assessment that leads him to conclude that 'tourism aims at the individuation of the self through the authentication of experience' (253). See also Harrison's (2003) con-siderations on Canadian tourists' desire to engage with residents of the visited populations as 'real persons' (65) and move beyond 'the generic category of "stranger"' (65).

10 See also Dahles (1998), and the parallel with Murphy's (2001: 61) notion of a 'feeling out' period, used in reference to the typical initial moments of a conversation in social interac-tions amongst backpackers.

11 Studies on sexual encounters between foreign women and local men in different tourist settings have also led several authors to highlight the multi-functionality of the relation-ships at stake (see for instance Dahles and Bras 1999b, Mullings 1999, Herold, Garcia and DeMoya 2001). Dahles and Bras (1999b: 287) thus write about 'multi-functional guides' in Indonesia, whereas Mullings (1999: 66) observes that 'sex workers often also play mul-tiple roles as holiday companions and tour guides as well as sex partners'.

12 This parallels Bowman's (1996: 90) remarks on street merchants in a Palestinian tourist market: 'Street merchants prided themselves on chameleon-like qualities, being able to shift language, religion, politics and even their national identity to suit what they perceived to be the tastes of potential customers.'

13 Several scholars of tourism have highlighted this potential. See in particular the seminal work of Graburn (1978 [1977], 1983), Causey's (2003: 167) remarks on 'utopic space' as the space that tourism offers for people to 'explore possible ways of being ... between real-ity and unrealizable desires', and Picard's (2011: 41) recent reflection on the 'kaleidoscope of possible roles and existences, of selves' potentiated by encounters happening through tourism.

14 Contrasting 'female sex workers' and male 'beach boys' in the Dominican Republic, Herold, Garcia and DeMoya (2001: 988) go so far as to suggest that 'because of the limited language skills of most of the female sex workers, it is very difficult for them to establish any kind of relationship with the male tourist other than a sexual one'. Other important factors related to gendered normativities may help explain this prevalence of sexual encounters (see chapter 2), but even though a similar tendency is perceptible in Cuba, I still found big differences in language skills amongst Cuban women. Indeed, there were many who managed to communicate and negotiate relationships with non-Spanish-speaking tourists that went far beyond the sexual domain (see chapter 8).

15 For street guides in Yogyakarta (Indonesia), Dahles (1998: 34) remarks for instance that 'success in the "tourist hunt" largely depends on communicative abilities, outward appear-ance, and mastery of foreign languages'.

16 See also Picard (2011: 41–43) for a compelling example of a guide's skilful 'performance' and 'role-play' on tours in La Reunion, which illustrate the importance of similar traits and

qualities. As Picard puts it: 'His performance was marked by changing rhythms and the staccato of dramaturgic turning points, by a juxtaposition of moments that created deep aesthetic emotions, feelings of heartbreaking sadness, thrills of erotic temptation, joyful happiness and profound sensations of existential human connectivity' (43).

17 Here we rejoin the considerations of Forshee (1999), Frohlick (2007) and Salazar (2010), who in different touristic contexts – studying pedicab drivers in Yogyakarta (Forshee), sexual and intimate relationships between female tourists and local men in Caribbean Costa Rica (Frohlick), and tourist guides in Yogyakarta and Arusha (Tanzania) (Salazar) – have likewise highlighted the 'cumulative knowledge' (Frohlick 2007: 149) of tourists' preferences, imaginaries and desires, and the peculiar cosmopolitanisms that members of a visited population can develop through their engagements in the tourism realm.

Chapter Five

1 Romeo y Julieta, Cohiba and Montecristo (the latter being respectively Fidel Castro's and Che Guevara's favourites), some of the most popular cigar brands in Cuba, were likely to be recognized by tourists.

2 The cigars were either smuggled out of factories or manufactured in alternative locations. The diversion of cigars or (as shown later) labels, guarantee seals and receipts from official channels likely required the complicity of state employees. However, data on this illegal traffic was hard to corroborate, in part because several contradictory stories circulated among my informants.

3 I am drawing here on Law and Singleton's reflections on objects as presences, which imply 'realities that are *necessarily* absent, that *cannot* be brought to presence; that are othered' (2005: 342). For more on how such conceptualization in terms of absences/presences can be used productively to uncover the workings of materialities in tourism destinations, see Ren (2009) and Simoni (2012a). In a chapter discussing the utility of actor-network theory in investigating tourism materialities, I have elaborated on the fruitful conver-gence between Law and Singleton's (2005) view and Callon's (1998a, 1998b) notions of framing/overflowing and entanglement/disentanglement in order to shed light on how tourism materialities actualize certain realities while also silencing others (Simoni 2012a). Accordingly, I have shown how framings trace boundaries between different realities: they internalize certain connections while externalizing others and generate presences and absences via processes of entanglement and disentanglement. The recent book edited by van der Duim, Ren, and Jóhannesson (2012), provides further examples and method-ological insights regarding actor-network theory's potential for social science research on tourism.

4 Stories about the circulation of 'fake Cuban cigars' and the possibility of being cheated date back to the seventeenth century at least. In a text published in Edinburgh in 1614, Dr William Barclay warned of the deceptive appearance of cigars whose external coats covered tobacco of inferior quality. Barclay thus came to the conclusion that the best tobacco was sold in leaves, and not rolled (Ortiz 2005 [1940]: 104–108).

5 The number of cigars offered to tourists by Viñales' farmers suggests that 'natural', 'local' cigars were produced and distributed along several chains. Some farmers admitted to

occasionally running out of their own tobacco stocks and having to ask neighbouring farms (located off the main tourism routes) to sell them some of theirs to satisfy visitors' demands. These same farmers also complained to me that some of their colleagues who did not even cultivate tobacco sold ready-made cigars that were not locally produced and could be bought very cheaply (one Cuban peso, CUP, each) at the village bodega, wrapping them up in palm leaves to give the bundle an 'organic', 'natural', 'local' look. Once again, as in street deals, claims and counterclaims about the provenance and nature of cigars abounded, the matter potentially becoming highly controversial and sensitive.

6 In their introduction to a recent special issue of the *Journal of the Royal Anthropological Institute* on 'The Return of Hospitality', Candea and da Col (2012) highlight more generally hospitality's instability as a locus of moral dilemmas and potentially conflicting events and transactions: 'Each major "event" of hospitality … encompasses a multiplicity of singular events and transactions where altruism and selfishness, trust and suspicion, benevolence and malice are present but never *co-present*. It is this careful *avoidance of simultaneity* which makes hospitality the locus of moral dilemmas – and generates its peculiarly charged affective space' (2012: 11, emphasis in the original). Candea and da Col's (2012) edited collection on hospitality attests to the vitality and long-standing potential of this subject of study in anthropology, 'highlighting the topic's connections to some of our discipline's most vibrant themes and concerns: ethical reasoning, materiality, temporality and affect, alterity and cosmopolitics, sovereignty and scale' (2012: 1) – issues that research on hospitality in contemporary tourism contexts may also be particularly good at illuminating (see e.g. Picard and Buchberger 2013).

7 Bourdieu (in Callon 1998a: 15) has shown how the time lag between gifts and counter-gifts 'is the decisive factor between the switch from one regime to another, from calculativeness to non-calculativeness'. The transitory character of the relationships examined here, and perhaps more generally of hospitality in the tourism realm, requires exchanges to unfold in a short time. This transience may increase the difficulty of preserving notions of generosity and non-calculativeness.

8 For a more detailed discussion of how competing scale-making projects and notions of scale played out in the Cuban tourism economy in relation to the production and distribution of cigars, see Simoni (2009).

Chapter Six

1 MacCannell (1973, 1976) famously made the quest for the 'real' and 'authentic' Other the key tenet of his theorization of tourism. Drawing on Goffman's (1959) front versus back distinction, MacCannell (1973: 589) maintained that modern tourists were longing to 'enter the back regions of the places they visited', regions 'associated with intimacy of relations and authenticity of experiences'. MacCannell saw this quest as ultimately doomed to failure, given that 'tourist settings are arranged to produce the impression that a back region has been entered even when this is not the case' (589). Since his pioneering conceptualization of tourism was first published, MacCannell's work has been much discussed and critiqued, giving way to more nuanced, constructivist approaches to authenticity (see in particular Cohen 1988, Bruner 1994).

2 I am indebted to sociologist Erhard Stölting for bringing these interactional dynamics to my attention, and for his remarks on 'coercive trust by rules of reciprocity' (personal communication, 4–5 May 2007). This is not to imply that any such 'rules' have universal applicability: differences between tourists, for instance, certainly existed on the matter, and their Cuban interlocutors were also likely to have some notion of the kinds of visitors and situations that could be more conducive to this kind of reciprocity.

3 Drawing on Harrison's (2003) conceptualization of touristic intimacy as 'part of a larger quest for connection that tourists seek in crossing international borders' (Frohlick 2007: 152), Frohlick pertinently points out that such intimacy is also 'the moral discourse that serves to justify international travel as a means through which cross-cultural understandings are gained' (152). Cubans could rely on very similar moral framings of tourism and travel when encouraging tourists to make friends with them, thus making friendship with locals a privileged pathway to achieving a true understanding of Cuba and its people.

4 In her article on Brazilian immigrants negotiating friendship in Lisbon (Portugal), Torresan considers that 'friendship between Brazilians and Portuguese created a bridge that crossed over cultural patterns which were then subsequently strengthened by the idea that friendship was only possible because someone in the relationship was an exception to the rule' (2010: 245).

5 See Simoni (2005b) on merchants' use of similar procedures in interaction with tourists in Ladakh, India.

6 A parallel can be drawn here with the 'good guest' discourses examined by Sant Cassia (1999) and Tucker (2001) in other tourism contexts, and discussed in chapter 5 in relation to cigar deals in Viñales.

7 Reflecting on 'lay views of friendship in Western societies', Allan has noted that 'while many friendships do involve instrumental assistance, they "must not be defined in these terms" (Allan 1989: 19–20)' (quoted in Killick and Desai 2010: 14). Drawing on research on the relationships between maids and their employers in Brazil, Rezende (1999) has considered how conceptions of friendship can accommodate asymmetries. But while 'emphasis on affinity does not imply that there are no differences between friends' (1999: 93), Rezende also remarks that in these relationships the 'stress falls on those aspects which make friends similar' (93). This is what my ethnographic material also seems to suggest. Once the stress fell instead on people's differences and asymmetries, the idioms of charity tended to replace those of friendship

8 See for instance most chapters in Bell and Coleman (1999a) and Desai and Killick (2010), and the articles of Dyson (2010), Mains (2013), Nisbett (2007), Santos-Granero (2007), and Torresan (2011).

9 In other words, my ethnography suggests that the version of friendship considered here did not develop independently of 'Western purified models', with, for instance, material support and affection seen as mutually constitutive and their entanglements left unquestioned. More generally, I would argue that the simple fact that 'material support' and 'affection' are problematized, teased out and conceptualized as separate may already be read as an indication that we are dealing with retrospective reassessments that assume purified ideals of relationships, affection and interest as a conceptual backdrop. By way of contrast, as Povinelli (2006) has shown, these interpretative grids may be unsuited to understanding forms of sociality that do not rely on these sorts of differentiations in the

first place. Drawing on Malinowski and on Mauss's reflection on gift giving to reassess the opposition between love and reciprocity, Povinelli, cited by Venkatesan (Venkatesan et al. 2011: 212), recently argued that 'the separation between love and reciprocity, and the qualities, essences and manifestations of each, is itself sociological – a separation that is worth exploring and not just accepting'. Building on Povinelli's insights, I am interested here in exploring whether and how touristic encounters in Cuba foster the circulation of purified relational idioms and their hybrids.

10 For Povinelli, 'autology' and 'genealogy' 'are two coexisting and intersecting forms of discipline that are constitutive of postcolonial governance' (Venkatesan et al. 2011: 225):

> 'Autology' refers to multiple discourses and practices which invoke the autonomous and self-determining subject, and which are therefore linked to, but not exhausted in, liberalism's emphasis on 'freedom' more narrowly conceived as a political philosophy. 'Genealogy', on the other hand, is taken to refer to discourses that stress social constraint and determination in processes of subject constitution and construe the subject as bound by 'various kinds of inheritances'.

11 Building on Carrier's (1999) work, Coleman (2010: 200) locates the roots of this purist stance in 'Aristotle's notion of perfect friendship as justified in and for its own sake', going on to argue that the 'altruistic giver and morally autonomous friend are products of the same ideological perspective, according to which purity of purpose and spontaneity can be contrasted with assumptions of the marketplace' (200). In emphasizing the aspirational dimension of these purified conceptions of friendship, my argument also draws on recent anthropological literature on love and companionate marriage, which describes how the ability to engage in 'romantic', 'selfless', 'pure' love can in certain contexts become a marker of modernization and of being an autonomous, self-determined subject (see e.g. the articles in Cole and Thomas 2009, Hirsch and Wardlow 2006, Padilla et al. 2007, Venkatesan et al. 2011, see also Faier 2007, Fernandez 2013, Hunter 2010, Patico 2009, Povinelli 2006). The approach adopted by Faier (2007) in her article on professions of love by Filipina migrants in rural Japan is particularly inspiring here, most notably when she argues that 'when professing love for their husbands, Filipina women … were claiming a sense of humanity, countering the stigma associated with their work in bars, and articulating a sense of themselves as cosmopolitan, modern, and moral women who possessed an emotional interiority' (149).

12 A fruitful parallel may be drawn with Patico's (2009) reflections on 'normalcy' in discussing how international matchmaking provides Russian women and American men with a way to seek normalcy in their personal lives. In the Cuban context, in her research on *jineteras* and their discourses of love for foreign tourists, de Sousa e Santos (2009: 422) similarly quotes an informant's argument that 'people here want to have what is normal to have, simply what any person in the world can have [the world here representing Western countries]'.

13 My reflections here are inspired by Ferguson's (2002, 2006) work on mimicry and membership, and by Piot's (2010) related insights on new cultural imaginaries taking shape in contemporary West Africa. Drawing on these authors, I read Cubans' claims of pure friendship as a way for them to 'embrace the future, through acts of mimetic engagement

with that which they desire' (Piot 2010: 10), that is, as wishful assertions of their member-ship in a world society (Ferguson 2006) that threatened to leave them behind, stuck in an undesirable state of exception.

14 In an article on how Western tourists and their Maghrebi hosts negotiate the moral ambi-guities of friendship, Buchberger (2014) also stresses the power of friendship in re-qualify-ing the nature and significance of economic exchanges between friends. She quotes Latif, one of her Maghrebi informants, who argues that 'there should not be any money issues between me and my friends' (2014: 48). Latif refers to the fact that '"real friends" should not expect reciprocity' and 'that you should give without expecting in return'– in other words, Buchberger continues, for Latif 'there is no need to create the illusion of equality in relationships qualified as friendships between unequal partners' (48). This finds an interest-ing parallel in the material presented in this section, which clearly shows that several of my Cuban interlocutors who became friends with foreigners regarded mutual recognition of the sentimental, disinterested nature of the relationship as also meaning that all material exchanges would escape any sort of calculation. The reasoning here is that friends give to each other without monitoring or measuring the balance of exchange (see Silver 1990 on the history of this ideal in Europe).

15 In contemplating these moral assessments of gift giving, we may also draw on Willerslev's insights, when, writing about love and the significance of ideals of love among Siberian Yukaghir hunters, he argues:

> The virtual ideal of the free gift given out of boundless love is implicitly at work in any concrete contexts of exchange, barter and even theft as an impossible phantasy or phan-tom ideal from which these actual transactions are given form, defined and morally judged. (Venkatesan et al. 2011: 231)

For Willerslev, the presence of such virtual ideals should be apprehended as an aspect of the real that has a significant impact on reality. Grounding his analysis in the notions of 'virtual' and 'actual' as advanced by Deleuze, he maintains more generally that 'the actual does not exist separately from the virtual', and 'the two dimensions are given as facets of one and the same expression or reality – that is, our actual existence duplicates itself all along with a virtual existence' (2011: 228). Bringing his reflection further, Willerslev ends up observing that 'anthropology will reach its analytical climax only at the moment that it invents a form of thinking that is capable of bypassing the actual and advancing into the virtual ideality of reality itself' (2011: 232). See Simoni and Throop (2014a) for a more thorough appraisal of this approach and its possible contributions to our reflections on friendship and its moral experience.

Chapter Seven

1 See Skinner's work (2011) on organized dancing tours in Cuba for more on this special-ized, 'niche' type of tourism, tour members' desires and expectations of the experience, and some of its implications in regards to interactions with Cuban people.

2 Here striking parallels emerge with what Herold, Garcia and DeMoya (2001: 986) observe in relation to the seduction process between 'beach boys' and female tourists in the Dominican Republic:

> When the tourist arrives at the disco, she will observe the beach boy displaying his dancing skills. This makes it easy for the beach boy to ask the woman to dance because he can offer to be her dancing instructor. It also provides him with the opportunity of flattering the woman when teaching her the dance routines. Most importantly, there is the opportunity for increased physical contact with the woman while on the dance floor. Popular dance music in the Dominican Republic such as the Meringue [sic] promotes close dancing and provides an ideal situation for the beach boy to initiate body touching. The lively music and dancing combined with drinks which have a high alcoholic content help to lower the tourist's inhibitions.

3 At the time of my fieldwork, salsa and *regeton* were arguably the two most popular types of music to which tourists and Cubans danced in clubs and discos. While Cuba's tourism image as 'the land of salsa' (Skinner 2011: 124) is well established, *regeton*, a much more recent phenomenon on the island that does not benefit from the same aura of authenticity, challenges 'dominant conceptions of Cuban national culture' (Baker 2009: 165), and continues to be at the centre of intellectual debates and moral controversies (Baker 2009, Birchler 2011).

4 One of Fairley's informants explicitly refers to the female movements in *regeton* as potentially a way to 'conquer a man' (2006: 480). In line with this semantic register are also Palmié's remarks (2004: 244) on *jineterismo* and the mermaid-like image of the *jinetera* who captures and conquers tourists.

Chapter Eight

1 Zigon (2010: 8) conceptualizes ethics as a 'moment of conscious reflection' on one's 'embodied moral dispositions', 'a conscious acting on oneself either in isolation or with others so as to make oneself into a more morally appropriate and acceptable person not only in the eyes of others but also for oneself'. Following moral breakdowns, people 'work on themselves by utilizing certain ethical tactics not only to return to the unreflective and unreflexive disposition of morality, but in so doing to create a new moral dispositional self. Thus, this moment of ethics is a creative moment, for by performing ethics, new moral persons and new moral worlds are created, even if ever so slightly' (9). As illustrated repeatedly throughout this book, I believe Zigon's (2008, 2009, 2010) approach to be an extremely productive one for drawing attention to and analysing the moral confrontations, tensions and (re)adjustments that touristic encounters can engender.

2 Here we can rejoin McCabe's (2005) considerations on the traveller-tourist dichotomy and the (relatively rare) instances in which the tourist identification is positively assumed. An interesting parallel may also be drawn with Brown's (1996: 40–41) remarks on the tourist-pilgrim opposition in a discussion of instances in which 'the tourist affirms himself as tourist' and rejects 'what he sees as the elitism and hypocrisy of the pilgrim'.

3 According to Cohen (1996: 301), experienced *farangs* (white foreigners) in Thailand end up preferring 'brief, mercenary encounters [with Thai women], in which money is paid for services rendered, free from illusions and further obligations', as opposed to engaging in long-term relationships permeated by the ambiguities of love and money. Interpreting this state of affairs, Cohen maintains that 'many old-timer *farangs* still fail to comprehend the ambiguity making open-ended prostitution in Thailand' (303). My analysis here moves beyond Cohen's in that it does not reduce these experienced tourists' stances to cognitive failure to understand 'the native point of view' (301). Instead, and in line with a more pragmatic approach to notions of culture (Simoni 2008a, 2011), I argue that their take on these sexual relationships cannot be dissociated from the specific purposes it achieved. In this sense, if their views failed to internalize conceptual ambiguities, it was precisely because their aim was to move beyond such uncertainties, rather than to grasp the perspective of the 'host socioculture' (Cohen 1996: 303).

4 This draws again on Zigon's view of 'morality as the embodied dispositions that allow for nonconsciously acceptable ways of living in the world', and as a way of 'being existentially comfortable in one's world' (2010: 5)

5 Cabezas (2004, 2009), in her work on sex and tourism in Cuba and the Dominican Republic, which I discussed in the Introduction, has highlighted the issue of resisting characterization as a sex worker and the need for analysts to sensibly account for such endeavours and recognize their potentially far-reaching implications.

6 With the money she received, Aurora bought herself the CD player she had been longing for. She had meant to buy an air conditioner first, but none was available in the stores at that moment. The CD player was her second choice. The washing machine story was made up for the Italians (in fact she did not have one, but getting it was not a priority as she could easily get her washing done at her neighbour's), mainly to inspire their pity and generosity. Indeed, after a little brainstorm we had together on the matter, we had all agreed that having to do all her washing by hand would elicit more compassion from the tourists than would suffering from heat (needing an air conditioner) or not being able to listen to music (needing a CD player). In play here was a reflexive and highly strategic assessment of the articulations between money, its purpose, and the morality of it (see Chapter 6).

7 A more detailed investigation of love and romance as they emerged from informal touristic encounters in Cuba remains out of the scope this book. These other forms of relationality are currently the subject of further research that builds on the analysis of sexual encounters presented here as well as the reflections on friendship developed in chapter 6 (see Simoni 2015a, 2015c, 2015d).

Conclusion

1 A useful parallel may be drawn here with Cole's (2009: 111) assessment of recent scholarship on African intimacies, which tends to foreground 'the instrumental, as opposed to the emotional, nature of intimate male-female relations ... either to highlight African agency despite difficult social and economic conditions or to illuminate the underlying logic behind seemingly promiscuous behaviour'. But putting too much emphasis on 'the strategic nature of relationships' (111), argues Cole, risks reproducing stereotypes of

Africans – and particularly African women – as 'purely instrumental' (111), a danger I could also detect in the case examined here.

2 Brennan's (2004) remarks on the normative expectations among female sex workers in the Dominican Republic, specifically regarding ways of talking about love with foreign partners, provide an interesting parallel to the Cuban case. As she puts it: 'Positing love could make Sosúan sex workers appear foolish. No matter what they feel for their foreign boyfriends, these women have an incentive to portray themselves as not naïve enough to actually fall in love' (96). As I already hinted in the Introduction, a similar moral expectation not to portray oneself as vulnerable or naïve seemed also to predominate among Cuban men and women as they and their peers discussed their relationships with foreign tourists. Elsewhere (Simoni 2015c), I elaborate further on how the adoption of these stances can be understood in relation to claims and expectations of belonging. In this sense, both casting tourists as an instrument for achieving economic goals and aspirations, and interpreting relationships with them as clearly economic in nature could help clarify where one's allegiance lay, positing Us-Cubans as the primary site of belonging.

3 Killick and Desai (2010: 11), for instance, have pointed out that the anthropological study of friendship may be ideally suited for this task, and thus become a rewarding research path to uncovering 'how contradictory models of personhood (and thus of relations between persons) do exist alongside one another'.

4 It is worth noting here that in several European countries, an analogous image circulating in current public (and often highly mediatized) debates on cross-border marriages involving Cuban nationals tends to promote the notion of 'sham' unions whose real goal is, allegedly, to enable the Cuban partner to migrate and obtain legal residence (see Anzil and Yzusqui 2014, Berg 2011, García Moreno 2010, García Moreno and Pujadas Muñoz 2011, and Roca 2013 for the case of Spain). Likewise, this image is insinuating itself in the governmental migratory policies and legal proceedings that patrol the boundaries of 'proper' marriages (Anzil and Yzusqui 2014). Here, in other words, we find a convergence of representations and moral assumptions operating at various levels and spheres – from Cuba to Europe, and from institutional to public discourse. I would argue that we need to be wary of any such convergence, which should be unpacked and reflexively accounted for in our investigations.

5 Other relational idioms, most notably those of charity and of love and romance, were also very present in the realm of tourism in Cuba. Though largely beyond the scope of this book, they certainly deserve further examination (see e.g. Cabezas 2009, Daigle 2013, de Sousa e Santos 2009, Fernandez 2013, Fosado 2005, Simoni 2015a, 2015b, 2015c, 2015d).

6 Notable exceptions included interactions informed by the idioms of charity and physical violence (as in the case of mugging), which I can only briefly mention here. In their own specific ways, charitable and violent engagements highlighted asymmetries between tourists and Cubans – their driving rationale – and were exceptions to ideals of reciprocal and mutual exchange. Contrary to the relational idioms that are the focus of Part Two of this book, charity and violence did not foster the long-term protraction of relationships but relied instead on punctual, abrupt manifestation.

7 See e.g. the chapters in the recent books edited by Cole and Thomas (2009), Hirsch and Wardlow (2006), and Padilla et al. (2007), as well as the writings of Povinelli (2006), Patico (2009), Faier (2007) and Hunter (2010).

8 Drawing on Willerslev's reflections on virtuality and actuality, which emphasize the former as an essential driving force of the latter (see Chapter 6), Zigon (2013: 203) also writes of love and moral subjectivity that 'as a motivating ethical demand ... love guides moral experience in ways that may not always be contained by the local' – a consideration that resonates well with the argument I am developing here.

9 In order to account, without condescension, for such mimetic endeavors, Piot (2010) urges us 'to fight the impulse to make theory adequate to political desire' and resist 'the romance of resistance' (169), and to be ready to 'measure "agency" through engagement with rather than rejection of Euro-otherness' (10).

10 We should heed Law's (1991) suggestion to attend to the techniques used to store power and eventually stabilize (unequal) relations between actors. Indeed, according to Law (1991: 174), 'one of the best strategies for stabilizing relations and their downstream power effects is ... precisely to embody them in durable materials: relations that tend, everything else being equal, to generate effects that last'. See also Latour (2005) for a similar argument about the importance that objects and non-human entities can acquire in the stabilization of power relations and inequality.

11 An interesting parallel to this way of reasoning, which is perhaps further testimony of its popularity and wide diffusion, can be found in Michel Houellebecq's (2002 [2001]) novel *Platform*.

REFERENCES

Abdallah-Pretceille, M. 1997. 'Du bon usage des malentendus culturels: Pour une pragmatique de la culturalité'. *Swiss Journal of Sociology* 23(2): 375–388.

Abram, S. 1997. 'Performing for Tourists in Rural France'. In S. Abram, J. Waldren and D.V.L. Macleod (eds), *Tourists and Tourism: Identifying with People and Places*. Oxford and New York: Berg, pp. 29–49.

Abram, S., and J. Waldren. 1997. 'Introduction: Tourists and Tourism: Identifying with People and Places'. In S. Abram, J. Waldren and D.V.L. Macleod (eds), *Tourists and Tourism: Identifying with People and Places*. Oxford and New York: Berg, pp. 1–11.

Abu-Lughod, L. 1990. 'The Romance of Resistance: Tracing Transformations of Power Through Bedouin Women'. *American Ethnologist* 17: 41–55.

Adams, V. 1992. 'Tourism and Sherpas, Nepal: Reconstruction of Reciprocity'. *Annals of Tourism Research* 19: 534–554.

Alcázar Campos, A. 2009. 'Turismo sexual, jineterismo, turismo de romance. Fronteras difusas en la interacción con el otro en Cuba'. *Gazeta de Antropología* 25(1). Retrieved 14 May 2012 from http://hdl.handle.net/10481/6856.

———. 2010. '"La Cuba de verdad". Construcción de alteridades y turismo en la contemporaneidad'. PhD dissertation. Granada, Spain: Universidad de Granada.

Allen, J.S. 2007. 'Means of Desire's Production: Male Sex Labor in Cuba'. *Identities: Global Studies in Culture and Power* 14(1–2): 183–202.

Anzil, V., and R. Yzusqui. 'El filtro de amor de los matrimonios mixtos: Análisis de los mecanismos institucionales de legitimación del amor transnacional'. In *Proceedings of the XIII Anthropology Congress of the Spanish Federation of Anthropology Associations (FAAEE)*. Tarragona: Universitat Rovira i Virgili, pp. 862–884.

Appadurai, A. 1986. 'Introduction: Commodities and the Politics of Value'. In A. Appadurai (ed.), *The Social Life of Things*. Cambridge: Cambridge University Press, pp. 3–63.

———. 1997. 'Fieldwork in the Era of Globalization'. *Anthropology and Humanism* 22(19): 115–118.

Aramberri, J. 2001. 'The Host Should Get Lost: Paradigms in the Tourism Theory'. *Annals of Tourism Research* 28(3): 738–761.

Argyriadis, K. 2005. 'El desarrollo del turismo religioso en La Habana y la acusación de mercantilismo'. *Desacatos* 18: 29–52.

Asamblea Nacional del Poder Popular. n.d. *Código Penal: Ley Nº 62*. Cubanet. Retrieved 6 February 2009 from http://www.cubanet.org.

Babb, F. 2011. *The Tourism Encounter: Fashioning Latin American Nations and Histories*. Stanford, CA: Stanford University Press.

Baker, C.P. 2004. *Cuba*. Emeryville, CA: Moon Handbooks.

Baker, G. 2009. 'The Politics of Dancing: Reggaetón and Rap in Havana, Cuba'. In R.Z. Rivera, W. Marshall and D.P. Hernandez (eds), *Reggaeton*. Durham, NC, and London: Duke University Press, pp. 165–199.

Bauer, T.G. and B. McKercher (eds). 2003. *Sex and Tourism: Journeys of Romance, Love, and Lust*. New York: The Haworth Hospitality Press.

Bell, S., and S. Coleman (eds). 1999a. *The Anthropology of Friendship*. Oxford and New York: Berg.

Bell, S., and S. Coleman. 1999b. 'The Anthropology of Friendship: Enduring Themes and Future Possibilities'. In S. Bell and S. Coleman (eds), *The Anthropology of Friendship*. Oxford and New York: Berg, pp. 1–19.

Berg, M.L. 2004. 'Tourism and the Revolutionary New Man: The Specter of *Jineterismo* in Late 'Special Period' Cuba'. *Focaal: European Journal of Anthropology* 43: 46–56.

———. 2011. *Diasporic Generations: Memory, Politics and Nation among Cubans in Spain*. New York and Oxford: Berghahn Books.

Bernstein, E. 2007. *Temporarily Yours: Intimacy, Authenticity, and the Commerce of Sex*. Chicago: Chicago University Press.

Birchler, B. 2011. '"I don't wan' it smooth, like salsa, I want a harsh sound bro": Negotiating a Rap Sound in Cuba'. *ASAonline* 1(5). Retrieved 14 May 2012 from http://www.theasa.org/downloads/asaonline/PDF/asaonline0105.pdf.

Bisogno, F. 2010. 'Vivere nell'informalità: *Luchar* nella Cuba post-sovietica'. PhD dissertation. Milan, Italy: Università degli Studi di Milano Bicocca.

Bloch, M. and J. Parry 1989. 'Introduction: Money and the Morality of Exchange'. In J. Parry and M. Bloch (eds), *Money and the Morality of Exchange*. Cambridge: Cambridge University Press, pp. 1–32.

Bohannan, P. 1955. 'Some Principles of Exchange and Investment among the Tiv'. *American Anthropologist* 57: 60–70.

Boissevain, J. (ed.) 1996. *Coping with Tourists: European Reactions to Mass Tourism*. Oxford: Berghahn Books.

Boltanski, L., and L. Thévenot. 2006 (1991). *On Justification: Economies of Worth*. Princeton, NJ: Princeton University Press.

Bowman, G. 1996. 'Passion, Power and Politics in a Palestinian Tourist Market'. In T. Selwyn (ed.), *The Tourist Image: Myths and Myth Making in Tourism*. Chichester: John Wiley and Sons, pp. 84–103.

Brennan, D. 2004. *What's Love Got to Do with It? Transnational Desires and Sex Tourism in the Dominican Republic*. Durham, NC: Duke University Press.

Brotherton, S. 2008. '"We Have to Think like Capitalists but Continue Being Socialists": Medicalized Subjectivities, Emergent Capital, and Socialist Entrepreneurs in Post-Soviet Cuba'. *American Ethnologist* 35(2): 259–274.

Brown, D. 1996. 'Genuine Fakes'. In T. Selwyn (ed.), *The Tourist Image: Myths and Myth Making in Tourism*. Chichester: John Wiley and Sons, pp. 33–47.

Browne, K.E. 2004. *Creole Economics: Caribbean Cunning under the French Flag*. Austin: University of Texas Press.

Bruner, E.M. 1994. 'Abraham Lincoln as Authentic Reproduction: A Critique of Postmodernism'. *American Anthropologist* 96(2): 397–415.

Buchberger, S. 2014. 'Can Social Unequals Be Friends? Western Tourists and Their Maghrebi Hosts Negotiate Moral Ambiguity'. *Suomen Antropologi*. 39(1): 37–52.

Bustamante, L. 2003. *Jineteras*. Barcelona: Altera.

Bunten, A.C. 2008. 'Sharing Culture or Selling Out? Developing the Commodified Persona in the Heritage Industry'. *American Ethnologist* 35(3): 380–395.

Cabezas, A.L. 2004. 'Between Love and Money: Sex, Tourism, and Citizenship in Cuba and the Dominican Republic'. *Signs* 29(4): 984–1015.

———. 2006. 'The Eroticization of Labor in Cuba's All-Inclusive Resorts: Performing Race, Class, and Gender in the New Tourist Economy'. *Social Identities* 12(5): 507–521.

———. 2009. *Economies of Desire: Sex and Tourism in Cuba and the Dominican Republic*. Philadelphia: Temple University Press.

Caillois, R. 2001 (1958). *Man, Play and Games*. Urbana and Chicago: University of Illinois Press.

Çalişkan, K., and M. Callon. 2009. 'Economization, Part 1: Shifting Attention from the Economy towards Processes of Economization'. *Economy and Society* 38(3): 369–398.

———. 2010. 'Economization, Part 2: A Research Programme for the Study of Markets'. *Economy and Society* 39(1): 1–32.

Callon, M. 1998a. 'An Essay on Framing and Overflowing: Economic Externalities Revisited by Sociology'. In M. Callon (ed.), *The Laws of the Markets*. Oxford and Malden, MA: Blackwell, pp. 244–269.

———. 1998b. 'Introduction: The Embeddedness of Economic Markets in Economics'. In M. Callon (ed.), *The Laws of the Markets*. Oxford and Malden, MA: Blackwell, pp. 1–57.

———. 2007. 'What Does It Mean to Say That Economics Is Performative?' In D. MacKenzie, F. Muniesa and L. Siu (eds), *Do Economists Make Markets? On the Performativity of Economics*. Princeton, NJ: Princeton University Press, pp. 311–357.

Callon, M., and V. Rabeharisoa. 2004. 'Gino's Lesson on Humanity: Genetics, Mutual Entanglements and the Sociologist's Role'. *Economy and Society* 33(1): 1–27.

Candei, M., and G. da Col. 2012. 'The Return of Hospitality'. *Journal of the Royal Anthropological Institute* N.S.: 1–19.

Carrier, J. 1999. 'People Who Can Be Friends: Selves and Social Relationships'. In S. Bell and S. Coleman (eds), *The Anthropology of Friendship*. Oxford and New York: Berg, pp. 21–38.

Carter, T. 2008. 'Of Spectacular Phantasmal Desire: Tourism and the Cuban State's Complicity in the Commodification of Its Citizens'. *Leisure Studies* 27(3): 241–257.

Cary, S.H. 2004. 'The Tourist Moment'. *Annals of Tourism Research* 31(1): 61–77.

Causey, A. 2003. *Hard Bargaining in Sumatra: Western Travellers and Toba Bataks in the Marketplace of Souvenirs*. Honolulu: University of Hawai'i Press.

Chambers, E. 1997. 'Introduction: Tourism's Mediators'. In E. Chambers (ed.), *Tourism and Culture: An Applied Perspective*. Albany: State University Press of New York, pp. 1–11.

———. 2000. *Native Tours: The Anthropology of Travel and Tourism*. Long Grove, IL: Waveland Press.

Cheong, S.-M., and M.L. Miller. 2000. 'Power and Tourism: A Foucauldian Observation'. *Annals of Tourism Research* 27(2): 371–390.

Clancy, M. 2002. 'The Globalization of Sex Tourism and Cuba: A Commodity Chains Approach'. *Studies in Comparative International Development* 36(4): 63–88.

Clark, G. (ed.). 1988. *Traders Versus the State: Anthropological Approaches to Unofficial Economies*. Boulder, CO, and London: Westview Press.

Clift, S., and S. Carter (eds). 2000. *Tourism and Sex: Culture, Commerce, and Coercion*. London and New York: Pinter.

Cohen, E. 1971. 'Arab Boys and Tourist Girls in a Mixed Jewish-Arab Community'. *International Journal of Comparative Sociology* 12: 217–233.

———. 1979. 'A Phenomenology of Tourist Experiences'. *Sociology* 13: 179–201.

———. 1984. 'The Sociology of Tourism: Approaches, Issues, and Findings'. *Annual Review of Sociology* 10: 373–392.

———. 1988. 'Authenticity and Commoditisation in Tourism'. *Annals of Tourism Research* 15(3): 371–386.

———. 1996. *Thai Tourism: Hill Tribes, Islands, and Open-Ended Prostitution*. Bangkok: White Lotus.

Colantonio, A., and R.B. Potter. 2006. *Urban Tourism and Development in the Socialist State: Havana during the 'Special Period'*. Aldershot: Ashgate.

Cole, J. 2009. 'Love, Money, and Economies of Intimacy in Tamatave, Madagascar'. In J. Cole and L. Thomas (eds), *Love in Africa*. Chicago and London: University of Chicago Press, pp. 109–134.

Cole, J., and L. Thomas (eds). 2009. *Love in Africa*. Chicago and London: University of Chicago Press.

Coleman, S. 2010. 'Afterword: Making Friendship Impure: Some Reflections on a (Still) Neglected Topic'. In A. Desai and E. Killick (eds), *The Ways of Friendship: Anthropological Perspectives*. New York and Oxford: Berghahn Books, pp. 197–206.

Comaroff, J.L., and J. Comaroff. 1997. *Of Revelation and Revolution, Vol. 2: The Dialectics of Modernity on a South-African Frontier*. Chicago and London: University of Chicago Press.

Constable, N. 2009. 'The Commodification of Intimacy: Marriage, Sex, and Reproductive Labor'. *Annual Review of Anthropology* 38: 49–64.

Corbett, B. 2002. *This Is Cuba: An Outlaw Culture Survives*. Cambridge, MA: Westview Press.

Couceiro Rodríguez, A.V. 2006. 'Los Pingueros y sus Clientes'. In *Proceedings of the VIII Conferencia Internacional de Antropología*, Havana, Cuba (CD-ROM).

Cousin, S. 2008 'L'Unesco et la doctrine du tourisme culturel: Généalogie d'un "bon" tourisme'. *Civilisations: Revue internationale d'anthropologie et de sciences humaines* 57(1–2): 41–56.

Cowie, L. 2002. 'El *jineterismo* como fenómeno social en la narrativa cubana contemporánea'. *Revista Mexicana del Caribe* 14: 207–215.

Crick, M. 1989. 'Representations of Tourism in the Social Sciences: Sun, Sex, Sights, Savings, and Servility'. *Annual Review of Anthropology* 18: 307–344.

———. 1992. 'Life in the Informal Sector: Streets Guides in Kandy, Sri Lanka'. In D. Harrison (ed.), *Tourism and the Less Developed Countries*. London: Belhaven Press; New York and Toronto: Halsted Press, pp. 135–147.

———. 1995. 'The Anthropologist as Tourist: An Identity in Question'. In M.-F. Lanfant, J.B. Allcock and E.M. Bruner (eds), *International Tourism: Identity and Change*. London: Sage, pp. 205–223.

Csikszentmihalyi, M. 1975. *Beyond Boredom and Anxiety*. San Francisco: Jossey-Bass.

References

Dahles, H. 1997. 'The New Gigolo: Globalization, Tourism and Changing Gender Identities'. *Focaal: European Journal of Anthropology* 30/31: 121–137.

———. 1998. 'Of Birds and Fish: Street Guides, Tourists, and Sexual Encounters in Yogyakarta, Indonesia'. In M. Oppermann (ed.), *Sex Tourism and Prostitution: Aspects of Leisure, Recreation, and Work*. New York: Cognizant Communication, pp. 30–41.

Dahles, H., and K. Bras (eds). 1999a. *Tourism and Small Entrepreneurs: Development, National Policy, and Entrepreneurial Culture: Indonesian Cases*. New York: Cognizant Communication.

———. 1999b. 'Entrepreneurs in Romance: Tourism in Indonesia'. *Annals of Tourism Research* 26(2): 267–293.

Daigle, M. 2013. 'Love, Sex, Money, and Meaning: Using Language to Create Identities and Challenge Categories in Cuba'. *Alternatives: Global, Local, Political* 38(1): 63–77.

Daniel, Y.P. 1996. 'Tourism Dance Performances: Authenticity and Creativity'. *Annals of Tourism Research* 23(4): 780–797.

de Albuquerque, K. 1998. 'In Search of the Big Bamboo'. *Transitions* 77: 48–57.

de la Fuente, A. 2001. *A Nation for All: Race, Inequality, and Politics in Twentieth-Century Cuba*. Chapel Hill and London: University of North Carolina Press.

de Sousa e Santos, D. 2009. 'Reading Beyond the Love Lines: Examining Cuban *Jineteras*' Discourses of Love for Europeans'. *Mobilities* 4(3): 407–426.

Desai, A. and E. Killick (eds). 2010. *The Ways of Friendship: Anthropological Perspectives*. New York and Oxford: Berghahn Books.

Dyson, J. 2010. 'Friendship in Practice: Girls' Work in the Indian Himalayas.' *American Ethnologist* 37(3): 482–498.

Edensor, T. 1998. *Tourists at the Taj: Performance and Meaning at a Symbolic Site*. London and New York: Routledge.

Ellis, K. 1999. *Traveller's Companion: Cuba*. Zollikofen: Kümmerly and Frey.

Elyachar, J. 2005. *Markets of Dispossession: NGOs, Economic Development, and the State in Cairo*. Durham, NC: Duke University Press.

Enken, T. 2004. 'Between Ideology and Pragmatism: The Revolution and the Private Sector before the Special Period'. *Cuba in Transition* 14: 212–223.

Enzensberger, H.M. 1996 (1958). 'A Theory of Tourism'. *New German Critique* 68: 117–135.

Evans-Pritchard, D. 1989. 'How "They" See "Us": Native American Images of Tourists'. *Annals of Tourism Research* 16: 89–105.

Faier, L. 2007. 'Filipina Migrants in Rural Japan and their Professions of Love'. *American Ethnologist* 34(1): 148–162.

Fairley, J. 2006. 'Dancing Back to Front: *Regeton*, Sexuality, Gender, and Transnationalism in Cuba'. *Popular Music* 25(3): 471–488.

Fassin, D. 2008. 'Beyond Good and Evil? Questioning the Anthropological Discomfort with Morals'. *Anthropological Theory* 8(4): 333–344.

Feifer, M. 1985. *Going Places: The Ways of the Tourist from Imperial Rome to the Present Day*. London: MacMillan.

Ferguson, J. 2002. 'Of Mimicry and Membership: Africans and the "New World Society"'. *Cultural Anthropology* 17(4): 551–569.

——— 2006. *Global Shadows: Africa in the Neoliberal World Order*. Durham, NC, and London: Duke University Press.

References

Fernández, D. 2000. *Cuba and the Politics of Passion*. Austin: University of Texas Press.

Fernandez, N. 1999. 'Back to the Future? Women, Race, and Tourism in Cuba'. In K. Kempadoo (ed.), *Sun, Sex, and Gold: Tourism and Sex Work in the Caribbean*. Lanham, MD: Rowman and Littlefield, pp. 81–89.

———. 2010. *Revolutionizing Romance: Interracial Couples in Contemporary Cuba*. New Brunswick, NJ, and London: Rutgers University Press.

———. 2013. 'Moral Boundaries and National Borders: Cuban Marriage Migration to Denmark'. *Identities: Global Studies in Culture and Power* 20(3): 270–287.

Figueras Pérez, M.A. 2004. 'El Turismo internacional y la formación de clusters productivos en la economía cubana'. In O.E. Pérez Villanueva (ed.), *Reflexiones sobre la economía cubana*. Havana: Editorial de Ciencias Sociales, pp. 85–99.

Formoso, B. 2001. 'Corps étrangers: Tourisme et prostitution en Thaïlande'. *Anthropologie et Sociétés* 25(2): 55–70.

Forshee, J. 1999. 'Domains of Pedaling: Souvenirs, *Becak* Drivers, and Tourism in Yogyakarta, Java'. In J. Forshee, C. Fink and S. Cate (eds), *Converging Interests: Traders, Travelers, and Tourists in Southeast Asia*. Berkeley: University of California at Berkeley, pp. 293–317.

Fosado, G. 2005. 'Gay Sex Tourism, Ambiguity and Transnational Love in Havana'. In D.J. Fernández (ed.), *Cuba Transnational*. Gainesville: University Press of Florida, pp. 61–78.

Franklin, A., and M. Crang. 2001. 'The Trouble with Tourism and Tourism Theory?' *Tourist Studies* 1(1): 5–22.

Freeman, C. 2007. 'Neoliberalism and the Marriage of Reputation and Respectability: Entrepreneurship and the Barbadian Middle Class'. In M. Padilla, J.S. Hirsch, M. Muñoz-Laboy, R.E. Sember and R.G. Parker (eds), *Love and Globalization: Transformations of Intimacy in the Contemporary World*. Nashville, TN: Vanderbilt University Press, pp. 3–37.

Frohlick, S. 2007. 'Fluid Exchanges: The Negotiation of Intimacy between Tourist Women and Local Men in a Transnational Town in Caribbean Costa Rica'. *City and Society* 19(1): 139–168.

———. 2008. 'Negotiating the Public Secrecy of Sex in a Transnational Tourist Town in Caribbean Costa Rica'. *Tourist Studies* 8(5): 19–39.

———. 2010. 'The Sex of Tourism? Bodies under Suspicion in Paradise'. In J. Scott and T. Selwyn (eds), *Thinking Through Tourism*. Oxford and New York: Berg, pp. 51–70.

Frohlick, S., and J. Harrison (eds). 2008a. 'Engaging Ethnography in Tourist Research'. Special issue, *Tourist Studies* 8(5).

———. 2008b. 'Engaging Ethnography in Tourist Research: An Introduction'. *Tourist Studies* 8(5): 5–18.

Fullagar, S. 2001. 'Encountering Otherness: Embodied Affect in Alphonso Lingis' Travel Writing'. *Tourist Studies* 1(2): 171–183.

Fusco, C. 1997. 'Jineteras en Cuba'. *Encuentro de la cultura cubana* 4/5: 52–64.

Gambetta, D. 2000. 'Can We Trust Trust?' In D. Gambetta (ed.), *Trust: Making and Breaking Cooperative Relations*. Oxford: Department of Sociology, University of Oxford, pp. 213–237.

Garcia, A. 2010. 'Continuous Moral Economies: The State Regulation of Bodies and Sex Work in Cuba'. *Sexualities* 13(2): 171–196.

García Moreno, C. 2010. 'Mujeres migrantes cubanas: "resolviendo" e "inventando" también en España'. PhD dissertation. Tarragona, Spain: Universitat Rovira y Virgili.

García Moreno, C., and J.J. Pujadas Muñoz. 2011. '"No es fácil..., y aquí tampoco". Trayectorias migratorias de mujeres cubanas en España'. *Revista de Dialectología y Tradiciones Populares* 66(2): 455–486.

Getfield, J. 2005. 'Tourist Harassment in Jamaica: Crime or Career?' In C. Jayawardena (ed.), *Caribbean Tourism: People, Service and Hospitality*. Kingston and Miami: Ian Randle, pp. 106–118.

Ginestri, G. n.d. 'Archivio Cuba si'. Blog. Retrieved 12 February 2009 from www.alinet.it/gin.cuba.si/capitoloD.html.

Glick Schiller, N. 2006. 'Introduction: What Can Transnational Studies Offer to the Analysis of Localized Conflict and Protest?' *Focaal: European Journal of Anthropology*, 47: 3–17.

Gloaguen, P. (ed.). 2007. *Le Guide du Routard: Cuba*. Paris: Hachette.

Goffman, E. 1959. *The Presentation of Self in Everyday Life*. Garden City, NY: Doubleday.

Gorry, C. 2004. *Lonely Planet: Cuba*. Footscray, Victoria: Lonely Planet.

Gottlieb, A. 1982. 'Americans' Vacations'. *Annals of Tourism Research* 9: 165–187.

Graburn, N.H.H. 1978 (1977). 'Tourism: The Sacred Journey'. In V.L. Smith (ed.), *Hosts and Guests: The Anthropology of Tourism*. Oxford: Basil Blackwell, pp. 17–31.

———. 1983. 'The Anthropology of Tourism'. *Annals of Tourism Research* 10(1): 9–33.

———. 2001. 'Secular Ritual: A General Theory of Tourism'. In V.L. Smith, and M. Brent (eds), *Hosts and Guests Revisited: Tourism Issues of the 21st Century*. New York: Cognizant Communication, pp. 43–50.

———. 2002. 'The Ethnographic Tourist'. In G.M.S. Dann (ed.), *The Tourist as a Metaphor of the Social World*. Oxon, NY: CABI, pp. 19–39.

———. 2012. 'The Dark Is on the Inside: The *Honne* of Japanese Exploratory Tourists'. In D. Picard and M. Robinson (eds.), *Emotion in Motion: Tourism, Affect and Transformation*. Farnham, Surrey, and Burlington, VT: Ashgate, pp. 49–71.

Graburn, N.H.H., and W. Mazzarella. 1994. 'Empty Meeting Grounds: Review Essay'. *Annals of Tourism Research* 21(2): 433–437.

Greenwood, D.J. 1978 (1977). 'Culture by the Pound: An Anthropological Perspective on Tourism as Cultural Commoditization'. In V.L. Smith (ed.), *Hosts and Guests: The Anthropology of Tourism*. Oxford: Basil Blackwell, pp. 129–138.

Guyer, J.I. 2004. *Marginal Gains: Monetary Transactions in Atlantic Africa*. Chicago: University of Chicago Press.

Hall, D. 1992. 'Tourism Development in Cuba'. In D. Harrison (ed.), *Tourism and the Less Developed Countries*. London: Belhaven Press; New York and Toronto: Halsted Press, pp. 102–120.

Hansing, K. 2006. *Rasta, Race and Revolution: The Emergence and Development of the Rastafari Movement in Socialist Cuba*. Berlin: LIT Verlag.

Harrison, J. 2003. *Being a Tourist: Finding Meaning in Pleasure Travel*. Vancouver and Toronto: University of British Columbia Press.

Hart, K. 1973. 'Informal Income Opportunities and Urban Employment in Ghana'. *Journal of Modern African Studies* 11(1): 61–89.

———. 2005. 'Formal Bureaucracy and the Emergent Forms of the Informal Economy'. Research Paper No. 2005/11: Expert Group on Development Issues, United Nations University, World Institute for Development Economics Research. Retrieved 20 September 2006 from http://www.rrojasdatabank.info.

Henare, A., M. Holbraad and S. Wastell. 2007. 'Introduction: Thinking through Things'. In A. Henare, M. Holbraad and S. Wastell (eds), *Thinking through Things: Theorising Artefacts Ethnographically*. Oxon and New York: Routledge, pp. 1–31.

Herold, E., R. Garcia and T. DeMoya. 2001. 'Female Tourists and Beach Boys: Romance or Sex Tourism?' *Annals of Tourism Research* 28(4): 978–997.

Herzfeld, M. 2005. *Cultural Intimacy: Social Poetics in the Nation State*. London and New York: Routledge.

———. 2012. 'Reciprocating the Hospitality of These Pages'. *Journal of the Royal Anthropological Institute* N.S.: 210–217.

Hirsch, J.S., and H. Wardlow (eds). 2006. *Modern Loves: The Anthropology of Romantic Love and Companionate Marriage*. Ann Arbor: University of Michigan Press.

Hitchcock, M. 1999. 'Tourism and Ethnicity: Situational Perspectives'. *International Journal of Tourism Research* 1: 17–32.

Hochschild, A.R. 1983. *The Managed Heart: Commercialization of Human Feeling*. Berkeley: University of California Press.

Hodge, D.G. 2001. 'Colonization of the Cuban Body: The Growth of Male Sex Work in Havana'. *NACLA Report on the Americas* 34(5): 20–44.

———. 2005. 'Sex Workers of Havana: The Lure of Things'. *NACLA Report on the Americas* 38(4): 12–15.

Hollan, D. 2008. 'Being There: On the Imaginative Aspects of Understanding Others and Being Understood'. *Ethos* 36(4): 475–489.

Hollan, D., and C.J. Throop. 2008. 'Whatever Happened to Empathy?' *Ethos* 36(4): 385–401.

Houellebecq, M. 2002 (2001). *Platform*. London: Heinemann.

Huizinga, J. 1950. *Homo Ludens: A Study of the Play Element in Culture*. Boston: Beacon Press.

Hume, L., and J. Mulcock (eds). 2004. *Anthropologists in the Field: Cases in Participant Observation*. New York and Chichester: Columbia University Press.

Humphrey, C. 2008. Reassembling Individual Subjects: Events and Decisions in Troubled Times. *Anthropological Theory* 8(4): 357–380.

Hunter, M. 2010. *Love in the Time of AIDS: Inequality, Gender and Rights in South Africa*. Indianapolis: University of Indiana Press.

Illouz, E. 1997. *Consuming the Romantic Utopia: Love and the Cultural Contradictions of Capitalism*. Berkeley: University of California Press.

Jack, G., and A. Phipps. 2005. *Tourism and Intercultural Exchange: Why Tourism Matters*. Bristol: Channel View.

Jackson, M. 1998. *Minima Ethnographica: Intersubjectivity and the Anthropological Project*. Chicago and London: University of Chicago Press.

———. 2007. 'Intersubjective Ambiguities'. *Medische Antropologie* 19(1): 147–161.

Jeffreys, S. 2003. 'Sex Tourism: Do Women Do It Too?' *Leisure Studies* 22: 223–238.

Jolly, M., and L. Manderson. 1997. 'Introduction: Sites of Desire/Economies of Pleasure in Asia and the Pacific'. In L. Manderson and M. Jolly, *Sites of Desire Economies of Pleasure: Sexualities in Asia and the Pacific*. Chicago and London: University of Chicago Press, pp. 1–26.

Kelski, K. 1999. 'Gender, Modernity, and Eroticized Internationalism in Japan'. *Cultural Anthropology* 14(2): 229–255.

———. 2001. *Women on the Verge: Japanese Women, Western Dreams*. Durham, NC, and London: Duke University Press.

Kempadoo, K. (ed.). 1999. *Sun, Sex, and Gold: Tourism and Sex Work in the Caribbean*. Lanham, MD: Rowman and Littlefield.

———. 2004. *Sexing the Caribbean: Gender, Race, and Sexual Labor*. New York and London: Routledge.

Killick, E., and A. Desai. 2010. 'Introduction: Valuing Friendship'. In A. Desai and E. Killick (eds), *The Ways of Friendship: Anthropological Perspectives*. New York and Oxford: Berghahn Books, pp. 1–19.

Ki-Moon, B. 2007. 'Remarks to the World Tourism Organization in Madrid'. 5 June 2007. Retrieved 3 July 2008 from http://www.un.org.

Kneese, T. 2005. 'La Mulata: Cuba's National Symbol'. *Cuba in Transition*. 15: 444–452.

Krippendorf, J. 1999 (1984). *The Holiday Makers: Understanding the Impact of Leisure and Travel*. Oxford: Butterworth-Heinemann.

Kruhse-MountBurton, S. 1995. 'Sex Tourism and Traditional Australian Male Identity'. In M.-F. Lanfant, J.B. Allcock and E.M. Bruner (eds), *International Tourism: Identity and Change*. London: Sage, pp. 192–204.

Kummels, I. 2005. 'Love in the Time of Diaspora: Global Markets and Local Meaning in Prostitution, Marriage and Womanhood in Cuba'. *Iberoamericana* 5(20): 7–26.

LaFlamme, A.G. 1981. 'Comment to Dennison Nash, "Tourism as an Anthropological Subject"'. *Current Anthropology* 22(5): 473.

Lambek, M. 2010. 'Toward an Ethics of the Act'. In: M. Lambek (ed.), *Ordinary Ethics: Anthropology, Language and Action*. Bronx, NY: Fordham University Press, pp. 39–63.

Latour, B. 2005. *Reassembling the Social: An Introduction to Actor-Network-Theory*. Oxford: Oxford University Press.

Law, J. 1991. 'Power, Discretion and Strategy'. In J. Law (ed.), *A Sociology of Monsters: Essays on Power, Technology and Domination*. London and New York: Routledge, pp. 165–191.

Law, J. and V. Singleton. 2005. 'Object lessons'. *Organization* 12(3): 331–355.

Lett, J. W. 1983. 'Ludic and Liminoid Aspects of Charter Yacht Tourism in the Caribbean'. *Annals of Tourism Research* 10(1): 35–56.

Lévy, J., S. Laporte and M. El Feki. 2001. 'Tourisme et Sexualité en Tunisie: Note de Recherche'. *Anthropologie et Sociétés* 25(2): 61–68.

Little, K. 2005. '"Paradise from the Other Side of Nowhere": Troubling a Troubled Scene of Tourist Encounter in Belize'. In D. Picard and M. Robinson (eds), *Proceedings of the International Conference Tourism and Performance: Scripts, Stages and Stories*, 14–18 July 2005, Centre for Tourism and Cultural Change, Sheffield Hallam University, Sheffield (CD-ROM).

Lundgren, S. 2011. 'Heterosexual Havana: Ideals and Hierarchies of Gender and Sexuality in Contemporary Cuba'. PhD dissertation. Uppsala, Sweden: Uppsala University.

MacCannell, D. 1973. 'Staged Authenticity: On Arrangements of Social Space in Tourist Settings'. *The American Journal of Sociology* 79(3): 589–603.

———. 1976. *The Tourist: A New Theory of the Leisure Class*. London: Macmillan.

———. 1992. *Empty Meeting Grounds: The Tourist Papers*. London and New York: Routledge.

———. 2008. 'Why It Never Really Was about Authenticity'. *Society* 45: 334–337.

Mains, D. 2013. 'Friends and Money: Balancing Affection and Reciprocity among Young Men in Urban Ethiopia'. *American Ethnologist* 40(2): 335–346.

Manderson, L., and M. Jolly (eds). 1997. *Sites of Desire, Economies of Pleasure: Sexualities in Asia and the Pacific*. Chicago and London: University of Chicago Press.

Mankekar, P., and L. Shein. 2004. 'Introduction: Mediated Transnationalism and Social Erotics'. *Journal of Asian Studies* 63(2): 357–365.

Massey, D. 1993. 'Power-Geometry and a Progressive Sense of Place'. In J. Bird et al. (eds), *Mapping the Futures: Local Cultures, Global Change*. London: Routledge, pp. 59–69.

Mattingly, C. 2006. 'Pocahontas Goes to the Clinic: Popular Culture as Lingua Franca in a Cultural Borderland'. *American Anthropologist* 108(3): 494–501.

———. 2010. *The Paradox of Hope: Journeys Through a Clinical Borderland*. Berkeley: University of California Press.

Maurer, B. 2006. 'The Anthropology of Money'. *Annual Review of Anthropology* 35: 15–36.

Mauss, M. 1969 (1925). *The Gift: Forms and Functions of Exchange in Archaic Societies*. London: Cohen and West.

McCabe, S. 2005. '"Who Is a Tourist?" A Critical Review'. *Tourist Studies* 5(1): 85–106.

Michel, F. 1998a. 'Des manières d'être et de faire du touriste et de l'anthropologue'. In F. Michel (ed.), *Tourismes, Touristes, Sociétés*. Paris: L'Harmattan, pp. 35–44.

———. 1998b. 'Le tourisme international: une bouée de sauvetage pour Cuba?' In F. Michel (ed.), *Tourismes, Touristes, Sociétés*. Paris: L'Harmattan, pp. 251–287.

MINTEL. 2007. *Market Research Report on Travel and Tourism in Cuba*. London: Mintel.

Mitchell, T. 2002. *Rule of Experts: Egypt, Techno-Politics, Modernity*. Berkeley: University of California Press.

Mody, P. 2008. *The Intimate State: Love-Marriage and the Law in Delhi*. Delhi: Routledge.

Montes, J. 2001. *La Jinetera*. Vigo: Ediciones Cardeñoso.

Moore, H.L. 2011. *Still Life: Hopes, Desires and Satisfactions*. Cambridge: Polity.

Morales, E. 2013. 'Año 2013: récord de remesas y viajeros a Cuba'. *Café Fuerte*, December 29. Retrieved 28 July 2015 from http://cafefuerte.com/cuba/9915-ano-2013-record-de-remesas-y-viajeros-a-cuba/

Mullings, B. 1999. 'Globalization, Tourism, and the International Sex Trade'. In K. Kempadoo (ed.), *Sun, Sex, and Gold: Tourism and Sex Work in the Caribbean*. Lanham, MD: Rowman and Littlefield, pp. 55–80.

———. 2000. 'Fantasy Tours: Exploring the Global Consumption of Caribbean Sex Tourism'. In M. Gottdiener (ed.), *New Forms of Consumption: Consumers, Culture, and Commodification*. Lanham, MD: Rowman and Littlefield, pp. 227–250.

Murphy, L. 2001. 'Exploring Social Interactions of Backpackers'. *Annals of Tourism Research* 28(1): 50–67.

Nachi, M. 2004a. 'Introduction: Dimensions du compromis. Arguments pour la constitution d'une théorie du compromis'. *Social Science Information* 43(2): 131–143.

———. 2004b. 'The Morality in/of Compromise: Some Theoretical Reflections'. *Social Science Information* 43(2): 291–305.

Nagel, J. 2000. 'States of Arousal/Fantasy Island: Race, Sex, and Romance in the Global Economy of Desire'. *American Studies* 41(2/3): 159–181.

———. 2003. *Race, Ethnicity, and Sexuality: Intimate Intersections, Forbidden Frontiers*. New York: Oxford University Press.

Narayan, K. 1993. 'How Native Is a "Native" Anthropologist?' *American Anthropologist* 95(3): 671–686.

Nash, D. 1978 (1977). 'Tourism as a Form of Imperialism'. In V.L. Smith (ed.), *Hosts and Guests: The Anthropology of Tourism*. Oxford: Basil Blackwell, pp. 33–47.

———. 1981. 'Tourism as an Anthropological Subject'. *Current Anthropology* 22(5): 461–481.

———. 1996. *Anthropology of Tourism*. Oxford: Pergamon.

Nisbett, N. 2007. 'Friendship, Consumption, Morality: Practising Identity, Negotiating Hierarchy in Middle Class Bangalore'. *Journal of the Royal Anthropological Institute* 13(4): 935–950.

Nuñez, T. 1978 (1977). 'Touristic Studies in Anthropological Perspective'. In V.L. Smith (ed.), *Hosts and Guests: The Anthropology of Tourism*. Oxford: Basil Blackwell, pp. 207–216.

O'Connell Davidson, J. 1996. 'Sex Tourism in Cuba'. *Race and Class* 38(1): 39–48.

O'Connell Davidson J. and J. Sánchez Taylor. 1999. 'Fantasy Islands: Exploring the Demand for Sex Tourism'. In K. Kempadoo (ed.), *Sun, Sex, and Gold: Tourism and Sex Work in the Caribbean*. Lanham, MD: Rowman and Littlefield, pp. 37–54.

Oficina Nacional de Estadísticas República de Cuba. 2005. *Capitulo XIII – turismo – tourism*. Retrieved 6 February 2006 from http://www.one.cu.

Oppermann, M. (ed.). 1999. *Sex Tourism and Prostitution: Aspects of Leisure, Recreation, and Work*. New York: Cognizant Communication.

Ortiz, F. 2005 (1940). 'Del "tabaco habano", que es el mejor del mundo, y del "sello de garantía" de su legitimidad'. *Catauro: Revista cubana de antropología* 7(12): 101–108.

Ortner, S. B. 1996. *Making Gender: The Politics and Erotics of Culture*. Boston: Beacon Press.

Padilla, M., J.S. Hirsch, M. Muñoz-Laboy, R.E. Sember and R.G. Parker (eds). 2007. *Love and Globalization: Transformations of Intimacy in the Contemporary World*. Nashville, TN: Vanderbilt University Press.

Paine, R. 1969. 'In Search of Friendship: An Exploratory Analysis in "Middle-Class" Culture'. *Man* 4(4): 505–524.

Palmié, S. 2004. *Fascinans* or *Tremendum*? Permutations of the State, the Body, and the Divine in Late-Twentieth-Century Havana. *New West Indian Guide* 78(3/4): 229–268.

——— 2013. 'Mixed Blessings and Sorrowful Mysteries: Second Thoughts about "Hybridity"'. *Current Anthropology* 54 (4): 463–482.

Parkin, D. 2000. 'Epilogue: Fieldwork Unfolding'. In P. Dresch, W. James and D. Parkin (eds), *Anthropologists in a Wider World: Essays on Field Research*. New York and Oxford: Berghahn Books, pp. 259–273.

Patico, J. 2009. 'For Love, Money, or Normalcy: Meanings of Strategy and Sentiment in the Russian-American Matchmaking Industry'. *Ethnos* 74(3): 307–330.

Pearce, P.L. 2005. 'The Role of Relationships in the Tourist Experience'. In W.T. Theobald (ed.), *Global Tourism*. 3rd edn. Oxford: Butterworth-Heinemann, pp. 103–122.

Pertierra, A.C. 2007. 'Anthropology that Warms Your Heart: On Being a Bride in the Field'. *Anthropology Matters Journal* 9(1). Retrieved 6 February 2009 from www.anthropology-matters.com.

Phillips, J. 2002. 'The Beach Boys of Barbados: Post-Colonial Entrepreneurs'. In S. Thorbek and B. Pattanaik (eds), *Transnational Prostitution: Changing Global Patterns*. New York: Zed Books, pp. 42–45.

Picard, D. 2011. *Tourism, Magic and Modernity: Cultivating the Human Garden*. Oxford and New York: Berghahn Books.

Picard, D., and S. Buchberger (eds). 2013. *Couchsurfing Cosmopolitanisms: Can Tourism Make a Better World?* Bielefeld: Transcript.

Picard, D., and M. Robinson. (eds) 2012. *Emotion in Motion: Tourism, Affect and Transformation*. Farnham: Ashgate.

Piot, C.A. 2010. *Nostalgia for the Future: West Africa after the Cold War*. Chicago and London: Chicago University Press.

Piscitelli, A. 2007. 'Shifting Boundaries: Sex and Money in the Northeast of Brazil. *Sexualities* (10)4: 489–500.

———. 2013. *Transitos: Brasileiras nos mercados transnacionais do sexo*. Rio de Janeiro: Editora da Universidade do Estado do Rio de Janeiro.

Pi-Sunyer, O. 1978 (1977). 'Through Native Eyes: Tourists and Tourism in a Catalan Maritime Community'. In V.L. Smith (ed.), *Hosts and Guests: The Anthropology of Tourism*. Oxford: Basil Blackwell, pp. 149–155.

Povinelli, E.A. 2002. 'Notes on Gridlock: Genealogy, Intimacy, Sexuality'. *Public Culture* 14(1): 215–238.

———. 2006. *The Empire of Love: Toward a Theory of Intimacy, Genealogy, and Carnality*. Durham, NC, and London: Duke University Press.

Pratt, M.L. 1992. *Imperial Eyes: Travel Writing and Transculturation*. Oxford and New York: Routledge.

Pruitt, D., and S. LaFont. 1995. 'Love and Money: Romance Tourism in Jamaica'. *Annals of Tourism Research* 22: 422–440.

Quintana, R., et al. 2005. *Efectos y futuro del turismo en la economía cubana*. Havana: Instituto Nacional de Investigaciones Económicas.

Rapport, N., and J. Overing. 2000. 'Stereotypes'. In N. Rapport and J. Overing (eds), *Social and Cultural Anthropology: The Key Concepts*. London and New York: Routledge, pp. 343–349.

Rebhun, L.-A. 1999. *The Heart Is Unknown Country: Love in the Changing Economy of Northeast Brazil*. Stanford, CA: Stanford University Press.

Reed, S.A. 1998. 'The Politics and Poetics of Dance.' *Annual Review of Anthropology* 27: 503–532.

Ren, C. 2009. 'Constructing the Tourist Destination: A Socio-Material Description'. PhD thesis. Esbjerg: University of Southern Denmark.

Rezende, C.B. 1999. 'Building Affinity through Friendship'. In S. Bell and S. Coleman (eds), *The Anthropology of Friendship*. Oxford and New York: Berg, pp. 79–97.

Ritter, A.R.M. 1998. 'Entrepreneurship, Microenterprise, and Public Policy in Cuba: Promotion, Containment, or Asphyxiation?' *Journal of Interamerican Studies and World Affairs* 40(2): 63–94.

———. 2005. 'Survival Strategies and Economic Illegalities in Cuba'. *Cuba in Transition* 15: 342–359.

Roca, J. (ed.). 2013. *Migrantes por amor: La búsqueda de pareja en el escenario transnacional*. Valencia: Editorial Germania.

Rodríguez Ruiz, P. 1997. 'Clases y razas en el context cubano actual'. *Revista de la Universidad Autónoma de Yucatan* 12(203): 16–34.

————. 2008. 'Espacios y contextos del debate racial actual en Cuba'. *Temas* 53: 86–96.

Roitman, J.L. 2005. *Fiscal Disobedience: An Anthropology of Economic Regulation in Central Africa*. Princeton, NJ: Princeton University Press.

Roland, L.K. 2011. *Cuban Color in Tourism and* La Lucha: *An Ethnography of Racial Meaning*. New York and Oxford: Oxford University Press.

Roux, S. 2007. 'Importer pour exister. Empower et le "travail sexuel" en Thaïlande'. *Lien social et Politiques* 58: 145–154.

————. 2010. 'Patpong, entre sexe et commerce'. *EspacesTemps.net*. Retrieved 3 April 2010 from http://espacestemps.net/document8075.html.

Ryan, C., and A. Martin. 2001. 'Tourists and Strippers: Liminal Theatre'. *Annals of Tourism Research* 28(1): 140–163.

Ryan, C., and M. Hall. 2001. *Sex Tourism: Marginal People and Liminality*. London: Routledge.

Sacchetti, E. 2004. 'Culturas del trabajo y estrategias de economia domestica en el cuentapropismo cubano: estudio de casos'. *Meeting of Latin American Studies Association*, Las Vegas, Nevada, 7–9 October 2004.

Salazar, N. 2010. *Envisioning Eden: Mobilizing Imaginaries in Tourism and Beyond*. Oxford and New York: Berghahn Books.

Salomon, C. 2009. 'Antiquaires et businessmen de la Petite Côte du Sénégal. Le commerce des illusions amoureuses'. *Cahiers d'études africaines* 193–194(1–2): 147–176.

Sanchez, P.M., and K.M. Adams. 2008. 'The Janus-Faced Character of Tourism in Cuba'. *Annals of Tourism Research* 35(1): 27–47.

Sánchez Taylor, J. 2000. 'Tourism and "Embodied" Commodities: Sex Tourism in the Caribbean'. In S. Clift and S. Carter (eds), *Tourism and Sex: Culture, Commerce and Coercion*. London and New York: Pinter, pp. 41–53.

Saney, I. 2004. *Cuba: A Revolution in Motion*. Black Point, Winnipeg: Fernwood; London and New York: Zed Books.

Sant Cassia, P. 1999. 'Tradition, Tourism and Memory in Malta'. *Journal of the Royal Anthropological Institute* 5(2): 247–263.

Santos-Granero, F. 2007. 'Of Fear and Friendship: Amazonian Sociality beyond Kinship and Affinity'. *Journal of the Royal Anthropological Institute* 13(1): 1–18.

Schmid, K.A. 2008. 'Doing Ethnography of Tourist Enclaves: Boundaries, Ironies, and Insights'. *Tourist Studies* 8(1): 105–121.

Schwartz, R. 1999. *Pleasure Island: Tourism and Temptation in Cuba*. Lincoln and London: University of Nebraska Press.

Selänniemi, T. 2003. 'On Holiday in the Liminoid Playground: Place, Time, and Self in Tourism'. In T.G. Bauer and B. McKercher (eds), *Sex and Tourism: Journeys of Romance, Love, and Lust*. New York: The Haworth Hospitality Press, pp. 19–31.

Selwyn, T. 1996. 'Introduction'. In T. Selwyn (ed.), *The Tourist Image: Myths and Myth Making in Tourism*. Chichester: John Wiley and Sons, pp. 1–32.

Sierra i Fabra, J. 2001. *Regreso a La Habana*. Barcelona: Ediciónes del Bronce.

Sierra Madero, A. 2013. 'Cuerpos en venta: Pinguerismo y masculinidad negociada en la Cuba contemporánea'. *Nómadas* 38: 167–183.

Silver, A. 1990. 'Friendship in Commercial Society: Eighteenth-Century Social Theory and Modern Sociology'. *American Journal of Sociology* 95(6): 1474–1504.

Simoni, V. 2005a. 'Informal Encounters between Foreign Tourist and Cubans in La Havana, Cuba'. In D. Picard and M. Robinson (eds), *Proceedings of the International Conference Tourism and Performance: Scripts, Stages and Stories*, 14–18 July, 2005, Centre for Tourism and Cultural Change, Sheffield Hallam University, Sheffield, (CD-ROM).

———. 2005b. '"Hello my friend! Have a look inside, special price!" Interazioni verbali tra commercianti e turisti in Ladakh (India)'. *Babylonia* 2(5): 58–61.

———. 2008a. '"Riding" Diversity: Cubans'/*Jineteros*' Uses of "Nationality-Talks" in the Realm of Their Informal Encounters with Tourists'. In P. Burns and M. Novelli (eds), *Tourism Development: Growth, Myths and Inequalities*. Wallingford and Cambridge, MA: CAB International, pp. 68–84.

———. 2008b. 'Shifting Power: The (De)Stabilization of Asymmetries in the Realm of Tourism in Cuba'. *Tsantsa* 13: 89–97.

———. 2009. 'Scaling Cigars in Cuba's Tourism Economy'. *Etnográfica* 13(2): 417–438.

———. 2011. 'L'interculturalité comme justification: Sexe 'couleur locale' dans la Cuba touristique'. In A. Lavanchy, F. Dervin and A. Gajardo (eds), *Anthropologies de l'interculturalité*. Paris: L'Harmattan, pp. 197–225.

———. 2012a. 'Tourism Materialities: Enacting Cigars in Touristic Cuba'. In R. van der Duim, C. Ren and G. T. Jóhannesson (eds), *Actor-Network Theory and Tourism: Ordering, Materiality and Multiplicity*. London: Routledge, pp. 59–79.

———. 2012b. 'Dancing Tourists: Tourism, Party and Seduction in Cuba'. In D. Picard and M. Robinson (eds), *Emotion in Motion: Tourism, Affect and Transformation*. Farnham: Ashgate, pp. 267–281.

———. 2013. 'Intimate Stereotypes: Becoming *Caliente* in Touristic Cuba'. *Civilisations* 62(1–2): 181–197.

———. 2014a. 'Revisiting Hosts and Guests: Ethnographic Insights on Touristic Encounters from Cuba'. *Journal of Tourism Challenges and Trends* 6(2): 39–62.

———. 2014b. 'The Morality of Friendship in Touristic Cuba'. *Suomen Antropologi* 39(1): 19–36.

———. 2014c. 'Coping with Ambiguous Relationships: Sex, Tourism and Transformation in Cuba'. *Journal of Tourism and Cultural Change* 12(2): 166–183.

———. 2014d. 'From Tourist to Person: The Value of Intimacy in Touristic Cuba'. *Journal of Tourism and Cultural Change* 12(3): 280–292.

———. 2015a. 'Breadwinners, Sex Machines and Romantic Lovers: Entangling Masculinities, Moralities, and Pragmatic Concerns in Touristic Cuba'. *Etnografica* 19(2): 389–411.

———. 2015b. 'Shaping Money and Relationships in Touristic Cuba'. In R. van der Duim, C. Ren, and G.T. Jóhannesson (eds), *Tourism Encounters: Ontological Politics of Tourism Development*. Farnham: Ashgate, pp. 21–38.

———. 2015c. forthcoming. 'True Love and Cunning Love: Negotiating Intimacy, Deception and Belonging in Touristic Cuba'. In C. Groes-Green and N.T. Fernandez (eds), *Global Intimacies, Intimate Migrations*. Oxford and New York: Berghahn Books.

———. 2015d. forthcoming. 'Intimacy and Belonging in Cuban Tourism and Migration'. *The Cambridge Journal of Anthropology* 33(2): 26–41.

Simoni, V., and S. McCabe. 2008. 'From Ethnographers to Tourists and Back Again: On Positioning Issues in the Anthropology of Tourism'. *Civilisations* 57(1–2): 173–189.

Simoni, V., and J. Throop. 2014a. 'Introduction: Friendship, Morality, and Experience. *Suomen Antropologi* 39(1): 4–18.

—— (eds). 2014b. *Friendship, Morality, and Experience*. Special Issue, *Suomen Antropologi*, 39(1).

Skinner, J. 2011. 'Displeasure on "Pleasure Island": Tourist Expectation and Desire on and off the Cuban Dancefloor'. In J. Skinner and D. Theodossopoulos (eds), *Great Expectations: Imagination and Anticipation in Tourism*. Oxford and New York: Berghahn Books, pp. 116–136.

Slater, D. 2002. 'From Calculation to Alienation: Disentangling Economic Abstractions'. *Economy and Society* 31(2): 234–249.

Smart, A. 1999. 'Expressions of Interest: Friendship and *Guanxi* in Chinese Societies'. In S. Bell and S. Coleman (eds), *The Anthropology of Friendship*. Oxford and New York: Berg, pp. 119–136.

Smith, M.E. (ed.). 1990. *Perspectives on the Informal Economy*. Lanham, MD, New York and London: University Press of America.

Smith, V.L. 1978 (1977). 'Eskimo Tourism: Micromodels and Marginal Men'. In V.L. Smith (ed.), *Hosts and Guests: The Anthropology of Tourism*. Oxford: Basil Blackwell, pp. 51–70.

—— (ed.) (1977). 1978. *Hosts and Guests: The Anthropology of Tourism*. Oxford: Basil Blackwell.

Spronk, R. 2012. *Ambiguous Pleasures: Sexuality and Middle Class Self-Perceptions in Nairobi*. Oxford and New York: Berghahn Books.

Stoller, P. 2002. *Money Has No Smell: The Africanization of New York City*. Chicago and London: University of Chicago Press.

Stout, N.M. 2007. 'Feminists, Queers and Critics: Debating the Cuban Sex Trade'. *Journal of Latin American Studies* 40: 721–742.

Strathern, M. 1988. *The Gender of the Gift: Problems with Women and Problems with Society in Melanesia*. Berkeley: University of California Press.

——. 1996. 'Cutting the Network'. *Journal of the Royal Anthropological Institute* 12(3): 517–535.

——. 2002. 'Externalities in Comparative Guise'. *Economy and Society* 31(2): 250–267.

——. 2005. *Kinship, Law and the Unexpected: Relatives Are Always a Surprise*. Cambridge: Cambridge University Press.

——. 2010. 'Afterword'. *Journal of Tourism Consumption and Practice* 2(2): 80–82.

Stronza, A. 2001. 'Anthropology of Tourism: Forging New Ground for Ecotourism and Other Alternatives'. *Annual Review of Anthropology* 30: 261–283.

Sudgen, J., and A. Tomlinson. 1995. 'Hustling in Havana: Ethnographic Notes on Everyday Life and Mutual Exploitation between Locals and Tourists in a Socialist Economy under Siege'. In G. McFee, W. Murphy and G. Whannel (eds), *Leisure Cultures: Values, Genders, Lifestyles*. Eastbourne: Leisure Studies Association, pp. 159–178.

Sweet, J.D. 1989. 'Burlesquing the "Other" in Pueblo Performance'. *Annals of Tourism Research* 16(1): 62–75.

Sykes, K. 2009. 'Residence: Moral Reasoning in a Common Place: Paradoxes of a Global Age'. In K. Sykes (ed.), *Ethnographies of Moral Reasoning: Living Paradoxes of a Global Age*. New York: Palgrave Macmillan, pp. 3–40.

Tabet, P. 1987. 'Du don au tarif: Les relations sexuelles impliquant compensation'. *Les Temps Modernes* 490: 1–53.

Tanaka, M. 2010. 'Being Cuban Is About Being (Im)Mobile: Spatial Imaginaries of Cubanness'. *Bulletin of the National Museum of Ethnology* 35(2): 337–362.

Tchak, S. 1999. *La prostitution à Cuba: Communisme, ruses et débrouille*. Paris: L'Harmattan.

Thomas, N. 1991. *Entangled Objects: Exchange, Material Culture, and Colonialism*. Cambridge, MA: Harvard University Press.

Throop, J.C. 2010. 'Latitudes of Loss: On the Vicissitudes of Empathy'. *American Ethnologist* 37(4): 771–782.

———. 2014. 'Morality, Friendship, and the Ethnographic Encounter'. *Suomen Antropologi* 39(1): 68–80.

Tiboni, L. 2002. 'Les papillons de la cinquième avenue. Entre tourisme et prostitution à Cuba: un regard sur l'espace vécu havanais.' MA thesis. Geneva: Université de Genève.

Time Out: Havana & the Best of Cuba. 2004. London: Penguin.

Timothy, D.J., and G. Wall. 1997. 'Selling to Tourists. Indonesian Street Vendors'. *Annals of Tourism Research* 24: 322–340.

Torresan, A. 2011. 'Strange Bedfellows: Brazilian Immigrants Negotiating Friendship in Lisbon'. *Ethnos* 76(2): 233–253.

Trumbull, C. 2001. 'Prostitution and Sex Tourism in Cuba'. *Cuba in Transition* 11: 356–371.

Tsing, A.L. 2005. *Friction: An Ethnography of Global Connection*. Princeton, NJ: Princeton University Press.

Tucker, H. 1997. 'The Ideal Village: Interactions through Tourism in Central Anatolia'. In S. Abram, J. Waldren and D.V.L. Macleod (eds), *Tourists and Tourism: Identifying with People and Places*. Oxford and New York: Berg, pp. 107–128.

———. 2001. 'Tourists and Troglodytes: Negotiating for Sustainability'. *Annals of Tourism Research* 28(4): 868–891.

———. 2003. *Living with Tourism: Negotiating Identities in a Turkish Village*. London and New York: Routledge.

Turner, V.W. 1977. 'Variations on a Theme of Liminality'. In S. Moore and B. Myerhoff (eds), *Secular Ritual*. Amsterdam: Van Gorcum, pp. 36–52.

Urry, J. 1990. *The Tourist Gaze: Leisure and Travel in Contemporary Societies*. London: Sage.

Valle, A. 2006. *Jineteras*. Bogotá: Planeta.

van den Berghe, P. 1980. 'Tourism as Ethnic Relations: A Case Study of Cuzco, Peru'. *Ethnic and Racial Studies* 3(4): 376–392.

———. 1994. *The Quest for the Other: Ethnic Tourism in San Cristóbal, Mexico*. Seattle and London: University of Washington Press.

———. 1996. 'Tourism'. In A. Barnard and J. Spencer (eds), *Encyclopaedia of Social and Cultural Anthropology*. London and New York: Routledge, pp. 551–552.

Van der Duim, R., C. Ren and G.T. Jóhannesson. 2012. *Actor-Network Theory and Tourism: Ordering, Materiality and Multiplicity*. London and New York: Routledge.

Veijola, S. and E. Jokinen. 1994. 'The Body in Tourism'. *Theory, Culture and Society* 11(3): 125–151.

Venkatesan, S., J. Edwards, R. Willerslev, E. Povinelli and P. Mody. 2011. 'The Anthropological Fixation with Reciprocity Leaves No Room for Love: 2009 Meeting of the Group for Debates in Anthropological Theory'. *Critique of Anthropology* 31(3): 210–250.

Venkatesh, S. 2002. '"Doin' the Hustle": Constructing the Ethnographer in the American Ghetto'. *Ethnography* 3(1): 91–111.

Waldren, J. 1996. *Insiders and Outsiders: Paradise and Reality in Mallorca*. Oxford and New York: Berghahn Books.

Werner, C. 2003. 'The New Silk Road: Mediators and Tourism Developments in Central Anatolia'. *Ethnology* 42(2): 141–159.

Wonders, N.A. and R. Michalowski. 2001. 'Bodies, Borders, and Sex Tourism in a Globalized World: A Tale of Two Cities: Amsterdam and Havana'. *Social Problems* 48(4): 545–571.

Zelizer, V.A. 2000. 'The Purchase of Intimacy'. *Law and Social Inquiry* 25(3): 817–848.

———. 2005. *The Purchase of Intimacy*. Princeton, NJ: Princeton University Press.

Zigon, J. 2008. *Morality: An Anthropological Perspective*. Oxford: Berg.

———. 2009. 'Morality within a Range of Possibilities: A Dialogue with Joel Robbins'. *Ethnos* 74(2): 251–276.

———. 2010. 'Moral and Ethical Assemblages: A Response to Fassin and Stoczkowski'. *Anthropological Theory* 10(1–2): 3–15.

———. 2013. 'On Love: Remaking Moral Subjectivity in Postrehabilitation Russia'. *American Ethnologist* 40(1): 201–215.

Zorn, E., and L.C. Farthing. 2007. 'Communitarian Tourism: Hosts and Mediators in Peru'. *Annals of Tourism Research* 34(3): 673–689.

INDEX

The (fictional) names of research participants are included where they appear in more than one place. Notes are indicated by 'n' (e.g. '226n17' refers to note 17 on page 226). Indicators referring purely to illustrations are indicated in italics (e.g. '*21*'). Where a 'see also' cross-reference refers to a subheading, it is placed in parentheses and 'see' is in lower case (e.g. '(*see also* trust)').

Salazar, Noel, 229n17
Salomon, Christine, 219n9
salsa, 154–5, 156, 158, 161, 234n3
Sánchez Taylor, Jacqueline, 42, 91, 96
Sant Cassia, Paul, 228n9, 231n6
Santa Maria beach, 20–*21*
   conversations, 61–62, 65
   languages, 98–99
   partying, 152, 153, 154, 167
   policing, 71, 73, 84–85, 167
   tourist perception of Cubans, 61–62, 65
Santos-Granero, Fernando, 137
scepticism, 211
   about Cubans, tourists', 102, 126,
      128–29, 130, 131, 195, 204, 227n4
      cigar deals, 112–13, 115
      Italians, 62–63
      jineterismo, 50, 65, 87
   money and sex, 187, 188, 191–92
   See also trust
Schmid, Karl Anthony, 217n14
Schwartz, Rosalie, 35, 36–37
secaderos, *117*, 118
seduction, 169–70, 204
   Cuban men, 55, 56, 64, 158–59,
      222n12
   Cuban women, 68, 97, 154, 159–60,
      169, 205–6
   dancing, 154, 158–63, 161, 162–63,
      164, 208, 234n2
   instrumentality, 92, 208
   mutuality, 165, 170, 189, 201
   partying, 149, 168, 208
   tourists' attitudes, 170, 173, 177, 178,
      183, 189–90, 191, 205–6
   Santa Maria beach, 20
segregation: tourists and residents, 2, 40,
   46, 66
sensuality: dancing, 152, 157–62, 163,
   164, 209
serendipity, 94–95, 168, 228n8
sex, money and, 165, 167, 169, 170,
   171–75, 176–7, 208, 209. *See also*
   commoditization: sex; prostitution
sex tourism, 165, 169, 170, 172, 180–84,
   189, 190
   bodily appearance, 89–91

desire for relationships, 56–58
history, 33–34, 37, 42–43, 49,
   219nn9–10
researcher, 24
tourists' relations with police, 83–85
See also prostitution
'sex worker', notion of, 12, 13
sexual arousal: partying, 152, 159–60
sexual encounters
   multi-functionality, 228n11
   research, 12
   Santa Maria beach, 20
sexual relationships, 165–92, 201, 204,
   208, 209, 212
   ambiguity, 165, 171, 176–80, 184–89,
      190, 191–92, 235n3
      lack of ambiguity, 182, 183, 184,
      187, 191
   instrumentality, 185, 192, 235n1
sexualization: images of Cubans, 41–2,
   90–91
Singleton, Vicky, 229n3
Slater, Don, 113, 125
slave trade, 34
slavery, sexualization and, 41–42
Smart, Alan, 15
Smith, Valene, 7, 98, 100
social distance, 7–8
socio-economic contextualization, 138–
   39, 174, 203, 208, 209, 210
Soviet Union: relationship with Cuba,
   37, 39
Sozzari, Pietro, 46
Spain: rule in Cuba, 34
Spanish language, 98–99
Special Period in Time of Peace, 33,
   39–40, 48, 51–53, 64, 221n5
'staged authenticity', 128, 204, 205
state and society, 221n9
stereotyping, 7–8, 96, 223n21, 227n6
   first encounters, 92, 93–94
   gender roles and norms, 190
   jineteras, 57, 91
   racial, 42–43, 90–91, 218n7, 222n12,
      235n1
   relationships, 201, 211, 213
Stout, Noelle M, 221n9